Entrepreneurship and Growth in Local, Regional and National Economies

Entrepreneurship and Growth in Local, Regional and National Economies

Frontiers in European Entrepreneurship Research

Edited by

David Smallbone

Professor of Small Business and Entrepreneurship, Small Business Research Centre, Kingston University, UK

Hans Landström

Professor in Business Administration, Institute of Economic Research, School of Economics and Management, Lund University, Sweden

Dylan Jones-Evans

Director of Research and Innovation, University of Wales, UK

IN ASSOCIATION WITH THE ECSB

Edward Elgar
Cheltenham, UK • Northampton, MA, USA

Published by
Edward Elgar Publishing Limited
The Lypiatts
15 Lansdown Road
Cheltenham
Glos GL50 2JA
UK

Edward Elgar Publishing, Inc.
William Pratt House
9 Dewey Court
Northampton
Massachusetts 01060
USA

A catalogue record for this book
is available from the British Library

Library of Congress Control Number: 2009930858

Mixed Sources
Product group from well-managed
forests and other controlled sources
www.fsc.org Cert no. SA-COC-1565
© 1996 Forest Stewardship Council

ISBN 978 1 84844 592 5

Printed and bound by MPG Books Group, UK

Contents

PART IV   BUSINESS EXITS

PART V   KNOWLEDGE-BASED ENTREPRENEURSHIP

PART VI   ENTREPRENEURSHIP AND SOCIAL INCLUSION

Contributors

A. Miguel Amaral, Technical University of Lisbon, Portugal

Rui Baptista, Technical University of Lisbon, Portugal

Niels Bosma, Utrecht University, Netherlands

Sara Carter, University of Strathclyde, UK

Philip Cooke, Cardiff University, UK

Pedro M. García-Villaverde, University of Castilla la Mancha, Spain

Ángela González-Moreno, University of Castilla la Mancha, Spain

Carole Howorth, Lancaster University, UK

Anders Isaksson, University of Gothenburg and Umeå University, Sweden

Trevor Jones, De Montfort University, UK

Dylan Jones-Evans, University of Wales, UK

Hans Landström, Lund University, Sweden

Francisco Lima, Technical University of Lisbon, Portugal

Colin Mason, University of Strathclyde, UK

Joana Mendonça, Technical University of Lisbon, Portugal

Colm O'Gorman, Dublin City University, Ireland

Vinit Parida, Luleå University of Technology, Sweden

Caroline Parkinson, Lancaster University, UK

Monder Ram, De Montfort University, UK

María J. Ruiz-Ortega, University of Castilla la Mancha, Spain

Francisco J. Sáez-Martínez, University of Castilla la Mancha, Spain

Veronique Schutjens, Utrecht University, Netherlands

David Smallbone, Kingston University, UK

Alan Southern, University of Liverpool, UK

Stephen Tagg, University of Strathclyde, UK

Nicholas Theodorakopoulos, De Montfort University, UK

Miguel Torres Preto, Technical University of Lisbon, Portugal

Vladimir Vanyushyn, Umeå University, Sweden

Friederike Welter, Jönköping University, Sweden

Mats Westerberg, Luleå University of Technology, Sweden

Foreword

With this book, the European Council for Small Business and Entrepreneurship (ECSB) presents the fourth volume in a series of papers from the annual Research in Entrepreneurship and Small Business Conference (RENT). RENT XXI was held in Cardiff in November 2007. Since its inauguration in 1996, RENT has grown to become one of Europe's best known and globally recognized conferences in the entrepreneurship field. RENT is organized jointly by the European Institute for Advanced Studies in Management (EIASM) and ECSB.

This book assembles selected best papers from RENT XXI, which centred on entrepreneurship and small business development making the difference in local, regional and national economies. Besides new venture creation and business exits, the papers in this book look at knowledge-based entrepreneurship and the role entrepreneurship can play related to social inclusion. Each of the papers went through a rigorous selection and review process. I thank the editors and reviewers who assisted in selecting papers, for their great effort. With this book and series, ECSB continues to offer a look into current European entrepreneurship research, thus facilitating knowledge transfer and international discussions.

Friederike Welter
President, ECSB

PART I

Introduction

1. Introduction

David Smallbone, Hans Landström and Dylan Jones-Evans

INTRODUCTION

This book provides a window on contemporary European entrepreneurship and small business research, through a selection of some of the best papers presented at the twenty-first Research in Entrepreneurship (RENT) Conference held in Cardiff in November 2007. The papers selected for inclusion demonstrate the applied nature of entrepreneurship research, as well as the various contributions that entrepreneurship can make to local, regional and national development, from both a social and an economic perspective. The papers also reveal the heterogeneity of the field of entrepreneurship, especially in terms of substantive content and the methodologies employed, with both quantitative and qualitative approaches well represented. This heterogeneity partly reflects different traditions and priorities in different European countries, which has always been part of the attraction and relevance of the RENT conference since its origin in 1986.

Following this introduction, the papers selected for inclusion have been grouped into five main themes: regional perspectives on entrepreneurship; new venture creation and growth; business exits; knowledge-based entrepreneurship; and entrepreneurship and social inclusion. While the division represents a convenient way of organizing the book, a number of the papers selected contribute to more than one theme. In addition, although RENT is primarily a scientific conference, all papers included in this volume have some implications for the contribution of entrepreneurship to economic development at the local, regional and/or national scales.

Although the nature and extent of the contribution of entrepreneurship to economic development is a well-established theme in the field, the papers included in this book offer new insights or perspectives on the topic, with potential implications for both policy makers and academics concerned with theories of entrepreneurship. Regional perspectives on entrepreneurship are important to policy makers because regional variations in economic development and resources affect the needs and priorities of regions from a policy perspective. As well as being at the heart of entrepreneurship as a field of study, both the level and qualitative characteristics of new venture creation are increasingly seen by policy makers as key factors influencing the performance of countries and regions in terms of economic development. Business exit is a topic that has been attracting increasing interest, not least because it is not easily defined by many academic studies. There is also growing recognition that entrepreneurial societies require easy exit from, as well as easy entry into, entrepreneurship, if scarce resources are to flow from less to more productive activities. Knowledge-based entrepreneurship is at the heart of the European Union's Lisbon Agenda, with entrepreneurship and innovation as key pillars influencing the competitiveness of the European economy in the twenty-first century. Alongside this, entrepreneurship is seen as an important contributor to social cohesion across Europe, although some academics have challenged the evidence base in this regard (Blackburn and Ram, 2006).

REGIONAL PERSPECTIVES ON ENTREPRENEURSHIP

In the first of two chapters explicitly concerned with entrepreneurship at the regional level, Philip Cooke presents new research on 'green' entrepreneurship, innovation and clusters (Chapter 2). This is the latest in a stream of papers over the last 20 years in which Cooke has argued that the regional level is particularly well suited to supporting the innovation activities of small and medium size enterprises (SMEs), through the myriad of public and private knowledge organizations that make up regional innovation systems. In drawing attention to the variation that exists between countries in political traditions, Cooke describes a concept of collective entrepreneurship, where the latter is induced at the regional level through subsidy, contrasting with more individualized notions of enterprise that are typically part of the Anglo-Saxon political tradition. The emergence of clusters is presented as a topic where the role of collective, as well as individual, entrepreneurship may be explored, illustrated with reference to the entrepreneurial networks that underpinned the emergence of industrial districts.

The core of Cooke's chapter is concerned with so-called 'green' innovation and green clusters, which he relates to technological convergence among diverse industries (e.g. biotechnology, ICT and clean technologies) within a particular geographic space. As well as referring to already documented clusters in California (agri-food, horticulture) and Denmark (solar thermal energy, wind turbine production), Cooke describes a recently 'discovered' cluster in Wales, which includes bioenergy from crops and other novel agricultural products. Cooke's analysis demonstrates the role of small enterprises, as well as some large firms, in the emergence of green clusters, together with the importance of an applied and basic research infrastructure, demonstrating the interdependence that exists within the context of regional innovation systems. Emphasizing the need for a multidisciplinary perspective and referring to both North American and European examples of green clusters, Cooke highlights the replication of processes that have historically underpinned industrial districts in the emergence of new economic activities.

In the second chapter in this section on regional perspectives (i.e. Chapter 3), Niels Bosma and Veronique Schutjens focus on the determinants of early-stage entrepreneurship in European regions. Their core proposition is that regional economic development depends on the type, as well as the level, of entrepreneurship. Using 400 000 individual observations from the Global Entrepreneurship Monitor (GEM) database, the authors focus on innovation and growth oriented entrepreneurship at the regional level. The analysis considers regional variations in innovation and growth oriented entrepreneurs, contrasting the pattern of entrepreneurs with and without a growth ambition. The empirical part of the chapter uses data from the GEM study to create indicators of regional entrepreneurial activity (dependent variables) and attitudes (independent variables), with additional regional level variables obtained from other sources. Four types of early stage entrepreneurship are distinguished: non-ambitious, ambitious, high growth and innovative. Analysis of harmonized entrepreneurship data over 225 regions in 18 countries shows differences between the four types in terms of their determinants. This has implications for the types of policies that are likely to be effective in stimulating different forms of entrepreneurship.

NEW VENTURE CREATION AND GROWTH

Four papers are included in the section on new venture creation and growth. The first, by Pedro García-Villaverde and María Ruiz-Ortega, is concerned with the advantages and risks associated with the entry timing of new ventures (Chapter 4). It is suggested that entry timing is important because of the need to compare windows of opportunity to gain competitive advantage and the liabilities of newness. The focus of the study is on the relationship between external environmental conditions and the capabilities of new ventures (particularly marketing and managerial capabilities), which the authors suggest affect entry timing.

The results confirm the interactive effects between the capabilities of a new venture, on the one hand, and market conditions on the other, on the timing of market entry. For example, the presence of managerial and marketing capabilities favours pioneer behaviour by new ventures in industries with a high level of imitation. This suggests that such capabilities may be used by entrepreneurs to create barriers to impede follower firms from reducing first mover advantages. As well as contributing to the literature on industrial organization, the authors identify implications for practitioners and specifically owners/managers of new businesses who are interested in assessing if their enterprises have suitable capabilities to take advantage of first mover advantages in unfavourable environmental conditions.

In Chapter 5, Miguel Torres Preto, Rui Baptista and Francisco Lima focus on the choice faced by individuals between paid employment and self-employment, from an economic perspective. While the economic theory of occupational choice suggests that differences in expected earnings are the main factor influencing this choice, this is not fully supported by empirical evidence. In this context, the chapter analyses the earnings of individuals who switch from paid employment to business ownership, in comparison with individuals who change firms but remain paid employees.

A longitudinal matched employer–employee data set from Portugal is used to investigate the mobility of workers and business owners during the period 1995–2003. Four models are presented to examine the effects of switching from paid employment to business ownership on individual incomes. Results suggest a severe income penalty in the short run for individuals who switch from paid employment to self-employment. Overall, the results show that opportunity costs play a significant role in influencing whether entering self-employment leads to an increase in earnings in the short run. This is reflected in observed differences between those entering self-employment from paid employment compared with those who were previously unemployed.

The next paper by Colm O'Gorman (Chapter 6) focuses on the financial needs of 'early-stage' entrepreneurs, suggesting that international differences in levels of entrepreneurship may be influenced by variations in the level of resources required to start a business. GEM data from 2002–06 are used to identify the mean and median planned financial requirements of early-stage entrepreneurs across nine Euro-zone countries. The results show significant differences between countries in the mean level of finance required to start a firm, although this appears to mainly reflect a high mean in the Netherlands and a low mean in Spain. More generally, O'Gorman finds there are not large differences between countries in the anticipated total finance required for market entry by nascent entrepreneurs. He also finds the expected financial requirements of early stage entrepreneurs to be low, with medians ranging from 20000 to 100000 euros across the nine countries studied. It should be stressed, however, that these are expected rather than actual start-up costs, since respondents are still at the pre-market or early market entry stage and not all of them will actually continue their efforts to start a business

In Chapter 7, Anders Isaksson and Vladimir Vanyushyn examine the link between growth attitudes and realized growth, using a conceptual frame drawn from the theory of planned behaviour. The focus of the chapter is an important topic, in view of the growing body of evidence emphasizing the link between an entrepreneur's motivation and aspirations and the growth performance of their enterprises. One of the distinguishing features of the research design is the attempt to measure attitudes to growth at one point in time and actual growth performance during a later time period. Moreover, unlike many other studies, the approach seeks a representative sample of enterprises rather than focusing on high performing firms, or firms where there are strong a priori reasons for expecting growth orientation (e.g. high-tech firms). As a result, the actual employment growth performance of enterprises during the study period included firms experiencing negative growth, as well as firms experiencing positive growth; although, not surprisingly perhaps, the majority showed no change in employment. Growth performance was analysed in relation to a four-fold classification of attitudes to growth. The results support the hypothesized link between intentions and outcomes, as stated by the theories of planned behaviour and reasoned action, although the association was weak and the differences in growth performance between high and low aspiration groups relatively small. This indicates the need to incorporate other factors when seeking to explain growth performance. In other words, entrepreneurs' attitudes to growth are important, but should not be considered in isolation.

BUSINESS EXITS

The next two papers deal with different aspects of business exits. Chapter 8 by Miguel Amaral, Rui Baptista and Francisco Lima is concerned with entrepreneurs' decisions to sell or dissolve their businesses, recognizing that business exit is not necessarily an indication of business failure, since some exit decisions are voluntary. Voluntary exit may be a result of an entrepreneur recognizing either a better business opportunity or more positive occupational prospects in, for example, paid employment. Voluntary exit by an entrepreneur may be achieved through winding up the firm or selling it. Part of the context for the chapter is the high proportion of individuals in the Portuguese economy who become entrepreneurs through acquisition, rather than 'de novo' start-up, which is reflected in high rates of business ownership but low start-up rates.

More specifically, the chapter investigates differences between individual and firm level factors that influence the mode of voluntary exit (i.e. sell-out and dissolution), which the authors seek to link to firm performance at the time of exit. A large longitudinal matched employer–employee database from Portugal is used to test a typology of voluntary exits, while addressing three key issues: firstly, the factors associated with exit from entrepreneurship; secondly, distinguishing features of individuals who exit entrepreneurship by discontinuing a firm compared with those who exit by selling the firm; and thirdly, how an individual's decision to sell or close a business relates to the performance of the latter in the market. Results from the logit model estimations for the two different modes of voluntary exit provide support for the hypothesized heterogeneity across forms of exit, in terms of individual and firm level characteristics. Interestingly, being the founder of a firm appears to impact negatively on the decision to leave the firm and exit entrepreneurship. This is interpreted as reflecting the fact that founders have assets that encourage and facilitate their persistence (such as specific business and market knowledge and a higher level of intrinsic involvement in the venture) than second or third generation owners. Not surprisingly perhaps, older firms are more likely to be the subject of voluntary exit than younger firms, with the negative association with the age of enterprise being stronger in the case of dissolution than for sell-out. Similarly, exit through dissolution is negatively associated with a firm's sales revenue, although the relation is not confirmed in the case of the decision to exit through sell-out.

In contrast to the paper by Amaral and his colleagues, the second chapter in this section, by Colin Mason, Sara Carter and Stephen Tagg, is concerned with business failure, or involuntary exit, focusing on its personal consequences for entrepreneurs (Chapter 9). The chapter is concerned with the position of small business owners in a risk society, where risk is equated with the personal financial consequences of the failure of their business. Two key questions are examined: firstly, the proportion of small business owners that are highly exposed to personal financial risk; and secondly, how this risk is distributed across different types of business owners. Data for the study undertaken by Mason and his colleagues were drawn from a large biannual survey of small businesses undertaken on behalf of one of the main membership associations representing small firms in the UK. The survey involved almost 19000 responses, and included a question asking respondents for a self-assessment of the consequences of business insolvency. The results showed a marked variation in the perceived consequences of insolvency, ranging from a more restrained lifestyle to more severe effects. Detailed analysis showed that entrepreneurs seeking to grow their businesses rapidly are potentially vulnerable to greater personal financial risk. By contrast, owners who are the least exposed to personal financial risk should their businesses fail, typically have little or no household wealth invested in the business, operate from home, and are engaged in service industries with low capital intensity. It is important to emphasize that the chapter is concerned with perceived sources of personal financial risk rather than actual business failure. Nevertheless, the findings have implications for the understanding of growth orientation in small firms, as well as contributing to the under-researched area of risk.

KNOWLEDGE-BASED ENTREPRENEURSHIP

This section contains three papers concerned with knowledge-based entrepreneurship. The first, by Joana Mendonça, Rui Baptista and Francisco Lima, is a policy oriented investigation of the role of higher education institutions in the formation of knowledge-based ventures (Chapter 10). The chapter is based on Portugal, which is a country where the higher education system has expanded considerably in the last 30 years, with the emergence of several new public and private universities. The focus is on the effect of the creation of these new higher education institutions on regional levels of entry by knowledge-based firms, based on comparing firm entry rates of regions with new universities with similar regions where the number of universities has remained constant. The data used enable short, medium and longer term effects to be identified over the period 1992–2002. The results indicate that the creation of a new higher education institution in a region has a positive impact on the share of new firm entry in knowledge intensive sectors. This emphasizes the contribution of universities in Portugal to the regional development of knowledge intensive activities, as well as the wider contribution of higher education institutions to the shift to a knowledge-based economy, not only through knowledge spillover effects from institutions, but also through the effect on the supply of more educated people.

Chapter 11 by Ángela González-Moreno and Francisco Sáez-Martínez focuses on cooperation with universities and research institutions for entrepreneurship in established firms rather than in new ventures. The aim of the chapter is to examine how a firm's innovation strategy influences the decision to engage in research and development cooperation with universities and research institutes, which includes a comparison between high-tech and low and medium technology industries. The chapter is based on data from the European Community's Innovation Survey in Spain, with a sample of 9684 firms in low and medium technology activities and 2094 in high technology sectors. The findings show that financial constraints are the main motive for cooperating with universities and research institutes in low and medium technology sectors, whereas in high-tech industries, it is a lack of market information and the perception of risk that are important. The findings also show that a firm innovation strategy affects its propensity to cooperate with universities and research institutes, as does increasing firm size, particularly in low and medium technology sectors. In low and medium technology activities, external cooperation of this type can act as a substitute for formal research and development activity in-house, although the frequency of such cooperation is typically less than in high technology sectors. More generally, firms that carry out internal research and development have a greater propensity to cooperate with universities and research institutes, suggesting that a firm's internal absorptive capacity influences it propensity to collaborate externally.

The third paper in the section (Chapter 12), by Vinit Parida and Mats Westerberg, is concerned with collaborative network structures involving small firms in the ICT sector. The study focuses on external relationships that contribute to a firm's revenue and are repetitive, in an attempt to concentrate on relationships that are important to the firms. Using entrepreneurial orientation (EO) as the dependent variable, the authors explore the relationship between the level of EO and different types of collaborative network, together with firm characteristics (age, size, etc.) and capabilities, specifically those related to networking and ICT. Hence, the purpose of the study was to investigate how different collaborative network structures of ICT-related small firms can be linked to ICT and networking capabilities and entrepreneurial orientation.

The analysis distinguishes four groups of firms. The first group ('stuck without contacts') comprises firms with few collaboration partners and low networking capacity, which is associated with low entrepreneurial orientation compared with other firms and low ICT capability. The second group ('on the move') consists of firms with few collaboration partners but high networking and ICT capabilities. Firms in this group also scored highly on entrepreneurial orientation. Firms in the third group ('stuck with contacts') have many collaborative partners but low networking capability, suggesting uncertain outcomes. Firms in this group are also low on ICT capability but exhibit a similar level of entrepreneurial orientation to firms in groups two and four. Firms in the fourth group ('at full potential') have many collaboration partners and high networking capability. They also have high ICT capability, which they combine to achieve high entrepreneurial potential. Across the sample as a whole, a link is identified between entrepreneurial orientation and ICT capability and networking, suggesting that firms not only need collaboration structures but also the tools to handle them. With regard to entrepreneurial orientation, the results suggest there are different ways for small firms in the ICT sector to achieve it, although further research is required to investigate the relationship with firm performance.

ENTREPRENEURSHIP AND SOCIAL INCLUSION

The final set of papers deal with different aspects of the relationship between entrepreneurship and social inclusion. Chapter 13 by Carole Howorth, Caroline Parkinson and Alan Southern is concerned with the discourse of enterprise and whether or not it has the power to enable or disable deprived communities. The chapter is inspired by the number of economic development initiatives in the UK that connect enterprise with deprived areas, which includes, but is not confined to, the promotion of social enterprise. Following a critical overview of UK enterprise policy with respect to deprived areas and a literature review, the authors analyse the discourse around enterprise policy and compare the language used by three different groups involved in social enterprise activities: support workers, social entrepreneurs and community leaders. This is based on a series of interviews with representatives of each group, in which qualitative data were gathered.

From their analysis of the language used by these three groups, the authors conclude that application of the enterprise discourse to the social enterprise agenda can potentially lock out certain players and activities. This can result from the exclusionary effects of less business-minded people and/or activities that do not comply with the legal forms of social enterprise organizations. Although all three groups interviewed echo the imperative of existing social organizations becoming more businesslike, unlike support workers, social entrepreneurs and community leaders establish discursive boundaries between being 'business like' and serving important social needs. Bordieu's concept of 'symbolic violence' is used as an interpretive frame, which refers to the gradual subordination of people to ideas and structures promulgated by the dominant groups in the society. The study uses a novel approach to an important topic that has implications for wider debates about enterprise culture, as well as specific implications for policy on enterprise in deprived areas.

Chapter 14, by Trevor Jones, Monder Ram and Nicholas Theodorakopoulos, is concerned with Somali entrepreneurs in Leicester, which is predicted to be the first city in the UK where ethnic minority people will become the majority. The study adopts a mixed embeddedness perspective to critically analyse the characteristics and behaviours of one of the more recently arrived immigrant groups in the UK. The approach adopted emphasizes the social embeddedness of immigrant and ethnic minority entrepreneurship, and particularly the economic and institutional context. The empirical focus of the chapter is on the extent to which UK-based Somalis are drawing on transnational links to establish and develop their small enterprises. In so far as they are, this may be interpreted as an extension of social capital into the international sphere through transnational trading and investment linkages. The study is part of a critical examination of transnationalism, which the authors describe as the latest fashion in ethnic exceptionalism. A qualitative research design was adopted to examine the nature of transnational links and the actual experiences of Somali business owners in Leicester, based on in-depth interviews with them.

The results show that, in some respects, transnational co-ethnic links act as an important resource for ethnic minority and/or immigrant small business activity. Examples include accessing finance, labour and commercially useful information. At the same time, the political-economic context is said to impose harsh constraints on Somali business activity that the mobilization of social capital at any spatial scale is unable to circumvent. In such conditions, the authors conclude that transnational entrepreneurship is likely to be the preserve of a minority of minorities.

The final paper (Chapter 15), by Friederike Welter and David Smallbone, deals with the emergence of entrepreneurial potential in economies in transition, which like the previous two chapters emphasizes the importance of interpreting entrepreneurship in its social context. Specifically, the chapter is concerned with the process of creation and development of new ventures in three of the Newly Independent States (NIS): Ukraine, Belarus and Moldova, which are all relatively harsh environments for the development of productive entrepreneurship. The authors use case studies to demonstrate the potential for venture creation from simple petty trading activities (or informal arbitrage activity), in a context where more conventional approaches to venture creation face serious resource and other constraints. The empirical evidence suggests that some of the activities operating outside the legal framework are adding value to the process of economic and social transformation in these countries. Conceptually, the evidence is used to challenge simplistic divisions between entrepreneurs and proprietors, opportunity and necessity entrepreneurs and the formal and informal economy. Instead, the cases are used to demonstrate the blurred nature of these boundaries empirically and thus the limitations of some of the related conceptualizations. Overall, the chapter demonstrates a need for entrepreneurship theory to be robust enough to be applicable in a variety of social contexts, of which the countries included here provide some of the harsh conditions for entrepreneurship to become established.

CONCLUSION

We very much hope that readers will find the selection of papers included in this collection stimulating and thought provoking. Entrepreneurship has grown rapidly as a field of study in Europe in recent years and this is demonstrated by the success of the RENT conference, which, in Cardiff, entered its twenty-first year. The dynamism of the field of study in Europe is also reflected in the emergence of entrepreneurship research groups in universities and research institutes across a growing number of countries. This is reflected in this volume, where contributions from Spain and Portugal feature prominently alongside the more traditional centres of research in the field in northern Europe. As editors of this volume, we are pleased to be able to report that, on the basis of the research presented at the RENT conference and specifically the contributions included in this book, European entrepreneurship research remains alive and well, both in terms of the heterogeneity of content and methods, and the vibrancy associated with emerging centres of research excellence.

REFERENCE

Blackburn, R. and M. Ram (2006), 'Fix or fiction? The contributions of small firms to social inclusion', *Entrepreneurship and Regional Development*, **18**(1), 73–89.

PART II

Regional Perspectives on Entrepreneurship

2. Regional innovation, collective entrepreneurship and green clusters

Philip Cooke

INTRODUCTION

The subject of this chapter is innovation and regions, highlighting new research on 'green' entrepreneurship, innovation and clusters. Accordingly it focuses particularly on the contribution that has been made to regional growth and prosperity through the operation of regional innovation systems and strategies. Of course a chapter on such a subject must recognize that the processes and outcomes being presented are not limited to regions alone. However, it has become increasingly clear during the past 15 years or so since the subject was first aired in the academic literature (Cooke, 1992) that the regional focus is particularly well suited to supporting the innovation activities of firms and knowledge organizations. The latter include university research centres and institutes, as well as public and private specialist research institutes outside the university sphere. These interact and display strong connectivity in robust regional innovation systems.

Knowledge flows to those who need it, and commercial opportunities arise. This is the aim, and in many cases the achievement, of democratic authorities, their agencies and private associations of firms and other innovation organizations that make up a regional innovation system. In recent years, such governance mechanisms have sometimes evolved with only light touch steering being applied, elsewhere they have been designed by a multilevel governance process. Some countries draw on traditions of enterprise, individualistic as well as collective; others induce it at regional level by subsidizing what may be deemed collective entrepreneurship. Collective entrepreneurship goes along with connective innovation in a systems approach to the subject.

Collective entrepreneurship is an interesting approach, which is comfortable with systems thinking and contrasting with the individualized notion of the entrepreneur. Systems centrally involve nodal points of power or influence and network connectivity between nodes; social systems are mainly open systems. The notion of entrepreneur as individual hero has dominated the field of study and action in entrepreneurship since Schumpeter (Schumpeter, 1975) although by that publication even he had evolved his thinking to recognize the element of teamwork that characterized corporate innovation. Entrepreneurship and innovation are not identical. A venture capitalist is entrepreneurial but his or her method is tried and tested. An innovator's offering is always to some degree novel, thus at risk. Mention of Schumpeter suggests an appropriate point at which to define some of the other key concepts that have been mentioned that will inform the following text. In this tradition (e.g. Freeman, 2008) innovation is defined with great clarity as: *the commercialization of new knowledge*. Thus its marketability differentiates *innovation* from *invention*. Innovation may be thought of as operating at a number of scales; global, international, national and *regional* (possibly also local in regard to innovative *clusters* – see below). Regional is taken as the meso-level of a country below the national and above the local level. Research has also been conducted into sectoral and technological innovation systems. However the former is increasingly somewhat constrained by a notion of 'sector' that seems increasingly to be breaking down given the prevalence of general purpose or 'platform' technological innovation, while the latter seems somewhat deterministic and hardware-focused given that innovation is increasingly concentrated in services and, currently, industries like agriculture (biofuels) or even culture (i.e. creative industries) that were only a few years ago widely thought rather low-tech or even no-tech (OECD, 1999; CEC, 2001). From this perspective, innovation takes five forms: product, process and organizational are the well-known ones found in, for example, the Frascati manual.

Even more interesting in some respects are Schumpeter's two other categories of innovation: *region* and *input*. The latter might include the quartz *input* to the (digital) watch. Of these, and for obvious reasons it is *region* as innovation type that is most fascinating for the purpose of this report. Sadly, however, Schumpeter left no well-formulated theory of regional innovation and entrepreneurship. But, as will be shown below, as with many things about Schumpeter, a combination of deep reflection, an appropriately informed empirical object, and a historical perspective can work wonders. Finally, from this work we observe five types of innovation process. The best known are *radical*; that is, 'root and branch', a total change in the whole system by which a commodity is supplied – a new classic being DVD rendering video obsolescent overnight, and Blu-ray doing the same to DVD. Incremental innovations involve improvements to existing products or processes such that, for example, cost is lowered and quality improved simultaneously. To these, recent proposals have been added: *sustaining* and *disruptive* innovation (Christensen, 1997). The former is, to stay with video/DVD competition, a firm producing better and better video recording equipment for a settled market segment (i.e. video in the media industry); while the latter offers typically cheaper, easier to use (e.g. DVD, now, as noted, being replaced by Blu-ray) technology.

Last is the type of innovation that Schumpeter thought was generic to all innovation in varying degrees, namely 'new combinations' (of existing knowledge) but this is too restrictive, leaving out the possible interaction of existing and wholly new knowledge. Spotting the 'new combinations' insight, Hargadon (2003) made the mistake of characterizing all innovation as 'recombinant', a topical term from biotechnology with its discoveries in recombinant DNA. In Cooke and Schall (1997, 2007) we proposed *recombinant* innovation to be that which recombined a specific innovation in numerous ways customized according to demand. Thus smart cards may be used to measure *temperature*, where a firm finds its bananas ripening too soon; *frequency* when a customer wants controls electronically applied around the clock to prevent, say, capacity overflows; or *pressure* in containers, engines or heaters and so on. Sensors have a similarly protean adaptability, as do increasing numbers of general purpose innovations (Helpman, 1998) in ICT, biotechnology and nanotechnology. Many of these converge in 'green innovation' as will be shown below.

The chapter proceeds as follows. The first section is devoted to the production of taxonomies of the above levels, categories and types of innovation accompanied by illustrative material. The second section highlights key aspects of entrepreneurship, notably of the collective kind, that is often overlooked in the relevant literature. The following section explores important evolutionary economic geography concepts, such as 'related variety', lateral absorptive capacity, proximity and portfolio, platform and platform policy, cluster mutation and Jacobian clustering. The third section examines four cases of green regional innovation systems based on Jacobian clustering. This is followed by a conclusion that sustains the notion that regional innovation is significantly responsible for creation of national value.

INNOVATION SYSTEM TAXONOMY

It is helpful to juxtapose the categorizations outlined above to investigate any important relationships such an exercise might reveal. At this stage of conceptualization, when we are primarily concerned with relating the five Schumpeterian innovation *categories* to the five neo-Schumpeterian innovation *intensities*, we are looking for elements of consistency along the columns and rows that help clarify the differential path dependencies or trajectories of innovation associated with underlying corporate strategies. When, later, we focus particularly strongly on Schumpeterian *regional innovation*, the interest in having observed corporate or cluster trajectories that are foundational for regional policy evolution will be to the forefront. The intersection between corporate culture and regional culture with respect to innovation and entrepreneurship choices is only now beginning to be explored in regional innovation system studies, utilizing a combination of 'varieties of capitalism', 'business systems' and 'worlds of production' frameworks (Cooke and Clifton, 2007; Casper et al., 1999; Whitley, 2000).

Innovation Intensity and Type: Some Regional Innovation Inferences

For the present, juxtaposing these innovation categories in an ex ante taxonomy (Table 2.1) reveals or underlines specific alignments that can be of use in regional innovation policy-making. The most important general point about the taxonomy is that it clearly shows the considerable range of innovation that occurs across the spectrum of economic activity from agro-food production to designer products, and financial services to information and communication technologies (ICT). This is important because, among other things, it shows hitherto deemed low-tech agriculture to be in the vanguard with respect to its contribution to renewable non-fossil fuels, in a context of climate change from greenhouse gases and 'peak oil' energy security concerns. But actually it reminds us that far from being low-tech,

Table 2.1   Innovation intensity and Schumpeterian category taxonomy

Innovation	Product	Process	Organizational	Region	Input
Radical	Computer	Pasteurization	On-line insurance	'Railroadization'	Laser
Disruptive	PC	Radiation	Budget airline	Trucking	Quartz watch
Recombinant	Smart card	SPV	Lean management	Biofuels	Sensors
Sustaining	HD TV	CAD-CAM	Customization	Artisan food	Designer goods
Incremental	3G cellphone	Wind energy	Call centres	Hybrids	2G biofuels

Notes: PC: personal computer; HD TV: high-definition TV; 3G: third generation; SPV: special purpose vehicle (see text); CAD-CAM: computer-aided design/manufacturing; 2G: second generation.

agro-food is one of the most science and technology intensive activities of all and has been since the onset of intensive and industrialized agriculture and food processing in the second half of the last century.

The illustrative selection of innovations is revealing for other reasons, particularly in clarifying differences among, for example, innovation intensities. Thus, as indicated earlier, radical innovation changes its context as well as commercializing unforeseen applications potential. Disruptive innovation, by contrast, is obsolescence-inducing and to some extent competence-destroying but essentially cheapens and 'democratizes' innovation, creating and broadening demand for new competences among its vastly increased user community. Recombinant innovation is *agile* in the adaptability of its fundamental properties to new combinations and contexts. One now notorious variant of recombinant innovation is the Special Purpose Vehicle (SPV).[1] Sustaining innovation, it becomes clear, involves moves up-market to escape competition. In this respect it is distinguished in this dimension also from disruptive innovation, which tends to cheapen. Finally, incremental innovation tends to offer more quality at less cost for a pre-existing innovation and is thus clearly different from sustaining innovation.

A further point of interest concerns *sustaining* innovation. As it clearly involves moving up-market to escape competition from disruptive and other innovators, it can be generalized to certain kinds of corporate or cluster organization where a particular regional mix of products or services is assailed by cheaper competition. The obvious regional exemplar of this as a cluster strategy supported by regional innovation policy is Emilia-Romagna and, it could be argued, the 'Third Italy' more generally. Thus CAD-CAM was introduced by the regional innovation system in the 1990s so that knitwear firms could escape developing country imitations and was made available to the collective entrepreneurs in the relevant industrial districts (Cooke and Morgan, 1998) by utilizing advanced technology with more agile design-intensive production at higher quality and cost than hitherto. Hence we could typify this and other appropriate Third Italy regions as having in the past and apparently for the future become locked in to a *sustaining innovation* developmental trajectory. This applies to all 'Made in Italy' production clusters such as shoes, leather goods, jewellery, clothing and furniture. In policy terms the emphasis on support for quality improvement has helped these traditional industry clusters to survive and thrive but whether it can continue so to do is an open question.

Penultimately, in regard to the illumination given to regional innovation by the taxonomy in Table 2.1, we may briefly indicate the rather unsurprising element of lock-in that also typifies *incremental innovation*. Unless it becomes disjointed, whereby it would arguably move into recombinant, it remains somewhat 'path dependent'. A good example of incremental product innovation occurs in telecom clusters like that for wireless communications at Aalborg in Denmark where what came to be called the NorCOM cluster collectively innovated the Global System for Mobile Communications (GSM) infrastructure system for supporting mobile telephony. Despite inward merger and acquisition by the likes of Texas Instruments, Motorola and Siemens, the cluster thrives and is innovating around third generation (3G) mobile telephony as well as researching 4G and 5G. In 2007 Denmark introduced regions, among whose obligations is that of supporting regional innovation.

Relatedly, in conjunction with medical technology innovation nearby, NorCOM has spawned an emergent BioMedico cluster of biotechnology firms in a process we elsewhere refer to as Jacobian cluster mutation. This evolutionary process is found in a number of innovative regions characterized by rapid knowledge flows among collective entrepreneurs and knowledge organizations. North Jutland is one example, California another, with Wales and the Central region of Israel yet others. This regional innovation process displays cross-fertilization among clusters in convergent industries that display 'platform-like' related variety (proposed by Jane Jacobs as the key driver of innovation in cities; Jacobs, 1969). Mutation occurs through high lateral absorptive capacity of knowledge spillovers among related industries and their entrepreneurs. Thus such external economies realize yet another form of collective entrepreneurship that is massively assisted by geographic proximity that avoids the 'portfolio' effect experienced in regions with low related variety, low knowledge spillovers and cognitive dissonance among firms rather than high lateral absorptive capacity. These are clear gains to regional innovation and growth performance where a single innovation might be adapted and applied in, say, six different contexts within the regional development platform.

Finally, we will look into Schumpeter's only writing to embrace the notion of 'region', which occurs in his discussion of a fourth kind of innovation that he exemplifies by the radical innovation process of 'railroadization'. This too had pronounced regional development platform elements, involving infrastructure, mobility, construction, agriculture and pedagogy of various kinds as well as collective and individual aspects of entrepreneurship. Railroadization was the process led by large railroad corporations as oligopolies opening up new agricultural lands. This happened wherever and whenever the railroad arrived. It was very evident on a vast scale in Eastern Europe and Russia; and on a smaller scale in Scandinavia, notably in Jutland, Denmark and of course North America. The railroad route was selected, towns were built at the train stations, land was made available cheaply to pioneer farmers, agricultural equipment entrepreneurs arrived, farm services were built at the railhead, insurance (the even earlier financial services innovations called 'futures' and 'options' occurred in connection with railroadization) and varieties of training were established, including setting up craft schools and agricultural extension colleges but also the distribution by the railroad companies of training manuals for would-be farmers, who helped each other get started in practical terms. Schumpeter refers to this as almost the purest form of radical innovation because it represents a disturbance to the general equilibrium of the national and even global economy by a significantly punctuated evolutionary moment. Traditions are overturned ('creative destruction'), productivity receives a massive boost from the greater efficiency and effectiveness of production, and bursts of innovation are set off in neighbouring sectors, such as the aforementioned futures and options markets, the organizational innovation of marketing complete farm equipment, including dwellings, through mail-order catalogues such as those of Sears and Roebuck, and much speedier product delivery, hence vast expansion of markets, again by railroad and by steamship. Later in this chapter railroadization is shown to explain the current proliferation of Jacobian clusters in the innovative growth region of north Jutland in Denmark. A taste of that analysis may be had by reflecting on the wind turbine blade innovations that branched from the railroadization era agricultural equipment (ploughs) and marine engineering (ships' propellers) industries that preceded wind turbines. The Danish national system subsidized the development of what became a highly successful strategic industry organized at the level of the north Jutland regional innovation system. As will emerge later in this report, collective entrepreneurship rather than public administration supplied the governance drivers for regional innovation in this, at the time, weakly 'regionalized' innovation system. As noted, in January 2007, well after the innovation had triumphed, Denmark defined its official regions, of which there are five – one being north Jutland.

COLLECTIVE ENTREPRENEURSHIP

In orthodox discussions on and research into entrepreneurship it has been traditional to place the focus of theoretical attention on attributes of individual entrepreneurs, for example psychological or behavioural dispositions, their status as recent immigrants, and so on. This approach unquestionably explains certain aspects of entrepreneurship as part of a larger, presumably more homogeneous adult population but it does not throw useful light on geographical variation in entrepreneurship. That is except insofar as recent immigrants might be expected to have located in or near ports, which can be shown historically to have higher than normal rates of entrepreneurship (Nijdam and de Langen, 2003). Nowadays mass air travel has diluted that observation to some extent, although port cities remain entrepreneurial places (Edvinsson, 2006).

Nevertheless, research on immigrant and/or ethnic entrepreneurship is often forced to relax individualistic theoretical assumptions and account for entrepreneurship in terms that highlight social networks of religious, linguistic or other cultural kinds. Notions like embeddedness, social capital, 'structural holes' and 'relational proximity' enter the discourse to capture the social dimension of economic activities that a more orthodox, not to say neo-classical approach neglects (Granovetter, 1992; Burt, 1992; Putnam, 1993; Cooke and Clifton, 2005; Boschma, 2005). In the analysis and empirical research that follows the notion of entrepreneurship that acts as a main vehicle for the emergence of Jacobian clusters is this kind of collective entrepreneurship. A compelling reason for this choice is the more structural and institutional analysis that the evolutionary economic geography implied by the key concept of regional innovation systems invokes. New economic geographic thinking about crucial questions, not least for policy observers let alone regional scientists, such as how and when do clusters *emerge* also necessarily takes us into a collective entrepreneurship rather than an individualist entrepreneurship discourse. That is not to say individual entrepreneurship is ignored in this perspective. Rather, where observable, as for instance with the notion of 'lead entrepreneur' and 'entrepreneurial' or 'triggering event', it plays a part. Though not studied in depth here, cluster emergence can be traced back in important ways in all empirical instances portrayed in this chapter, such as the NorCOM cluster genesis in north Jutland, Denmark (*SP Radio*, 1948, ship-to-shore radio), the wireless cluster in San Diego (*Linkabit*, 1968, military communications; Simard and West, 2003), photovoltaics in Wales (*Thales Optronics*, 1957, lenses), and software firewalls in Israel (*NDS*, 1977, encryption algorithms). However, in all cases these entrepreneurial events were accompanied by swiftly imitating spin-offs (Klepper, 2002) that together with elements of public investment and academic knowledge resulted in cluster emergence.

Hence, these elements of origination through interaction, among those capable in exploration (research), examination (testing) and exploitation (commercialization), lie at the heart of modern collective entrepreneurship. In earlier periods, the *networks* sustaining collective entrepreneurship had been more community-based forms of embeddedness as found in industrial districts. Something distinctive from this, which may have been more corporately induced but still retaining numerous collective considerations, can be envisaged with Schumpeter's notion of North American 'railroadization' with its responsibilities for soft and hard infrastructure, pedagogy and so on in newly opened lands. Elements of this style of western coop- erative competition form the core of Saxenian's (1994) study of Silicon Valley. Finally, establishment of self-organized, publicly supported tech- nology institutes and craft schools inter alia in new communities, with reli- gious worship also sustaining pioneer communities (as in California too), were common in the early modernization of Jutland, Wales and Israel. Evolving over time, such that religious embeddedness elements became attenuated, and venture capital and/or the state as key support investor rose in its place, nevertheless, it has been shown by Kristensen (1992), Saxenian (1994), Avnimelech (2008), also Teubal et al. (2002) and Cooke (this chapter, below) that collective entrepreneurship in regional innova- tion systems (RIS) is a viable and valid way of understanding regional evolution in the cases examined.

RECENT ADVANCES IN RIS RESEARCH

One of the most interesting research areas opened up in RIS research in the recent past concerns the insights of Jane Jacobs (1969) and can also be referred to as addressing the challenging issue of 'cluster emergence'. In particular by examining the emergence of a number of 'green clusters' on a regional canvas, we see emphasis in 'green innovation' on technological convergence among diverse industries. These include biotechnology, infor- mation technology and nanotechnology (but not limited to these high- tech activities) and among them we also see a process of cluster 'species mutation'. Of particular fascination here is that some regions have the capability relatively rapidly to mutate many 'Jacobian' clusters – so-called because although different they display evolutionary characteristics of 'related variety' (Boschma, 2005).

Jacobian Clusters

One such region is northern California whose ICT, biotechnology and clean technology clusters overlap in proximity to San Francisco but also near various agro-food clusters like wine in the Napa, Sonoma and Russian River valleys and varieties of horticulture in the San Joaquin and Sacramento River valleys (see Figure 2.1). But notice, Figure 2.1 also shows southern California having prominent Jacobian clusters in Los Angeles and San Diego (Cooke, 2008). North Jutland in Denmark is another such region, as apparently is Wales in the UK, as we shall see (Cooke, 2008, 2009). The important points here are the importance of national policy for regional innovation and the importance of regional

⊖	Clean Technology
⊘	Biotechnology
●	Wireless
⊖	ICT
◑	Agro-Food
☺	Wine
○	Film

Figure 2.1   California's Jacobian clusters

innovation for national growth. North Jutland's economy is the global centre of the wind turbine production industry, whose profile and evolutionary trajectory were key beneficiaries from the outset of varieties of innovation. As will be shown, this recently 'discovered' cluster has all the required characteristics to warrant the cluster designation, conjoining university research at, for example, Ålborg and Århus Universities, the Danish Technological Institute (DTI) also at Århus, and both spinout firms and larger, indigenously established firms that are involved in 'green innovation'. This is captured in data from the European Commission that shows Denmark as a whole being one of the Cleantech leaders. Thus in 2007, according to the European Commission:

environmental technology is one of Denmark's largest business clusters, and includes 420 companies (60,000 employees) . . . analysis showed a number of 'strongholds' for potential to develop new environmental technologies clusters. They include offshore turbines and water purification. (European Commission, 2007)

The Danish Ministry of Economic and Business Affairs (FORA) report (Environment Ministry, 2006) shows that a further 46 knowledge institutions consider themselves to be primarily active in environmental technology research. The FORA report shows one means by which the emergence of 'green innovation' clusters may be performed partly at the behest of government activity. This is referred to elsewhere as 'articulation of discourse' (Davenport and Leitch, 2009), which is a powerful cognitive and ideological process by means of which a discourse of action and promotion occurs within the state apparatus but articulated both to wider, global concerns, the interests and concerns of local business, and a modernizing discourse expressing a policy-advisory consensus, in this case privileging clusters, innovation and climate change. For illustrative purposes, clearly, on inspection, the quote from the European Commission (2007) report is taken directly from the FORA report. This report shows how the FORA business and economic research unit defined environmental businesses and mapped a Danish cluster. This cluster occupies the abstract space of Denmark's national environmental industry. It is the loosest definition of 'clustering' as promulgated by Porter (1990).

Hence apart from being in Denmark the 'cluster' has no geographical specificity of the kind Porter (1998, p. 199) was rather more sensitive towards. He referred there to a cluster as: 'a geographically proximate group of interconnected companies and associated institutions in a particular field, linked by commonalties and complementarities'.

With regard to such clusters the most important analytical task is to establish the extent of interconnections, commonalities and complementarities since this is what distinguishes a localized cluster, its specialization or differentiation and its potential for exploiting knowledge spillovers for competitive advantage.

In the FORA exercise, the first step was to identify the 'clump' of environmental technology firms throughout Denmark prior to articulating that they constitute a cluster. Next, the 'cluster' is divided into sub-clusters based on the environmental challenge faced by the company or knowledge institution; that is, into which sub-category of the abstracted cluster do specific actors 'fit'? Eight of these were identified. Next a pilot project was run examining three of these sub-clusters: energy/climate change, water and chemicals. The rationale for selecting these first for further analysis was scale ('three sizeable clusters'), including high-tech smaller and large Danish companies, and areas in which Danish research institutes are perceived to be conducting world-class research and development (R&D). The two target groups, firms and research institutes were then invited to profile their extent of 'green innovation', market expectations of their chosen course of action, and extent of collaboration (key to clustering) with others in this pursuit. Next, these answers were assessed in relation to sub-cluster critical mass (unspecified), knowledge (world class or not), and market potential (preferably global). Hence the articulated discourse of what have now become Denmark's environmental technology clusters draws on global excellence, innovativeness, collaboration and scale. Interestingly, photovoltaics, another pronounced cluster in north Jutland is not highlighted in this report.

Therefore on this basis five promising clusters were selected:

- Wind energy turbines (pioneered in Denmark since the 1970s, see below).
- Water purification (well-established businesses).
- Industrial biotechnology (well established, e.g. fermentation, enzymes).
- Biofuels (spin-offs from existing industry, for development).
- Fuel cells (spin-offs from existing industry, for development).

Companies in such industries were then asked what frame conditions (i.e. government support) would help them to evolve their potential or actual 'stronghold' status. These included regulation, stimulus to collaboration, public research funding and entrepreneurship. In the Appendix reporting contacts with research institutes only, some 10 per cent of these seem to have occurred outside Copenhagen, indicating the official 'cluster' discourse probably has a geography (and a 'scale' bias) that is centred on the capital city, even though substantial economic activity takes place in Jutland and elsewhere. This shows how national innovation systems leaders favour core over periphery, giving impetus to collective action at the periphery, as will be suggested below. Such an interpretation is reinforced in respect of the large scale of business interviewees, thus only a few, larger Jutland firms like Vestas and Siemens Wind Power (wind turbines), Grundfos and Danfoss (both engineering) feature among the total number of environmental technology interviewees.

FURTHER EVIDENCE OF JACOBIAN CLUSTERS

Jacobian Clusters in Jutland

We noted above the presence of Jacobian clusters in the Californian RIS, commenting how such convergence was rendered more visible by examining green innovation, which is necessarily highly convergent. Continuing in this vein and focusing for the moment on wind energy, the question of whether what is in North Jutland is a wind-turbine cluster had first to be addressed. On this, Andersen et al. (2006) point to the wind energy industry having passed through an early phase characterized by numerous small and medium-sized enterprises (SMEs) producing domestically scaled wind power for individual farms and householders. But latterly, especially since the government subsidy to domestic consumers was removed in 2000, exports have risen, the scale of equipment has increased tenfold and sea power from large-scale offshore wind farms has come to predominate. As wind turbines have only some ten years life expectancy, most early wind turbines in rural Denmark will soon disappear if they have not already done so. So the current industry structure is large Danish (*Vestas*) or foreign (*Siemens, Gamesa, Suzlon*) producers and a supply platform of SMEs. There may be less local sourcing of key equipment like gearboxes than in the early days when North Jutland shipbuilding firms could adapt to meet the nascent wind energy demand. Services and special logistics firms, the latter capable of transporting the now typically massive fibreglass turbine blades, also exist in proximity as do a great many components suppliers (Figure 2.2).

Stoerring (2007) agrees with this evolutionary profile, pointing out that scale was also partly induced in the early 1980s by huge demand for wind turbines from the US and more particularly California. Then, in the late 1980s this market collapsed because California's state administration removed its subsidy regime and the Reagan administration cut alternative energy research budgets. At this time, many US turbines malfunctioned badly and even the superior Danish three-blade design was prone to breakdowns. Thereafter, the industry recovered as demand in European and Asian markets rose. Nowadays around half global production capacity is accounted for by Danish firms, like world leader *Vestas Wind Systems* of Randers, near Århus (acquirer of Danish firms *NEG-Micon; Nordtank; Wind World*) and *Siemens* (*Bonus*) at Brande and Ålborg. *Gamesa Wind Engineering*, Spain's largest producer of turbines is at Silkeborg. *Suzlon*, India's leader is located at Århus. *LM Glasfiber* of Lunderskov near Århus in Jutland is the leading supplier of fibreglass wind turbine blades, and so on. Of the Danish Wind Industry Association's 70 members, 50 are in Jutland, mostly north-central Jutland.

Unrealized until now, overlapping this substantial and globally leading wind turbine technology cluster is the main Danish solar thermal energy cluster (Figure 2.3). This consists of largely indigenous firms and their suppliers, which involve firms in two types of supply chain as follows:

Key:

Manufacturer   Materials

Services   Logistic   Components

Source: Drawn from Danish Wind Industry Association statistics.

Figure 2.2   The North Central Jutland wind turbine cluster

Source: Composed from ESTIF data.

Figure 2.3 North Jutland's solar thermal energy cluster

- Solar collectors
- Glazed (roofs):
  - (Flat plate collectors):
    - Glass
    - Heat absorbent copper/aluminium
    - Coatings, paint
    - Pipes welded to absorber plate
  - Vacuum collectors:
    - Parallel glass tubes
    - Absorber
    - Transfer pipes
    - Vacuum is insulator
- Unglazed (swimming pools) long tubes

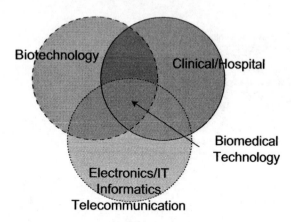

Cluster Evolution and Species Multiplication in Aalborg?

BIOMEDICO Cluster Emergence: Aalborg, Denmark

Source: Stoerring (2007).

Figure 2.4   Jacobian cluster emergence in North Jutland

- Synthetic absorbent material
- Hydraulics in pool filtration system
- Heat storage and back-up heating
- Plumbing and Installation.

Finally, exemplifying North Jutland's Jacobian cluster profile it is worth considering Figure 2.4 and 2.5, the first of which reveals established cluster evolution in the shape of the NorCOM wireless communications cluster at Ålborg and the possibly emergent and overlapping biomedical technology cluster in close proximity (Stoerring, 2007). Here, the long-established wireless telecommunications cluster (Stoerring and Dalum, 2007) has given rise to possible cluster mutation by interaction with the healthcare activities associated with clinical trials and testing related to biomedical equipment. Many of these activities are closely associated with science and technology commercialization through academic entrepreneurship at Ålborg University. In Figure 2.5 are shown the most prominent (though many have yet to be fully researched) of North Jutland's Jacobian clusters, which are characterized as emergent clusters or established ones by their 'related variety' characteristics in relation to each other. This may be understood as follows:

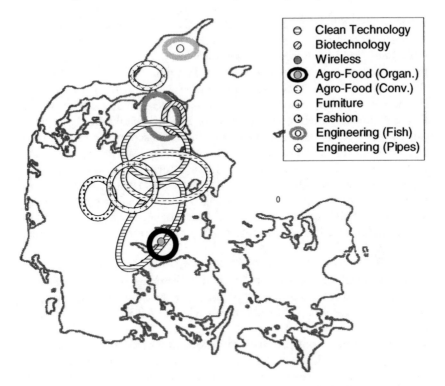

Figure 2.5 North Jutland's Jacobian clusters and related variety

- Clean technology is path dependent on agricultural and marine engineering (e.g. wind turbine blades replicate plough and propeller design).
- Biotechnology is path dependent on Wireless ICT and Medical Tech.
- Wireless technology is path dependent on ship-to-shore marine technology.
- Agro-food became established with the 'railroadization' of Jutland; organic agro-food is a reaction against conventional intensive food production in Jutland (mostly dairy).
- Furniture is path dependent on 'railroadization', craft schools and the local forestry tradition.
- Fashion clothing evolved for women from craft schools skilling farmers' wives.
- Modern fish equipment and pipework engineering is path dependent on fishing and marine engineering.

There is insufficient space to offer a satisfying explanation for the Jacobian cluster mutation process in North Jutland but Kristensen (1992) underlines 'railroadization' as a key process where Jutland as a whole was opened up on a smaller scale but with similar inspiration to that of the Frontier West in the nineteenth-century USA. With this came two key movements. The first was the farmers' cooperative movement, where farmers supplied their own production and household needs, including banks. The second movement was the craft schools, established in over 350 centres; followed by the still flourishing Danish Technological Institutes from 1907. Together these made a form of social or collective entrepreneurship possible; in other words, the infrastructure, education, technical support, finance and markets. Hence 'social capital' remains an important dimension of the SME-based collective entrepreneurship of North Jutland. It makes technological branching by means of related variety evolution possible.

Finally, the existence of an RIS infrastructure of technological institutes, technical and craft schools and universities sustains entrepreneurship and localized knowledge transfer. Hence this is a strong case, probably as much as California, of an RIS animated by a tradition of collective entrepreneurship rather than administratively guided. Much the same can be said of our penultimate regional illustration. From the ruins of Wales' FDI-led RIS strategy and the under-performance of its generic entrepreneurship successor, has emerged a related variety platform of mostly rurally based innovation excellence driven by research laboratories and spinouts in the broad agro-food platform, which is now rapidly being augmented by biofuels and biomass energy innovation. In a brief final subsection the generalization of RIS-based Jacobian clustering around these convergent technologies is extended to Israel.

Bioenergy from Crops in Wales

One of the most surprising, perhaps, but unquestionably innovative developments in the bioenergy field has occurred in recent years in Wales. Descriptively speaking it involves patented knowledge derived by the Institute for Grassland and Environmental Research (IGER) based at Aberystwyth in rural, central Wales. This UK Biological Research Council-funded research institute has, for 70 years to 2007, been the UK's main, specialist grassland research institute. It was tasked from the outset with improving the quality of fodder for cattle and sheep feedstock, which is mainly grass. By the early 1980s, research involved not simply breeding richer grasses but understanding the rumen of these ruminative animals. It had revealed that a limit to quality on these mountain-bred animals occurred because the enzymes that broke down fodder into protein were actually consuming a significant portion of the nutritional value of the fodder eaten by the animal.

Following many years of lengthy field trials and laboratory research, cross-breeding the basic ryegrass commonly utilized for cattle and sheep fodder with breeds possessing enhanced sugar content produced optimal results. The enzymes took some of the enhanced sugar content, transforming it directly into energy, but left a substantial portion for the animal, sufficient for the amount, nutritional value and flavour of the animal to be significantly enhanced. A patent was approved for this in 1987. This came to the market at a time when consumer demand for leaner meat of the type raised in mountainous areas rose significantly and continuous improvement to the original *AberDart* strain of ryegrass, marketed by *Germinal Holdings*, over the intervening years led to it reaching 50 per cent of the UK market. It further secured the status of Welsh black beef and Welsh lamb as premium products and enabled significant improvements to occur in comparable upland cattle breeds, such as Aberdeen Angus.

In 2003, it was realized that IGER had, in the form of these SugarGrasses, an indigenous product to add to its burgeoning portfolio of biofuels. Tests had shown that SugarGrass had twice the calorific value of sugar cane, the source of much of the world's biofuel. IGER thus evolved a second string to its grassland expertise by developing a renewables research division. One of the biofuel feedstocks in which it became supreme early on was the growing and processing of *Miscanthus*, more popularly known as Elephant Grass, an Asian tall grass that grows on marginal land. Accordingly it doesn't compete for land with food crops, one of the criticisms of the US and Europe's 'bolt for biofuels'. This has seen the ears and cobs of wheat and corn being turned into ethanol because of easy availability and major subsidy, causing up to 40 per cent increases in the price of such cereals, and grief in developing country food markets.

Tellingly, IGER is widely perceived as in a global class of its own in these specific bioenergy sub-fields. The official view is that maybe the University of California, Berkeley is a serious rival, now they have received a $500 million endowment for a Climate Change research institute from British Petroleum (BP). Apart from the University of Illinois, also mentioned as a possible future competitor (but only those two), IGER has a current lead on both of them. But in any case, SugarGrass is also twice as calorific as *Miscanthus* and SugarGrass is thus favoured as the technology with the best long-term prospect to replace oil. Willow woodchip has also been researched for renewable biomass energy and is seen as a leading candidate for combustion power generation. IGER has the patent for SugarGrass, currently earning royalties of £100 000 per year from sales of seed varieties for fodder. But as the world awakens to the relatively simple processes of biorefining the product, these are likely to grow substantially. So much so that agreement has been reached with Welsh government officials about the promise of funds to help build an experimental biorefinery. Thinking had gone as far as to speculate that when oil ceases to be refined at the huge Milford Haven refineries in neighbouring Pembrokeshire, the pool of talent and infrastructural sunk costs would make them ideal candidates for becoming SugarGrass (and *Miscanthus*) biorefineries. These would continue to meet a huge share of the UK's future energy. But it is not simply a spinout venture capital model that is in mind, possibly because a spinout model doesn't yet work as well as a commercialization out-sourcing model in this nascent field. For example, *Molecular Nature*, the spinout identified in Figure 2.6, burnt up its venture capital, but because of the value of its patent for biofuels potential as well as its fodder market, it was acquired by spin-in company *Summit*. Moreover, true to the tra-ditions of collective entrepreneurship among Welsh mountain farmers, IGER promotes a new vision of mixed farming whereby groups of farmers grow *Miscanthus* on their poorest soil, devote some fields for SugarGrass fuel cropping and raise quality Welsh lamb or Welsh black beef on their best SugarGrass land.

Precision farming, whereby seed is automatically sown in varying intensities according to GPS field data on variability in soil humidity and fertility, held in the laptop in the farmer's tractor cab, makes for enhanced efficiency and effectiveness in this increasingly high-tech farming model (Pedersen and Pedersen, 2006). But the prospect is that farmer coop-eration would enable them to undertake local, small-scale biorefining. SugarGrass is fermentable for extracting the juice that becomes ethanol to be used on the farm or sold. But the dried remnants can also be used either as fodder, or as feedstock for yet another bioenergy variant, in biomass power station burning. A bio-revolution seems to be afoot in rural Wales, as not only biofuels but biocomposites are also being researched and experimentally produced among groups of entrepreneurial farmers linked to Bangor University in north Wales. Mercedes cars use hemp-based insulation material of the kind being produced by an eight-farm group in Snowdonia and 'Future Farmers of Wales', which is a 140-strong associa-tion of younger farmers willing to diversify into biofuels, functional foods and cosmeceuticals, is thriving.

Hence, Figure 2.7 attempts to delineate key interactions in the emer-gence of a biocomposites, biofuels and related agro-biotechnology *plat-form* of inter-connected and emergent clusters in north Wales, while Figure 2.8 maps the photovoltaics cluster, again in north Wales but also the networks of photovoltaics producers throughout Wales. In this

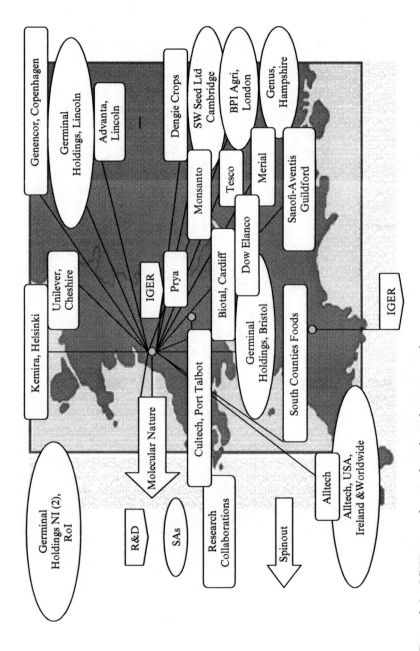

Figure 2.6 IGER – novel agricultural products research

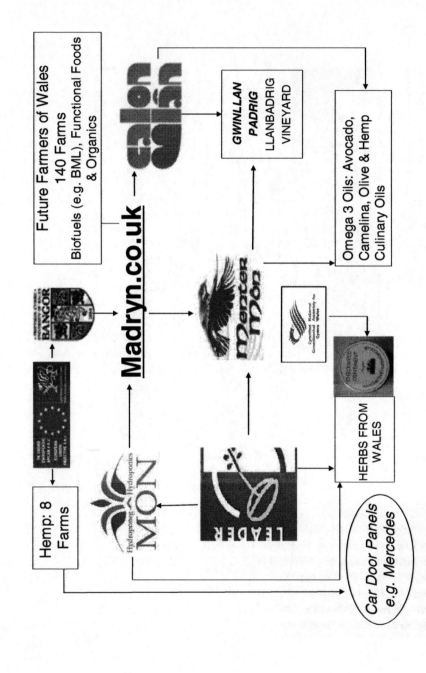

Figure 2.7 Green cluster emergence: North Wales

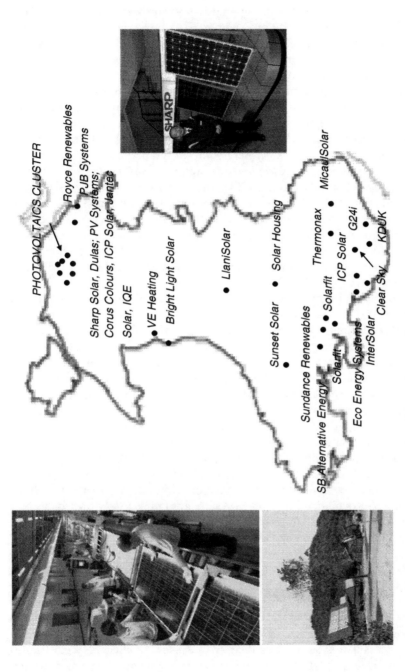

Figure 2.8   30 solar energy equipment manufacturers in Wales

emergent and relatively sub-regional innovation system a number of key organizations are found. For example, EU Convergence Funding plays a role in a project whereby a number of farms experiment with hemp as a biocomposite of the kind utilized by automotive firms, such as *Mercedes* as insulation in car body panels.

Partnership with Bangor University's Biocomposites Centre is a means by which knowledge generated in the Centre is exploited commercially. However, also important to the network is *Madryn*, an intermediary firm that acts as a combination of 'knowledge aggregator' and 'entrepreneurship accelerator'. It works closely with, on the one hand, an association of farmers seeking to diversify into agro-bio and sustainable product development and marketing, while, on the other, engaging in serial entrepreneurship itself and entrepreneurship acceleration among other businesses. These range from firms producing 'green cosmeceuticals' (herbal make-up) to functional foods and locally grown culinary oils enriched with, for example Omega-3 oils. These include relatively recently introduced olive trees that survive the hitherto cold winters of north Wales as a consequence of climate change.

Photovoltaics produce solar thermal energy as in North Jutland. In Wales, this has been studied by authors (Hendry et al., 2003) comparing the broader opto-electronics cluster, which also specializes in fibre-optic cabling, with those such as that associated with *Carl Zeiss* in Jena, eastern Germany. However, in relation to this present discussion about 'green clusters', it is the photovoltaics capability that comes to the fore. Figure 2.8 reveals the presence of sub-divisions of multinationals such as Japanese electronics corporation *Sharp* whose *Sharp Solar* subsidiary is based at St Asaph alongside Corus Colours, a subsidiary of Corus, the UK–Dutch steel manufacturer, acquired in 2007 by Indian giant *Tata Steel*. This company has developed the radical innovation of solar energy paint that can be applied to steel-clad buildings: 100 000 square metres of steel cladding yields the equivalent of 50 medium-sized wind farms. Other firms in the photovoltaics cluster at St Asaph are indigenously owned, such as Cardiff headquartered microprocessor firm *IQE* and 'green engineering' firm *Dulas*, headquartered in mid-Wales.

Hence, in conclusion, we see that numerous indications of clustering among small firms, but also some large enterprises, together with an applied and basic research infrastructure, characterize important locations of 'green clusters', mainly, in this analysis, focused on the production of non-fossil fuel energy that contributes to the moderation of global warming. A key feature to be discussed in the concluding section of this chapter is that in some cases there is an element of cluster 'species' multiplication that, from an evolutionary economic geography perspective can

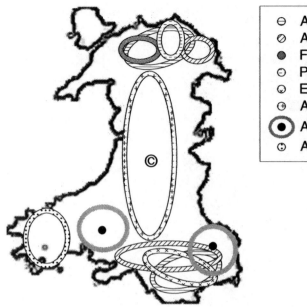

⊖	Aerospace
⊘	Automotives
●	Fibre Optics
⊙	Photovoltaics
⊙	Electronics
⊕	Agro-Food ©
⦿	Agro-Food (O)
⊙	Arts & Crafts

Figure 2.9   Jacobian clusters in Wales

readily be hypothesized. As shown in Figure 2.1, the Californian clean technology clusters are to be found in juxtaposition to the ICT and biotechnology, food and wine clusters of the San Francisco region of northern California and the wireless telecom and biotechnology clusters of San Diego in southern California. Indeed, so-called *Cleantech* is widely seen as arising from the combination of biotechnology (including biopolymers and biofuels), ICT (sensors) and nanotechnology (catalysts and filtration membranes). However, while agro-food is also one of California's key industries, agro-food path and agro-engineering[2] RIS Jacobian cluster mutation are more pronounced in the cases of Jutland and Wales (Figures 2.5 and 2.9), as we have seen, while in yet another case forestry is important to Sweden's biofuels cluster in Örnsköldsvik (Cooke, 2007).

A final, comparable instance is shown in Figure 2.10 in relation to Israel. Agro-food had long been a predominating industry there. Until the 1990s it had supplied the largest share of Israeli exports. But immigration from post-Soviet Russia brought numerous highly qualified scientists and engineers, for whom the Israeli government designed an innovation system programme involving construction of some 200 incubators where small start-up businesses could locate, and a public–private venture capital system to finance the best prospects. Some two to three thousand

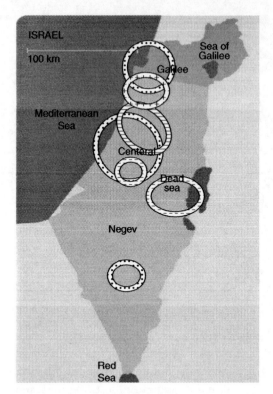

Figure 2.10   Israel's Jacobian clusters

such new firms, many in software and other ICT activities, medical technology, biotechnology and, most recently, *Cleantech* have been founded
(Avnimelech, 2008).

CONCLUSIONS AND IMPLICATIONS

By virtue of an examination of the emergence of new RIS green clusters,
often involving the production of new forms of non-fossil fuel energy
aimed at lessening the overall greenhouse gas (GHG) emissions derived
from human economic activity, a curious feature of economic evolution
has been revealed. The clue lies in the element of convergence that charac-
terizes green innovation. As hinted at in the cases of northern and southern California, not studied in detail here but examined elsewhere (Cooke,
2007), the type of 'Cleantech' industry emerging in the clustered form
described by Burtis et al. (2004, 2006) evolves from agro-food, ICT and

biotechnology. In North Jutland, we see something comparable having occurred. Thus the wind turbine and solar thermal clusters are found in the more agricultural and marine engineering regions of Denmark. In writing the history of the former industry, Karnøe and Jørgensen (1996) and Jørgensen and Karnøe (1995) note how the Danish design of wind turbines defeated the main global competitor from where a significant renewable technology demand also arose simultaneously from the 1970s, namely California. As noted, Danish wind turbine blade design was influenced by the agricultural engineering industry, notably the design of modern ploughing equipment. In the experimental innovation phase when some 30 firms engaged in the design of prototype turbine blades, knowledge spillovers from the design of propellers by marine engineers in the Jutland shipbuilding industry were also absorbed. This resulted in a three blade solution and the idea that the greater efficiency in the operation of such blades came from pointing them into the wind. California's aeronautics tradition, by the 1970s predominantly relying on jet propulsion, led to the recovery of historic knowledge of propeller-driven aeroplanes. This suggested a two-blade solution pointing downwind. The Danish solution proved far superior to the Californian in this technological contest.

Hence in these multi-cluster locations, it is clear that a good deal of technological convergence is possible and probably necessary. But, interestingly, comparable technological assets do not necessarily produce optimum solutions from such Schumpeterian 'new combinations'. Nevertheless, it is clear that in some regions cluster forms can evolve quite readily from other cluster forms; the cluster 'species' multiplication giving the region more of a cluster 'platform' characteristic to its industrial organization. On further inspection, both California and Jutland prove to have spawned many clusters. In the former case, wine clusters overlap the horticultural zones, Hollywood's film cluster is well known and Porter (1998) also profiles other, sometimes highly specialized clusters, such as the alloy golf club cluster at Carlsbad in the southern Californian desert. Further inspection of the cluster history of Jutland (Figure 2.5) reveals the detailed cases of Salling (furniture) and Ikast (clothing), the even more closely studied NorCOM wireless telephony cluster at Ålborg (Stoerring and Dalum, 2007), the emergent BioMedico cluster also at Ålborg, as well as so far unexamined cluster candidates in insulated pipework near Ålborg, and fish processing equipment near Skagen, at Jutland's northern tip. At Barritskov, east Jutland, is the estate that sustains the *Årstiderne Organic Food Network*, a cooperative retail network that delivers 30 000 boxes per week of organic food throughout Denmark. It could also be argued that there is a high degree of knowledge transfer from varieties of agricultural production to bioenergy production in Wales leading to possibly nascent cluster formation, but also from glass technology to fibre-optic cables and then photovoltaics by a different route into renewable energy in a multi-functional opto-electronics cluster. Species multiplication or muta- tion of this kind would be perfectly consistent with an underlying theory of evolutionary economic geography, especially that part referring to the opportunities for innovation and growth arising where there is *related variety* among industries. Absorptive capacity for adaptation to new com- binations based on easily understood knowledge spillovers would be the mechanism by which such species multiplication is explained, as the case of Jutland's wind turbine technology illustrates especially clearly.

In other cases, focusing on 'green innovation' cluster specialization, as ascribed to Marshall–Arrow–Romer (MAR) thinking, seems on the face of it to be more convincing than the idea of Jacobian clustering. Yet even where limited clustering occurs, as in Rhineland or Brazil, previously exist- ing industries, whether the coal, steel and chemicals super-clusters of the Ruhr Valley (bioremediation) or the sugar producing industry on Brazil (bioethanol), are suggestive of the presence of important spillovers from knowledge of filtration and ventilation in the former and fermentation in the latter cases. These were of profound importance to the evolution of new, convergent combinations of innovative products and processes. This tends to confirm the widespread and common sense policy experience that clusters cannot be easily built *in vacuo* but may find a less rigorous evolutionary trajectory to emergence, where the regional context gives opportunities for Schumpeterian 'new combinations' from regionalized 'related variety'. Where such related variety is more attenuated, as perhaps with biofuels in Brazil or north-east England (biodiesel), fewer 'Jacobian clusters' emerge.

However, that is not the whole of the explanation for Jacobian cluster mutation; rather it is an important contextual factor as noted, for example, in the work of Cantwell and Iammarino (2003). Other key features that may be hypothesized, but further research is needed to test, are that Jacobian clustering benefits from other more social, institutional, and organizational assets, such as those listed below, in addition to more economic assets concerning related variety, knowledge spillovers and high lateral absorptive capacity:

- Social capital
- Collective entrepreneurship
- Technological branching ('new combinations' opportunities)
- Peripherality (perceived distance from key governance core)
- Infant industry subsidy
- Innovation system – regional research and technological institutes
- Universities, regional innovation platform policy and funding.

The key concluding point of this section is that, for the first time in regard to new industries, we see replication of processes that have historically underpinned successful regional economies that once spawned many traditional industrial districts or clusters. Evolutionists like Klepper (2002), for example, would also highlight the transfer of routines from one industry to another by means of 'mobility of talent', as in the cases of the US, German and Italian automotive and engineering industries (see also Boschma and Wenting, 2007). Probably the key findings of this contribution in relation to evolutionary theory are the following. First, while Schumpeter had little to say about regional innovation, his concept of innovation by 'railroadization' proves to be highly apposite as an explanation of, at least, the case of Denmark's opening up of North Jutland and elsewhere in the west in the nineteenth century, and its modern evolution into an arena of Jacobian clustering in related variety industries. It may prove to be, on further historical reflection, also the case in Wales. Second, the green perspective has somehow thrown the evolution of this kind of industry organization into clearer perspective because it focuses on a horizontal and convergent technology 'platform concept' rather than a more traditional industrial economics perspective that emphasizes vertical structures like sectors or clusters. Finally, regarding cluster emergence within a Regional Innovation Systems context, the research reported showed the importance of social capital, which even in California may be considered strong, as the work of Saxenian (1994) on Silicon Valley showed, as an evolutionary driver of certain kinds of regional innovation system. Indeed, whether as 'bonding', or more institutional 'bridging' social capital, it is the key element of the hidden power of networks, both social and institutional, that has always been at the heart of the RIS approach to evolutionary science.

This means RIS thinking may usefully be linked to a general policy perspective that aims to enhance related variety industrial structures, especially where these can be embedded in established skills and capabilities suitably adapted and modernized. The aim must always involve building 'bridging' social capital between regional institutions and organizations, not least because these enhance the transmission of knowledge spillovers. It seems that single or few knowledge centres are also able to maximize their innovation effect, where there is a related variety platform to interact with. Geographical proximity and the possibility of Jacobian cluster mutation can be profoundly dynamic economic development vehicles in such circumstances, as demonstrated. Finally, policy organization itself must be transformed away from vertical sector and specialized cluster approaches into more horizontal, 'joined-up' and lateral project-based policy activity. A portfolio of relevant innovation policy instruments such as those described, including financial, infrastructural and skills-related instruments, must be made available as flexible packages for entrepreneurs. But this may also have to be conducted in a much more pragmatic way, whereby public management targeting is de-emphasized and, when it comes to subsidizing infant innovative industries, subsidies to customers to be able to purchase innovations should be considered in some contexts, such as green innovation, as possibly superior support instruments than those normally provided only to producers.

NOTES

1. This was innovated in Hollywood as a mean of financing films by placing revenues in a special off-balance sheet account; hence if a film lost money it didn't affect the health of the film company, while if it was successful it was off-balance sheet so did not attract taxation until it was on the balance sheet. It was later to feature in the energy industry as the vehicle by means of which Enron and others fraudulently avoided declaring huge trading losses, finally bringing the firm to bankruptcy. Tarnished by association with Enron, recently SPV have spawned many new variants in financial services as the entities into which 'sliced and diced' sub-prime mortgage debt was traded through variable interest entities (VIEs) or 'conduits', special investment vehicles (SIVs) and collateralized debt obligations (CDO), in 2007 leading to numerous bank collapses.
2. In Wales the cluster mutation path dependences move from agro- and mining engineering to automotive and aerospace and latterly to ICT, then opto-electronics and photovoltaics. Conventional agriculture led to alternative agriculture in functional, organic/ artisan foods, biocomposites and latterly biomass and biofuels industries that show signs of potential as emergent clusters. As in Denmark arts and crafts are intimately interactive with rural skills such as weaving, ceramics and painting – nowadays tied closely to 'cultural' tourism.

REFERENCES

Andersen, P., M. Borup and M. Olesen (2006) 'Innovation in energy technologies', *Risø Energy Report*, **5**, 21–27.
Avnimelech, G. (2008) *An Evolutionary Model of Startup-Intensive and Venture Capital-Backed High Tech Cluster Development*, Be'er Sheva: Ben Gurion University of the Negev.
Boschma, R. (2005) 'Proximity and innovation: a critical assessment', *Regional Studies*, **39**, 61–74.
Boschma, R. and R. Wenting (2007) 'The spatial evolution of the British automobile industry: does location matter?', *Industrial and Corporate Change*, **16**, 213–38.
Burt, R. (1992) *Structural Holes: The Social Structure of Competition*, Cambridge, MA: Harvard University Press.
Burtis, P., R. Epstein and R. Hwang (2004) *Creating the California Cleantech Cluster*, San Francisco, CA: Natural Resources Defence Association.
Burtis, P., R. Epstein and N. Parker (2006) *Creating Cleantech Clusters*, San Francisco, CA: Natural Resources Defence Association.

Cantwell, J. and S. Iammarino (2003) *Multinational Corporations and European Regional Systems of Innovation*, London: Routledge.

Casper, S., M. Lehrer and D. Soskice (1999) 'Can high technology industries prosper in Germany? Institutional frameworks and the evolution of the German software and biotechnology industries', *Industry and Innovation*, **6**, 5–24.

CEC (2001) *Regions: Statistical Yearbook 2001*, Luxemburg: Commission of the European Communities.

Christensen, C. (1997) *The Innovator's Dilemma: When New Technologies Cause Great Firms to Fail*, Boston, MA: Harvard Business School Press.

Cooke, P. (1992) 'Regional innovation systems: competitive regulation in the new Europe', *Geoforum*, **23**, 365–82.

Cooke, P. (2007) *Growth Cultures: The Global Bioeconomy and Its Bioregions*, London: Routledge.

Cooke, P. (2008) '*Cleantech* and an analysis of the platform nature of life sciences: further reflections upon platform policies', *European Planning Studies*, **16**, 1–19.

Cooke, P. (2009) 'Green clusters: green innovation and Jacobian cluster mutation', *Geografiska Annaler*, **1**, forthcoming.

Cooke, P. and N. Clifton (2005), 'Social capital, firm embeddedness and regional development', *Regional Studies*, **39**, 1065–78.

Cooke, P. and N. Clifton (2007) 'Evolving a conceptual framework: from RIS analysis to "worlds" and "varieties" of regional economy and governance Culture', Background Paper for EU FP 6 *Corporate Culture and Regional Embeddedness (CURE)* Research Project, Cardiff, Centre for Advanced Studies.

Cooke, P. and K. Morgan (1998) *The Associational Economy*, Oxford: Oxford University Press.

Cooke, P. and N. Schall (1997) 'How do firms innovate?', *Regional Industrial Research Paper 29*, Cardiff: Centre for Advanced Studies.

Cooke, P. and N. Schall (2007) 'Schumpeter and varieties of innovation', in H. Hanusch and A. Pyka (eds), *The Companion to Neo-Schumpeterian Economics*, Cheltenham, UK and Northampton, MA, USA: Edward Elgar publishing.

Davenport, S. and S. Leitch (2009) 'Creating space for the successor: the discourse strategies of pro- and anti-GM factions regarding the future of agriculture in New Zealand', *European Planning Studies*, **17** (7), 943–61.

Edvinsson, L. (2006) 'Aspects of the city as a knowledge tool', *Journal of Knowledge Management*, **10**, 6–13.

Environment Ministry (2006) *Environmental Technology Strongholds in Denmark*, Copenhagen: Environment Ministry and FORA.

European Commission (2007) 'The European Cluster Memorandum: promoting European innovation through clusters – an agenda for policy action', available at: www.clusterobservatory.eu.

Freeman, C. (2008) *Systems of Innovation: Selected Essays in Evolutionary Economics*, Cheltenham, UK and Northampton, MA, USA: Edward Elgar publishing.

Granovetter, M. (1992) 'Problems of explanation in economic sociology', in N. Nohria and R. Eccles (eds), *Networks and Organisations: Structure, Form and Action*, Boston, MA: Harvard Business School Press.

Hargadon, A. (2003) *How Breakthroughs Happen*, Boston, MA: Harvard Business School Press.

Helpman, E. (ed.) (1998) *General Purpose Technologies and Economic Growth*, Cambridge, MA: MIT Press.

Hendry, C., J. Brown, H. Ganter and S. Hilland (2003), 'Facilitating innovation in opto-electronics in a national, global, and regional context', *Environment and Planning C: Government and Policy*, **21**, 53–70.

Jacobs, J. (1969) *The Economy of Cities*, New York: Vintage.

Jørgensen, U. and P. Karnøe (1995) 'The Danish wind turbine story: technical solutions to political visions', in A. Rip, T. Misa and J. Schot (eds), *Managing Technology in Society: The Approach of Constructive Technology Management*, London: Pinter.

Karnøe, P. and U. Jørgensen (1996) *The International Position and Development of the Danish Wind Turbine Industry*, Copenhagen: AKF.

Klepper, S. (2002) 'Capabilities of new firms and the evolution of the US automobile industry', *Industrial and Corporate Change*, **11**, 645–66.

Kristensen, P. (1992) 'Industrial districts in West Jutland, Denmark', in F. Pyke and W. Sengenberger (eds), *Industrial Districts and Local Economic Development*, Geneva: International Institute for Labour Studies.

Nijdam, M. and P. de Langen (2003) *Leader Firms in the Netherlands Maritime Cluster*, Delft: Delft University Press.

OECD (1999) *S&T Indicators: Benchmarking the Knowledge-Based Economy*, Paris: Organisation for Economic Co-operation and Development.

Pedersen, S. and J. Pedersen (2006) 'Innovation and diffusion of site-specific crop management', in J. Sundbo, A. Gallina, G. Serin and J. Davis (eds), *Contemporary Management of Innovation*, London: Palgrave.

Porter, M. (1990) *The Competitive Advantage of Nations*, New York: The Free Press.

Porter, M. (1998) *On Competition*, Boston, MA: Harvard Business School Press.

Putnam, R. (1993) *Making Democracy Work*, Princeton, NJ: Princeton University Press.

Saxenian, A. (1994) *Regional Advantage*, Cambridge, MA: Harvard University Press.

Schumpeter, J. (1975) *Capitalism, Socialism & Democracy*, New York: Harper.

Simard, C. and J. West (2003) 'The role of founder ties in the formation of San Diego's "Wireless Valley"', paper presented at DRUID summer conference *Creating, Sharing and Transferring Knowledge*, 'Geographical Agglomerations' theme, Copenhagen, 12–14 June.

Stoerring, D. (2007) 'Emergence and growth of high technology clusters', PhD thesis, Department of Business Studies, Aalborg University.

Stoerring, D. and B. Dalum (2007) 'Cluster emergence: a comparative study of two cases in North Jutland, Denmark', in P. Cooke and D. Schwartz (eds), *Creative Regions: Technology, Culture and Knowledge Entrepreneurship*, London: Routledge.

Teubal, M., G. Avnimelech and A. Gayego (2002) 'Company growth, acquisitions and access to complementary assets in Israel's data security sector', *European Planning Studies*, **10**, 933–54.

Whitley, R. (2000) 'The institutional structuring of innovation strategies: business systems, firm types and patterns of technical change in different market economies', *Organization Studies*, **21**, 855–86.

3. Determinants of early-stage entrepreneurial activity in European regions: distinguishing low and high ambition entrepreneurship

Niels Bosma and Veronique Schutjens

INTRODUCTION

Entrepreneurship has received increasing attention in the past three decades and has been shown to be one of the engines of regional economic growth (Acs et al., 2003; Audretsch and Keilbach, 2004; Wennekers, 2006). Theoretically, entrepreneurship and new firm formation contribute to economic growth in at least three ways. First, in the Schumpeterian vocabulary, a direct economic effect is a result of the fact that entrepreneurs themselves are the people making 'Neue Kombinationen' of products and markets (Schumpeter, 1934). Schumpeter regarded an entrepreneur as 'a master innovator, as a force behind economic development' (Etzioni, 1987, p. 177). Among the many other scientists who defined entrepreneurship, ranging from Marshall's 'coordinator of economic resources' in 1890 to Casson's 'decision maker' (see Van Praag, 1999 for an overview), Schumpeter stood out in stressing that innovativeness is the key characteristic of an entrepreneur. This type of entrepreneur introduces new products, new processes, new market applicants and new organization structures. In the end, this innovative entrepreneurship fuels productivity growth of individual firms – and at a higher level, regional economic development. A second direct effect of entrepreneurship relates to employment creation. In particular, gazelles (rapidly growing firms, who succeed in combining resources and opportunities) fuel employment growth (Henrekson and Johansson, 2008). Many of these gazelles turn out to be young firms, who grow more organically than older gazelles (Henrekson and Johansson, 2008, p. 11). Finally, a third, more indirect, effect of entrepreneurship on economic growth, relates to the competition effect of new market entry, leading to passive and active learning of incumbents, and eventually to an increase in productivity.

In conceptualizing the economic effects of new firm formation, a key notion is entrepreneurial variety. Not all firms can be characterized as truly 'entrepreneurial' (Wennekers and Thurik, 1999) and entrepreneurial activities in the region, shaped by institutions forming the rules of the game, need not be 'productive' (Baumol, 1990). In reality many new firms walk well-trodden paths and can be regarded as imitators instead of innovators (Schutjens and Wever, 2000). Setting up a new firm is a risky business, and 'playing safe' by entering familiar markets with familiar products, can at least partly lift the burden of uncertainty. Although even imitators are necessary for knowledge diffusion, market expansion and industry development, stimulating the genuine entrepreneurial pioneers in innovation and growth presumably has the largest multiplier effects in the regional economy (Carree and Thurik, 2003). It seems that not only the level of regional entrepreneurship matters to the regional economy, but also the type of entrepreneurship, especially its quality (in surviving) and potential (in growth and innovative productivity). In our view the distinction between high and low ambition entrepreneurship is key to recent propositions of the role of 'entrepreneurship capital' (Audretsch et al., 2006) or entrepreneurship as the 'knowledge filter' (Acs et al., 2003) in fuelling economic growth. However, in seeking empirical support for this, predominantly measurements of entrepreneurship have been used that also include non-ambitious entrepreneurs; while a large share of these can, in economic terms, be in fact considered as labour or at most resemble managerial business owners with a limited distinctive impact on growth. Positive exceptions to this are studies focusing on entrepreneurship in specific sectors.

Because of their relatively large direct economic effects, it is innovation and growth-oriented entrepreneurship we focus on in this chapter. Following Davidsson et al. (2006) we argue that both firms' growth and innovative potential are strongly determined by the aspirations and expectations of the entrepreneurs at the time of start-up. As argued above, most new entrepreneurs have low growth ambitions, and show satisfying behaviour in running a firm (small business ownership, shopkeeping or refugee firms), which is reflected in relatively low survival or growth rates of new firms. But many people who start off with high ambitions about future growth and innovation, eventually turn their young business into a 'gazelle' in terms of number of employees (Birch, 1979) or into a real innovative business. Wong et al. (2005) came up with empirical evidence that high growth oriented early stage entrepreneurial activity significantly stimulated GDP growth per worker, while overall early stage entrepreneurial activity did not. With respect to employment effects, Autio (2007) showed that nascent and new firms with high job growth ambitions (10 per cent of the sample) represented 80 per cent of total expected job creation. This is in line with the work of Wiklund (2006), who stated that firm performance depends on entrepreneurial strategy, which can be captured by a company's entrepreneurial orientation measured by innovation, proactiveness and risk taking.

It has been shown that most explanations of differences in entrepreneurship rates can be found at the sub-national level, instead of the national level (Reynolds et al., 2005; Sternberg, 2000; Tamásy, 2006; Bosma and Schutjens, 2009). Furthermore, there is empirical evidence of regional differences in growth- and innovation-oriented entrepreneurship (Bosma and Schutjens, 2007). What we propose is to study regional prevalence rates of ambitious, early-stage entrepreneurial activity, identified at the individual level, in a similar fashion as Wong et al. (2005) did at the national level. However, where Wong et al. focused on economic effects in linking prevalence rates to economic growth, we investigate the determinants of regional variation in ambitious entrepreneurship.

In this chapter we therefore analyse whether some regions perform better than others in innovative- and growth-oriented entrepreneurship, and whether the regional pattern of ambitious (new) entrepreneurship in Europe differs from the pattern of non-ambitious entrepreneurship. Furthermore, in search for underlying processes we investigate potential determinants of the regional patterns of both non-ambitious and ambitious entrepreneurship. As we include factors at both the regional and the national level, this is a multilevel exercise. Studying determinants of both non-ambitious and ambitious entrepreneurship over regions and countries enables us to disentangle *specific regional attributes* (e.g. market opportunities), *regional demography effects* (an overrepresentation of groups of individuals with high entrepreneurial and/or ambitious spirits), and an *institutional component* consisting of informal institutions (culture, values, norms) and formal institutions (rules, laws, regulations) (North, 1990). The results are relevant to policy makers in two ways. First, a high prevalence of innovative and high growth oriented early stage entrepreneurs at present, may in the near future boost employment growth or innovation at the firm level, and economic growth at the regional level (Autio et al., 2007). Second, the outcomes give insight into which spatial levels of intervention and which specific policy instruments can be most effective to stimulate promising entrepreneurial activities.

In the next section we explore the literature on explanations of regional variations in entrepreneurship and, more specifically, ambitious entrepreneurship. Next, we pay attention to the data and methodology we use for obtaining measures of ambitious entrepreneurial activity in European regions. Based on entrepreneurship rates calculated from over 400000 individual observations from the Global Entrepreneurship Monitor (GEM), we show regional patterns of people's involvement in different types of early-stage entrepreneurial activity in 125 (mainly) Nuts1 regions in 18 European countries. In the following section we explain regional variation in four different types of entrepreneurship. The last section concludes and discusses our findings.

EXPLAINING REGIONAL DIFFERENCES IN ENTREPRENEURSHIP: LITERATURE REVIEW WITH A FOCUS ON AMBITIOUS ENTREPRENEURSHIP

The literature on explaining differences in regional entrepreneurship rates – albeit low or high ambitious entrepreneurship – shows that its underlying processes play at different analytical levels (Schutjens and Wever, 2000). As the basic decision to start a firm lies within the individual, the event of taking this step highly depends on the balance between economic opportunities and individual values, preferences, personality and capabilities (Frank et al., 2007). At the regional level, for instance, local availability of (mainly cheap) business premises, regional market perspectives, employment possibilities, competition structure and accessibility may affect personal opportunities. Also at the regional level, the population composition influences firm entry, as an aggregate of individual entrepreneurial capabilities and personal attitudes towards entrepreneurship. At a higher level, both analytically and spatially, socio-cultural values and attitudes towards firm ownership or even national regulatory impediments matter to individual values and individual assessments of capabilities and opportunities. As a consequence, regional differences in entrepreneurship may be the effect of both specific *regional economic attributes* (e.g. job or market opportunities), a *regional demography component* (an overrepresentation of groups of individuals with high entrepreneurial spirits or actual entrepreneurial behaviour), and *an institutional component* encompassing informal (national or regional values concerning self-employment) and formal (national or regional regulations to employment protection, tax policies) factors.

Regional Economic Attributes

At the regional level, specific 'opportunity-related' factors may enhance or limit entrepreneurship rates. In the view of traditional industrial economics, the carrying capacity of the market indicates whether there is room left for new firms. Market entry and exit arise from the confrontation of demand and supply. The industry structure involved plays an important role here, especially with respect to firm size, innovativeness, competition and job opportunities. Market concentration (Tödtling and Wanzenböck, 2003), a high share of small and medium sized firms (Fritsch, 1992), and high entry and exit barriers negatively affect new firm entrance. It has also been stated that turbulent and high growth industrial sectors generate more innovative start-ups than mature industries (Schumpeter, 1942). A negative relation exists between high shares of alternative job opportunities and entrepreneurship. On the demand side, market potential and market growth, as well as GDP change, influence firm formation. Market conditions both at the national and the regional level influence entrepreneurial activity: good market opportunities will trigger new entrepreneurs. Originally based on the urban incubator hypothesis, the large market potential in terms of both customers and suppliers and high knowledge intensity are important benefits for potential entrepreneurs (Tödtling and Wanzenböck, 2003). With respect to agglomeration economies, the current debate is whether the presence of similar types of firms or different firm types stimulates new firm formation (localization and urbanization effects respectively) (Fotopoulos and Louri, 2000, Rocha and Sternberg, 2005). Also, regional unemployment rates may affect start-up rates, in the sense that for the unemployed the opportunity costs of self-employment are relatively low.

The Regional Demography Component

As starting a firm is an individual decision, individual characteristics are important determinants of new firm formation. Therefore many scholars in the field of entrepreneurship use the labour market approach, instead of the business stock perspective, when explaining regional rates of entry (Bosma et al., 2008c). As in the latter perspective entrepreneurship or firm formation rates are calculated as a percentage of the existing business stock, it assumes that characteristics of the incumbent firms, such as numbers or average firm size, lie behind firm formation. In contrast, the labour market approach, in which the rate of new firms is measured with labour market size as the denominator, emphasizes that individual decisions depend on personal characteristics or – at a regional level – on population structure (Santarelli and Vivarelli, 2007). According to this labour market approach to firm formation (Koster, 2007), age structure, gender and education structure of the population play a central role in explaining firm formation rates (Delmar and Davidsson, 2000). In their study on the effects of social capital on new firms, Liao and Welsch (2003) stress that in the early firm formation stage, getting access to resources is crucial, and that social capital 'can be a substitute for other resources' (p. 152). A relatively recent but popular contribution to this view is the work of Florida (Lee et al., 2004), pointing to the positive effect of a creative class on entrepreneurship and especially new firm formation.

An Institutional Component

As regards *informal* institutions, there is a widely held view that entrepreneurial perceptions precede entrepreneurial activity (see e.g. Arenius and Minniti, 2005; Freytag and Thurik, 2007). For instance in the GEM conceptual model that is used to guide the GEM data collection, entrepreneurial perceptions – in particular perceived opportunities and perceived capabilities – are thought to be intermediate states between so-called 'Entrepreneurial Framework Conditions' (EFCs) and entrepreneurial activity.[1] Levie and Autio (2008) extensively describe these relationships and test the impact for one of these entrepreneurial framework conditions: entrepreneurship education and training. For high income countries they find that there is a positive link between the EFC on 'Higher education' and the perceived opportunities to start a business, controlling for other relevant factors.[2] They also find a positive link between perceived opportunities and early-stage entrepreneurial activity – overall as well as high growth oriented early-stage entrepreneurial activity – and that perceived opportunities are moderating the effect of higher education on entrepreneurial activity. Freytag and Thurik (2007) did not find a direct link between measures of national entrepreneurial culture and entrepreneurial activity, even though the relationship between national entrepreneurial culture and entrepreneurial preference was significant. A possible explanation is the spatial level applied in their work. Attitudes to entrepreneurship may, as discussed above, differ within countries and therefore impact entrepreneurial activity at the regional level rather than the national level.

At the regional level, indeed, a positive relationship exists between entrepreneurial perceptions and entrepreneurial activity (Bosma and Schutjens, 2009). Regions with higher levels of entrepreneurial perceptions show higher levels of entrepreneurial activity. This in itself does not exclusively point at a positive impact of entrepreneurial attitudes on entrepreneurial activity; it is also established that the reverse effect may hold: entrepreneurial activity can manifest 'contagiously' in the region. Bosma et al. (2008b) found in an empirical study on three Dutch regions (based on the GEM survey) that for more than half of the early-stage entrepreneurs another entrepreneur – or firm – served as an example when setting up their firms. Over 70 per cent of the entrepreneurial role models worked in the same labour market area. Also, the vast majority of people who personally knew someone who started their business in the past two years lived in the same labour market area. These findings point at a reinforcing mechanism between entrepreneurial perceptions and entre- preneurial activity. The results of this study also make clear that the net- working activities by individuals – the 'personification' of this reinforcing mechanism – largely take place within the region.

A second noteworthy issue is that there could be regional and national forces at play that hinder (or reinforce) a direct 'transition' from attitudes to activity. For example, if region A is characterized by an abundance of good job opportunities, or a high degree of social security, thus increas- ing the *opportunity costs* of entrepreneurship for individuals, the observed entrepreneurial activity may be lower than what could be expected from observed entrepreneurial attitudes. These interaction effects should be taken into account. A regional indicator comprising (individual) attitudes toward entrepreneurship and business ownership, may contribute to our understanding of variations in (different types of) entrepreneurship rates, especially if it is also possible to take the abovementioned opportunity costs of entrepreneurship into account.

From the studies focusing on international differences in *formal* insti- tutions related to entrepreneurship, the impact of national factors on entrepreneurial attitude and maybe even subsequently activity is striking. The World Bank report (2005) has revealed enormous national differences with respect to laws, regulations and procedures in entrepreneurship regis- tration. These regulatory obstacles may discourage entrepreneurial spirit.[3] Therefore national institutional forces (regulations, policy instruments) also affect entrepreneurial activity. With respect to entrepreneurship policy, large national differences exist – and have always existed, accord- ing to an extensive international comparison of policy in ten countries (Stevenson and Lundström, 2001). Within many European countries, spe- cific regional policy instruments have been used to affect entrepreneurship rates, but the most influential factors (taxes, regulations, and laws) are still set out by national policy makers.

Ambitious Entrepreneurship

As mentioned earlier, it is a stylized fact that entrepreneurship has many different faces. Not all entrepreneurs start a firm that survives and eventually grows into a large or innovative business, as the distinctions between managerial business owners, imitative and innovative entrepre- neurs (Wennekers and Thurik, 1999; Koellinger, 2008), 'real' entrepre- neurs and 'revolving door' entrepreneurs (Santarelli and Vivarelli, 2007, p. 464) or 'mice, gazelles and elephants' (Acs and Mueller, 2008) indicate.

The employment and innovation effect of new firms shows enormous variation, which has to be taken into account in linking economic growth to entrepreneurship (Baumol, 1990). In explaining actual firm growth and innovation, factors of different spatial levels come up: individual factors, firm characteristics, industry effects, business cycle effects, (regional) market size and growth. However, there is only limited empirical evidence of factors explaining actual firm growth or innovative performance of *new firms*, mainly because of the longitudinal data needed. A notable exception is the seminal work of Davidsson (1991), who conducted a longitudinal analysis on realized firm growth showing that growth motivation of the entrepreneur had a significantly positive effect. Vivarelli and Audretsch (1998) also found empirical evidence of a positive effect of innovative propensity on post-entry performance, both in economic returns, employment growth and export growth. In another study, Arrighetti and Vivarelli (1999) also found that innovative motivation and previous innovative experience positively correlated with post-entry performance.

However, this is not to say that growth motivation is the only factor affecting firm growth, as evidence shows that despite high aspirations many new entrepreneurs do not reach their goals. Also the other way around: firm growth may occur even among entrepreneurs without explicit growth ambitions. The same goes for entrepreneurial intentions with respect to innovation, of which a realistic assessment at the time of start-up is almost impossible. According to Koellinger et al. (2007), many new entrepreneurs are overconfident about their own entrepreneurial capacities and are overoptimistic about future prospects. This incapacity to grasp market and competition reality at the time of start-up and the inability to manage internal and external threats to and opportunities for the firm in the early stages of its life course are the main reasons why growth ambition and actual firm growth are not perfectly correlated. Furthermore, entrepreneurial growth intentions may change over time, especially in the first period after a venture is initiated (Kreuger, 2000; Dutta and Thornhill, 2008). However, we may conclude that entrepreneurial ambition is a strong predictor of actual firm performance in later stages.

In our search for explanations of regional differences in ambitious entrepreneurship rates, again we seek refuge in the labour market perspective. As we support the view that at the basis of entrepreneurship is a person taking the step to start a business, conditioned by individual and personality characteristics, we believe these aspects are even more important when we focus on his or her ambitions or intentions related to this firm. Eventually, especially in the early stages, firms are embodied by the person or persons who founded them and the ambitions of the new firm can then be equated with the ambitions of the entrepreneur involved

(Garnsey et al., 2006). Our focus on the individual level is also justified by the extensive literature overview on drivers of initial growth intention carried out by Dutta and Thornhill (2008), who found many more studies with empirical evidence on effects of individual factors, than with evidence of organizational or environmental effects.

Turning back to Davidsson's finding that entrepreneurial motivations affect actual outcomes, he also showed that this motivation depends on the entrepreneur's ability, opportunity and need to grow. However, even more interesting was his conclusion that not only objective measures of ability, opportunity and need matter, but also the entrepreneur's individual *perception* of ability, opportunity and need. He concluded that objective aspects only explain part of actual growth. In this view, variables related to the personal characteristics of the entrepreneur, the firm or the environment, are less important.

If perceptions of individual ability, opportunity and need are important to firm growth motivation, what then explains these individual perceptions? The theory of planned behaviour (Ajzen, 1985, 1991) sheds light on this relation between motivations, perceptions and actual behaviour. The idea is that a person's value attached to certain behaviour is strongly affected by the expected consequences of this particular behaviour (Wiklund et al., 2003). If nascent entrepreneurs perceive high administrative burdens associated with hiring and firing employees, their ambitions in terms of firm size will be relatively low. This line of reasoning also applies to positive effects: when regional income and welfare are high or growing, people expect market growth they can take advantage of by starting a new ambitious firm. In this sense, GRP growth might trigger highly ambitious entrepreneurs. From their empirical study on revenue aspirations of nascent entrepreneurs, Liao and Welsch (2003) conclude that social capital (both network size and trust) positively influences growth aspiration, while human capital variables (experience and education) have no effect. A significant positive effect of financial capital on growth aspirations, however, existed, together with a positive influence of cognitive capital; that is, strong shared norms and values.

Based on both Ajzen's theory of planned behaviour and the findings of Liao and Welsch, it can be expected that traditional explanations based on entrepreneurial characteristics such as age and education level only partially explain ambitious entrepreneurship. In the explanatory studies on firm growth ambitions of Wiklund et al. (2003), Davidsson (1991) and Liao and Welsch (2003), personal characteristics of the entrepreneur, the firm or the environment, are less important than perceptions, personal strategies and shared values. Koellinger (2008) also found empirical evidence for the importance of perceptions in explaining innovative aspirations of nascent entrepreneurs. These innovative ambitions strongly correlated with perceptions of both individual skills and regional opportunities, next to gender, education level, working status and national economic development. Based on this, compared to general entrepreneurial activity, in analysing ambitious entrepreneurship we might expect lower explanatory power of entrepreneurial personal characteristics, and stronger effects of entrepreneurial attitudes, values and perceptions towards future firm growth or innovation (Koellinger, 2008; see also Wiklund et al., 2003). Both hypotheses on ambitious entrepreneurship – that is: (1) compared to non-ambitious entrepreneurship, the relatively limited significance of traditional determinants in explaining regional differences in ambitious entrepreneurship, and (2) compared to non-ambitious entrepreneurship, the relatively large effect of (regional) entrepreneurial attitudes in studying ambitious entrepreneurship – are tested in this chapter.

DATA AND METHODOLOGY

We use data from the Global Entrepreneurship Monitor (GEM) for creating indicators on regional entrepreneurial activity (dependent variables) and attitudes (independent variables). Additional independent variables at the regional level are obtained from Cambridge Econometrics, European Regional Data and at the national level from the OECD. The selection of countries included in our study is restricted by data availability. First, we require GEM participation for at least three years in the 2001–06 period. This results in indices on entrepreneurial activity and entrepreneurial perceptions over 125 larger regions in 18 countries.[4] By mapping these indicators we are able initially to explore cultural, institutional and urbanization effects relating to our four measures of entrepreneurial activity. We then proceed with empirically investigating determinants of each type of entrepreneurial activity. To this end, we first identify some dense regions situated in the previously identified larger regions; if the sample size permits us to do so, we abstract these dense regions and treat them separate from the larger region they are part of. An example is the Munich metropolitan area. This area is situated in the Nuts1 region of Bavaria. However, based on the literature we can expect different patterns of entrepreneurial activity in the Munich area as compared to the rest of Bavaria. Therefore we identify Munich and the Bavarian region excluding Munich as two separate regions in our empirical analysis. In sum, this exercise leads to an augmented sample of 147 regions.[5] Because of data availability for the independent variables and our restriction of a sample size of at least 750 valid cases per region, we end up with 121 observations over 16 countries in the regression analysis.

Dependent Variables

Since 1999 GEM has provided several *national* indicators on entrepreneurial activity for an increasing number of countries (see Reynolds et al., 2005; Bosma et al., 2008a). The indicators are based on telephone surveys among the adult population. A key GEM indicator is the early-stage entrepreneurial activity (ESEA) rate.[6] This measure is defined as the prevalence rate (in the 18–64 population) of individuals who are involved in either nascent entrepreneurship or involved as an owner-manager in a new firm existing for up to 42 months. Nascent entrepreneurs are identified as individuals who are, at the time of the GEM survey, setting up a business. Moreover they have indicated: (1) that they have 'done anything to help start a new business, such as looking for equipment or a location, organizing a start-up team, working on a business plan, beginning to save money, or any other activity that would help launch a business'; and (2) that they will be the single owner or a co-owner of the firm in gestation. Also, they have not paid any salaries, wages or payment in kind (including to themselves) for more than three months – if they have they are considered to be an owner-manager of a (new) firm.

While the ESEA rate is an 'overall' measure of early-stage entrepreneurial activity, identifying different types is also possible. An example of a specific type of entrepreneurship is 'high growth-expectation' entrepreneurship (see e.g. Autio, 2007). We make a similar distinction but identify three different groups of growth orientation:

1. Early-stage entrepreneurial activity with low growth ambitions (ESEAGR_LO): Individuals in early-stage entrepreneurial activity who expect to have no more than one employee in the next five years
2. Early-stage entrepreneurial activity with modest growth ambitions (ESEAGR_MD): Individuals in early-stage entrepreneurial activity who expect to have between two and nine employees in the next five years
3. Early-stage entrepreneurial activity with high growth ambitions (ESEAGR_HI): Individuals in early-stage entrepreneurial activity who expect to have ten or more employees in the next five years

A second type of entrepreneurship involves the innovative orientation of early-stage entrepreneurs. All entrepreneurs have been asked to indicate if all, many or none of their (potential) customers consider this product or service new and unfamiliar (answers: all/some/none). Also, they have indicated if many, few, or no other businesses are offering the same products or services to their (potential) customers. We identify early-stage entrepreneurs to be oriented towards innovation if they indicate that at least some customers consider the product or service new and unfamiliar *and* not many businesses are offering the same products or services.

4. Early-stage entrepreneurial activity with innovative ambitions ESEAINNOV: Individuals in early-stage entrepreneurial activity who expect (i) at least some customers to consider the product or service new and unfamiliar *and* (ii) not many businesses to be offering the same products or services.

We acknowledge that this last measure may not be perfect for innovative entrepreneurship, but at least it gives some indication of the innovative ambitions, in terms of new product–market combinations, of individuals in the region. At the regional level the indicator reveals innovative entrepreneurial ambitions, but we should keep in mind that individuals in some regions may tend to be more optimistic than in other regions, and some of them may be highly overoptimistic.

One important finding of the GEM studies so far is that cross-country variation in early-stage entrepreneurial activity is very persistent over years. As it has been shown empirically that regional variation in entrepreneurship is also persistent (Parker, 2005; Fritsch and Mueller, 2007), we merge the GEM data for six subsequent years (2001–06). This merging exercise results in *regional* indicators on the three measures of growth-oriented entrepreneurial activity and perceptions that pertain to the 2001–06 period. Due to data availability the indicator on entrepreneurial activity with innovative ambitions is obtained by merging the data for 2002–06.

Note that all dependent variables are obtained from individual data, so whether or not a person is involved in any of the four types of early-stage entrepreneurial activity has been determined at the individual level. It is also important to point out that each individual involved in innovative oriented early-stage entrepreneurship is also classified in either of the three growth orientation categories. As could be expected, early-stage entrepreneurs were relatively often in the category of high-growth orientation: of all high-growth oriented individuals involved in ESEA, 25 per cent were also characterized as innovative, whereas the percentages for the medium and low levels of growth orientation were 19 and 16 respectively. These percentages show that, even though there is a positive correlation between early-stage entrepreneurship with growth ambitions and innovative ambitions, high levels of innovative orientation certainly do not necessarily coincide with growth ambitions.[7]

The regional pattern of the different types of entrepreneurship in Europe, as pictured in Figures 3.1–3.4, shows large differences, pointing to the

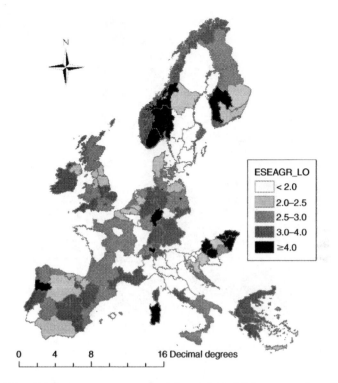

*Figure 3.1   Early-stage entrepreneurial activity with low growth ambitions
(0–1 employees)*

importance of distinguishing regions instead of merely nations. The average non-growth regional entrepreneurship rate (ESEAGR_LO) pictured in Figure 3.1 is 2.8 per cent and ranges from 1.2 per cent in the western part of France to 6.0 per cent in Western Transdanubia (Hungary). The rate of high-growth oriented ESEA in Figure 3.3 ranges from 0.6 per cent in the French Bassin Parisien to 2.6 per cent in the Hamburg area. We should note that, since the indicators are *estimates* rather than actual values, there are confidence intervals attached to these estimates. These may be quite high in some cases even though the minimum sample per region is set at 750. Therefore, when examining the maps one should especially focus on general patterns and not so much on the outcome for a particular region.

Although we can still figure out national borders in these European maps, regional variations within countries are also large. Focusing on the main differences between lower ambitious types of entrepreneurship (Figures 3.1 and 3.2) and higher ambitious types of entrepreneurship (Figures 3.3 and 3.4), we see some remarkable differences. In general, the

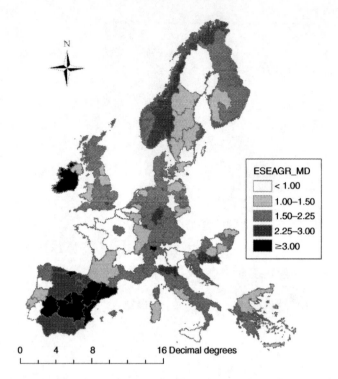

Figure 3.2   Early-stage entrepreneurial activity with modest growth
ambitions (2–9 employees)

growth and innovation oriented entrepreneurship rates appear to be somewhat higher in or around densely populated regions. In addition, there
appear to be some country-specific effects. In many Spanish areas there
are quite a lot of early-stage entrepreneurs with low or modest growth
ambitions, but the rate of ambitious ones is relatively low. The same goes
for northern Portugal and Greece. In Italy, it seems that for the northern
regions there is relatively little participation in ESEA with low growth orientation, but the scores on ambitious entrepreneurship are clearly higher.
In this respect the western part of Slovenia connects to northern Italy.

France and Sweden are examples of countries showing low overall
entrepreneurship rates, but performing much better on ambitious entrepreneurship. The Stockholm and Paris areas in particular, as well as the
northern part of Sweden and the Mediterranean region in France, have a
relatively large number of ambitious entrepreneurs. Regions performing
relatively badly in all types of entrepreneurship are situated in the east
of France, and to a lesser extent, some Swedish regions and the whole

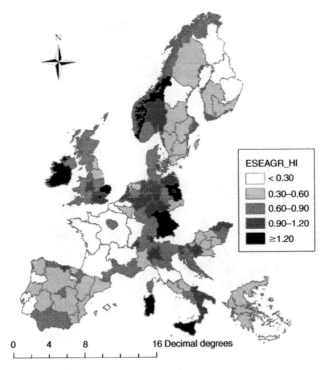

*Figure 3.3   Early-stage entrepreneurial activity with high growth
ambitions (10 or more employees)*

of Belgium. Finally we observe some interesting differences between
high-growth oriented ESEA and innovation oriented ESEA. In France,
for example, the Paris and Mediterranean regions stand out concerning
growth orientation, while the regional pattern is more mixed if we look at
orientation towards innovation. Here the Mediterranean area seems to be
outstanding compared to the rest of France.[8]

Independent Variables

We include determinants in our conceptual framework identifying regional
composition and regional economic attributes, as well as indicators reflecting regional (informal) and national institutions. Informal institutions are
captured by variables measuring perceptions of entrepreneurship. These
variables measure perceived opportunities, perceived capabilities and fear
of failure – all related to early-stage entrepreneurship. Included economic
attributes are gross regional product (GRP) per capita in purchasing

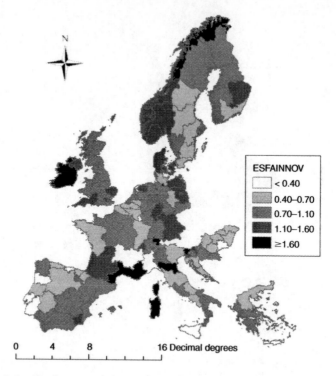

ESFAINNOV

☐	< 0.40
▨	0.40–0.70
▦	0.70–1.10
▩	1.10–1.60
■	≥1.60

0   4   8   16 Decimal degrees

Figure 3.4   Early-stage entrepreneurial activity with innovative ambitions

power parities, GRP growth, unemployment rates and a variable designed
to capture opportunity costs. We have defined this measure as the ratio
between GRP per capita and compensation per employee: high scores
reflect lower wages relative to regional output and are therefore associated with lower opportunity costs to entrepreneurship. Although this is an
imperfect measure of the opportunity costs to entrepreneurship, which are
hard to capture at the regional level, it denotes the difference between production and wages and indicates a region's relative advantage of entrepreneurship (compared to wages). Data on economic attributes at the regional
level are mainly drawn from the Cambridge Econometrics database on
European regions. In case of missing values (e.g. for unemployment rates)
we used the Eurostat regional database. Both data sources are also used
for deriving regional composition attributes (population growth, share of
people aged 18-34). National indicators on employment protection and
immigration were obtained from the OECD. See Table 3.1 for descriptions and sources of the independent variables entering the regressions.
Table 3.2 shows the descriptive statistics for the variables (only for the

Table 3.1   Independent variables: definitions

Variable	Description	Data source
Regional informal institutional effects		
Perceived skills	Percentage of adult population 18-64 years indicating to have required knowledge and skills to start a firm	GEM Adult Population Surveys 2001–06
Perceived opportunities	Percentage of adult population 18-64 years perceiving good opportunities for start-ups in the area where they live	GEM Adult Population Surveys 2001–06
Fear of failure	Percentage of adult population 18-64 years indicating that fear of failure would prevent them from starting a business	GEM Adult Population Surveys 2001–06
Regional demographic and economic attributes		
Know start-up entrepreneurs	Percentage of adult population 18–64 years (nascent entrepreneurs and business owner-managers excluded) who personally know someone who started a business in the past two years	GEM Adult Population Surveys 2001–06
Share 18–34 years	Share of people aged between 18–34 years in the 18–64 population	Eurostat Regional Database
Population growth	Growth in total population, 1999–2004	Cambridge Econometrics Database
Opportunity costs	Ratio of GRP per capita to compensation per employee, 2003	Cambridge Econometrics Database
Population density	Number of inhabitants per km², 2003	Cambridge Econometrics Database
GRP per capita	GRP in PPS (European Union = 100), 2003	Cambridge Econometrics Database
GRP growth	Growth in GRP, 1999–2004	Cambridge Econometrics Database
Unemployment rate	Number of unemployed as percentage of labour force, 2003	Cambridge Econometrics Database & Eurostat Regional Database
National effects		
Employment protection	OECD Employment protection index (version 2), 2003	OECD
Immigration	OECD Factbook	OECD

Table 3.2 Descriptive statistics

	Mean	Std. dev	Correlation matrix														
			1	2	3	4	5	6	7	8	9	10	11	12	13	14	15	16
1 ESEA low growth orientation	2.8	0.9																
2 ESEA modest growth orientation	1.9	0.8	0.29															
3 ESEA high growth orientation	0.7	0.4	0.42	0.29														
4 ESEA innovative growth orientation	0.9	0.5	0.34	0.36	0.64													
5 Perceived skills	41	5.8	0.40	0.46	0.26	0.14												
6 Perceived opportunities	32.4	12.7	0.00	0.35	0.24	0.35	0.23											
7 Fear of failure	39	9	−0.08	0.19	−0.21	−0.08	−0.03	−0.24										
8 Know start–up entrepreneurs	34.8	6.6	0.17	0.07	0.25	0.30	−0.15	0.30	0.06									
9 Share 18–34 years	0.36	0.04	0.04	0.39	0.06	−0.02	0.24	0.07	0.05	−0.07								
10 Population growth	2.3	3.6	−0.09	0.44	0.04	0.21	0.25	0.41	0.03	−0.14	0.50							
11 Opportunity costs	1.73	0.35	0.12	0.04	0.39	0.27	0.26	0.28	−0.05	0.13	−0.05	0.15						
12 Population density	0.4	0.9	0.12	0.06	0.34	0.20	0.07	0.00	−0.17	−0.08	0.22	0.03	0.32					
13 GRP per capita	109.3	53.5	−0.10	0.05	0.15	0.19	0.00	0.20	−0.12	0.14	−0.04	0.12	0.39	0.24				
14 GRP growth	12.4	7.3	0.08	0.28	−0.10	0.00	0.44	0.09	0.12	−0.18	0.46	0.37	0.02	−0.05	−0.07			
15 Unemployment rate	7.27	4.48	−0.09	0.07	−0.23	−0.17	−0.16	−0.30	0.57	0.07	0.14	−0.19	−0.40	−0.01	−0.17	0.11		
16 Employment protection	2.35	0.62	−0.18	0.15	−0.35	−0.33	−0.31	−0.09	0.48	0.19	0.31	0.22	−0.19	−0.12	−0.09	−0.06	0.34	
17 Immigration	10.79	4.82	−0.01	−0.18	0.17	0.22	0.24	−0.18	−0.01	−0.08	−0.22	−0.04	0.39	0.03	0.09	−0.16	−0.24	−0.40

Note: All descriptive statistics are based on 121 observations (regions) over 16 countries entering the regressions.

regions included in the empirical analysis). We intended to include social security rates in accordance with Hessels et al. (2007). However, in tests for multicollinearity, the high correlation between social security rates and employment protection gave some problems. We decided to include the employment protection index because this measure is more specific and because we are particularly interested in its effect on ambitious types of early-stage entrepreneurial activity. Individuals who have the potential to become a growth or innovation oriented entrepreneur may prefer to remain employed if there are strong employment benefits.

Potential reversed causality issues at the individual level (I am ambitious because I have succeeded so far versus I am ambitious and therefore I will be successful) are to some extent prevented by adopting the regional level rather than the individual level. However, as described earlier, also at the regional level reversed causality is not ruled out. One should also be cautious when interpreting our results with respect to informal effects measured by perceptions of entrepreneurship. Significantly positive results are more likely to be interpreted as a two-way reinforcing mechanism between perceptions and activity. Therefore, we initially run a regression model excluding the variables measuring perceptions of entrepreneurship. This enables us to better grasp the effects informal institutions can have and to what extent they interplay with the other determinants. The regression analysis has been conducted for the dependent variables separately, using multilevel analysis (allowing for random intercepts for country levels). The likelihood ratio tests all suggested that we should indeed consider the national level as a relevant spatial scale.[9]

RESULTS AND IMPLICATIONS

What now determines the regional variation in the four distinguished types of early-stage entrepreneurship? The estimation results are described in Table 3.3. Each type of entrepreneurship is assessed by two models; the first excluding informal institutional effects and the second including these determinants. All dependent and independent variables have been standardized before they entered the regression. A first overview of the table gives support to the hypothesis that non-ambitious entrepreneurship has different determinants as compared to ambitious entrepreneurship. In particular the explanations for the first two types of early-stage entrepreneurship (models 1 and 2) differ from those for the high-growth oriented ESEA (model 3) and innovation oriented ESEA (model 4). Early-stage entrepreneurial activity with no growth orientation is largely explained by perception of skills and knowledge to start a business

Table 3.3 Estimation results: explaining different types of early-stage entrepreneurial activity (ESEA) at regional level[a]

	ESEA low growth orientation		ESEA modest growth orientation		ESEA high growth orientation		ESEA innovative orientation	
	Model 1a	Model 1b	Model 2a	Model 2b	Model 3a	Model 3b	Model 4a	Model 4b
Regional informal institutional effects								
Perceived skills		0.67		0.46		0.18		−0.03
		(0.13)***		(0.11)***		(0.11)		(0.12)
Perceived opportunities		0.32		0.44		0.22		0.31
		(0.17)*		(0.15)***		(0.15)		(0.16)*
Fear of failure		0.34		−0.01		−0.17		0
		(0.18)*		(0.15)		(0.15)		(0.16)
Regional demographic and economic attributes								
Know start-up entrepreneurs	0.42	0.14	0.18	−0.12	0.40	0.26	0.39	0.3
	(0.15)***	(0.15)	(0.13)	(0.13)	(0.12)***	(0.13)**	(0.13)***	(0.14)**
Share 18−34 years	0.06	−0.06	0.05	−0.02	0.22	0.19	0	0
	(0.12)	(0.11)	(0.1)	(0.09)	(0.1)**	(0.1)**	(0.11)	(0.11)
Population growth	0.01	−0.02	0.05	−0.06	−0.04	−0.12	0.23	0.16
	(0.11)	(0.1)	(0.1)	(0.09)	(0.09)	(0.1)	(0.1)**	(0.11)
Opportunity costs	0.08	0.07	0.01	−0.09	0.17	0.11	0.02	−0.05
	(0.13)	(0.12)	(0.11)	(0.11)	(0.11)*	(0.11)	(0.12)	(0.12)
Population density	0.07	0.07	0.15	0.15	0.22	0.22	0.19	0.2
	(0.1)	(0.08)	(0.08)*	(0.07)**	(0.08)***	(0.08)***	(0.09)**	(0.09)**
GRP per capita	−0.09	−0.06	0.05	0.04	−0.27	−0.28	−0.09	−0.1
	(0.11)	(0.1)	(0.1)	(0.09)	(0.09)***	(0.09)***	(0.1)	(0.1)
GRP per capita, squared	0.00	−0.02	−0.03	−0.01	0.06	0.07	0.02	0.03
	(0.04)	(0.03)	(0.03)	(0.03)	(0.03)**	(0.03)**	(0.03)	(0.04)

	(1)	(2)	(3)	(4)	(5)	(6)	(7)	(8)
GRP growth	0.07	−0.04	0.02	−0.03	0.06	0.06	0.05	0.07
	(0.15)	(0.14)	(0.13)	(0.12)	(0.12)	(0.12)	(0.13)	(0.13)
Unemployment rate	−0.02	0.07	−0.06	0.01	−0.12	−0.07	0.01	0.02
	(0.13)	(0.12)	(0.12)	(0.11)	(0.11)	(0.11)	(0.12)	(0.12)
National effects								
Employment protection	−0.11	0.00	−0.19	0.03	−0.49	−0.32	−0.53	−0.44
	(0.24)	(0.29)	(0.22)	(0.23)	(0.2)**	(0.22)	(0.19)***	(0.21)**
Immigration	0.00	−0.18	−0.05	−0.04	−0.01	0.06	0.08	0.2
	(0.21)	(0.26)	(0.2)	(0.21)	(0.17)	(0.2)	(0.17)	(0.18)
Constant	0.08	0.22	−0.17	−0.15	−0.24	−0.26	−0.09	−0.14
	(0.24)	(0.28)	(0.22)	(0.22)	(0.2)	(0.21)	(0.19)	(0.19)
Log restricted-likelihood	−159.38	−147.29	−143.93	−133.75	−136.37	−135.95	−149.21	−148.08
Wald Chi-squared	15.68	57.98***	15.82	49.62***	79.02***	89.97***	46.74***	42.29***
LR test vs. linear regression: Chi²	29.43***	34.78***	55.17***	45.61***	42.90***	47.38***	20.86***	23.12***

Notes:
*** $p < 0.01$, ** $p < 0.05$, * $p < 0.10$. Standard errors in parentheses. All regressions are based on 121 observations (regions) over 16 countries.
[a] All regressions performed using Stata (xtmixed) with random intercept for each country.

(model 1b). If we exclude perceptions to entrepreneurship (model 1a) the explained variance decreases significantly and partly shifts to the factor of knowing entrepreneurs who started a business. We did not find a relationship with any of the economic attributes. Also we found no impact of national levels of employment protection. Hence, involvement in non-growth oriented entrepreneurship at the regional level seems to be largely determined by processes reflecting an 'I can also do this' mentality, a combination of perceptions and seeing other early-stage entrepreneurs rather than a rational choice on economic grounds. Knowing people in ESEA personally may also enhance the self-perceived skills to start a business. We should note that we were not able to include some potentially relevant attributes, such as education levels. Perceptions are also important in explaining the early-stage entrepreneurship with modest growth orientation. In addition a positive but weakly significant effect is found for population density.

For growth oriented early-stage entrepreneurship the picture is clearly different. We find very limited evidence on the importance of informal institutional effects. Perceived skills, perceived opportunities and fear of failure are all insignificant. However, we do find a significant and positive effect for the variable measuring a network effect; that is, knowing entrepreneurs who recently started a business (note that entrepreneurs themselves were not included when deriving this measure from the representative sample of the regional adult population). An important finding is that ambitious entrepreneurs, both in terms of job growth orientation and in terms of innovation, are predominantly prevalent in densely populated areas. Furthermore we find that the share of younger people has a positive impact on ESEA with high growth orientation. Interestingly, the degree of employment protection has a negative effect on ambitious entrepreneurship concerning orientation to both employment growth and innovation, see models 3a and 4a. There are two possible explanations that may complement each other. First, in a regime with high degrees of employment protection, potential high-ambition entrepreneurs – whether these ambitions reflect desire for growth or for innovation – may feel fewer incentives to engage in entrepreneurship and prefer safer and fairly generous employment. Second, new entrepreneurs may lower their expectations for high growth because of the regime of high employment protection. We observe that the impact of employment protection disappears (in model 3b) or weakens (in model 4b) when we include informal institutional effects, even though these effects themselves are not found to be significant. In our view this result points out that the effects of formal institutions may not only impact individuals' activities but also their perceptions. Indeed Table 3.2 indicates that the correlation of national levels of employment protection with regional aggregates of individuals' perceived skills to start a business is considerably negative (–0.31), and the correlation with fear of failure is substantial and positive (0.48). Thus, the distinction between informal institutions (in our exercise: perceptions to entrepreneurship) and formal institutions (employment protection) may not be as clear-cut as is sometimes proposed.

DISCUSSION AND CONCLUSIONS

This chapter contributes to field of entrepreneurship studies by presenting and analysing harmonized entrepreneurship data over European regions *and* countries in two ways. First, by mapping patterns in both general and ambitious entrepreneurial activity for 125 regions over 18 countries, we initially showed that the regional level is an appropriate level to study entrepreneurship. The second main contribution is the distinction between several types of entrepreneurial activity and analysing their determinants. Based on the existing literature we expected that the determinants for higher ambitious types of entrepreneurship would differ from those of lower ambitious types of entrepreneurship. Our empirical analysis on regional rates of ambitious entrepreneurship showed that only part of the determinants of lower growth oriented entrepreneurial activity played a significant role, as expected. For instance, population density does not matter for lower ambitious entrepreneurship rates, but is related to ambitious entrepreneurship. Furthermore, a subdivision of ambitious entrepreneurship in growth oriented and innovation oriented entrepreneurship shows that also here, the impact of regional and national factors varies to some extent. While growth oriented entrepreneurship is positively associated with the share of younger people and exhibits a U-shaped relationship with regional wealth levels, population growth is positively linked to innovation oriented entrepreneurship. Common determinants are network effects (measured by the degree to which people – excluding entrepreneurs – personally know someone who started a business in the past two years), population density and a negative effect of the national degree of employment protection.

Our hypothesis regarding a higher impact of regional entrepreneurial perceptions on ambitious entrepreneurship rates than on overall entrepreneurship rates, however, was not confirmed. Whereas regional levels of self-perceived attitudes towards start-up skills are of significant importance in explaining lower ambitious early-stage entrepreneurial activity, none of the three regional attitude indices was significant in explaining ambitious early-stage entrepreneurial activity. The influence of perceived skills on non-ambitious entrepreneurship needs some more detailed inspection. Observing the regional variation in the maps (see also Bosma and Schutjens, 2009 for maps displaying perceptions of entrepreneurship), we have reason to believe that starting a business is being considered less as a special event (put differently, an event embedded in society) in southern Europe and therefore people may perceive that fewer skills and less knowledge are required for starting a business. It may even be the case that the 'average' business in some countries is perceived differently in other countries (or regions) – and therefore the perceptions of opportunities and required capabilities relating to start-ups may differ substantially. Also we should note that the variables included in our study relate to starting a business rather than *growing* a business or starting an *innovative* business.

As regards formal institutions at the national level, these appear to affect total early-stage entrepreneurial activity to some extent, even in our case with 16 countries across Europe. We find some evidence of negative impacts; that is, of employment protection on growth and innovation oriented entrepreneurial activity. This finding certainly asks for further research. Our results indicate that this effect, as an example of a 'formal institutional' effect, may to some extent also be captured in variables measuring individual perceptions of entrepreneurship. This calls for more research on how formal institutions affect informal institutions and vice versa.

The limitations of our study are fourfold. First, our focus on regional entrepreneurship levels obscures the influence of individual characteristics on both the decision to start a firm, and second, the growth and innovation ambitions with respect to this new firm. According to many studies based on the labour market perspective, it is exactly this individual level at which the most decisive determinants can be found: age, gender, education level, income level, network (see e.g. Davidsson, 1991). In our study we circumvented this omission of the individual level by including regional demographic characteristics, but we are aware that the regional composition effect at best proxies the individual characteristics involved in the quite personal decision of becoming an (ambitious) entrepreneur. New research findings are under way in which we do control for this individual level.

Second, our focus on the ambitions of entrepreneurs in the period before or soon after the start-up does not permit inferences on realizations of job growth and innovation. As explained in the literature overview, this relation is not straightforward because of high uncertainty about existing and future markets, competition and capabilities to cope with internal and external challenges, especially in the exciting first phases of the firm's life course. Longitudinal analysis is needed to track down post start-up performance of new firms.

A third limitation of our contribution is that we have to distinguish rather large regions, because of limited data availability and small sample sizes on a lower spatial scale. Ideally we would have worked with Nuts3 regions only but this is currently not feasible in the GEM research design. For some countries we have abstracted smaller, dense areas from the larger areas. Another consequence of using regional aggregates of individual observations is that we had to merge 2001–06 data for obtaining regional measures on entrepreneurial activity and entrepreneurial perceptions. This boils down to a cross-sectional analysis and interpretations on causality, especially concerning the relationship between entrepreneurial perceptions and activity, should be made with care.

Finally, more data are needed at the regional level in order to grasp the possible effects of economic specialization, knowledge intensity, and agglomeration economies on entrepreneurship in general and innovation oriented entrepreneurship in particular. In addition, regional data on unemployment levels may improve explanations of not only non-ambitious entrepreneurship, but also growth oriented entrepreneurship as low labour costs may increase growth aspirations. Finally, data on the regional firm size structure, especially small-size businesses and new and young firms, may shed light on our finding that regional networks as proxied by knowing other new entrepreneurs, positively relate to regional entrepreneurship rates.

Our outcomes can be of relevance to policy makers aiming at stimulating the most promising types of entrepreneurship. In stimulating new firm formation by specific national regulations and institutions, one should be aware that this does not automatically positively affect ambitious entrepreneurship. In order to address this group of firms in particular, making employment more flexible could be a key trigger. Further research should be conducted in this area. As regards policy implications at the regional level, a general message from our results is that one should be aware that densely populated areas have advantages for fostering ambitious entrepreneurship, in line with traditional agglomeration economies stimulating concentration of economic activity. Not only are dense areas directly associated with ambitious entrepreneurial activity; dense areas also tend to have relatively high shares of younger populations and more networking possibilities (i.e. people in dense areas will know more people, and probably also more people who recently started a firm). Entangling the exact mechanisms underlying these urban advantages for ambitious entrepreneurship, in order to develop policy instruments, now is a challenge to both academics and policy makers.

ACKNOWLEDGEMENT

The authors would like to thank all the GEM teams for sharing their data. Although GEM data were used, their interpretation and use are the sole responsibility of the authors. The chapter has benefited from useful comments of two anonymous referees. All errors are ours.

NOTES

1. The GEM conceptual model is described in most annual GEM Global Reports (see for instance Bosma et al., 2008a) and more thorough theoretical underpinnings are supplied by Levie and Autio (2008).
2. The EFC 'Higher education' is a composite factor on the scores of three items in the annual 'National Expert Survey' that is held annually among experts in the field of entrepreneurship (see Reynolds et al., 2005). The items relate to the degree to which, according to the experts, (i) colleges and universities (ii) the level of business and management education, and (iii) the vocational, professional and continuing education systems provide good and adequate preparation for starting-up and growing new firms. See for more details Levie and Autio (2008).
3. The World Bank 'Doing Business' Indicators, including those related to start-ups, are based on regulations involving business with 250 employees or more. Therefore the World Bank figures do not allow a very good measurement of the link between formal institutions and start-up activity. However, one could argue that the perceptions to institutional barriers may be correlated with the World Bank measures related to start-ups.
4. In this first selection we have indices for 125 regions corresponding to the classification used by ESRI. This classification comprises of Nuts1 levels for Belgium, France, Germany, Greece, Ireland, the Netherlands and the United Kingdom. Nuts2 levels are applied for Croatia, Denmark, Finland, Hungary, Norway, Portugal, Slovenia and Sweden, and a combination of Nuts1 and Nuts2 for Italy, Spain and Switzerland.
5. The abstracted regions that are not shown in Figures 3.1–3.4 are Antwerp and Ghent (Belgium); Aarhus (Denmark); Helsinki (Finland); Duisburg-Essen, Düsseldorf, Köln, Rhein-Main, Stuttgart and Munich (Germany); Budapest (Hungary); Dublin, 'Border/Midlands/Western', 'Southern/Eastern' (Ireland); Amsterdam, Rotterdam, The Hague and Utrecht (Netherlands); Barcelona, Valencia, Seville and Malaga (Spain).
6. This is the same measure as what is known as 'TEA' in most GEM reports. We have chosen to use the abbreviation ESEA because it better reflects the early-stage nature of the measure.
7. The correlations between the dependent variables are all positive and significant at the .05 level, ranging from 0.29 (ESEAGR_LO and ESEAGR_MD) to 0.64 (ESEAGR_HI and ESEAINNOV).
8. This region includes the Sophia–Antipolis cluster.
9. If we did not find the country level to be important, we could have modelled all four dependent variables simultaneously in a Seemingly Unrelated Regression (SUR). SUR estimation takes the potential correlation of residuals of the equations into account. However, SUR estimation is to our knowledge not available in a multilevel setting.

REFERENCES

Acs, Z., D. Audretsch, P. Braunerhjelm and B. Carlsson (2003), *The Missing Link: The Knowledge Filter and Endogenous Growth*, Stockholm, Sweden: Center for Business and Policy Studies.

Acs, Z. and P. Mueller (2008), 'Employment effects of business dynamics: mice, gazelles and elephants', *Small Business Economics*, **30**, 85–100.

Ajzen, I. (1985), 'From intentions to actions: a theory of planned behaviour', in J. Kuhl and J. Bechmann (eds), *Action-Control: From Cognition to Behaviour*, Heidelberg: Springer, pp. 11–39.

Ajzen, I. (1991), 'The theory of planned behaviour', *Organizational Behaviour and Human Processes*, **50**, 179–221.

Arenius, P. and M. Minniti (2005), 'Perceptual variables and nascent entrepreneurship', *Small Business Economics*, **24** (3), 233–47.

Arrighetti, A. and M. Vivarelli (1999), 'The role of innovation in the post entry performance of new small firms: evidence from Italy', *Southern Economic Journal*, **65**, 927–39.

Audretsch, D.B. and M. Keilbach (2004), 'Entrepreneurship capital and economic performance', *Regional Studies*, **38** (8), 949–60.

Audretsch, D.B., M.C. Keilbach and E.E. Lehmann (2006), *Entrepreneurship and Economic Growth*, Oxford: Oxford University Press.

Autio, E. (2007), *Global Entrepreneurship Monitor; 2007 Global Report on High-Growth Entrepreneurship*, London: Babson College, London Business School, and Global Entrepreneurship Research Association (GERA).

Autio, E., M. Kronlund and A. Kovalainen (2007), 'High-growth SME support initiatives in nine countries: analysis, categorization, and recommendations', report prepared for the Finnish Ministry of Trade and Industry.

Baumol, W.J. (1990), 'Entrepreneurship: productive, unproductive, and destructive', *Journal of Political Economy*, **98** (5), 893–921.

Birch, D. (1979), *The Job Generation Process*, Cambridge, MA: MIT Program on Neighbourhood and Regional Change.

Bosma, N.S. and V.A.J.M. Schutjens (2007), 'Outlook on Europe: patterns of promising entrepreneurial activity in European regions', *Tijdschrift voor Economische en Sociale Geografie*, **98** (5), 675–86.

Bosma, N.S. and V.A.J.M. Schutjens (2009), 'Mapping entrepreneurial activity and entrepreneurial attitudes in European regions', *International Journal of Entrepreneurship and Small Business*, **7** (2), forthcoming.

Bosma, N.S., K. Jones, E. Autio and J. Levie (2008a), *Global Entrepreneurship Monitor 2007, Executive Report*, London: Babson College, London Business School and Global Entrepreneurship Research Association.

Bosma, N.S., V.A.J.M. Schutjens and K. Suddle (2008b), *Whither a Flat Landscape? Regional Differences in Entrepreneurship in the Netherlands*, EIM Scales paper H200805, Zoetermeer: EIM.

Bosma, N.S., A.J. Van Stel and K. Suddle (2008c), 'The geography of new firm formation: evidence from independent start-ups and new subsidiaries in the Netherlands', *International Entrepreneurship and Management Journal*, **4** (2), 129–46.

Carree, M.A. and A.R. Thurik (2003), 'The impact of entrepreneurship on economic growth', in Z. Acs and D.B. Audretsch (eds), *Handbook of Entrepreneurship Research*, Dordrecht: Kluwer, pp. 437–72.

Davidsson, P. (1991), 'Continued entrepreneurship: ability, need, and opportunity as determinants of small firm growth', *Journal of Business Venturing*, **6** (6), 405–29.

Davidsson, P., F. Delmar and J. Wiklund (2006), 'Entrepreneurship as growth; growth as entrepreneurship', in P. Davidsson, F. Delmar and J. Wiklund (eds), *Entrepreneurship and the Growth of Firms*, Cheltenham, UK and Northampton, MA, USA: Edward Elgar publishing, pp. 21–38.

Delmar, F. and P. Davidsson (2000), 'Where do they come from? Prevalence and characteristics of nascent entrepreneurs', *Entrepreneurship and Regional Development*, **12**, 1–23.

Dutta, D.K. and S. Thornhill (2008), 'The evolution of growth intentions: toward a cognition-based model', *Journal of Business Venturing*, **23**, 307–32.

Etzioni, A. (1987), 'Entrepreneurship, adaptation and legimation', *Journal of Economic Behavior and Organization*, **8**, 175–89.

Fotopoulos, G. and H. Louri (2000), 'Location and survival of new entry', *Small Business Economics*, **14**, 311–21.

Frank, H., M. Lueger and C. Korunka (2007), 'The significance of personality in business start-up intentions, start-up realization and business success', *Entrepreneurship and Regional Development*, **19**, 227–51.

Freytag, A. and A.R. Thurik (2007), 'Entrepreneurship and its determinants in a cross-country setting', *Journal of Evolutionary Economics*, **17** (2), 117–31.

Fritsch, M. (1992), 'Regional differences in new firm formation: evidence from West Germany', *Regional Studies*, **25**, 233–41.

Fritsch, M. and P. Mueller (2007), 'The persistence of regional new business formation-activity over time – assessing the potential of policy promotion programs', *Journal of Evolutionary Economics*, **17**, 299–315.

Garnsey, E., E. Stam and P. Heffernan (2006), 'New firm growth: exploring processes and paths', *Industry and Innovation*, **13** (1), 1–20.

Henrekson, M. and D. Johansson (2008), *Gazelles as Job Creators*, IFN Working Paper No. 733, Stockholm: Research Institute of Industrial Economics.

Hessels, J., A.J. Van Stel, P. Brouwer and A.R.M. Wennekers (2007), 'Social security arrangements and early-stage entrepreneurial activity', *Comparative Labour Law and Policy Journal*, **28** (4), 743–74.

Koellinger, P. (2008), 'Why are some entrepreneurs more innovative than others?', *Small Business Economics*, **31**, 21–37.

Koellinger, P., M. Minniti and C. Schade (2007), 'I think I can, I think I can . . . a study of entrepreneurial behaviour', *Journal of Economic Psychology*, **28** (3), 502–27.

Koster, S. (2007), 'The entrepreneurial and replication function of new firm formation', *Tijdschrift voor Economische en Sociale Geografie*, **98** (5), 667–74.

Krueger, N.F. (2000), 'The cognitive infrastructure on opportunity emergence', *Entrepreneurship Theory and Practice*, **24**, 5–23.

Lee, S.Y., R. Florida and Z.J. Acs (2004), 'Creativity and entrepreneurship: a regional analysis of new firm formation', *Regional Studies*, **38** (8), 879–91.

Levie, J. and Autio, E. (2008), 'A theoretical grounding and test of the GEM model', *Small Business Economics*, **31** (3), 235–63.

Liao, J. and H. Welsch (2003), 'Social capital and entrepreneurial growth aspirations: a comparison of technology and non-technology-based nascent entrepreneurs', *Journal of High Technology Management Research*, **14**, 149–70.

North, D.C. (1990), *Institutions, Institutional Change and Economic Performance*, Cambridge: Cambridge University Press.

Parker, S.C. (2005), 'Explaining regional variations in entrepreneurship as multiple equilibria', *Journal of Regional Science*, **45**, 829–50.

Reynolds, P.D., N.S. Bosma, E. Autio, S. Hunt, N. de Bono, I. Servais, et al. (2005), 'Global Entrepreneurship Monitor: data collection design and implementation 1998–2003', *Small Business Economics*, **24** (3), 205–31.

Rocha, H. and R. Sternberg (2005), 'Entrepreneurship: the role of clusters. Theoretical perspectives and empirical evidence from Germany', *Small Business Economics*, **24** (3), 267–92.

Santarelli, E. and M. Vivarelli (2007), 'Entrepreneurship and the process of firms' entry, survival and growth', *Industrial and Corporate Change*, **16** (3), 455–88.

Schumpeter, J.A. (1934), *The Theory of Economic Development*, Cambridge, MA: Harvard University Press.

Schumpeter, J.A. (1942), *Capitalism, Socialism and Democracy*, New York: Harper & Row.

Schutjens, V.A.J.M. and E. Wever (2000), 'Determinants of new firm success', *Papers in Regional Science*, **79** (2), 135–53.

Sternberg, R. (2000), 'Gründungsforschung – Relevanz des Raumes und Aufgaben der Wirtschaftsgeographie', *Geografische Zeitschrift*, **88**, 199–219.

Stevenson, L. and A. Lundström (2001), 'Patterns and trends in entrepreneurship/ SME policy and practice in ten economies', *Entrepreneurship Policy for the Future Series*, **3**, Swedish Foundation for Small Business Research.

Tamásy, C. (2006), 'Determinants of regional entrepreneurship dynamics in contemporary Germany: a conceptual and empirical analysis', *Regional Studies*, **40** (4), 364–84.

Tödtling, F. and H. Wanzenböck (2003), 'Regional differences in structural characteristics of start-ups', *Entrepreneurship and Regional Development*, **15**, 351–70.

Van Praag, C.M. (1999), 'Some classic views on entrepreneurship', *De Economist*, **147** (3), 311–35.

Vivarelli, M. and D.B. Audretsch (1998), 'The link between the entry decision and post-entry performance: evidence from Italy', *Industrial and Corporate Change*, **7**, 485–500.

Wennekers, A.R.M. (2006), 'Entrepreneurship at country level; economic and non-economic determinants', ERIM PhD Series Research in Management, Erasmus University Rotterdam.

Wennekers, A.R.M. and A.R. Thurik (1999), 'Linking entrepreneurship and economic growth', *Small Business Economics*, **13**, 27–55.

Wiklund, J. (2006), 'The sustainability of the entrepreneurial orientation–performance relationship', in P. Davidsson, F. Delmar and J. Wiklund (eds), *Entrepreneurship and the Growth of Firms*, Cheltenham, UK and Northampton, MA, USA: Edward Elgar, pp. 141–55.

Wiklund, J., P. Davidsson and F. Delmar (2003), 'What do they think and feel about growth? An expectancy-value approach to small business managers' attitudes towards growth', *Entrepreneurship Theory and Practice*, **27** (3), 247–66.

Wong, P.K., Y.P. Ho and E. Autio (2005), 'Entrepreneurship, innovation, and economic growth: evidence from GEM data', *Small Business Economics*, **24** (3), 335–50.

World Bank (2005), *Doing Business in 2005: Removing Obstacles to Growth*, Washington, DC: World Bank.

PART III

New Venture Creation and Growth

4. Can new ventures develop pioneer behaviour in industries with unfavourable conditions? The role of capabilities

Pedro M. García-Villaverde and María J. Ruiz-Ortega

INTRODUCTION

Most studies on entry timing have focused on analysing the direct and indirect influence of the moment of market entry on the firm's performance (for example, Coeurderoy and Durand, 2004; Shamsie et al., 2004). We have found few empirical studies that focus on analysing the advantages and risks of entry timing for new ventures (for example, Shepherd et al., 2000; Williams et al., 1991). However, none of these empirical studies on the factors that influence entry timing is focused on new ventures (Mitchell, 1989; Robinson et al., 1992; Schoenecker and Cooper, 1998). We think that entry timing and entrepreneurship studies are strongly linked because of the shared need to compare windows of opportunity to gain competitive advantage and the liabilities of newness (Shepherd and Shanley, 1998).

We believe that environmental conditions determine new ventures' expectations to obtain first mover advantages and, therefore, bring about the moment of entry into the market (Covin et al., 2000). While the extant literature highlights the importance of the competitive dynamic, stating that the pioneer strategy can affect the competitive position of competitors in a relevant way (Geroski, 1995), we analyse the *level of imitation* and *rivalry* in the industry, which are two unfavourable environmental conditions to develop first mover advantages (Kerin et al., 1992).

Following population ecology (Hannan and Freeman, 1977), new ventures that perceive important potential advantages of early entry tend to enter a new market quickly if they have suitable resources and capabilities to allow it (Schoenecker and Cooper, 1998). The possession of certain complementary resources and capabilities can encourage new ventures to develop a pioneer behaviour to succeed in the marketplace, even when the environmental conditions are unfavourable for obtaining first mover advantages (Teece, 1986; Makadok, 1998). Besides, under unfavourable environmental conditions, the availability of certain capabilities can encourage new ventures to develop late follower type behaviour because late entry will enable new ventures to learn from the pioneers' mistakes, so providing better adaptation to the unfavourable environmental conditions. We expect to demonstrate that a high level of imitation and rivalry favours late follower behaviour of new ventures and that the possession of several capabilities affects the influence of these environmental conditions on the entry timing of the new ventures.

The contributions of our study are fourfold. First, we include the level of imitation among the analysed environmental conditions. Though excluded from the great majority of developed studies about entry timing, this variable is linked with the sustainability of first mover advantages and its inclusion in an empirical study allowed us to establish important conclusions (Lee et al., 2000). Second, we have included two kinds of capabilities hardly included before in this field of research; that is, managerial and marketing capabilities.[1] We include managerial capabilities, which can be a basic factor for the sustainability of first mover advantages, through organizational flexibility, the firm's adaptation capability to environmental changes and constant innovation. We also include marketing capabilities, which can have strong implications in the exploitation of potential advantages derived from pioneer entry into the market (Schoenecker and Cooper, 1998). Third, we correct methodological biases from previous studies (for example, Shepherd and Shanley, 1998; Lieberman and Montgomery, 1998; Covin et al., 2000). In particular, we have measured the moment of entry as a continuous variable, avoiding the bias arising from self-classification (Shepherd and Shanley, 1998). Finally, we develop the empirical study in a high-technology industry, in which the advantages of a pioneer strategy are not as evident as in more mature industries (Golder and Tellis, 1993).

The rest of the chapter is divided into four sections. Next, we provide the theory development. Then, we give an overview of the methods followed by the results obtained. Finally, we close with the discussion and conclusions.

THEORY DEVELOPMENT AND HYPOTHESES

Environmental Conditions and Pioneering New Ventures

Several studies in industrial organisation (for example, Bain, 1956) have stated the influence of environmental conditions on the decision of new ventures' entry timing (Levesque and Shepherd, 2004). From this perspective, the sector structure is the determining factor in a new venture's behaviour, influencing its goals, strategies, practices and performance (Robinson, 1998). Evolutionary economics regards competition as a dynamic process, in which firms try to adapt their strategies to market conditions and, at the same time, by means of their strategic decisions, to develop actions that allow them to influence environmental conditions (Nelson and Winter, 1982). From this standpoint, in a market without balance, new ventures will be able to tap into the constant opportunities that appear in the market (Geroski, 1995; Dean and Meyer, 1996). Accordingly, new ventures face uncertainty, either because of the lack of information about their industry and competitors, or from their concern over the adverse effects of the market environment on survival and success (Chrisman et al., 1998). In the present study, we analyse the influence of two environmental variables that the literature has traditionally considered unfavourable for the development of pioneer behaviour: imitation capability of the competitors and rivalry (Shepherd and Shanley, 1998; Covin et al., 2000; Levesque and Shepherd, 2004).[2]

New ventures may develop pioneer type behaviour in appropriate emergent segments, achieve scale economies, dominate industry standards or control distribution channels, which can allow them to achieve a strong market position (Golder and Tellis, 1993). The pioneer new ventures usually make an important effort in R&D investment, market development and customer education, which could entail high risk. The chances of taking advantage of the pioneer's effort by means of imitation is one of the advantages that the follower companies can achieve, but only if these companies have suitable imitation capabilities (Shepherd et al., 2000). New ventures will enter later into the market if there is a positive difference between the innovation costs and the imitation costs (Kerin et al., 1992). As a result, new ventures' perception of a high level of imitation in the industry favours late follower behaviour (Levesque and Shepherd, 2004), because it has a negative influence on their expectation to obtain sustainable first mover advantages (Durand and Coeurderoy, 2001). Hence,

H1: A greater level of imitation in an industry favours late follower type behaviour for new ventures.

High market rivalry can decrease the profits that pioneer new ventures expect to obtain at the monopoly stage (Romanelli, 1989).[3] This is because the intense pressure on resources that is generated in hostile environments limits the available resources and capabilities to develop and introduce new products into the market (Miller and Friesen, 1984). In addition, constant price wars and scant consumer loyalty lead new ventures to develop late entry into the market, avoiding the risks of early entry (Lieberman and Montgomery, 1998). In hostile environments there are disadvantages related to business climate, supply conditions and strict regulations that lead the new ventures to develop late follower behaviour (Kerin et al., 1992). Not surprisingly, Zahra (1996) showed that in highly hostile environments new ventures tend to behave as followers.[4] From these arguments we propose the following hypothesis:

H2:   Greater rivalry in an industry favours late follower type behaviour for new ventures.

Capabilities, Environmental Conditions and Pioneering New Ventures

Under population ecology, environmental conditions are the main factor that determines a firm's behaviour and performance (Hannan and Freeman, 1977). Somewhat opposed to industrial organization and evolutionary economics, population ecology acknowledges the important role of a firm's resources and capabilities. In doing so, population ecology highlights that strategic behaviour is the way in which firms within a population exploit the resources and opportunities that exist in a niche (Hannan and Freeman, 1977). In consequence, a firm tends to spread out rapidly when its key capabilities match the capabilities needed to survive in a new market (Brittain and Freeman, 1980). We argue that the interactions between the new venture's specific capabilities and market conditions have the greatest influence on entry timing.

New ventures that have suitable capabilities to gain first mover advantages in favourable environmental conditions will have greater incentives to enter early into the market (Williams et al., 1991).[5] In contrast, several studies have highlighted that, when first mover advantages in an industry are not strong enough, a new venture's resource position does not influence the timing of entry in a significant way. Along these lines, Schoenecker and Cooper (1998) point out that in particular industries, early entrants may have been unusually efficient in the specific technology, or 'lucky' in their R&D efforts so that they were ahead of rivals. We posit that, even when market conditions are unfavourable for obtaining first mover advantages, the possession of certain complementary resources and capabilities to achieve success in the market can encourage these new ventures to develop pioneer type behaviour (Giarratana, 2004). Thus, we think that the possibility of creating strong resource position barriers can generate expectations for new ventures to obtain sustainable first mover advantages.[6] In contrast to studies that have been solely focused on the influence of market conditions or a new venture's resources and capabilities on the pioneer or follower type behaviour, we have included the interactive effects. These effects between the perception of the environmental conditions and the possession of certain resources and capabilities explain the moment of market entry (Lieberman and Montgomery, 1988; Suárez and Lanzolla, 2005).

As mentioned previously, a new venture's perception of the *industrial level of imitation* influences the moment of market entry significantly, favouring later entry of this new venture into the market. However, even when there are strong imitation and entry threats in an industry because of the lack of entry barriers, if new ventures have certain key resources and capabilities that can develop 'resource position barriers', they will achieve and even maintain first mover advantages for a long period of time (Makadok, 1998). Therefore, competitors that have suitable resources can imitate certain attributes of the product or actions linked to the market pioneer, but cannot imitate complex actions, especially when tacit skills are involved (Lippman and Rumelt, 1982).[7]

Lieberman and Asaba (2006) stress that the success or failure of the commercialization of a new product can take months, and that market uncertainties of new technologies can take a few years to disappear. However, the organizational innovations created by means of *managerial capabilities* are characterized by longer gestation lags and more residual uncertainty. Thus, managerial and organizational processes promote the flexibility to respond quickly to changes as well as constant learning and innovation (Nadler and Tushman, 1997). These factors are basic in order to develop an early market entry because of the difficulties of achieving the product benefits when the firm's competitors exert a strong threat of imitation.

Managerial and organizational capabilities appear as a basic factor for obtaining first mover advantages in imitation environments (Teece et al., 1997). In this context, followers cannot gain advantages when they do not have the resources to imitate. This effect is bigger when the complexity, understood as the tacit character or the causal ambiguity of certain managerial capabilities, prevents them from understanding the pioneers' innovations (Lieberman and Asaba, 2006). Therefore, we consider that new ventures that have strong managerial and organizational capabilities will tend to develop pioneer type behaviours, and will achieve first mover advantages that will be very difficult to imitate by competitors with strong imitation capabilities.

First mover advantage will have a shorter life if a firm's competitors are capable of quickly imitating a new product's strengths and attributes (Lee et al., 2000). We argue that when companies in an industry have high imitation capabilities, those new ventures with a higher commitment to their successful products will neither have incentives to develop and introduce new products into the market, nor incentives to react in the first stages of their development. Higher commitment is reflected in the accumulation of specialized *marketing capabilities*. These new ventures will only draw on their capabilities to enter early into the market when the innovations are incremental. However, when there is a strong imitation threat, the new ventures with strong marketing capabilities will not want to develop radical innovations for fear of cannibalization with their own products (Taylor and Anderson, 2001). We consider that these new ventures will tend to develop late follower behaviour. In consequence,

H3:   In industries with a high level of imitation, greater managerial capabilities favour pioneer type behaviour for new ventures, and greater marketing capabilities favour late follower type behaviour.

In *hostile environments* there are constant threats against new ventures' viability (Zahra and Bogner, 1999). Therefore, when the rivalry is low, pioneer new ventures can use the monopoly conditions to control the market, develop economies of scale and strengthen their position. In this context, the pioneer new ventures can create entry barriers that will allow them to achieve and maintain strategic and economic advantages (Shankar et al., 1998). When the competitive rivalry is high, new ventures face constant price wars and difficulties in maintaining consumers' loyalty.[8] Then, there is a strong competition for resources and opportunities in the industry. The pioneer new venture's expectations to gain profits with regard to suppliers, consumers or followers will mainly depend on the availability of complementary resources linked to the new product's exploitation (Mitchell, 1989).[9]

Following Carpenter and Nakamoto (1994), we regard *marketing resources and capabilities* as essential for the market success of new products, especially when there is strong rivalry among competitors to influence the formation of consumer preferences. Thus, pioneer new ventures' strengths in advertising, promotion and educational capabilities can allow them to achieve consumers' loyalty and to lead and form consumer preferences. Furthermore, these strengths favour product differentiation and the creation of a strong brand image that consumers can identify with the standard of the product in the market. Whereas the distinctiveness of the pioneers' product offering can allow them to command a premium price in hostile environments, the follower companies will have to compete on the basis of price, because their products will be less differentiated (Covin et al., 2000).

In hostile environments, where growth opportunities are limited, pioneer new ventures can also enter and saturate the market with greater potential profits if they have control of distribution channels. Thus, selective control of distribution channels will allow the pioneer new ventures to attract the most desirable market segments, forcing follower companies to gain access to the rest (Makadok, 1998). Furthermore, a new venture's possession of downstream capabilities will allow it to open new geographic markets in which to establish, broadening its opportunities of growth (Giarratana, 2004).

We have noted that *managerial resources and capabilities* are linked to planning, learning and adaptation. In line with Day and Schoemaker (2001), we consider that these capabilities can lead new ventures to adopt defensive behaviour – maintaining their strategic commitment with the successful products and markets – given the risk that new ventures face in high hostile environments. Thus, new ventures with strong managerial capabilities can obtain advantages from developing late follower behaviour when their viability has been proved. Then, in hostile environments, the late entry could allow new ventures to obtain greater levels of performance than the pioneer new ventures (Conant et al., 1990).

We believe that in highly hostile environments, new ventures that have strong marketing capabilities will have expectations of appropriating the rents that are derived from the early introduction of new products into the market and, therefore, these firms will tend to adopt pioneer type behaviour. On the contrary, those new ventures that have strong managerial capabilities will probably tend to develop late follower type behaviour. Therefore:

H4: In industries with high levels of rivalry, greater marketing capabilities favour pioneer type behaviour for new ventures, and greater managerial capabilities favour late follower type behaviour.

SAMPLE AND METHODS

Sample

To carry out the empirical study, we have chosen to focus on the information and communications technology sector in Spain, starting by combining information from five data bases: ANIEL, Census of Exporters, Promotion of the Production, Europage and Camerdata. To avoid heterogeneity problems because of firm size, and following Spanos and Lioukas (2001), we dropped from the sampling frame firms with fewer than ten employees, as well as firms with missing data. Besides, we only included non-diversified new ventures; that is, companies that make at least 70 per cent of their income from their main activity (Rumelt, 1974). This yielded an initial sample frame of 283 new ventures created between 1991 and 2002.[10] After sending the questionnaire once, and then again three weeks later, we received 104 valid questionnaires; an acceptable response rate of 36.75 per cent.

With regard to the sampling error, for a confidence level of 95 per cent, and the least favourable situation of $p = q = 0.5$, we have an error of 7.6 per cent. We developed a T-test for all the variables included in the study between the firms that responded during the first three weeks (76) and the firms that responded later (28). We did not find any significant differences between these two groups. Furthermore, we compared the mean level of the size variable between the whole population and the firms included in the sample, and obtained very similar values for both groups. Therefore, following Armstrong and Overton (1977), a 'non-response bias' was not detected.

Measurement

The questionnaire design was developed from a wide review of the literature, which allowed us to measure the great majority of analysed variables from valid scales. In order to improve the content validity (Hambrick, 1981), we developed a pre-test with nine new ventures within the sector. We sent a lengthy questionnaire, in which the managers could indicate the degree of comprehensibility of the questions, as well as express their opinion on whether the questions were appropriate for the proposals that we were trying to make. Likewise, we also had in-depth discussions with academics and experts on the design of the questionnaires. In these meetings, we went through the questionnaire, so that these experts could suggest possible critiques and improvements. We made sure that, for every variable, we were choosing the best possible scale of measure (see Appendix Table 4A.1).

Control Variables

Age
The variable *age* is usually included in the studies about entrepreneurship in order to control its influence on a firm's survival. In this sense, as a new venture's age increases, the risk of failure decreases, with a consequent positive influence on firm performance (Chandler and Hanks, 1994).

Size

This variable is frequently included in studies to control the effect that it can have on new ventures' performance. Large firms can own more resources to obtain a better position in the market and develop scale economies that will help them achieve a better performance (McEvily and Zaheer, 1999). This variable has been included through the natural logarithm of the number of employees (Spanos and Lioukas, 2001; Tsai, 2001).

Origin

There are several studies that analyse the influence of a new venture's *origin* (independent or corporate) on the pioneer strategy and on a firm's performance (Roure and Maidique, 1986; Zahra, 1996; Shepherd and Shanley, 1998). These authors highlight that independent new ventures will tend to develop a pioneer behaviour because these firms can anticipate the customers' needs. This anticipation will allow the independent new ventures to be successful in developing new products.

Dynamism

Market *dynamism* reflects the difficulty of predicting industrial changes (Dess and Beard, 1984) and a steady movement of entry and exit in the industry (Miller and Friesen, 1984). In this case, after revising several scales we decided to include an adaptation of the scale proposed by Miller (1987), because we consider it to be the most suitable scale for our study. This variable was measured by means of a four-item scale. The scale is as follows: *the opportunities in the environment to grow strongly; the technology in my sector changes frequently; the innovation in processes and products or services grow strongly;* and *the research and development activity in my sector grows strongly* (Cronbach's alpha of 0.726).

Dependent Variable

We have included 'entry timing' as the dependent variable. This variable was measured with a three-item scale adapted from the study of Covin et al. (2000).[11] This scale is as follows: *we compete heavily on the basis of being first to the market with new product; we typically precede our major competitors in bringing new products to the market;* and *we offer products that are unique and distinctly different from those of our major competitors* (Chronbach's alpha of 0.712). This scale has allowed us to use a variable that reflects the new ventures' propensity to develop a pioneer type behaviour, which is not exactly to create a new product or to enter in a specific market, but a way of going about making decisions and taking actions

(Covin et al., 2000). We have used a five-point Likert scale that, though it supports some bias derived from subjective valuation of the moment of entry in the market, eliminates the tendency of the late follower group that existed in the PIMS database to self-exclude (Golder and Tellis, 1993).

In order to establish the response consistency of the moment of entry variable we examined the correlation between the moment of entry and the competitive proactivity variable,[12] which is measured with two items adapted from Venkatraman (1989) (Chronbach's alpha of 0.772). The results obtained show a level of correlation of 0.548 positive and significant to 99 per cent, so that we may consider the response consistency established.

Independent Variables

Environmental conditions

We have measured environmental conditions by means of requesting the new ventures' chief executive officers to value their perceptions of the industrial level of imitation and market rivalry. Thus, we could analyse the influence of these variables on the decision of when to enter the market. For these, and for all the variables included in this study, the new ventures' chief executive officers have valued their perceptions of them. We believe that the perceptions of the market environment are most relevant for studies that focus on new ventures' specific actions, such as the choice of entry timing (Boyd et al., 1993). We asked the managers about their view of industry conditions, because managers' views of their firms' main industry shape their strategic choices (Covin et al., 2000; Keats and Hitt, 1988).

Imitation. We can define the imitation level in the sector as the group of market reactions to a new product's introduction (Chaney et al., 1991). This means the imitation level will be high if, when a new product is introduced into the market, there are many actions to imitate it. Conversely, the imitation level will be low if there are hardly any actions to imitate it at all. In this case, we have not found a validated scale for measuring this variable, so we have created a measurement scale. This variable was measured with a two-item scale created[13] from Lee et al. (2000). The scale is as follows: *the firms in the sector usually imitate new products introduced into the market rapidly*; and *competitors have unique capabilities of imitating new products introduced into the market* (Cronbach's alpha of 0.783).

Rivalry. Rivalry reflects an unfavourable business climate, with intense competition for resources and market opportunities (Iansiti, 1995). This variable was measured by a five-item scale adapted from Covin et al. (2000). The scale is as follows: *the number of firms that fail in my sector is high*; *the competitive intensity based on quality is high in my sector*; *the competitive intensity based on service is high in my sector*; *the competitive intensity based on prices is high in my sector*; and *the number of competitors is high in my sector* (Cronbach's alpha of 0.705).

Capabilities

In relation to the measurement of firm capabilities we have reviewed several studies in order to select the most suitable scales (Chandler and Hanks, 1994; Li and Calantone, 1998; Lilien and Yoon, 1990; Makadok, 1998; Miller, 1996; Robinson et al., 1992; Shepherd et al., 2000; Spanos and Lioukas, 2001; Williams et al., 1991).[14] Finally, we have included part of the scale[15] proposed by Spanos and Lioukas (2001) because we consider it to be the most suitable scale for our study. Thus, we have included two kinds of capabilities:[16] managerial and marketing capabilities.

Managerial capabilities.   These capabilities are linked to organizational and managerial processes. The construct includes seven items: *firms' climate, efficiency in the organisational structure, mechanisms of efficient coordination, knowledge and skills of employees, managerial competences,* the procedures of *strategic planning* and the *ability to attract creative employees* (Cronbach's alpha of 0.842).

Marketing capabilities.   These capabilities refer to the output-based competences. The construct includes four items: the *advantages in the relations with clients*, the *customer 'installed base', control and access to the distribution channels* and *market knowledge* (Cronbach's alpha of 0.796).

Interaction terms.   As explained previously, we have hypothesized that the interactions between a new venture's specific capabilities and market conditions have an influence on entry timing. In order to measure these interactions we need to create the interaction terms among market conditions (imitation and rivalry) and new ventures' capabilities (managerial and marketing). We have built these interaction terms by multiplying both groups of variables (Cohen and Cohen, 1983).

Analysis

After measuring variables we developed several statistical techniques in order to test the hypotheses specified in our research. First, we developed a correlation analysis to verify that there are no multicollinearity problems between the variables included in the models. Then we developed a hierarchical regression analysis. The hierarchical approach is necessary since an interaction effect exists if, and only if, the interaction term gives a significant contribution over and above the main effects only model (Cohen and Cohen, 1983).

RESULTS

Before expounding the results of the regression analysis, we first calculated the means and standard deviations for all variables and a correlation matrix (Appendix Table 4A.2). In Table 4.1 we present the value inflation factors (VIFs). As these values are all below five, they are well below the benchmark (Hair et al., 1998), indicating that multicollinearity is unlikely to be a problem.

We have tested the hypotheses using hierarchical regression analysis. The results are displayed in Table 4.2. All the variables included in the study were standardized in order to interpret the results[17] correctly. The control variables of age, organizational size, origin and dynamism, the environmental variables of imitation and rivalry, and the variables of a new venture's capabilities were first entered in a base model that explained a statistically significant share of the variance of a firm's performance (0.135). The results obtained show that the level of imitation in the industry has a significant influence on the decision concerning the timing of market entry. The sign of the regression coefficient shows that the firms will enter later (minus sign) when the level of imitation of the firm's

Table 4.1   Tolerance and VIF

Variables	Tolerance	VIF
Age	.770	1.289
Size	.759	1.317
Origin	.756	1.323
Dynamism	.798	1.254
Imitation	.700	1.428
Rivalry	.644	1.553
Managerial capabilities	.492	2.032
Marketing capabilities	.549	1.821
Imitation × managerial capabilities.	.249	4.022
Imitation × *marketing* capabilities	.221	4.528
Rivalry × managerial capabilities	.260	3.843
Rivalry × *marketing* capabilities	.227	4.405

Table 4.2   Regression analysis

Variables	Main-effects-only model		Full model	
	β	t-statistics	β	t-statistics
Age	.030	.303	.028	.290
Size	.007	0.065	−.021	−.190
Independent or corporative	−.152	−.1417	−.130	−1.208
Dynamism	.178	1.707*	.180	1.816*
Imitation	−.282	−2.676***	−.298	−2.814***
Rivalry	−.035	−.316	.081	.721
Managerial capabilities	.135	1.160	.246	2.059**
Marketing capabilities	.175	1.534	.161	1.484
Imitation × managerial capabilities			.497	2.920***
Imitation × *marketing* capabilities			−.176	−.981
Rivalry × managerial capabilities			−.446	−2.755***
Rivalry × *marketing* capabilities			.349	2.019**
Model				
R²		.206***		.317****
Adjusted R²		.135***		.221****
Change in R²				.086***

Notes: * $p < 0.1$; ** $p < 0.05$; *** $p < 0.01$; **** $p < 0.001$.

competitor is high (β = −0.282, $p < 0.001$). From the results obtained we can accept hypothesis *H1*. With regard to the influence of market rivalry on the moment of market entry, the results obtained show a negative influence. However, it is not significant, so we cannot draw a significant conclusion from it and therefore, we cannot accept hypothesis *H2*. With regard to the two capability variables, managerial and marketing capabilities, the results obtained show that these have a positive influence on the promptness of entry, although none of them are significant. Therefore, from this base model we cannot draw conclusions regarding the influence of the capabilities on the decision about the moment of entry.

Full Model

After developing the main effects only model, we added to the regression analysis the interaction terms between unfavourable environment conditions (level of imitation and rivalry) and the new ventures' capabilities.[18]

The addition of the interaction terms gives an explanatory contribution over and above that of the base model ($\Delta R^2 = 0.086$, $p < 0.001$). This suggests that interaction effects are indeed present, thus the interactive effects between imitation and rivalry – and a firm's capabilities – influence the decision concerning the timing of entry into the market. Specifically, the results show that greater managerial capabilities ($\beta = .246$, $p < 0.005$), greater environmental dynamism ($\beta = .180$, $p < 0.01$) and a lower level of imitation ($\beta = -.298$ $p < 0.001$) favour prompt entry into the market.

In relation to the interactive effects the results obtained allow us to state that, as proposed in *H3* and *H4*, in environments with high levels of imitation and rivalry, the possession of certain kinds of capabilities will influence the new ventures' decision concerning the moment of market entry. Specifically the results show that the availability of managerial capabilities in sectors with high levels of imitation ($\beta = .497$, $p < 0.001$) favours pioneer type behaviour, whereas the possession of greater marketing capabilities favours later follower type behaviour, although not in a significant way. Furthermore, the results obtained show that in industries with high levels of rivalry, greater marketing capabilities favour early entry into the market ($\beta = .349$, $p < 0.005$) whereas greater managerial capability ($\beta = -.446$, $p < 0.001$) favours late entry into the market. From the results obtained we can accept *H3* (partially) and *H4*.

DISCUSSION AND CONCLUSIONS

With regard to the environmental conditions, the results obtained show that only the level of imitation in the industry creates a significantly unfavourable environment in order to develop pioneer type behaviour by new ventures. However, rivalry does not influence in a significant way the new ventures' moment of entry into the market. With regard to the influence of the new ventures' managerial and marketing capabilities, we have verified that, although their influence on the promptness of the moment of entry is always positive, there are none that are significant. Only in the full model did we find that greater managerial capabilities favour pioneer type behaviour in the new ventures. As expected, the interactive effects between the new ventures' capabilities and market conditions have a strong influence on the moment of market entry. In industries with a high level of imitation, those new ventures with greater managerial capabilities will enter earlier into the market. In more hostile environments, greater marketing capabilities favour an earlier entry. However, greater managerial capabilities favour later entry.

The results obtained also show that new ventures adapt their activity to the environmental conditions and their evolution. With regard to the level of imitation, we also obtained the expected result, because imitation leads to later entry of the new ventures into the market. Thus, new ventures avoid the potentially negative effect of pioneer entry when there is imitation (Lee et al., 2000). These results add empirical evidence to studies that suggest that a high ability for a competitor to imitate negatively affects the expectations of achieving a sustainable competitive advantage with pioneer market entry (Bowman and Gatignon, 1995; Durand and Coeurderoy, 2001).

With regard to the influence of market rivalry on the moment of entry the results obtained are not conclusive. In our research the opposite effects raised in the entry timing literature have been highlighted (Zahra and Bogner, 1999; Levesque and Shepherd, 2004). Therefore, as Miller and Friesen (1984) observed, market rivalry does not only have one possible relationship with the moment of market entry, so it would be necessary to include other moderating variables that allow us to explain this relationship.

Furthermore, with regard to the influence of resources and capabilities on the moment of entry into the market (Lieberman and Montgomery, 1998), we have not found conclusive results. In this sense, only in the full model did managerial capabilities have a positive and significant influence on entry timing. These results reflect the doubts we have found in the market literature about the direct effect of certain resources and capabilities on the timing of the entry of new ventures into the market (Williams et al., 1991; Kerin et al., 1992; Deeds et al., 1999). With regard to studies that have demonstrated how certain resources favour early entry into the market (Mitchell, 1989; Robinson et al., 1992; Schoenecker and Cooper, 1998; Thomas, 1996), this can be explained by the fact that these studies are mostly developed in industries whose characteristics favour the obtaining of first mover advantages by those new ventures that have suitable capabilities (Henderson, 1993; Henderson and Clark, 1990).

Of particular relevance are the results obtained regarding the influence of the availability of certain capabilities in unfavourable environmental conditions on the new ventures' moment of entry into the market. Managerial and organizational capabilities favour pioneer type behaviour by new ventures in industries with a high level of imitation. These capabilities are based on organizational innovations characterized by longer gestation lags and more residual uncertainty (Lieberman and Asaba, 2006). Thus, by means of early entry, new ventures can exploit their managerial capabilities, creating strong resource position barriers that impede follower firms from damaging first mover advantages, although they have strong imitation capabilities. With regard to the influence of the marketing capabilities in environments with high levels of imitation, the results obtained show the negative influence of this variable on the promptness of the new ventures' moment of entry, although these results are not statistically significant. This seems to be an unfavourable situation for obtaining first mover advantage. The availability of marketing capabilities can favour the development of follower behaviour, given the risk of cannibalizing their own products – not late follower behaviour but early follower behaviour. In this sense, the availability of marketing capabilities, traditionally linked to early follower behaviour (Schoenecker and Cooper, 1998; Lee et al., 2000), would explain both the negative influence that we have obtained in the regression analysis and the lack of significant influence. This is mainly because these capabilities favour an intermediate entry between the pioneer and the late follower.

The results obtained show that, in environments with high levels of rivalry, marketing capabilities favour earlier entry into the market. These capabilities are the most relevant complementary assets in order for pioneer new ventures to obtain commercial success from new product exploitation in environments with strong competition for opportunities and market resources (Shepherd et al., 2000). This is because these capabilities allow the firms to influence the formation of consumer preferences, avoiding price wars and the scarce loyalty to products that is usual in hostile environments. Furthermore, the control of distribution channels allows pioneer new ventures to tap into the most attractive market segments, forcing the follower companies to gain access to the rest.

In contrast, greater managerial capabilities lead to later entry in highly hostile industries. In this sense, given the high risk that new ventures face in environments with high rivalry, these capabilities, which are linked to planning, learning and adaptation, can lead a new venture to defensive behaviour – maintaining its strategic commitment with successful products and markets (Day and Schoemaker, 2001; Mitchell, 1989). In this sense, those new ventures with greater managerial capabilities in highly hostile environments will make use of their experience and management teams in a better way if they adopt late entry into the market.

One of the main contributions of this study involves analysing how the possession of a certain kind of resource in an industry with specific unfavourable characteristics will influence new ventures' behaviour with regard to the moment of entry into the market.[19] It confirms the need to study the interactive effects of market conditions and a firm's capabilities, previously raised by several authors (for example, Teece et al., 1997). With this study we give empirical support to the industrial organization and evolutionary economy approaches, because the obtained results support the influence of market conditions on new ventures' behaviour (Levesque and Shepherd, 2004). However, the main contribution of our results is linked to the population ecology approach. We appreciate that, when new ventures have key capabilities that coincide with the capabilities needed for survival and success in a new market, they enter early into the market (Brittain and Freeman, 1980), even when they perceive unfavourable environmental conditions.

We can conclude that new ventures will tend to develop late follower type behaviour if they perceive unfavourable conditions in the industry linked to the threat of competitors' imitation, because these conditions can both increase the survival risk and make obtaining first mover advantages difficult. Nevertheless, the availability of relevant managerial capabilities to face an unfavourable environment leads a new venture to develop pioneer type behaviour. However, we have not found that rivalry leads to developing late follower type behaviour in new ventures. We have found that the availability of strong marketing capabilities in new ventures to face a highly hostile environment successfully favours pioneer type behaviour. Similar to Makadok (1998), given a new venture's perception of unfavourable environmental conditions, the availability of key capabilities to develop and market new products in a constant way and the possibility of creating strong 'resource position barriers' will favour pioneer behaviour on its part.

With this study we contribute to overcoming several methodological biases in studies that have analysed the new ventures' moment of entry (e.g. Zahra, 1996; Shepherd and Shanley, 1998; Zahra and Bogner, 1999; Covin et al., 2000; Levesque and Shepherd, 2004). We have included traditional control variables (age and size) and the independent or corporate origin of new ventures, because the firm's origin can affect its strategic behaviour (Zahra, 1996) and initial success (Chrisman et al., 1998; Shrader and Simon, 1997). We have also included the perception of the market dynamism that the neo-Austrian perspective highlights as a variable both favouring the generation of new opportunities (Hill and Deeds, 1996) and affecting the strategic behaviour of new ventures (Dean and Meyer, 1996). Furthermore, following the suggestions developed by Shepherd and Shanley (1998) and Covin et al. (2000), we have considered the variable entry timing as continuous, spreading from market pioneer to late follower. This scale has allowed us to use a variable that reflects a firm's propensity to develop pioneer behaviour.[20] Moreover, we have included adolescent firms among the population of new ventures (Bantel, 1998). We include these firms because in technological industries, the influence of environmental factors and capabilities on a new venture's behaviour and performance can appear across a number of years (Chandler and Hanks, 1994).[21]

In the development of the present study, we note several limitations that may affect the results obtained. First, we must indicate the cross-sectional and non-longitudinal nature of the study. Nevertheless, we think that, because of the detailed information required to achieve our research aims, a longitudinal study would be excessively complex.

In addition, the perceptions of the CEOs with regard to industry conditions and new venture capabilities will not necessarily coincide exactly with objective reality, which might lead to possible limitations in the results obtained. However, we consider that the managerial perceptions reflect the new ventures' view of reality in their industry, relative capabilities and entry timing (Zahra, 1996; Shepherd et al., 2000). Furthermore, the measurement of entry timing as a continuous variable and its high correlation level with proactivity reinforces the validity of the measurement of this variable (Covin et al., 2000).

From the results obtained, we can expound several implications for new ventures' managers. In this sense, we consider that managers must judge if their firms have suitable capabilities to take advantage of first mover advantages given unfavourable environmental conditions. They must also evaluate the joint risks derived from pioneer entry given unfavourable conditions and the high risk of new ventures in their early years (Williams et al., 1991; Zahra and Bogner, 1999; Shepherd et al., 2000). In this sense, the managers of new ventures can develop and exploit certain capabilities in order to take advantage of the opportunities of early entry in industries with imitation and rivalry.

The conclusions of this chapter lead us to establish a series of proposals for future studies. A possible line of research would be its extension to other sectors of industrial activity, as well as to service sector companies. We also propose the inclusion of new market conditions, such as the heterogeneity or market potential, and new resources and capabilities that are specific to the analysed sector. This would allow deeper study of the influence of new interactions on the entry timing of new ventures into the market. We also consider it would be interesting to analyse several environmental conditions in a joined-up way (for example, imitation, rivalry and dynamism). Finally, a possible extension of this study would be to compare the direct and interactive effects of environmental conditions and new ventures' capabilities on entry timing among independent and corporate new ventures.

NOTES

1. In this chapter, we have not included technological capabilities that have been analysed in previous studies (Mitchell, 1989; Schoenecker and Cooper, 1998; Thomas, 1996).

2. The environmental factors are reflected in the managers' perceptions of their firm's major industry, because we consider that managerial perceptions are the main factors that determine the firms' strategic behaviour (Covin et al., 2000).

3. The *rivalry* is generally associated with reductions in the profitability of the industry (Porter, 1985). Zahra and Bogner (1999) identify rivalry with hostility.

4. Zahra and Bogner (1999) determine that in both 'price' and 'no price' hostile environments, early entry into the market is negatively associated with the new ventures' performance.

5. Mitchell (1989) points out that the new ventures that perceive important potential advantages of an early market entry will tend to enter quickly into the new market if their resources and capabilities allow it.

6. Makadok (1998) suggests that these advantages will be resistant to the entry of new competitors, even in industries with few entry and imitation barriers.

7. Rivkin (2000) highlights that the imitation process can become unprofitable if it is necessary to imitate many elements and interactions to achieve success.

8. Boulding and Christen (2003) consider that if there are limited entry barriers after a pioneer entry, the follower firms will take advantage of the pioneer's previous investments in product design and marketing.

9. Several authors have pointed out that market hostility does not have only one relationship with the firm's innovation (Miller and Friesen, 1984). In this sense, it highlights the need to study which are the new venture's capabilities that favour early market entry in a highly hostile industry (Teece et al., 1997).

10. We established a maximum age of 12 years to define the population of new ventures, according to Chandler and Hanks (1994) and Bantel (1998).

11. We excluded one of the items of the Covin et al. (2000) scale in order to improve its coherence and to get a better adaptation to our study.

12. We have examined the correlation between the moment of entry and competitive proactiveness (Venkatraman, 1989) because according to Covin et al. (2000), these two variables reflect a similar firm's behaviour, and when we prove that these variables are correlated we can consider the response consistency established.

13. We have created a scale for measuring imitation. We have included these two items in the scale because after reviewing the literature we concluded that these two items reflected the firms' behaviour we wanted to measure.

14. Several of these papers analyse the new ventures.

15. The scale proposed by Spanos and Lioukas (2001) distinguishes among three kinds of capabilities: managerial, marketing and technical capabilities.

16. In this sense, as we have explained previously, we want to analyse the influence of managerial and marketing capabilities on the moment of entry, and this scale (Spanos and Lioukas, 2001) gathers these variables.

17. The values for mean and standard deviation are included in the table of correlations and were calculated before to standardize the variables.

18. We developed the hierarchical approach because an interaction effect exists if, and only if, the interaction term gives a significant contribution over and above the main effects only model (Cohen and Cohen, 1983).

19. As we proposed in the hypothesis, we have proved that if a new venture has the capabilities needed to face the competitive market conditions, this will directly influence its moment of market entry.

20. Thus, we eliminate the biases derived from the utilization of self-definition measures, like those established in the PIMS database, avoiding the tendency for self-exclusion of the late follower group.

21. We have included the variable *age* in order to control its effect on the moment of entry into the market.

REFERENCES

Armstrong, J.S. and T. Overton (1977), 'Estimating nonresponse bias in mail surveys', *Journal of Marketing Research*, **14**, 396–402.

Bain, J.S. (1956), *Barriers to New Competition*, Cambridge, MA: Harvard University Press.

Bantel, K.A. (1998), 'Technology-based, adolescent firm configurations: strategy identification, context, and performance', *Journal of Business Venturing*, **13**, 205–30.

Boulding, W. and M. Christen (2003), 'Sustainable pioneering advantage: profit implications of market entry order', *Marketing Science*, **22** (3), 371–92.

Bowman, D. and H. Gatignon (1995), 'Determinants of competitor response time to a new product introduction', *Journal of Marketing Research*, **23**, 42–53.

Boyd, B., G.C. Dess and A. Rasheed (1993), 'Divergence between archival and perceptual measures of the environment: causes and consequences', *Academy of Management Review*, **18**, 204–26.

Brittain, J. and J. Freeman (1980), 'Organizational proliferation and density dependent selection', in J. Kimberly and R. Miles (eds), *The Organization Life Cycle*, San Francisco, CA: Jossey-Bass, pp. 291–338.

Carpenter, G.S. and K. Nakamoto (1994), 'Reflections on consumer preference formation and pioneering advantage', *Journal of Marketing Research*, **31**, 570–3.

Chandler, G.N. and S.H. Hanks (1994), 'Market attractiveness, resource-based capabilities, venture strategies, and venture performance', *Journal of Business Venturing*, **9**, 331–49.

Chaney, P.K., T.M. Devinney and R.S. Winer (1991), 'The impact of new product introductions on the market value of firms', *Journal of Business*, **64**, 573–610.

Chrisman, J.J., A. Bauerschmidt and C.W. Hofer (1998), 'The determinants of new venture performance: an extended model', *Entrepreneurship Theory and Practice*, **23** (1), 5–29.

Coeurderoy, R. and R. Durand (2004), 'Leveraging the advantage of early entry: proprietary technologies versus cost leadership', *Journal of Business Research*, **57**, 583–90.

Cohen, J. and P. Cohen (1983), *Applied Multiple Regression/Correlation Analysis for the Behavioural Sciences*, 2nd edn, Hillsdale, NJ: Lawrence Erlbaum Associates, Inc.

Conant, J., M.P. Mokwa and P.R. Varadarajan (1990), 'Strategic types, distinctive marketing competencies and organizational performance: a multiple-measures based study', *Strategic Management Journal*, **11**, 365–83.

Covin, J.G., D.P. Slevin and M.B. Heeley (2000), 'Pioneers and followers: competitive tactics, environment, and firm growth', *Journal of Business Venturing*, **15**, 175–210.

Cronbach, L.J. (1951), 'Coefficient alpha and the internal structure of test', *Psychometrika*, **31**, 93–6.

Day, G. and P. Schoemaker (2001), 'Avoiding the pitfalls of emerging technologies', *California Management Review*, **42**, 8–33.

Dean, T.J. and G.D. Meyer (1996), 'Industry environments and new venture formations in U.S. manufacturing: a conceptual and empirical analysis of demand determinants', *Journal of Business Venturing*, **11**, 107–32.

Deeds, D.L., D. De Carolis and J. Coombs (1999), 'Dynamic capabilities and new product development in high technology ventures: an empirical analysis of new biotechnology firms', *Journal of Business Venturing*, **15** (3), 211–30.

Dess, G.G. and D.W. Beard (1984), 'Dimensions of organizational task environments', *Administrative Science Quarterly*, **29**, 52–73.

Durand, R. and R. Coeurderoy (2001), 'Age, order of entry, strategic orientation, and organizational performance', *Journal of Business Venturing*, **16**, 471–94.

Geroski, P.A. (1995), 'What do we know about entry?', *International Journal of Industrial Organization*, **13**, 421–40.

Giarratana, M.S. (2004), 'The birth of a new industry: entry by start-ups and the drivers of firm growth. The case of encryption software', *Research Policy*, **33**, 787–806.

Golder, P.N. and G.J. Tellis (1993), 'Pioneer advantage: marketing logic or marketing legend?', *Journal of Marketing Research*, **30**, 158–70.

Hair, J.F., R.E. Anderson, R.L. Tatham and W.C. Black (1998), *Multivariate Data Analysis*, New York: Prentice Hall International.

Hambrick, D.C. (1981), 'Environment, strategy and power within top management teams', *Administrative Science Quarterly*, **26**, 253–76.

Hannan, M.T. and J. Freeman (1977), 'The population ecology of organizations', *American Journal of Sociology*, **82** (5), 929–64.

Henderson, R. (1993), 'Underinvestment and incompetence as responses to radical innovation: evidence from the photolithographic alignment equipment industry', *Rand Journal of Economics*, **24** (2), 248–70.

Henderson, R.M. and K.B. Clark (1990), 'Architectural innovation: the reconfiguration of existing product technologies and the failure of established firms', *Administrative Science Quarterly*, **35**, 9–30.

Hill, C.W.L. and D.L. Deeds (1996), 'The importance of industry structure for the determination of firm profitability: a neo-Austrian perspective', *Journal of Management Studies*, **33** (4), 429–51.

Iansiti, M. (1995), 'Shooting the rapids: managing product development in turbulent environments', *California Management Review*, **38** (1), 37–58.

Keats, B. and M.A. Hitt (1988), 'A casual model of linkages among environmental dimensions, macro organizational characteristics, and performance', *Academy of Management Journal*, **31**, 570–98.

Kerin, R., R.R. Varadarajan and R. Peterson (1992), 'First-mover advantage: a synthesis, conceptual framework, and research propositions', *Journal of Marketing*, **56** (4), 33–52.

Lee, H., K.G. Smith, C.M. Grimm and A. Schomburg (2000), 'Timing, order and durability of new product advantages with imitation', *Strategic Management Journal*, **21** (1), 23–30.

Levesque, M. and D.A. Shepherd (2004), 'Entrepreneurs' choice of entry strategy in emerging and developed markets', *Journal of Business Venturing*, **19**, 29–54.

Li, T. and R.J. Calantone (1998), 'The impact of market knowledge competence on new product advantage: conceptualization and empirical examination', *Journal of Marketing*, **62**, 13–29.

Lieberman, M.B. and S. Asaba (2006), 'Why do firms imitate each other?', *Academy of Management Review*, **31** (2), 366–85.

Lieberman, M.B. and D.B. Montgomery (1988), 'First mover advantages', *Strategic Management Journal*, Summer Special Issue, **9**, 41–58.

Lieberman, M.B. and D.B. Montgomery (1998), 'First mover (dis)advantages: retrospective and link with the resource-based view', *Strategic Management Journal*, **19**, 1111–25.

Lilien, G.L and E. Yoon (1990), 'The timing of competitive market entry: an exploratory study of new industrial products', *Management Science*, **36** (5), 568–85.

Lippman, S.A. and R.P. Rumelt (1982), 'Uncertain imitability: an analysis of inter-firm differences in efficiency under competition', *Bell Journal of Economics*, **13**, 418–38.

McEvily, B. and A. Zaheer (1999), 'Bringing ties. A source of firm heterogeneity in competitive capabilities', *Strategic Management Journal*, **20**, 1133–56.

Makadok, R. (1998), 'Can first-mover and early-mover advantages be sustained in an industry with low barriers to entry/imitation?', *Strategic Management Journal*, **19** (7), 683–96.

Miller, D. (1987), 'Strategy making and structure: analysis and implications for performance', *Academy of Management Journal*, **30** (1), 7–32.

Miller, D. (1996), 'Configurations revisited', *Strategic Management Journal*, **17**, 505–12.

Miller, D. and P.H. Friesen (1984), *Organizations: A Quantum View*, Englewood Cliffs, NJ: Prentice Hall.

Mitchell, W. (1989), 'Whether and when? Probability and timing of incumbents entry into emerging industrial subfields', *Administrative Science Quarterly*, **34**, 208–30.

Nadler, D.A. and M. Tushman (1997), *Competing By Design: The Power of Organizational Architecture*, New York: Oxford University Press.

Nelson, R.R. and S.G. Winter (1982), *An Evolutionary Theory of Economic Change*, Cambridge, MA: Harvard University Press.

Porter, M. (1985), *Competitive Advantage: Creating and Sustaining Superior Performance*, New York: Free Press.

Rivkin, J.W. (2000), 'Imitation of complex strategies', *Management Science*, **46**, 824–44.

Robinson, K.C. (1998), 'An examination of the influence of industry structure on eight alternative measures of new venture performance for high potential independent new ventures', *Journal of Business Venturing*, **14**, 165–87.

Robinson, W.T., C. Fornell and M. Sullivan (1992), 'Are market pioneers intrinsically stronger than later entrants?', *Strategic Management Journal*, **13**, 609–24.

Romanelli, E. (1989), 'Environments and strategies of organization start-up: effects on early survival', *Administrative Science Quarterly*, **34**, 369–87.

Roure, J.B. and M.A. Maidique (1986), 'Linking pre-funding factors and high-technology venture success: an exploratory study', *Journal of Business Venturing*, **1** (3), 295–306.

Rumelt, R.P. (1974), 'Towards a strategic theory of the firm', in R. Lamb (ed.), *Competitive Strategic Management*, Englewood Cliffs, NJ: Prentice Hall, pp. 556–70.

Schoenecker, T.S. and A.C. Cooper (1998), 'The role of firm resources and organizational attributes in determining entry timing: a cross-industry study', *Strategic Management Journal*, **19**, 1127–43.

Shamsie, J., C. Phelps and J. Kuperman (2004), 'Better late than never: study of late entrants in household electrical equipment', *Strategic Management Journal*, **25**, 69–84.

Shankar, V., G. Carpenter and L. Krishnamurthi (1998), 'Late mover advantage: how innovative late entrants outsell pioneers', *Journal of Marketing Research*, **35**, 54–70.

Shepherd, D.A. and M. Shanley (1998), *New Venture Strategy. Timing, Environment Uncertainty, and Performance*, Thousand Oaks, CA: Sage Publications.

Shepherd, D.A., R. Ettenson and A. Crouch (2000), 'New venture strategy and profitability: a venture capitalist's assessment', *Journal of Business Venturing*, **15**, 449–67.

Shrader, R.C. and M. Simon (1997), 'Corporate versus independent new ventures: resource, strategy, and performance differences', *Journal of Business Venturing*, **12**, 47–66.

Spanos, Y.E. and S. Lioukas (2001), 'An examination into the causal logic of rent generation: contrasting Porter's competitive strategy framework and the resource based perspective', *Strategic Management Journal*, **22**, 907–34.

Suárez, F.Y. and G. Lanzolla (2005), 'The half-truth of first mover advantages', *Harvard Business Review*, **83** (4), 121–7.

Taylor, A. and P. Anderson (2001), 'Note on first mover advantage', Working Paper, the Ruck School of Business at Dartmouth.

Teece, D.J. (1986), 'Profiting from innovation', in D.J. Teece (ed.), *The Competitive Challenge*, New York: Harper & Row, pp. 26–54.

Teece, D.J., G. Pisano and A. Shuen (1997), 'Dynamic capabilities and strategic management', *Strategic Management Journal*, **20**, 509–33.

Thomas, L.A. (1996), 'Brand capital and entry order', *Journal of Economics and Management Strategy*, **5** (1), 107–29.

Tsai, W. (2001), 'Knowledge transfer in intra-organizational networks. effects of network position and absorptive capacity on business unit innovation and performance', *Academy of Management Journal*, **44** (5), 996–1004.

Venkatraman, N. (1989), 'Strategic orientation of business enterprises', *Management Science*, **35** (8), 942–62.

Williams, M.L., M.H. Tsai and D. Day (1991), 'Intangible assets, entry strategies, and venture success in industrial markets', *Journal of Business Venturing*, **6**, 315–33.

Zahra, S.A. (1996), 'Technology strategy and financial performance: examining the moderating role of the firm's competitive environment', *Journal of Business Venturing*, **11**, 189–219.

Zahra, S.A. and W.C. Bogner (1999), 'Technology strategy and software new venture performance', *Journal of Business Venturing*, **15**, 135–73.

APPENDIX

Table 4A.1   Variables and scales*

Control variables
Dynamism (Miller, 1987)
The opportunities of the environment grow strongly
The technology in my sector changes frequently
The innovation in processes and products or services grows strongly
The research and development activity in my sector grows strongly
Dependent variable
Entry timing (Covin et al., 2000)
We compete heavily on the basis of being first to the market with new products
We typically precede our major competitors in bringing new products to the market
We offer products that are unique and distinctly different from those of our major competitors
Proactiveness (Venkatraman, 1989)
With regard to competitors, my firm is, normally, the first in developing actions which are responded by competitors
With regard to competitors, my firm is, very frequently, the first in introducing new products, new services . . .
Environmental variables
Imitation (Lee et al., 2000)
The firms in the sector usually imitate new products introduced into the market rapidly
Competitors have unique capabilities for imitating new products introduced into the market
Rivalry (Covin et al., 2000)
The number of firms that fail in my sector is high
The competitive intensity based on quality is high in my sector
The competitive intensity based on service is high in my sector
The competitive intensity based on prices is high in my sector
The number of competitors is high in my sector
Capabilities
Managerial capabilities (Spanos and Lioukas, 2001)
Firms' climate
Efficiency in the organizational structure
Mechanisms of efficient coordination
Knowledge and skills of employees
Managerial competences
Strategic planning
Ability to attract creative employees

Table 4A.1   (continued)

Marketing capabilities (Spanos and Lioukas, 2001)
Advantages in the relations with clients
Customer 'installed base'
Control and access to the distribution channels
Market knowledge

Note: *As we have explained in the chapter, some of these scales are adapted from the original.

Table 4A.2 Correlations

	Size	Age	Dynamism	Imitation	Rivalry	Mana. Cap	Mark. Cap	I×MC	I×MkC	R×MC	R×MkC	Mom. Entry
Mean	143.5	1995.4	3.547	3.668	3.822	3.719	3.746	.109	.122	0.127	.0648	3.211
SD	465.6	2.99	.815	1.003	.815	.634	.680	.680	.735	.879	.901	.881
Size	1											
Age	0.041	1										
Dynamism	.214*	.108	1									
Imitation	.108	-.096	.238*	1								
Rivalry	.264**	-.107	.054	.378**	1							
Mana.Cap	.036	.097	.290**	.203*	.204*	1						
Mark.Cap	.050	-.035	.155	.093	.248*	.517**	1					
IxMC	-.012	.211*	-.035	-.206*	-.155	-.180	-.084	1				
IxMkC	-.023	.188	-.010	-.222*	-.326**	-.133	-.070	.337**	1			
RxMC	.040	.138	-.115	-.215*	-.215*	-.399	-.192	.343**	.321**	1		
RxMkC	-.029	.185	-.095	-.329**	-.233*	-.241*	-.119	.368**	.364**	.340**	1	
Mom.Entry	.151	.122	.170	-.236*	-.053	.233*	.252**	.052	.143	.139	.143	1

Notes: * $p < 0.1$; ** $p < 0.05$.

5. Switching from paid employment to entrepreneurship: the effect on individuals' earnings

Miguel Torres Preto, Rui Baptista and Francisco Lima

INTRODUCTION

The role played by the characteristics and preferences of individuals, as well as general and specific human capital in determining whether individuals choose wage employment or self-employment, has been addressed by some key theoretical and empirical works in the discipline of economics (Lucas, 1978; Kihlstrom and Laffont, 1979; Evans and Leighton, 1989a; Blanchflower and Oswald, 1998; and Lazear, 2005). While theoretical models highlight differences in expected earnings as the main factor determining the decision, empirical evidence does not provide clear support that earnings differentials play a significant (or, at least, the most significant) role in the choice between these two occupations (Parker, 2004). Moreover, empirical evidence on earnings differentials between the self-employed and wage employees does not favour the former (Hamilton, 2000).

The main objective of this chapter is to look at the pecuniary impact of becoming a business owner after being employed in a firm. We use data that allow us to observe individual and firm level effects on incomes simultaneously, thus avoiding misspecification problems associated with panel studies that only include personal data. We account for multiple determinants of wage earnings, such as individual attributes (age, education), employer characteristics (firm size, economic sector, and administrative region), and individuals' career paths.

In line with labour economics research, while estimating individual earnings, we estimate different types of earnings models, each including different kinds of information concerning wage determinants. We first consider individual attributes such as age, schooling and tenure, while controlling for firm characteristics, including firm size, industry and region. Secondly, we include mobility variables for two specific groups, namely individuals switching from paid employment to business ownership and those switching from paid employment in one firm to paid employment in another firm. Thirdly, we account for specific pecuniary effects for those individuals who leave their current job to become entrepreneurs. Finally, information about the individuals' careers is included as our data comprise historical employment data for individuals.

The following section reviews the literature on earnings differentials between waged workers and the self-employed. The third section discusses the data and methodological issues. The fourth section presents the empirical specification of the study. The fifth section displays the estimation results and summarizes the main findings, while the final section concludes.

BACKGROUND

Economic models of occupational choice between wage employment and self-employment are mostly based on the expectation that individuals are attracted to business ownership because of higher expected earnings relative to paid employment. In other words, paid employment earnings are the opportunity cost for entrepreneurs. However, the majority of recent evidence suggests that for comparable levels of education and experience, most self-employed individuals earn less than paid employees. An important stream of literature shows that over-optimism about future earnings as an entrepreneur plays a role in explaining this fact (Kahneman and Lovallo, 1993; Camerer and Lovallo, 1999). However, over-optimism does not explain persistence in self-employment by individuals who earn less than they could if they were paid employees. Some researchers argue that the evolution of earnings over time should show sharper increases for the self-employed than for paid employees as the self-employed do not share the rents of their investments in human capital (Becker, 1975). Others contend that earnings for waged workers should increase more sharply over time, in order to discourage shirking because of agency problems, especially given that as a wage worker progresses up the job ladder, shirking becomes more costly to the firm (Lazear and Moore, 1984).

A stream of literature examines the difference between the earnings of waged employees and those of the self-employed. While most studies using cross-sectional data find that the self-employed have lower earnings than paid employees (Bregger, 1963; Ray, 1975; Fain, 1980; Becker, 1984; Haber et al., 1987; and Carrington et al., 1996), studies using longitudinal data find that mean earnings are to some extent analogous (Rees and Shah, 1986; Gill, 1988; Borjas and Bronars, 1989). Some of these latter studies indicate that initial earnings growth for entrepreneurs in a new business is larger than the growth in wages for salaried employees starting a new job (Brock and Evans, 1986; Rees and Shah, 1986; Borjas and Bronars, 1989; Evans and Leighton, 1989a; and Hamilton, 2000). Other empirical studies report an average income advantage for the self-employed (Form, 1985; Borjas, 1986; Carroll and Mosakowski, 1987; Ferber and Waldfogel, 1998; Quadrini, 1999; and Fairlie, 2004). There are multiple determinants explaining the decision to become self-employed. Hsu et al. (2007) highlight the importance of financial and opportunity cost-based determinants. Individuals are more likely to start new firms if their opportunity costs are lower; that is, they have relatively low current wage earnings and their liquidity constraints are less binding than for others (Evans and Jovanovic, 1989; Amit et al., 1995; Iyigun and Owen, 1998; Blanchflower and Oswald, 1998; Dunn and Holtz-Eakin, 2000). Additionally, employees are more likely to leave their existing organization and become self-employed when there is a slowdown in sales growth (Gompers et al., 2005). Other studies find a negative correlation between tax rates and self-employment in lower tax brackets (Blau, 1987).

Human capital theory proposes a positive relationship between factors such as formal education or professional experience with labour productivity (Mincer, 1974; Becker, 1975). Theoretical models of entrepreneurial choice and dynamics, such as those by Lucas (1978) and Jovanovic (1982), posit that entrepreneurial ability (whether pre-determined or learned) is a fundamental determinant of occupational choice. While experienced and educated wage workers are expected to be more productive and are consequently rewarded with higher earnings in the labour market, Casson (2003) argues that the skills that make good entrepreneurs are not necessarily the same as those embodied in formal qualifications. Even if individuals are not endowed with the complete set of skills necessary to start a business, they can acquire those skills. Lazear (2005) suggests that entrepreneurs should be generalists while those who work for others should be specialists, implying that human capital investments differ between those who end up as entrepreneurs and those who end up in salary or waged work. While Evans and Leighton (1989a) and Evans and Jovanovic (1989) find no connection between formal education and entrepreneurial earnings, Silva (2006) finds that changes in the spread of knowledge across different fields do not necessarily increase the prevalence of entrepreneurship.

Some studies show that relative earnings do not play a significant role in labour market status (i.e. self-employment vs. paid employment), suggesting that pecuniary rewards may not be the primary motivation for choosing self-employment. Parker (2003) stresses that, in general, occupational choice between self-employment and paid employment is not robustly related to pecuniary factors. Taylor (1999) suggests that individuals are attracted to self-employment by the freedom from managerial constraints that it offers. Hamilton (2000) argues that non-pecuniary benefits of self-employment are substantial, because entrepreneurs persist in business even when they have both lower initial earnings and lower earnings growth than they could obtain in paid employment. Following the literature on over-optimism, Koellinger et al. (2007) find strong evidence that subjective, and often biased, perceptions have a crucial impact on new business creation.

The study of actual transitions from paid employment to entrepreneurship has attracted less attention. In an important study, Carrasco (1999) finds that the unemployed are more likely to enter self-employment, but their businesses generate lower earnings and face higher failure rates. Hamilton (2000) finds that the earnings of individuals entering self-employment are not significantly different from those of waged employees. In a recent study, Ñopo and Valenzuela (2007), using data for Chile, find that individuals switching from paid employment to self-employment experience positive average increases in income. The present chapter aims to contribute to this particular segment of the literature by examining and comparing the determinants of the earnings of individuals who switch from paid employment to self-employment with those of individuals who change firms while remaining paid employees.

DATA AND METHODOLOGY

As pointed out above, the present study concentrates on the earnings of those individuals who switch from paid employment to entrepreneurship, and of those individuals who change firms but remain paid employees. Additionally, paid employees who do not change firms represent our control group. We estimate earnings equations for paid employees and business owners as a function of individual/personal characteristics, while controlling for the characteristics of the firm, such as size, industry and region. The availability of matched employer–employee data allows for this kind of analysis.

Hamilton (2000) considers different measures of self-employment earnings, namely: net profit, draw, and equity-adjusted draw. Net profit from running an enterprise is the standard measure widely used in the literature as measure of self-employment income. Given the potential under-reporting problem associated with net profit, other measures constitute good alternatives, such as 'draw', which is the amount of consumption the business generates for the owner. Another measure less frequently used is the draw plus the growth in business equity. This measure is adjusted to account for the opportunity cost of business equity. In fact, the measurement of entrepreneur income constitutes a problem established in the literature (Parker, 2004). Typically, four types of problems exist in this regard, namely income under-reporting by the self-employed; relatively high non-response rates to survey income questions by the self-employed; failure to deal properly with negative incomes; and erroneous income reporting.

Since we lack specific data on entrepreneurs' income, we use the earnings of the highest paid employee in each firm as a proxy for the business owner's income. While the proxy chosen in the present study might in most cases understate the true business owner's earnings, the earnings distribution of the highest paid employee in a new firm is likely to be similar to the true earnings distribution of the business owner during the first years after start-up, as the firm has not yet had time to accumulate profits and generate capital gains.

The main data source is the 'Quadros de Pessoal' (QP) micro-data, a longitudinal matched employer–employee data set including extensive information on worker mobility and business owners for 1995 through to 2003. QP includes annual data from all establishments with at least one wage-earner in Portugal. There are over two million workers in each annual survey who can be traced over time through the use of a unique identification number associated with the Portuguese social security system. Data for each business owner and paid employee include occupation, tenure, schooling and careers.

The population under analysis focuses on all male individuals, paid employees and business owners, aged between 16 and 65 years old who are observable in the data set by 1995 and traceable through to 2003. For the purpose of this research, a broad definition of 'business owner' is used. It includes all individuals who are reported as owning a business with at least one waged employee (sole contractors are excluded), regardless of whether they have full or partial ownership, and have started, acquired or inherited the business. We choose not to delve into a conceptual distinction between the terms business owner, self-employed and entrepreneur.

Individual earnings equations are defined for all the periods from 1995 to 2003. Individuals are compared using earnings as the variable of interest for paid employees and the earnings of the highest paid employee as a proxy for entrepreneurial income. We compute for each year and for each firm the earnings of the highest paid employee and assign that wage to the business owner of the firm. Controls for the events are defined as mobility across firms, distinguishing those workers who remain as paid employees from those who become business owners. Age, education, tenure, and firm characteristics are also controlled. As we know the hierarchical level of the worker, we also control for promotions and demotions.

EMPIRICAL SPECIFICATION

We begin by estimating a typical earnings equation (Mincer, 1974) using a log-linear wage function:

$$\ln y_{it} = a + X_{it}\beta + D_{it}\gamma + u_{it} \tag{5.1}$$

where y_{it} is the monthly wages received by individual i in year t; X_{it} is a vector of both individual characteristics – including age (and its squared term), education (three dummy variables), and tenure (and its squared term) – and firm characteristics – including firm size, industry and administrative region (which can be varying or invariant over time); D_{it} represents the dummy variables accounting for transitions; and u_{it} is the equation error term.

In our analysis we also apply a panel data methodology as to control for individual unobserved heterogeneity. We define a fixed effects model for wage equation as:

$$\ln y_{it} = \alpha + X_{it}\beta + D_{it}\gamma + \upsilon_i + \varepsilon_{it} \tag{5.2}$$

where υ_i is a vector of unobservable individual time-constant effects, and ε_{it} is the error term reflecting time-varying unobservable factors.

As previously mentioned, the period under study starts in 1995 and concludes with 2003. The analysis is restricted to males, who account for 61 per cent of all individuals present in the data set in 1995. Individuals aged between 16 and 65 in 1995 correspond to 97 per cent of the original sample. The dependent variable in the earnings equations is the natural logarithm of monthly wage calculated by the sum of basic wage with regular payments, deflated using the Consumer Price Index. Overtime payments are not included as part of the dependent variable.

Table 5.1 shows the descriptive statistics. The mean age is nearly 44 for business owners and 39 for paid employees. Business owners are better educated, having achieved a university level education. On average, the tenure of business owners is little lower than the tenure of individuals who are always paid employees.

Education is included in the model through three dummy variables accounting for (1) individuals who completed the nine years of Portugal's

Table 5.1   Descriptive statistics, 1995–2003

Variables	Statistics	All individuals	Paid employees	Business owners
	N	6170011	5810330	359681
Monthly wage (log)	Mean	6.610	6.620	6.446
	St. dev.	0.547	0.548	0.491
Age (years)	Mean	39.593	39.291	44.472
	St. dev.	10.606	10.585	9.717
Nine years education	Mean	0.155	0.154	0.165
(dummy)	St. dev.	0.362	0.361	0.372
Secondary education	Mean	0.125	0.125	0.126
(dummy)	St. dev.	0.330	0.330	0.332
College education (dummy)	Mean	0.034	0.033	0.048
	St. dev.	0.180	0.178	0.213
Tenure (years)	Mean	9.574	9.613	8.946
	St. dev.	9.357	9.441	7.840
Firm size (log)	Mean	4.364	4.500	2.172
	St. dev.	2.309	2.301	0.899
Entry into business	Mean	0.006	0.001	0.076
ownership (BO) (dummy)	St. dev.	0.076	0.038	0.265
Paid employees (PE) firm	Mean	0.098	0.105	0.000
change (dummy)	St. dev.	0.298	0.306	0.000
Direct transition into BO	Mean	0.003	0.001	0.036
(dummy)	St. dev.	0.051	0.025	0.185
PE firm change: get	Mean	0.020	0.022	0.000
promoted (dummy)	St. dev.	0.142	0.146	0.000
PE firm change: stay	Mean	0.057	0.061	0.000
current level (dummy)	St. dev.	0.233	0.239	0.000
PE firm change: get	Mean	0.016	0.017	0.000
demoted (dummy)	St. dev.	0.125	0.129	0.000
Promotion (dummy)	Mean	0.043	0.044	0.043
	St. dev.	0.204	0.204	0.203
Demotion (dummy)	Mean	0.029	0.029	0.027
	St. dev.	0.167	0.167	0.164

Note: Monthly wage is calculated by summing base wage with regular payments, deflated by the Consumer Price Index. The size of the firm is measured by number of employees. *Age* and *tenure* are measured in years. *Nine years of education, secondary education, college education, entry to business ownership, paid employees firm change, direct transition to business ownership, promotion* and *demotion* are defined as dummy variables. When the worker changes firm, promotion and demotion are identified by comparing the hierarchical level before and after the move. The direct transition into business ownership is the event where an employee leaves the firm and become a business owner within a one-year window.

compulsory education; (2) individuals who completed their secondary education; and (3) individuals who completed tertiary education, which usually corresponds to a university degree. Table 5.1 shows that only a very small percentage of individuals have tertiary education.

Our study follows two types of individuals, namely those who switch from paid employment to business ownership, observed through a binary variable accounting for entry into business ownership, and those who switch from paid employment in one firm to paid employment in another firm, identified by a binary variable tracking such changes. Paid employees who do not switch firms in the period covered by the study are used as a control group.

A central concern of this chapter is to understand the role of opportunity costs in determining the pecuniary effect of switching from waged employment to self-employment. In order to shed light on this, we differentiate between individuals who enter self-employment directly from paid employment (thus facing an opportunity cost equal to their previous wage) from those entering from unemployment (thus facing a comparably lower opportunity cost). We consider individuals who take less than one year between leaving wage employment and becoming self-employed in the former category. The rationale behind this observation is twofold: firstly, individuals who pay an opportunity cost to enter self-employment are more likely to have discovered a profitable entrepreneurial opportunity, and also face fewer liquidity constraints that may lead to a sub-optimal start-up size; secondly, even if the human capital required for entrepreneurship does not correspond directly with formal education, it is more likely to be acquired while employed. Therefore people who have spent significant time unemployed before becoming a business owner are less likely to have significant stocks of human capital. Thus it is expected that individuals who enter self-employment directly from paid employment will have relatively higher self-employment earnings.

In order to address the relationship between the evolution of wages and occupational mobility, we control not only for demographic variables, but also for firm characteristics across time, such as firm size, economic sector and the administrative region where the firm is located. The variable size is measured using the natural logarithm of the number of employees in the firm, for individual i at time t. For sector, we consider five groups of economic sectors, namely, primary sector (ISIC code 1–14), total manufacturing (ISIC code 15–37), energy and construction (ISIC code 40–45), services (ISIC code 50–74), and community social and personal services (ISIC code 75-99). For the regional variable, we follow the NUTS 2 level of aggregation that consists of seven different regions in Portugal (five regions in mainland Portugal plus the two autonomous regions).

Table 5.2   Entry into business ownership by firm characteristics

Variables	All individuals (%)	Last year as employee (%)	First year as business owner (%)
Firm size			
Micro businesses	20.24	37.26	71.20
Small businesses	27.78	33.75	25.65
Medium businesses	22.54	17.12	2.66
Large businesses	29.44	11.87	0.48
Hierarchical levels			
Apprentices, interns, trainees	2.84	3.89	0.01
Non-qualified professionals	8.3	4.31	0.37
Semi-qualified professionals	11.84	7.7	0.36
Qualified professionals	50.21	55.35	5.91
Higher qualified professionals	6.93	7.23	0.75
Supervisors, team leaders	6.28	7.22	0.71
Intermediary managers	3.76	5.24	1.33
Top managers	9.84	9.06	90.56

Note: Firm size is measured by number of workers and is divided into five categories: micro firms (1–9 employees), small firms (10–49 employees), medium firms (50–249 employees), and large firms (over 250 employees). *QP* discriminates employee hierarchy in the firm according to the eight different levels from apprentices, interns and trainees (level 1) to top managers (level 8).

Table 5.2 presents the percentage of individuals who enter business ownership (even if they pass through a unemployment spell in between) at two specific times, the last year as paid employees and the first year as business owners, per size of the firm and per hierarchical level.

About 29 per cent of individuals switching from wage employment to business ownership were previously employed by medium or large firms (50 employees or more). About 97 per cent of individuals who become business owners do so in micro and small businesses (fewer than 50 employees). Over 55 per cent of individuals leaving paid employment to become business owners are 'qualified professionals', that is, individuals with specialized knowledge acquired through formal education and/or on-the-job training. Over 90 per cent of individuals who become business owners take up a 'top manager' position in the firm, which means they are responsible for the coordination of the firm's fundamental activities. As a consequence, more than 90 per cent of the business owners are likely to earn an income equal to, or greater than, the highest wage paid by the firm, thus validating at least partially our choice of proxy variable for entrepreneurial income.

Lastly, we also identify career paths, following from one year to the next for career events such as promotions and demotions. We also add an interaction variable that simultaneously reconciles paid employees, firm change and the evolution of hierarchical levels. Here, we consider the three hypotheses, namely individuals promoted with the firm change, which means the worker experiences an upward movement to a higher hierarchical level; individuals remaining at the same hierarchical level after the firm change; and individuals demoted with the firm change, which means the worker moves to a lower hierarchical level. When a worker moves from one firm to another, the data do not allow us to identify the reason for that change and the worker can quit or be dismissed. Those who quit have a higher probability of finding a better job with a higher hierarchical position (i.e. of getting promoted). Those who were made redundant have a higher probability of taking a job with a lower hierarchical position (i.e. of getting demoted). Promotion and demotion are here used in an informal way given that we are comparing hierarchical levels in two different firms and not within the same firm.

RESULTS

We begin by presenting the pooled regression results, followed by the fixed effects results for all the models. Model (i) includes as independent variables individual attributes, namely: age, education, tenure, and firm characteristics, specifically the logarithm of firm size, and industry and regional dummies. Model (ii) adds two mobility dummies, one accounting for entry into business ownership and the other accounting for firm changes by paid employees. Model (iii) contains a new variable that considers direct transitions into business ownership as a determinant of individual wages. Finally, in model (iv) information about employees' careers event is introduced.

Pooled Regression

Results for models (i)–(iv) are presented in Table 5.3, which shows pooled cross-section regression coefficients for our initial wage equation, as described in equation (5.1). Dummies measuring specific effects concerning years, industries and regions are included for all models. Most of the coefficients are statistically significant at the 1 per cent level.

The linear coefficient of the age variable is positive. Educational attainment level also has a positive effect on income. Better educated individuals are more likely to earn higher wages than those with secondary or lower

Table 5.3   Wage equations, pooled cross-section regressions, 1995–2003

Variable	Model (i)	Model (ii)	Model (iii)	Model (iv)
Age	0.0390***	0.0388***	0.0388***	0.0391***
	[0.0002]	[0.0002]	[0.0002]	[0.0002]
Age^2 × 10^{-2}	−0.0407***	−0.0405***	−0.0405***	−0.0408***
	[0.0003]	[0.0003]	[0.0003]	[0.0003]
9 years education	0.1950***	0.1949***	0.1949***	0.1941***
	[0.0010]	[0.0010]	[0.0010]	[0.0010]
Secondary education	0.3662***	0.3662***	0.3662***	0.3646***
	[0.0012]	[0.0012]	[0.0012]	[0.0012]
College education	0.9530***	0.9528***	0.9527***	0.9499***
	[0.0024]	[0.0024]	[0.0024]	[0.0024]
Tenure	0.0108***	0.0114***	0.0114***	0.0110***
	[0.0001]	[0.0001]	[0.0001]	[0.0001]
Tenure^2 × 10^{-2}	−0.0128***	−0.0141***	−0.0141***	−0.0132***
	[0.0004]	[0.0004]	[0.0004]	[0.0004]
Firm size (log)	0.0717***	0.0717***	0.0717***	0.0719***
	[0.0002]	[0.0002]	[0.0002]	[0.0002]
Entry into business ownership (BO)		0.0203***	−0.0090**	−0.0121***
		[0.0038]	[0.0045]	[0.0045]
Direct transition to BO			0.0639***	0.0659***
			[0.0077]	[0.0077]
Paid employees (PE) firm change		0.0148***	0.0148***	
		[0.0007]	[0.0007]	
PE firm change: get promoted				0.0352***
				[0.0013]
PE firm change: stay current level				0.0332***
				[0.0008]
PE firm change: get demoted				−0.0800***
				[0.0014]
Promotion				0.0597***
				[0.0009]
Demotion				0.0461***
				[0.0011]
Year dummies	Yes	Yes	Yes	Yes
Industry dummies	Yes	Yes	Yes	Yes
Region dummies	Yes	Yes	Yes	Yes
Intercept	5.0782***	5.0791***	5.0790***	5.0719***
	[0.0042]	[0.0042]	[0.0042]	[0.0042]
F test	48663.34	45069.93	43468.18	38511.22
R-squared	0.443	0.443	0.443	0.444
Observations	6174625	6174625	6174625	6174625
Number of individuals	1302927	1302927	1302927	1302927

Table 5.3   (continued)

Notes:
Dependent variable is the natural logarithm of monthly wage. *Age* and *tenure* are measured in years. *Nine years of education, secondary education, college education, entry to business ownership, paid employees firm change, direct transition to business ownership, promotion* and *demotion* are defined as dummy variables. Robust standard errors are in brackets.
* Significant at 10%; ** significant at 5%; *** significant at 1%.

educational levels. As expected, the dummy variable for nine-year education has less influence on wage evolution than the secondary education
dummy, while the dummy for tertiary education has a stronger effect on
wage evolution than the dummy for secondary education. Firm size is
statistically significant and positively associated with wage, which is in line
with the literature suggesting that smaller firms pay lower wages (Evans
and Leighton, 1989b; Brown et al., 1990; Oi and Idson, 1999).

According to model (i), individuals see their wage increased by almost
1 per cent for every additional year of tenure. Both human capital and
matching theories predict that the conditional mean of wages should rise
with tenure, as discussed by Becker (1975) in the context of the development and exposition of the theory of human capital, and Jovanovic
(1979a, 1979b, 1984) for the job matching argument. When we introduce
dummies accounting for firm change and entry into business ownership,
this variable keeps the same magnitude. By analysing model (ii), individuals entering business ownership see their estimated income increase
by almost 2 per cent, while workers who remain paid employees but move
to a different firm benefit from a wage increase of 1.5 per cent. Model (iii)
includes a binary variable that differentiates direct transitions from waged
employment to business ownership from transitions occurring after a spell
of unemployment. This variable is positively associated with income. The
incomes of individuals who move directly from paid employment into
self-employment rise by more than 6 per cent. Model (iv) shows that those
individuals who make a direct transition from paid employment to self-
employment increase their income, even controlling for career events such
as demotions or persistence at the same hierarchical level in their previous
firm, so opportunity costs matter even when some dissatisfaction may
occur in the previous wage job.

Fixed Effects Regression

Results for models (i)–(iv) are presented in Table 5.4, showing fixed effects
(within) regression coefficients for the wage equation described in equation (5.2). Most of the coefficients are statistically significant at the 1 per

cent level. The fixed effects estimation displays very similar effects of age, education and firm size to the pooled regression.

Model (i) indicates that the effect of tenure is still significant, but the size of the coefficient reveals that individuals see their income increase by less that 0.2 per cent (instead of 1 per cent in the pooled model), for every additional year of previous experience in the firm. This result suggests that the effect of tenure may vary with unobserved individual characteristics. Model (ii) shows that individuals entering business ownership suffer a drastic income penalty of about 14 per cent, while workers who remain as paid employees, but switch to a different firm, experience an insignificant impact on their wage level. However in model (iii), when differentiating direct transitions from waged employment to self-employment, as compared with transitions from unemployment to self-employment, we observe that those who switch from paid employment directly into self-employment see their incomes rise by nearly 4 per cent, while those who move from unemployment into self-employment experience a decrease in income of about 16 per cent when compared with their last wage before becoming unemployed. The wage change for paid employees who switch firms remains insignificant. In model (iv) we observe that paid employees switching firms who were demoted in the process suffer a wage decrease of about 7 per cent; those who remain at the same hierarchical level experience a small positive change (0.6 per cent); and those who move to a higher hierarchical level receive wage premium of over 4 per cent. While unrelated to self-employment, these last results strongly suggest that wages are also determined by job assignment and career events, as proposed by Baker et al. (1994) and Gibbons and Waldman (1999, 2006).

CONCLUSION

The aim of this chapter is to examine the effect of switching from paid employment to business ownership on individuals' earnings. Using a longitudinal matched employer–employee data set from Portugal we have followed the mobility of workers and business owners for the period 1995–2003, estimating personal and firm level effects on incomes simultaneously, and accounting for multiple determinants of wage earnings, such as individual attributes, employer characteristics, and individuals' organizational careers.

The wages of individuals are determined by several factors including occupational and firm mobility, personal attributes and career events. The four models presented have attempted to examine the effect of switching

Table 5.4   Wage equations, fixed effects (within) regressions, 1995–2003

Variable	Model (i)	Model (ii)	Model (iii)	Model (iv)
Age	0.0544***	0.0553***	0.0553***	0.0551***
	[0.0002]	[0.0002]	[0.0002]	[0.0002]
$Age^2 \times 10^{-2}$	−0.0374***	−0.0379***	−0.0379***	−0.0377***
	[0.0003]	[0.0003]	[0.0003]	[0.0003]
9 years education	0.0055***	0.0058***	0.0058***	0.0057***
	[0.0008]	[0.0008]	[0.0008]	[0.0008]
Secondary education	0.0189***	0.0192***	0.0192***	0.0188***
	[0.0011]	[0.0011]	[0.0011]	[0.0011]
College education	0.0948***	0.0954***	0.0954***	0.0943***
	[0.0016]	[0.0016]	[0.0016]	[0.0016]
Tenure	0.0022***	0.0018***	0.0018***	0.0016***
	[0.0001]	[0.0001]	[0.0001]	[0.0001]
$Tenure^2 \times 10^{-2}$	0.0038***	0.0040***	0.0039***	0.0042***
	[0.0003]	[0.0003]	[0.0003]	[0.0003]
Firm size (log)	0.0406***	0.0399***	0.0399***	0.0403***
	[0.0003]	[0.0003]	[0.0003]	[0.0003]
Entry into business ownership (BO)		−0.1395***	−0.1565***	−0.1566***
		[0.0041]	[0.0052]	[0.0052]
Direct transition to BO			0.0380***	0.0381***
			[0.0080]	[0.0080]
Paid employees (PE) firm change		0.0001	0.0001	
		[0.0004]	[0.0004]	
PE firm change: get promoted				0.0437***
				[0.0009]
PE firm change: stay current level				0.0055***
				[0.0005]
PE firm change: get demoted				−0.0678***
				[0.0010]
Promotion				0.0196***
				[0.0004]
Demotion				0.0063***
				[0.0006]
Year dummies	Yes	Yes	Yes	Yes
Industry dummies	Yes	Yes	Yes	Yes
Region dummies	Yes	Yes	Yes	Yes
Intercept	4.8402***	4.8213***	4.8214***	4.8257***
	[0.0055]	[0.0055]	[0.0055]	[0.0055]
F test	1627.44	1575.34	1523.49	1533.58
R-squared	0.019	0.020	0.020	0.024
Observations	6170011	6170011	6170011	6170011
Number of individuals	1301750	1301750	1301750	1301750

Table 5.4   (continued)

Notes:
Dependent variable is the natural logarithm of monthly wage. *Age* and *tenure* are measured in years. *Nine years of education, secondary education, college education, entry to business ownership, paid employees firm change, direct transition to business ownership, promotion* and *demotion* are defined as dummy variables. Robust standard errors are in brackets.
* Significant at 10%; ** significant at 5%; *** significant at 1%.

from paid employment to business ownership on individuals' incomes. Model (i) considered individual attributes as well as firm characteristics as determinants of earnings. Model (ii) included mobility variables for two specific groups: those individuals who switch from paid employment to business ownership; and those who switch from paid employment in one firm to paid employment in another firm. Model (iii) considered direct transitions from paid employment to self-employment as opposed to transitions with a significant (at least two years) spell of unemployment occurring in-between jobs. Finally, model (iv) introduced information about the individuals' organizational careers, based on changes in hierarchical levels within firms.

The results indicate a concave relation between income and age. We also observe a bell-shaped relationship between wages and tenure. However, the return on age decreases a lot more quickly than that on tenure. Age and education are always positively associated with income. Results show that, on average, there is an earnings penalty for those who enter self-employment, and that smaller start-ups pay lower wages, confirming results from previous empirical work.

When information about individuals who switch from paid employment to self-employment and those who switch firms while remaining paid employees is included, fixed effects estimation results indicate a severe income penalty in the short run for those individuals who become entrepreneurs. However, when differentiating those who switch directly from paid employment to entrepreneurship from those who enter self-employment from unemployment, we find that the former actually capture an earnings premium, while there is an earnings penalty for novice entrepreneurs. Results also show that switching firms while in paid employment only has a strong positive effect on wages when such transition implies a progression in terms of hierarchical levels within organizations.

As entrepreneurs that switch directly from paid employment to self-employment create more income than those entrepreneurs who enter self-employment after a stint in unemployment, we would expect their impact on economic growth to be greater. However, we should be cautious about suggesting that policy makers should focus exclusively on promoting opportunity entrepreneurship in the sense of those individuals who enter self-employment directly from paid employment. Block and Wagner (2009) discuss this issue, arguing that we do not know enough about the marginal effects of money spent on promoting what they called necessity or opportunity entrepreneurship.

Overall, results clearly show that opportunity costs play a significant role in determining whether entering self-employment leads to an increase in earnings in the short run. Individuals in paid employment are more likely to search for entrepreneurial opportunities that provide them with greater chances of higher earnings from self-employment at the outset. Even though our results control for firm size, it is also possible to speculate that they should also be better able to raise the necessary financing to launch such types of ventures. From a policy perspective, further research might compare those individuals who enter self-employment directly from paid employment, thus facing an opportunity cost equal to their previous wage, and those individuals who become business owners after a spell in unemployment, who should face a comparatively lower opportunity cost. One would expect significant differences in entrepreneurial income, firm performance, and job creation ability between these types of business owners, leading to important implications for public policy.

ACKNOWLEDGEMENTS

The authors thank the GEP (Gabinete de Estratégia e Planeamento from Ministério do Trabalho e Solidariedade Social) for providing the data used in this study. Miguel Torres Preto is grateful to the Fundação para a Ciência e Tecnologia (FCT) for their financial support (grant number SFRH/BD/22648/2005). The authors are also grateful to FCT for their financial support for this line of research (project number PTDC-ESC-71080-2006).

REFERENCES

Amit, R., E. Muller and I. Cockburn (1995), 'Opportunity costs and entrepreneurial activity', *Journal of Business Venturing*, **10** (2), 95–106.
Baker, G., M. Gibbs and B. Holmstrom (1994), 'The internal economics of the firm: evidence from personnel data', *Quarterly Journal of Economics*, **109** (4), 881–919.

Becker, E. (1984), 'Self-employed workers: an update to 1983', *Monthly Labor Review*, **107** (7), 14–18.

Becker, G.S. (1975), *Human Capital: A Theoretical and Empirical Analysis, with Special Reference to Education*, 2nd edn, New York: Columbia University Press.

Blanchflower, D.G. and A.J. Oswald (1998), 'What makes an entrepreneur?', *Journal of Labor Economics*, **16** (1), 26–60.

Blau, D.M. (1987), 'A time-series analysis of self-employment in the United States', *Journal of Political Economy*, **95** (3), 445–67.

Block, J. and M. Wagner (2009), 'Necessity and opportunity entrepreneurs in Germany: characteristics and earnings differentials', *Schmalenbach Business Review*, forthcoming.

Borjas, G.J. (1986), 'The self-employment experience of immigrants', *Journal of Human Resources*, **21** (4), 485–506.

Borjas, G.J. and S.G. Bronars (1989), 'Consumer discrimination and self-employment', *Journal of Political Economy*, **97** (3), 581–605.

Bregger, J. (1963), 'Self-employment in the United States, 1948–1962', *Monthly Labor Review*, **86** (Jan.), 37–43.

Brock, W.A. and D.S. Evans (1986), *The Economics of Small Businesses: Their Role and Regulation in the U.S. Economy*, New York: Holmes & Meier.

Brown, C., J. Hamilton and J.L. Medoff (1990), *Employers Large and Small*, Cambridge, MA: Harvard University Press.

Camerer, C.F. and D. Lovallo (1999), 'Overconfidence and excess entry: an experimental approach', *American Economic Review*, **89** (1), 306–18.

Carrasco, R. (1999), 'Transitions to and from self-employment in Spain: an empirical analysis', *Oxford Bulletin of Economics and Statistics*, **61** (3), 315–41.

Carrington, W.J., K. McCue and B. Pierce (1996), 'The role of employer/employee interactions in labour market cycles: evidence from the self-employed', *Journal of Labor Economics*, **14** (4), 571–602.

Carroll, G.R. and E. Mosakowski (1987), 'The career dynamics of self-employment', *Administrative Sciences Quarterly*, **32** (4), 570–89.

Casson, M. (2003), *The Entrepreneur: An Economic Theory*, 2nd edn, Cheltenham, UK, and Northampton, MA, USA: Edward Elgar.

Dunn, T. and D. Holtz-Eakin (2000), 'Financial capital, human capital, and the transition to self-employment: evidence from intergenerational links', *Journal of Labor Economics*, **18** (2), 282–305.

Evans, D.S. and B. Jovanovic (1989), 'An estimated model of entrepreneurial choice under liquidity constraints', *Journal of Political Economy*, **97** (4), 808–27.

Evans, D.S. and L.S. Leighton (1989a), 'Some empirical aspects of entrepreneurship', *American Economic Review*, **79** (3), 519–35.

Evans, D.S. and L.S. Leighton (1989b), 'Why do smaller firms pay less?', *Journal of Human Resources*, **24** (2), 299–318.

Fain, T. (1980), 'Self-employed Americans: their number has increased', *Monthly Labor Review*, **103** (11), 3–8.

Fairlie, R. (2004), 'Does business ownership provide a source of upward mobility for Blacks and Hispanics?', in D. Holtz-Eakin and H. S. Rosen (eds), *Public Policy and the Economics of Entrepreneurship*, Cambridge, MA: MIT Press, pp. 153–79.

Ferber, M.A. and J. Waldfogel (1998), 'The long-term consequences of non-traditional employment', *Monthly Labor Review*, **121** (5), 3–12.

Form, W.H. (1985), *Divided We Stand: Working Class Stratification in America*, Urbana, IL: University of Illinois Press.

Gibbons, R. and M. Waldman (1999), 'A theory of wage promotions dynamics inside firms', *Quarterly Journal of Economics*, **114** (4), 1321–58.

Gibbons, R. and M. Waldman (2006), 'Enriching a theory of wage and promotion dynamics inside firms', *Journal of Labor Economics*, **24** (1), 59–107.

Gill, A.M. (1988), 'Choice of employment status and the wages of employees and the self-employed, some further evidence', *Journal of Applied Econometrics*, **3** (3), 229–34.

Gompers, P., J. Lerner and D. Scharfstein (2005), 'Entrepreneurial spawning: public corporations and the genesis of new ventures, 1986-1999', *Journal of Finance*, **60** (2), 577–614.

Haber, S., E. Lamas and J. Lichtenstein (1987), 'On their own: the self-employed and others in private business', *Monthly Labor Review*, **110** (5), 17–23.

Hamilton, B.H. (2000), 'Does entrepreneurship pay? An empirical analysis of the returns to self-employment', *Journal of Political Economy*, **18** (3), 604–31.

Hsu, D.H., E.B. Roberts and C.E. Eesley (2007), 'Entrepreneurs from technology-based universities: evidence from MIT', *Research Policy*, **36** (5), 768–88.

Iyigun, M.F. and A.L. Owen (1998), 'Risk, entrepreneurship, and human capital accumulation', *American Economic Review*, **88** (2), 454–57.

Jovanovic, B. (1979a), 'Firm specific capital and turnover', *Journal of Political Economy*, **87**, 1246–60.

Jovanovic, B. (1979b), 'Job matching and the theory of turnover', *Journal of Political Economy*, **87**, 972–90.

Jovanovic, B. (1982), 'Selection and the evolution of industry', *Econometrica*, **50** (3), 649–70.

Jovanovic, B. (1984), 'Matching, turnover, and unemployment', *Journal of Political Economy*, **92**, 108–22.

Kahneman, D. and D. Lovallo (1993), 'Timid choices and bold forecasts: a cognitive perspective on risk taking', *Management Science*, **39** (1), 17–31.

Kihlstrom, R. and J. Laffont (1979), 'A general equilibrium entrepreneurial theory of firm formation based on risk aversion', *Journal of Political Economy*, **87** (4), 719–40.

Koellinger, P., M. Minniti and C. Schade (2007), 'I think I can, I think I can – over-confidence and entrepreneurial behaviour', *Journal of Economic Psychology*, **28** (4), 502–27.

Lazear, E.P. (2005), 'Entrepreneurship', *Journal of Labor Economics*, **23** (4), 649–80.

Lazear, E.P. and R.L. Moore (1984), 'Incentives, productivity, and labour contracts', *Quarterly Journal of Economics*, **99** (2), 275–96.

Lucas, R.E. (1978), 'On the size distribution of business firms', *Bell Journal of Economics*, **9** (2), 508–23.

Mincer, J. (1974), *Schooling, Experience, and Earnings*, New York: Columbia University Press.

Ñopo, H. and P. Valenzuela (2007), 'Becoming an entrepreneur', IZA Discussion Paper No. 2716.

Oi, W.Y. and T. Idson (1999), 'Firm size and wages', in O. Ashenfelter and D. Card (eds), *Handbook of Labor Economics*, Vol. 3, Amsterdam: Elsevier Science, pp. 2165–214.

Parker, S.C. (2003), 'Does tax evasion affect occupational choice?', *Oxford Bulletin of Economics and Statistics*, **65** (3), 379–94.

Parker, S.C. (2004), *The Economics of Self-employment and Entrepreneurship*, Cambridge: Cambridge University Press.

Quadrini, V. (1999), 'The importance of entrepreneurship for wealth concentration and mobility', *Review of Income and Wealth*, **45** (1), 1–19.

Ray, R. (1975), 'A report on self-employed Americans in 1973', *Monthly Labor Review*, **98** (1), 49–54.

Rees, H. and A. Shah (1986), 'An empirical analysis of self-employment in the UK', *Journal of Applied Econometrics*, **1** (1), 101–8.

Silva, O. (2006), 'The jack-of-all-trades entrepreneur: innate talent or acquired skill?', *Economics Letters*, **97** (2), 118–23.

Taylor, M.P. (1999), 'Survival of the fittest? An analysis of self-employment duration in Britain', *Economic Journal*, **109** (454), 140–55.

6. The financial requirements of early-stage entrepreneurs

Colm O'Gorman

INTRODUCTION

How much finance do early-stage entrepreneurs expect to use when starting a firm? Does the level of finance required to start a firm differ across countries? Do country differences in aspects of the institutional environment that shape the choices of individuals – who becomes an entrepreneur; the nature of entrepreneurship; in what sectors does entrepreneurship occur; and the cost of market entry – lead to variation in the financial requirements of nascent entrepreneurs?

In seeking to influence levels of entrepreneurial activity, the policy maker faces two significant problems. First, to effectively influence the scale and scope of entrepreneurial activity policy makers need to understand 'what determines the supply of productive entrepreneurship' (Baumol, 1993, p. 16) or, phrased differently, what factors influence a country's 'entrepreneurial capital', defined by Audretsch and Keilbach, as the 'regional milieu of agents that is conducive to the creation of new firms' (2004, p. 420). Clearly not all national economic systems are equally good at supporting entrepreneurship or new market entry, as evidenced by variations in the levels of entrepreneurial activity across national context (Acs et al., 2004; Audretsch et al., 2002; Scarpetta, 2003), within national contexts (Johnson, 2004; Reynolds et al., 1994), and over time (Carree et al., 2002; Chandler, 1990). Policy choices made at national and regional levels give rise to the evolution of differing institutional arrangements between countries and within countries. Providing direct and indisputable evidence of the relationship between any given institutional arrangements and entrepreneurial activity is a 'difficult and perhaps an impossible task' (Davidsson and Henrekson, 2002, p. 89). As such there is still ambiguity about which aspects of context explain variation in entrepreneurial activity, and therefore, what policies might be appropriate for encouraging more entrepreneurial activity (Storey, 2000).

Second, even if the appropriate set of conditions for increased entrepreneurial activity are identified, it may not be clear how the policy maker can best influence the environment to cause an increase in the supply of entrepreneurs. Baumol suggests that many of the factors that influence the supply of entrepreneurial activity may be difficult to influence, as the process of change is 'slow and undependable' (1993, p. 17). For example, in countries where a collectivistic, high uncertainty avoidance culture is seen as an inhibitor of entrepreneurial activity, a policy intervention in the education system may be considered appropriate (Mueller and Thomas, 2001). However, a long period of time may need to elapse before an education initiative targeted at, say, primary school children might be expected to impact on levels of entrepreneurial activity. Similarly, if low levels of entrepreneurial activity reflect current industry structure, as Davidsson and Henrekson (2002) argue is the case in Sweden, how does the policy maker seed the development of new industries?

Recognizing these two difficulties, Baumol calls on researchers and policy makers to identify aspects of the current environment that can be modified 'to stimulate the volume and intensity of entrepreneurial activity' (1993, p. 17). One factor that might influence the level of entrepreneurship and be subject to influence by policy makers is the level of financial resources needed to start a new business. As entrepreneurship policy becomes increasingly important in developed economies, there is evidence of attempts by policy makers to remove barriers to market entry (for example, deregulation) and to reduce the time and cost of starting a new business. In a recent review of government policies towards business, Gilbert et al. argued that entrepreneurship policies 'are emerging as one of the most essential instruments for economic growth' (2004, p. 313). The rhetoric and actions of many policy makers suggest that they increasingly believe this to be so. For example, in the recent EU Action Plan: The European Agenda for Entrepreneurship, the Commission of the European Communities sought to outline how member states of the European Union could reduce the deficit in entrepreneurial activity and capacity in EU member countries (Commission of the European Communities, 2004).

We suspect that the financial resources required to start a firm are an important determinant of the level of entrepreneurial activity. While ex ante entrepreneurs cannot know how much in terms of financial resources will be required to start a business, they must make an informed guess as to whether they will be able to start the business, and this guess involves an implicit or explicit estimation of the resources required. In this chapter we study the planned financial requirements of nascent entrepreneurs. We explore two research questions: first, what level of finance do entrepreneurs expect to use in starting a firm; and second, are there differences across countries in the anticipated level of finance needed to start a firm?

We use the Global Entrepreneurship Monitor data set to identify the mean and median level of planned financial requirement of early-stage entrepreneurs. We then compare the planned financial requirements of early-stage entrepreneurs across nine Euro-zone countries.

LITERATURE REVIEW AND RESEARCH QUESTIONS

Planned Financial Requirements of Entrepreneurs

A nascent entrepreneur is someone who initiates serious activities that are intended to culminate in a viable business start-up (Reynolds et al., 1994). To create a new organization a nascent entrepreneur requires access to resources (Aldrich, 1999). The tangible and intangible resources that a nascent entrepreneur requires include, among others things, a product idea, technical know-how, personal contacts, financial resources, and customer orders (Vesper, 1990). The level of planned financial resources will be influenced by personal, sector and country-level factors. First, at the level of the individual, existing personal financial resources will influence the level of planned finance required for the start-up. Saxenian (1990) argues that access to local networks is critical to understanding how entrepreneurs amass the resources required to start a new firm. Second, minimum capital requirements and barriers to entry differ across sectors and will influence the level of finance required to start a new firm. Third, country level factors such as minimum required capital to form a company, licensing costs and the cost of doing business will all influence the amount of capital the nascent entrepreneur needs to start a business.

While these factors might suggest that there will be variations in the level of finance required to start a firm, there is also the argument that given the uncertainty associated with new firm creation, nascent entrepreneurs will only be able to access small amounts of finance. So while there may be differences in the level of finance required by nascent entrepreneurs reflecting personal and sector factors, the overall level of finance that entrepreneurs anticipate they will be able to access may be low. This might be expected because of the uncertainty and market judgements inherent to the entrepreneurial process (Knight, 1921; Casson, 2003). Uncertainty as to the likely success of a new venture and information asymmetries between entrepreneurs and investors make it difficult for investors to identify entrepreneurial successes. This results in entrepreneurs facing difficulties in accessing external finance during the early stage of venture creation. Furthermore nascent entrepreneurs and the new organizations they seek to create typically lack legitimacy with customers and resource providers. Consequently we expect most entrepreneurs to start with limited resources.

This argument is supported by some empirical research. Prior research on the financial resource endowments of new firms suggests that many firms start with relatively few resources. Empirical evidence suggests that in terms of two critical resources that entrepreneurs need to create a new business, financial and human, resource requirements of founding are very low. Typically, most entrepreneurs start with little capital and with few, if any, employees (Aldrich, 1999). Financial resources are particularly important to nascent entrepreneurs as they allow the nascent entrepreneur to access other resources. Aldrich presents evidence suggesting that the majority of new firms start with fewer than five employees and that the majority of entrepreneurs might need as little as US$5000 (based on survey data collected in 1987) to start a new business. Bhidé (2000) suggests that new ventures are 'unremarkable in their origins', with the fastest growing new ventures being characterized by significant capital constraints, with nearly 80 per cent of INC 500 companies starting with less than $50 000; and that new ventures are improvised; that is, they 'replicated or modified an idea they encountered through previous employment or by accident' (Bhidé, 2000). Bygrave has shown that nascent entrepreneurs typically rely on their own resources and those of close family members during the early stages of venture creation (Bygrave et al., 2003; Bygrave, 2005). There is also evidence that some entrepreneurs seek to reduce their resource requirements by adopting bootstrapping strategies and by using 'resources at hand' (Baker, Miner and Eesley, 2003; Winborg and Landström, 2001).

In this chapter we study the level of finance that entrepreneurs expect to need to start a new firm, and the extent to which entrepreneurs expect to use small amounts of financial resources in starting firms. This leads to our first research question: what level of finance do entrepreneurs expect to use in starting a business?

Cross-country Variation in the Planned Financial Requirements of Nascent Entrepreneurs

If the level of finance an entrepreneur expects to use reflects their personal resources, the sector of activity, and the institutional context that the new venture is created in, it is likely that the cost of entry will differ across countries. There is evidence that variation in these factors impacts on the level of entrepreneurship. For example, variation in industrial structure across regions may partly explain variation in entrepreneurial activity

(Johnson, 2004). Differences in reported levels of entrepreneurial activity may reflect the composition of industry sector as entry and exit rates differ by sector and by time within sectors (periods of high entry and low entry as products or technologies mature) (Scarpetta, 2003). Audretsch (1995) concluded that new firm start-up activity tends to be substantially more prevalent under what he terms the 'entrepreneurial regime', a period when small firms account for the bulk of innovative activity, rather than under the 'routinized regime', when large incumbents account for the bulk of innovative activity. Davidsson and Henrekson (2002) concluded that low levels of entrepreneurial activity in Sweden partly reflected the lack of entrepreneurial opportunity in the service sector because of the relative high taxes on labour and a political choice to produce some services in the public sector.

Differences in levels of entrepreneurial activity may also reflect the institutional environment in terms of the cost and time required to start a business. Djankov et al. (2002) demonstrated that there are differences in both the numbers of procedures required to register in a new country and the relative cost of company registration across different countries. They attributed these differences to variations in institutional regimes, with countries characterized by more democratic governments and by lighter governments having looser regulations. Relative to the 85 countries they studied, the countries in the European Union would be characterized as 'more' democratic.

The OECD (Scarpetta, 2003) has recently argued that entrants to new markets in the US are smaller, as compared to selected European countries.[1] Market entrants in the US tend to be smaller and grow faster, what they refer to as a process of 'market experimentation'. In the 'market experimentation' model entrepreneurs pursue opportunities in the short term to identify if opportunities prove worthy of start-up or prove to be poor choices that should be abandoned (Carter et al., 1996). In contrast, in the European countries studied, entrants tend to be larger, suggesting to the OECD that there is more 'pre-market selection'. They suggest that these differences in market entry processes reflect differences in regulatory and policy considerations surrounding the ease of start-ups, new firm access to finance, and access to markets. While the OECD notes that there is no evidence that one model dominates the other in terms of increasing productivity, 'in a time of significant technological change it might be that the longer-term advantage will accrue to countries characterised by the "market experimentation" model' (Scarpetta, 2003, pp. 155–6).

In this chapter we explore whether the amount of finance planned differs across countries. This is important as such differences may partly explain variation in levels of entrepreneurial activity. It might be expected that there will be differences in the planned financial investment of early-stage entrepreneurs. These differences reflect institutional differences that shape the choices of individuals in terms of who decides to become an entrepreneur, the availability of own and external finance to entrepreneurs, the sectors that new firms are started in, and the costs associated with starting a new firm. While personal, sector and country effects might be expected to explain the level of finance required, we only explore country effects in this chapter. As country level institutional factors shape both the individual's access to capital and the distribution by sector of entrepreneurship, comparing planned financial investments of nascent entrepreneurs across countries should reflect the inherent differences in institutional contexts for entrepreneurship within these countries. This leads to our second research question: does the level of finance required for market entry via entrepreneurship vary across countries?

METHODOLOGY

We use the Global Entrepreneurship Monitor (GEM) databases for 2002, 2003, 2004, 2005 and 2006 (see Levie and Autio, 2008 and Reynolds et al., 2005, for a full description and explanation of the GEM model and methodology). Based on a population survey in each participating country, the GEM project seeks to identify levels of early-stage entrepreneurial activity, including nascent entrepreneurial activity and those that have started a firm within the previous 42 months, by directly asking people if they are engaged in such activity. Within GEM an early-stage entrepreneur is someone classified as either a nascent entrepreneur or a new firm entrepreneur. A nascent entrepreneur is someone who responded positively to the following statement: 'you are, alone or with others, currently trying to start a new business, including any self-employment or selling any goods or services to others', provided they have not yet paid themselves a wage for more than three months. A new firm entrepreneur is someone who at least part owns and manages a new business that is between 4 and 42 months old and has not paid salaries for longer than this period. Such people are asked a number of questions that capture aspects of their personal context and aspects of the business they are trying to start.

For the period 2002–06 we use GEM data for nine of the 12 Euro-zone countries. These are Belgium, Finland, France, Germany, Greece, Ireland, Italy, Netherlands, and Spain. The missing three countries are Austria, Luxembourg, and Portugal.

For these nine countries there were 5112 early-stage entrepreneurs who responded to a question about the financial requirements of the new

Table 6.1 Sample sizes for nine Euro-zone countries

Country	Early-stage entrepreneurs	
	n	% of *n*
Belgium	142	2.8
Finland	135	2.6
France	117	2.3
Germany	1006	19.7
Greece	188	3.7
Ireland	379	7.4
Italy	106	2.1
Netherlands	209	4.1
Spain	2830	55.4
Total	5112	100

venture. A small number of countries have particularly large samples and where this is combined with a high rate of entrepreneurial activity, they account for a large proportion of our sample (Table 6.1). The anticipated total financial resources required to start a business was captured by asking 'how much money, in total, will be required to start this new business?' The responses are in euros.

The analysis was done using the SPSSx package. We calculated the mean and median anticipated finance required for each country. We compared the nine countries, exploring for differences in the anticipated finance required. We used ANOVA to compare the means for each country, using the Welch and Brown-Forsythe tests and the Scheffe test to identify differences between countries.

RESULTS

Levels of Finance

The sample mean is €101 875 and the sample median is €30 000. Table 6.2 presents mean and median anticipated total financial resource requirements. The amount of finance required ranges from a low of €58 403 in Spain to a high of €328 965 in the Netherlands. The median figure ranges from a low of €20 000 in Ireland to a high of €100 000 in Italy. The median planned investment is less than €30 000 in three countries, Ireland, Finland, and France; less than €40 000 in Germany, Spain, and Belgium; €40 000 in the Netherlands and €45 000 in Greece; and €100 000 in Italy.

Table 6.2   Anticipated total finance required: nine Euro-zone countries

Country	Cost of entry: anticipated total finance required – €	
	Mean	Median
Belgium	172049	37500
Finland	130481	27000
France	123315	28500
Germany	144154	30000
Greece	91553	45000
Ireland	139830	20000
Italy	141988	100000
Netherlands	328965	40000
Spain	58403	35000

Cross-country Variation in Levels of Finance

There are differences in the mean level of finance required to start a firm. Using the Kruskal Wallis test procedure these differences are statistically significant – the H-value for total anticipated finance required is 94, significant at the .000 level. Comparing means using ANOVA and the Scheffe test we report that the differences are not across all countries but are a result of the relatively high mean in the Netherlands and the relatively low mean in Spain (Table 6.3).

DISCUSSION

In this chapter we set out to explore the level of financial resources early-stage entrepreneurs require to start firms. The cost of entry represents the resources that an entrepreneur must amass prior to entry. The cost of entry is considered an important determinant of entrepreneurial activity as it is an important component of the risk–reward trade-offs that entrepreneurs are assumed to make. Prior literature has demonstrated that the resource endowments of new organizations are low. Aldrich (1999) has argued that new organizations are typically founded with few resources, and that a consequence of this, combined with a lack of external legitimacy, is that new organizations fail at a higher rate than established organizations. In this study we present empirical evidence of the planned resource requirements of early-stage entrepreneurs. The evidence from the data set is that many early-stage entrepreneurs plan to enter new markets with relatively

Table 6.3   Differences in means: Scheffe[a, b] test for country differences

Country	N	Subset for alpha = .05		
		1	2	3
Spain	2830	58403		
Greece	188	91553	91553	
France	117	123315	123315	
Finland	135	130481	130481	
Ireland	379	139830	139830	
Italy	106	141988	141988	
Germany	1006	144154	144154	
Belgium	142		172049	
Netherlands	209			328965
Significance		.309	.406	1.000

Notes: Means for groups in homogeneous subsets are displayed.
[a] Uses harmonic mean sample size = 193.464.
[b] The group sizes are unequal. The harmonic mean of the group sizes is used. Type I error levels are not guaranteed.

small amounts of resources. For example, half of the entrepreneurs across the nine countries plan to start with €30 000 or less.

We also explored whether there is variation across countries in the level of finance required to start up. We find that the cost of entry differs across some countries. However we find that there are not large differences between countries in the anticipated total finance required for market entry via entrepreneurship.

What are the policy implications of these findings? In the EU policy makers have begun to address the direct cost and time required to incorporate in Europe. However the differences in capital requirements we identified are much broader than this as they refer to the amount of money that nascent entrepreneurs believe they need to enter a market (not just to incorporate). The implication of this for policy makers is that they need to identify what aspects of the environment impact on the resources required to start a new business. The policy of lowering entry costs assumes that entrepreneurs will continue to enter markets even if there are high levels of failure. Even though new businesses experience high failure rates, there is an inherent logic in policies that allow entrepreneurs to start new ventures with relatively low resource endowments. If an 'entrepreneur is someone who specialises in taking judgmental decisions about the coordination of scarce resources' (Casson, 2003, p. 20) and 'an opportunity for pure profit cannot, by its nature, be the object of systematic search' (Kirzner, 1997,

p. 71), by starting small entrepreneurs can test their judgements, and in the process generate new knowledge that may assist them (for example, 'I am not good at running a business' or 'there is little demand for my specialized services') or others in launching a new business. McGrath (1999) argues that such failures can create system level learning, and so the individual failures of specific entrepreneurs may be important in facilitating innovation by others. Therefore, it could be argued that policy makers should seek to facilitate entry by reducing the costs of entry.

However, there is a policy dilemma as the policy of providing direct supports that encourage more market entry is not uniformly accepted (Storey, 1994). For example, more entries might lead to displacement among existing businesses; and the collective cost of entry in terms of the financial and time commitments of new entrants is high and might be more productively used in other activities. Furthermore, low entry costs essentially decrease the barriers to market entry and therefore may reduce the profitability of incumbent firms. It could be argued that higher entry costs might discourage entry that would otherwise lead to displacement. The counter argument is that economic 'churn' is an important contributor to economic growth and development as it is a mechanism for new innovations to be brought to market and for increased competition that leads to better utilization of resources.

CONCLUSIONS

The chapter makes a number of important empirical contributions. First, we show that the financial requirements of early-stage entrepreneurs are relatively low, with a sample median of €30 000 and medians ranging from €20 000 to €100 000 across nine countries. Second, we show that there are relatively small differences across countries in the mean anticipated cost of start-up. The empirical data we present contribute to our understanding of the resources required to create new commercial organizations (Aldrich, 1999); to the determinants of entrepreneurial activity (Baumol, 1993); and to how government policies might be important in encouraging entrepreneurial activity (Chandler, 1990).

There are a number of limitations associated with this study. It looks at early-stage entrepreneurs. While this has the advantage of capturing entrepreneurial activity at a very early stage in its development (all market entrants via entrepreneurship must, by definition, have been nascent entrepreneurs for some period of time), it also raises a number of questions. First, as early-stage entrepreneurs are still at the pre-market or early market entry stage, they might be systematically under-estimating or over-estimating the cost of entry. Second, not all early-stage entrepreneurs will continue their efforts at start-up. While this may be the outcome of an assessment by the entrepreneur of the viability of the venture or of the risk and rewards associated with the venture, there also appears to be a group of nascent entrepreneurs that Reynolds refers to as 'hobby' nascent entre- preneurs – nascent entrepreneurs who appear to continuously explore their business idea without ever acting on it. Their estimates of the cost of entry might distort upwards or downwards the reported means and medians. Third, the focus on early-stage entrepreneurs means that market entry by established firms is excluded from our analysis. A further limitation of our work is that we did not explore the effect of different sector composi- tion of early-stage entrepreneurial activity on the cost of entry. Instead we chose to focus on country differences. The next stage of the analysis will be to shift our focus from country effects only to a study of how individual, sector and country combine to determine the anticipated finance required by early-stage entrepreneurs.

In conclusion, the history of economic growth suggests that stimulat- ing productive economic activity is neither an easy process nor a 'natural' outcome in a democratic free market economy (North, 1990). North has argued that institutional change is both incremental and path depend- ent. According to evolutionary theories such as the population ecology model, evolutionary change depends on diversity in economic actions (Aldrich, 1999). In an economic context, such change partly reflects the independent actions of entrepreneurs. Therefore it is generally assumed that entrepreneurial activity is important. The argument is that the entry by, among others, nascent entrepreneurs into markets explains the Schumpeterian process of 'creative destruction'. If the 'cost of entry' matters to entrepreneurial activity and economic growth and develop- ment, as is assumed in much of the extant literature and the policy choices of many governments, it is important to know the 'cost of entry' and how countries differ in 'cost of entry'. In this chapter we have provided initial data on the level of the anticipated cost of starting a new business in nine Euro-zone countries.

ACKNOWLEDGEMENTS

Data used in this chapter were collected by the Global Entrepreneurship Monitor Consortium. The analysis and interpretation are the sole responsibility of the author.

NOTE

1. The Organisation for Economic Co-operation and Development research is based on ten
    OECD countries (the US, Germany, France, Italy, the UK, Canada, Denmark, Finland,
    the Netherlands, and Portugal). The data are based on entry and exit of firms (not estab-
    lishments) and exclude single-person firms. The OECD suggests that this size threshold
    may not be a major shortfall based on a sensitivity analysis of the Finnish data (using 5
    employees and 20 employees as the cut-off yielded similar results).

REFERENCES

Acs, Z., P. Arenius, M. Hay and M. Minniti (2004), *Global Entrepreneurship Monitor:
2004 Executive Report*, London: Babson College and London Business School.

Aldrich, H. (1999), *Organizations Evolving*, London: Sage.

Audretsch, D. (1995), 'Innovation, growth and survival', *International Journal of
Industrial Organisation*, **13** (4), 441–57.

Audretsch, D., M. Carree, A. van Stel and R. Thurik (2002), 'Impeded industrial
restructuring: the growth penalty', *Kyklos*, **55** (1), 81–98.

Audretsch, D. and M. Keilbach (2004), 'Does entrepreneurship capital matter?',
Entrepreneurship Theory and Practice, **28** (5), 419–29.

Baker, T., A. Miner and D. Eesley (2003), 'Improvising firms: bricolage, account
giving and improvisational competencies in the founding process', *Research
Policy*, **32** (2), 255–76.

Baumol, W. (1993), *Entrepreneurship, Management, and the Structure of Payoffs*,
Cambridge, MA: MIT University Press.

Bhidé, A. (2000), *The Origin and Evolution of New Businesses*, New York: Oxford
University Press.

Bygrave, W. (2005), *Financing Entrepreneurial Ventures: Global Entrepreneurship
Monitor Financing Report*, London: Babson College and London Business
School (with Stephen Hunt).

Bygrave, W., M. Hay, E. Ng and P. Reynolds (2003), 'Executive forum: a study
of informal investing in 29 nations composing the Global Entrepreneurship
Monitor', *Venture Capital*, **5** (2), 101–16.

Carree, M., A. van Stel, R. Thurk and S. Wennekers (2002), 'Economic development and business ownership: an analysis using data of 23 OECD countries in
the period of 1976–1996', *Small Business Economics*, **19** (3), 271–90.

Carter, N., W. Gartner and P. Reynolds (1996), 'Exploring start-up event
sequences', *Journal of Business Venturing*, **11** (3), 151–66.

Casson, M. (2003), *The Entrepreneur: An Economic Theory*, Cheltenham, UK and
Northampton, MA, USA: Edward Elgar.

Chandler, A. (1990), *Scale and Scope: The Dynamics of Industrial Capitalism*,
London and Cambridge, MA: Belknap Press.

Commission of the European Communities (2004), *Action Plan: The European
Agenda for Entrepreneurship*, Communication from the Commission to the
Council, the European Parliament, the European Economic and Social Committee
and the Committee of the Regions, Brussels, 11.02.2004, COM(2004).

Davidsson, P. and M. Henrekson (2002), 'Determinants of the prevalence of
start-ups and high-growth firms', *Small Business Economics*, **19** (2), 81–94.

Djankov, S., R. La Porta, F. Lopez-De-Silanes and A. Shleifer (2002), 'The regulation of entry', *Quarterly Journal of Economics*, **117** (1), 1–37.

Gilbert, B., D. Audretsch and P. McDougall (2004), 'The emergence of entrepreneurship policy', *Small Business Economics*, **22** (3/4), 313–23.

Johnson, P. (2004), 'Differences in regional firm formation rates: a decomposition analysis', *Entrepreneurship Theory and Practice*, **28** (5), 431–45.

Kirzner, I. (1997), 'Entrepreneurial discovery and the competitive market process: an Austrian approach', *Journal of Economic Literature*, **35** (1), 60–85.

Knight, F. (1921), *Risk Uncertainty and Profit*, Boston, MA: Kessinger Publishing.

Levie, J. and E. Autio (2008), 'A theoretical grounding and test of the GEM model', *Small Business Economics*, **31** (3), 235–63.

McGrath, R.G. (1999), 'Falling forward: real options reasoning and entrepreneurial failure', *Academy of Management Review*, **24** (1), 13–30.

Mueller, S. and A. Thomas (2001), 'Culture and entrepreneurial potential: a nine country study of locus of control and innovativeness', *Journal of Business Venturing*, **16** (1), 51–75.

North, D. (1990), *Institutions, Institutional Change and Economic Performance*, Cambridge: Cambridge University Press.

Reynolds, P., N. Bosma, E. Autio, S. Hunt, N. De Bono, I. Servais, et al. (2005), 'Global Entrepreneurship Monitor: data collection design and implementation 1998–2003', *Small Business Economics*, **24** (3), 205–31.

Reynolds, P., D. Storey and P. Westhead (1994), 'Cross-national comparisons of the variation in new firm formation rates', *Regional Studies*, **28** (4), 443–56.

Saxenian, A. (1990), 'Regional networks and the resurgence of Silicon Valley', *California Management Review*, **33** (1), 89–112.

Scarpetta, S. (2003), *The Sources of Economic Growth in OECD Countries*, Paris: Organisation for Economic Co-operation and Development.

Storey, D.J. (1994), *Understanding the Small Business Sector*, London: Routledge.

Storey, D.J. (2000), 'Six steps to heaven: evaluating the impact of public policies to support small businesses in developed economies', in D. Sexton and H. Landström (eds), *The Blackwell Handbook of Entrepreneurship*, Oxford: Blackwell Publishers, pp. 176–93.

Vesper, K. (1990), *New Venture Strategies*, Englewood Cliffs, NJ: Prentice Hall.

Winborg, J. and H. Landström (2001), 'Financial bootstrapping in small businesses: examining small business managers' resource acquisition behaviours', *Journal of Business Venturing*, **16** (3), 235–54.

7. An examination of the link between growth attitudes and realized growth

Anders Isaksson and Vladimir Vanyushyn

INTRODUCTION

The growth of new ventures and SMEs has long been recognized as an important stream of research in the field of small business and entrepreneurship (Delmar et al., 2003; Storey, 1994; Birch, 1987; Boswell, 1973). The volume of literature on the subject offers a range of insights into the nature and causes of growth, two of which are of particular importance to this study. The first is recognition of the fact that growth is a complex multidimensional phenomenon that requires sophisticated tools to capture and analyse, since the use of classical measures such as employment, sales, or market share may obscure the complexity of the phenomenon under scrutiny (Gilbert et al., 2006). The second is the acknowledgement of the importance of the entrepreneur's motivation and aspirations when studying growth, as entrepreneurs may defy the narrow profit maximization imperative and choose not to grow in order to preserve the atmosphere of a small organization (Wiklund et al., 2003).

In this study, we investigate the link between growth attitudes and realized growth. The theoretical arguments for the link between growth attitudes and realized growth can be traced back to the fundamental psychological theory of reasoned action (TRA) (Ajzen and Fishbein, 1980; Fishbein and Ajzen, 1975; Sheppard et al., 1988) and the theory of planned behaviour (TPB) (Ajzen, 1991). TRA suggests that a person's behavioural intention depends on the person's attitude toward the behaviour and subjective norms (Ajzen and Fishbein, 1980; Fishbein and Ajzen, 1975). In other words, if a person intends to pursue a certain line of action then it is likely that the person will do so. TRA assumed that most human social behaviour is under volitional control and, therefore, can be predicted from intentions alone (Ajzen, 2002). The theory of planned behavior has further advanced the TRA by adding perceived behavioural control as a

Entrepreneurship and growth

new component. Perceived behavioural control (self-efficacy and control-lability) is the self-belief that one can successfully execute the behaviour required to produce the outcomes (Fishbein and Cappella, 2006; Ajzen, 2002).

The theory of reasoned action and the theory of planned behaviour are well suited for research into entrepreneurial behaviours and have been used in numerous studies. For instance, Kolvereid and Isaksen (2006) used the theory of planned behaviour, finding that salient beliefs concerning self-employment determine attitudes toward self-employment. Florin et al. (2007) studied attitudinal dimensions of entrepreneurial drive in business education and Maula et al. (2005) used the theory to study determinants of business angels' investments in entrepreneurial firms. TRA and TPB are also of great interest for policy makers in order to decide whether promoting entrepreneurship and growth among entrepreneurial firms should focus on changing attitudes or behaviour (see Dreisler et al., 2003, for a discussion regarding attitudes vs. behaviour).

Previous studies generally confirm the positive relationship between motivation and actual growth, however, with noticeable variability in the results. Part of this variability may be attributed to how the growth/size is conceptualized and measured. At the conceptualization stage, there is a debate about heterogeneity versus homogeneity (Yolande et al. 2006) with respect to growth. The second part, namely the problem of measurement, is not unique to the field of entrepreneurship and small business management. For example, a meta-analytic study of the relationship between firm innovativeness and size (Camison-Zornoza et al., 2004) has shown that the magnitude and direction of the relationship are affected by the operationalization of size (i.e. the number of employees, financial indicators, physical capacity), and whether direct or logarithmic measures were used.

Wiklund et al. (2003), in their seminal paper examining attitudes towards growth, suggested investigating the link between attitudes and actual growth as an important area for future research. In a different study that appeared in the same year (Wiklund and Shepherd, 2003), the authors looked more closely at the link between motivation and actual growth, pointing out that, despite the interest in and importance of the topic, only four published studies were available at the time. The reason for this paucity was suggested to be the demands placed on the research design that would involve measuring motivations at one point of time and actual growth later:

> The relative scarcity of such studies may be attributed to research design requirements, as temporal separation of motivation and growth outcomes is necessary. Firm growth is not instantaneous. The motivations and behaviours

of today will affect size changes into the future. Therefore, it is important to assess motivation at one point of time and size changes from that point onwards. (Wiklund and Shepherd, 2003, p. 1920)

Thus, the overarching purpose of this study is to investigate whether attitudes to growth motivation have an influence on actual growth. The design of the study reflects this purpose, in that we measure attitudes at one point of time and actual growth over a later time period. While pursuing this objective, we employ multiple measures to assess the levels of motivation, relative change in employment, and relative change in sales as measures of subsequent growth.

Furthermore, the objective of our study is to analyse the attitudes and growth of firms in a region. In other words, we will not focus on high-growers or larger SMEs and will restrict analysis to one relatively homogeneous geographic area, as opposed to regions with a high concentration of high-tech firms. By limiting ourselves to the Västerbotten county of Sweden, we believe that we get a cross-section of such a region. Västerbotten County is situated in the northern part of Sweden and is the second largest county in Sweden in terms of territory (at around one-eighth of the total area), but is inhabited by only 3 per cent of the Swedish population. Business in the county is based largely on basic industries, such as forestry, mining and hydropower. The gross domestic product (GDP) per capita in the region is close to the national average. If entrepreneurial activity is measured as newly started enterprises per capita, the authors have estimated from official statistics that the region is slightly above the national average (with 313 newly started firms per 1000 people in comparison with the national average of 280 firms per 1000).

The rest of the chapter is structured as follows. The next section describes the research design, sampling and measurement issues, followed by a presentation of the analytical procedures and the results. Then, we discuss the results and how they relate to the existing body of knowledge, and summarize the key points in the conclusions.

THE RESEARCH DESIGN AND METHOD

The Sample

The data for this study come from two sources: a survey that contained measures of the attitudes to growth, and external data on the actual growth of businesses over a four-year period. The survey was mailed out in April 2004. The questionnaire was sent to managers and/or owners of all

Table 7.1   Population and sample description

	Population (N = 4573)	Respondents (N = 1601)
Size group, % of firms		
1	30	30
2–5	46	46
6–10	12	12
11–20	6	7
21–50	4	3
51–250	2	1
Total	100	100
Average number of employes	6.2	6.7
Average turnover, thousand SEK	9359	9655

Note: Approximate exchange rates, April 2004: 1 USD ≈ 7.7 SEK ≈ .84 EUR.

limited liability companies in the county of Västerbotten with between one and 250 employees. Addresses of the firms were collected from Affärsdata (http://www.ad.se), which is a database that contains information on all registered companies in Sweden. After some adjustments (e.g. bankruptcy, moved to other region, missing address data), our population contained 4573 firms.

Out of the total mail-out, 1601 firms responded (after one reminder), corresponding to a response rate of 35 per cent. We were not able to find any statistically significant differences between responding and non-responding firms in foundation year, industry affiliation, and size (both number of employees and turnover) and thus ruled out non-response bias. Table 7.1 presents the descriptive statistics of both the population and the sample, including the average number of employees and turnover for the total sample (*N*: 4573 firms) and respondents (*N*: 1601). Both the t-tests and non-parametric tests did not show any significant differences between the groups. The distribution within different size-classes reported in Table 7.1 was also very even, further emphasizing the representativeness of the sample.

At the second step, we collected annual report data for the financial years 2002 to 2005. Only firms with a complete set of annual reports for the period were analysed. For the purpose of this study, we concentrated on the following components: detailed code for industry affiliation, foundation year, composition and changes in ownership and/or management, number of employees, and sales.

Of the original responding firms, 1443 (or 90.1 per cent) were still registered as active in 2007. Thirteen of these firms lacked one annual report or more and were removed, leaving 1430 firms. Fourteen firms that had annual reports that were out of date (i.e. the most recent report was from 2004 or older) were also removed from selection (leaving 1416 firms). To conclude, the final sample consisted of 1416 firms that correctly filled in the questionnaire and had full annual report data for the four financial years 2002–05.

A caveat needs to be made at this point. The data suggest exits were about 10 per cent, although it should be noted that the fact that a firm ceased to be registered as active does not necessarily mean that it went out of business or became bankrupt. While for some of the exits this certainly was the case, other firms may have simply changed organizational form, merged with or were acquired by other firms. There are other events that might require a firm to change its legal identification number. Thus, these 10 per cent should not be interpreted as a 'death rate'.

Measurement

The questionnaire contained both direct and indirect measures of attitudes to growth, such as growth versus lifestyle businesses (Churchill and Lewis, 1983) and an assessment of external factors, such as the perceived level of competition (Roper, 1998). The question measuring growth intention (i.e. *GGgoal*) has been used in previous studies in Sweden as a proxy for identifying growth firms (Olofsson and Berggren, 1998; Olofsson, 1994). Overall, five measures were employed. The first question asked directly whether sales growth was a goal for the firm and was used as a measure of growth aspiration. The second evaluated entrepreneurs' perception of growth as a competitive necessity. Items three and four captured the extent to which a firm is a bread-and-butter provider, checking whether it is a significant source of employment and income for the owners. The last question assessed whether running a firm is a hobby-like endeavour for the owner.

The exact wording of the questions, italicized variable labels, means, standard deviations and correlations are reported in Table 7.2. Item number 5, that is the question 'the firm is almost a hobby', produced a very low mean value, which was only marginally different from 1 (strongly disagree), and was excluded from further analysis.

The relative, or percentage, change in employment served as a platform for measuring realized growth (Gilbert et al., 2006). First, we calculated the relative change in employment during the years 2004–05, which was a period immediately after the survey data were collected. The relative

Table 7.2 Correlation matrix for attitude variables

	Mean	S.D.	2	3	4	5
1 Strong growth in sales is an important goal for our firm (*GGoal*)	3.52	1.16	.59*	.08*	−.03	−.10*
2 In our line of business strong growth is a competitive necessity (*GNecessity*)	3.08	1.18	1.00	.07*	−.04	−.07*
3 Economies of the firm and its owners are very closely related (*ERelated*)	3.65	1.32		1.00	.38*	.07*
4 The most important objective of the firm is to provide employment and salary to the owners(*EmplSalary*)	3.34	1.41			1.00	.05
5 The firm is almost a hobby (*Hobby*)	1.28	.82				1.00

Note: * Significant at $p < .01$. All questions are measured on a 5-point scale 'strongly agree'–'strongly disagree'.

change in employment was used to form three growth groups. Firms in the negative group exhibited negative growth, firms in the zero group exhibited no change in the number of employees, and in the positive group, the number of employees increased. We also calculated the relative change in sales for the same period, in order to examine the association between change in employment and sales. The same procedure was applied for the annual reporting period 2002–05: a period that roughly corresponds to a one-year pre-survey and two-year post-survey performance.

Working with groups rather than continuous measures offers certain benefits from an analytical standpoint, when the objective is to identify the presence and direction of an effect, rather than its magnitude. While many of the earlier studies used regressions or covariance structure analysis, the authors of these studies focused primarily on the significance (presence) and sign (direction of the effect) of the coefficients.

ANALYSIS AND RESULTS

During the post-survey period 2004–05, the composition of the growth groups was as follows: 16 per cent of firms belong to the negative growth group; 63 per cent to the zero growth group; and 22 per cent to the positive growth group. For the period 2002–05, the composition of the groups is somewhat more even: 25 per cent negative; 45 per cent zero; and 30 per cent positive growth. One immediate result is that there are a large number of firms that remain stable in terms of the number of the employees during both the one year and three year periods of time.

We then used an ANOVA procedure to examine the differences among mean values of the attitudinal variables *GGoal*, *GNecessity*, *ERelated* and *EmplSalary*. Tables 7.3 and 7.4 report the mean values of each variable, significance levels, the results of Bonferroni-corrected post hoc t-tests. The last two columns present in Tables 7.3 and 7.4 report the results of partitioning the between-groups sums of squares into linear and quadratic trend components. To aid the interpretation, Figure 7.1 plots the mean values of the variables of interest against the growth groups, or fixed factor values, for the post-survey period.

The assumption of the equality of variances was met for both periods 2004–05 and 2002–05, with the significance levels of Levene's statistic in excess of 0.1; with the variable 'Relative change in sales 2002–05' being the only exception. Given the large sample size, the Welch and Brown-Forsythe statistics could be used as alternatives to the usual F test. These also were significant and indicated difference between group means. The robust test was also significant for the variable 'Relative change in sales 2004–05' ($p < .00$).

Given that the levels of the fixed factor are ordered, that is, negative–zero–positive growth in employment, it is possible to partition the between-groups sums of squares into trend components. The visual inspection of the plot of means presented in Figure 7.1, and of the results of post hoc tests of individual differences represented by subscripts in Tables 7.3 and 7.4, suggests that both the linear and quadratic trends might be present. For example, variable *GGoal* appears to exhibit a linear trend, that is, an increase across the ordered values of relative change in employment; while variable *EmplSalary* suggests the presence of quadratic shape.

The last two columns in the tables showing the ANOVA results present the condensed findings from partitioning the variation between groups into linear and quadratic trends for both periods. As the full ANOVA table with trends is rather cumbersome, only F-statistic and *p*-values for the weighted trend are reported. In the tables, the low *p*-values signify the presence of the trend. For the period 2004–05, which was the one after the survey was completed, variable *GGoal* exhibits both linear and quadratic trends; with the variable *GNecessity* following the same pattern. Note, however, the F-statistic values are much higher for the quadratic term, which means that the between-groups sum of squares associated with this term are much higher. Variables *ERelated* and *EmplSalary* show highly

Table 7.3 Comparisons between negative, zero and positive growth groups, period 2004–05

	Negative	Zero	Positive	F; p	Partitioning into trend components	
					Linear	Quadratic
GGoal – Strong growth in sales is an important goal for our firm	3.50_a	3.44_a	3.70_b	5.08; .01	4.82; .03	5.34; .02
GNecessity – In our line of business strong growth is a competitive necessity	3.25_a	2.92_b	3.35_a	16.87; .00	3.14; .08	30.6; .00
ERelated – Economies of the firm and its owners are very closely related	3.53_a	3.76_b	3.50_a	5.44; .00	.510; .48	10.37; .00
EmplSalary – The most important objective of the firm is to provide employment and salary to the owners	2.96_a	3.56_b	2.94_a	29.66; .00	1.72; .19	57.6; .00
Relative change in sales 2004–05; %	$-.10_a$	$.62_a$	$.35_a$	.87; .42	.28; .60	1.46; .23

Note: Different subscripts indicate that the mean differences were significant in Bonferroni-corrected post hoc t-tests at $p < .05$.

146

Table 7.4 Comparisons between negative, zero and positive growth groups, period 2002–05

	Negative	Zero	Positive	F; p	Partitioning into trend components	
					Linear	Quadratic
GGoal – Strong growth in sales is an important goal for our firm	3.34_a	3.42_a	3.71_b	10.74; .00	18.66; .00	2.82; .09
GNecessity – In our line of business strong growth is a competitive necessity	3.04_a	2.91_a	3.29_b	12.66; .00	9.8; .01	15.42; .00
ERelated – Economies of the firm and its owners are very closely related	3.55_a	3.83_b	3.50_a	9.47; .00	.61; .44	15.42; .00
EmplSalary – The most important objective of the firm is to provide employment and salary to the owners	3.00_a	3.66_b	3.09_a	32.44; .00	.54; .81	64.82; .00
Relative change in sales 2002–05; %	$-.08_a$	$.35_b$	$.95_c$	16.75; .00	33.08; .00	.40; .52

Note: Different subscripts indicate that the mean differences were significant in Bonferroni-corrected post hoc t-tests at $p < .05$.

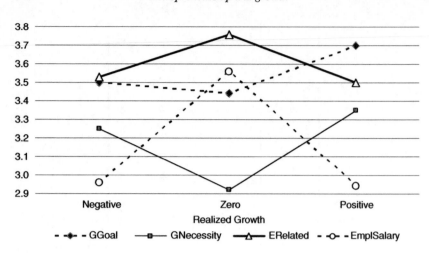

*Figure 7.1   Means of ratings of growth motives plotted against realized
              growth groups, post-survey period 2004–05*

significant quadratic and insignificant linear terms. The results for relative
change in sales 2004–05 are not significant; however, this conclusion is
suspect for the reasons explained above.

The results for the four-year period 2002–05 follow a similar pattern.
The notable differences are that the linear component is much more pronounced for the variable *GGoal* and the relative change in sales 2002–05
is linear. In sum, one may conclude, with certain reservations, that the
pronounced differences observed in the plots of means presented in Figure
7.1; and the ANOVA tables are statistically significant.

DISCUSSION

The purpose of this study is to examine the relationship between growth
attitudes and actual growth outcomes. The preliminary results have generally confirmed the presence of a weak positive relationship between
growth aspirations and actual growth outcomes. For both time periods
covered, firms that exhibited positive growth assigned significantly higher
ratings to the question *GGoal*. The marginal significance, given the sample
size, of the quadratic component ($F = 5.34$, $p = .02$) in the post-survey
period suggests that firms in the negative and positive growth groups are
somewhat similar in their perception of growth as an objective. Over the
long term, however, the linear component dominates ($F = 18.66$, $p = .00$),
which is a result that is more consistent with earlier research that suggested

a positive linear form of relationship between growth aspirations and realized growth. The same long-term pattern holds true for the relationship between growth in sales and growth in number of employees. While there was no discernible pattern for the period 2004–05, when a longer-term period is considered (see the last row in Table 7.4), the positive and linear relationship between growth in sales and growth in employment is present and significant, in line with previous research (Gilbert et al., 2006).

We have also identified the presence of a large group of zero-growth firms that did not exhibit even a slight change in number of employees in the one-year post-survey period (63 per cent of the sample) and three-year period (45 per cent of the sample). The firms in this group turned out to be different from both the positive-growth and negative-growth groups in their attitude towards growth as a competitive necessity, as manifested by the high significance of the quadratic component in both periods studied (F = 30.6, p = .00 and F = 15.42, p = .00). Figure 7.1 also suggests that the owners of these firms, as compared to firms in the other two groups, perceived their firms as an important source of income and employment. On the other hand, firms that had either grown or declined during the time periods studied exhibited a relatively high degree of similarity in attitudes to and perception of growth, a finding that provides a tentative indication of the win-or-lose type of outcome in the firms that aspire to grow.

Even though the mean differences for the attitude variables are statistically significant, they may appear small from a practical standpoint. This is not surprising per se, as the low estimates of the model fit are not uncommon in similar studies. For example, Wiklund and Shepherd (2003) report adjusted R^2 of .06 for the model linking actual growth, aspirations, and control variables. They have also shown that the bivariate correlations between growth and growth aspirations are not significantly different from 0, even if aspiration is multiplied by other variables, such as education, experience, and financial capital, to account for the interaction effect.

Our sample is also different from those used in similar studies. We use a representative cross-section of a region where the bulk of the firms (76 per cent) have five or fewer employees (Table 7.1). Thus, our conclusions may differ somewhat from the studies where the bulk of the firms employed more than five employees. Furthermore, we did not exclusively focus on high or consistent growth firms. In our sample, only 4 per cent of the firms exhibited consistent growth in employment over the four-year period, and 90 per cent of these growers employed more than ten people: a result that is drastically different from the sample and population. In terms of sales, 27 per cent of firms had shown consecutive positive increase over the four-year period.

Hence, our results indicate that the basic theoretical link between intentions and outcome stated by theories of reasoned action and planned behaviour (Ajzen, 1991; Ajzen and Fishbein, 1980) seems to be confirmed. Our results also confirm results from previous research, such as Kolvereid and Bullvåg (1996), who also found a small positive relationship between growth intentions and achieved growth. However, some important considerations need to be mentioned.

While our results do not provide strong support to the TPB/TRA (as the difference between high and low aspiration groups is very small in Figure 7.1), the small magnitude of the differences in no way invalidates the theories or makes them any less useful in the field of small business and entrepreneurship. This situation is rather typical for research that relies on, or explores TRA/TPB. Bagozzi and Warshaw (1992) stated, for instance, that research investigating the attitude–behaviour relation typically indicates a slight connection at best.

In the theory of planned behaviour, behavioural control is an important factor that moderates the link between aspiration and behaviour. In our study, we only consider the direct influence of growth intention and actual growth. On the other hand, one can also argue that our measures of growth intention capture some aspects of the entrepreneurs' behavioural control. Entrepreneurs who have an intention to grow have also taken into account the presence of the resources and opportunities that are the behavioural controls they need to grow. In other words, our measure of growth intention might also, to some extent, capture behavioural control.

As mentioned previously, the magnitude of the relationship between growth aspiration and growth outcomes is not very large from a practical standpoint. It has been established that small business growth is affected by a wide range of factors, from general macroeconomic conditions to work climate in a firm, although our study did not include the moderating variables. In the study of growth aspiration and achieved growth, Wiklund and Shepherd (2003) found the presence of (small but significant) interaction effects in the form of education, experience and environmental dynamism. Our data limit us to the analysis of the entrepreneurs' behavioural control, but following the results of previous research, the link might be even stronger than what we would have found if these factors had been included.

Overall, our study suggests that other measures have to be considered when looking for growth firms. From the policy viewpoint, our study implies that growth attitudes per se are important in discerning between growth and non-growth entrepreneurs, although that value is limited if used in isolation.

Limitations

This study has several important limitations that need to be addressed. First, while the formation of negative, zero, and positive growth groups may be justified, grouping does result in some information loss. Second, the average firm size in each group varied, with the smallest firms located in the zero-growth group. While there is empirical evidence from studies conducted in a similar environment that business size is not related to growth or growth aspirations (Wiklund and Shepherd, 2003), such conclusions may not apply to the smallest firms. Third, our analysis is limited to only two measures of growth and the time span between measuring aspirations and outcomes is one and a half years. Consequently, expanding the analysis by using other measures of growth and collecting more growth data is necessary. As this study will benefit from additional annual report data, these deficiencies will be remedied in future work. A more serious limitation and the one that cannot be changed retrospectively is that the findings reported here may be country- and even region-specific. Therefore, a more thorough investigation of the empirical evidence collected in different countries and settings is required in order to examine the applicability of the reported findings to different contexts.

CONCLUSIONS

Overall, our study has confirmed the presence of a weak positive relationship between growth aspirations and actual growth outcomes. We have also identified the presence of a large group of zero-growth firms that did not exhibit even a slight change in number of employees in either the one-year post-survey period or the three-year period. The firms in this group turned out to be different from both positive- and negative-growth groups in their attitude towards growth as a competitive necessity. The owners of these firms also perceived their firms as a primary source of income and employment. On the other hand, firms that had either grown or declined during the time periods studied exhibited a high degree of similarity in attitudes to and perception of growth; a finding that provides a tentative indication of the win-or-lose type of outcome in the firms that aspire to grow.

REFERENCES

Ajzen, I. (1991), 'The theory of planned behaviour', *Organizational Behavior and Human Decision Processes*, **50** (2), 179–211.

Ajzen, I. (2002), 'Perceived behavioural control, self-efficacy, locus of control, and the theory of planned behaviour', *Journal of Applied Social Psychology*, **2** (4), 665–83.

Ajzen, I. and M. Fishbein (1980), *Understanding Attitudes and Predicting Social Behavior*, Englewood Cliffs, NJ: Prentice Hall.

Bagozzi, R. and P.R. Warshaw (1992), 'An examination of the etiology of the attitude–behaviour relation for goal-directed behaviours', *Multivariate Behavioural Research*, **27** (4), 601–34.

Birch, D. (1987), *Job Creation in America*, New York: Free Press.

Boswell, J. (1973), *The Rise and Decline of Small Firms*, London: Allen & Unwin.

Camison-Zornoza, C., R. Lapiedra-Alcami, M. Segarra-Cipres and M. Boronat-Navarro (2004), 'A meta-analysis of innovation and organizational size', *Organization Studies*, **25** (3), 331–61.

Churchill, N.C. and V.L. Lewis (1983), 'The five stages of small business growth', *Harvard Business Review*, **61** (3), 30–39.

Delmar F., P. Davidsson and W.B. Gartner (2003), 'Arriving at the high-growth firm', *Journal of Business Venturing*, **18** (2), 189–216.

Dreisler, P., P. Blenker and K. Nielsen (2003), 'Promoting entrepreneurship – changing attitudes or behaviour?', *Journal of Small Business and Enterprise Development*, **10** (4), 383–92.

Fishbein, M. and I. Azjen (1975), *Belief, Attitude, Intention Research*, Reading, MA: Addison-Wesley.

Fishbein, M. and J.N. Cappella (2006), 'The role of theory in developing effective health communications', *Journal of Communication*, **56** (Supplement), 1–17.

Florin, J., R. Karri and N. Rossiter (2007), 'Fostering entrepreneurial drive in business education: an attitudinal approach', *Journal of Management Education*, **31** (1), 17–42.

Gilbert, B.A., P.P. McDougall and D.B. Audretsch (2006), 'New venture growth: a review and extension' *Journal of Management*, **32** (6), 926–50.

Kolvereid, L. and E. Bullvåg (1996), 'Growth intentions and actual growth: the impact of entrepreneurial choice', *Journal of Enterprising Culture*, **4** (1) 1–17.

Kolvereid, L. and E. Isaksen (2006), 'New business start-up and subsequent entry into self-employment', *Journal of Business Venturing*, **21** (6), 866–885.

Maula, M., E. Autio and P. Arenius (2005), 'What drives micro-angel investments?', *Small Business Economics*, **25** (5), 459–75.

Olofsson, C. (1994), 'Små och medelstora företags finansiella villkor – en enkätstudie' ['Financial conditions for SMEs – a survey'], in Näringsdepartementet [Ministry for Trade and Commerce], *Småföretagens riskkapitalförsörjning [Risk Capital Supply for SMEs]*, Ds 1994:52, Stockholm: Näringsdepartementet, pp. 131–60.

Olofsson, C. and B. Berggren (1998), *Finansiella villkor för mindre företag [Financial Conditions for SMEs]*, CEF Working Report 1998:102, Uppsala: CEF.

Roper, S. (1998), 'Entrepreneurial characteristics, strategic choice and small business performance,' *Small Business Economics*, **11** (1), 11–24.

Sheppard, B.H., J. Hartwick and P.R. Warshaw (1988), 'The theory of reasoned action: A meta-analysis of past research with recommendations for modifications and future research', *Journal of Consumer Research*, **15**, 325–43.

Storey, D.J. (1994), *Understanding the Small Business Sector*. London: Routledge.

Wiklund, J., P. Davidsson and F. Delmar (2003), 'What do they think and feel about growth? An expectancy-value approach to small business managers' attitudes toward growth', *Entrepreneurship Theory and Practice*, **27** (3), 247–70.

Wiklund, J. and D. Shepherd (2003), 'Aspiring for, and achieving growth: the moderating role of resources and opportunities', *Journal of Management Studies*, **40** (8), 1919–41.

Yolande, E.C., B. Niraj and T.S. Christopher (2006), 'Having arrived: the homogeneity of high-growth small firms', *Journal of Small Business Management*, **44** (3), 426–40.

PART IV

Business Exits

8. Becoming an ex-entrepreneur: firm performance and the sell-out or dissolution decision

A. Miguel Amaral, Rui Baptista and Francisco Lima

INTRODUCTION

A significant amount of research in entrepreneurship and market dynamics focuses on the determinants of firm entry and survival as a way of understanding business performance (Santarelli and Vivarelli, 2006). The most common views underlying this research suggest that firm dissolution relates mostly with failure (Caves, 1998), thus supporting the argument that firm survival is an adequate indicator for measuring entrepreneurial success. However, there are obvious inconsistencies between this view and reality. For instance, an individual may cease to be an entrepreneur by giving up ownership of his/her firm, meaning that there can be entrepreneurial exit without firm exit or dissolution. It may also happen that exiting firms were performing better before closing than surviving firms. Such discrepancies have led to the recognition of 'entrepreneurial exit' as a heterogeneous phenomenon that is distinct from, but related to, firm exit.

By looking solely at the life duration of a firm one cannot completely capture its performance, since not all firms are compulsorily liquidated and not all entrepreneurs' decisions to exit are involuntary. Taylor (1999) investigated the duration of self-employment spells, differentiating between involuntary and voluntary terminations. The author found that while a relatively small percentage of self-employment terminations were a result of bankruptcy, leading to individuals' unemployment, the highest percentage of businesses terminated with a move of the entrepreneur to a better or different alternative activity. Chrisman and McMullan (2000) have also detected that dissolution through bankruptcy is a relatively rare event.

Hence, exit can also be seen as a voluntary decision of the entrepreneur, driven by lack of willingness to continue in business. Voluntary entrepreneurial exit is associated with diverse factors; namely, recognition of a better business opportunity (McGrath and Macmillan, 2000; Shane, 2000), resource allocation to better markets (McGrath, 1999), positive occupational prospects as a paid employee (Van Praag, 2003; Bates, 2005) or re-entrance as an entrepreneur through starting-up or acquiring a different firm in the market (Westhead and Wright, 1998). Furthermore, voluntary exit of the entrepreneur can either take place through discontinuation of the firm or through sell-out where the firm continues operating with a different owner (Holmes and Schmitz, 1995, 1996; Bates, 1999).

The fact that exit can be voluntary implies that when investigating entrepreneurial 'success', one should consider both the entrepreneurs' and the firms' thresholds of performance. Entrepreneurial exit may not occur because firm performance is insufficient to meet the requirements of the market, but because the entrepreneur deems that same performance to be insufficient. We have therefore a different set of determinants for firm dissolution (associated with competitive conditions in the industry, firm and individual characteristics) and for entrepreneurial exit (associated with individual preferences in which the entrepreneur establishes a 'threshold' for business performance below which he/she chooses to exit) (Gimeno et al., 1997; Headd, 2003).

The purpose of the present study is to further explore differences between the individual and firm-level factors influencing the modes of entrepreneurial exit (i.e. 'sell-out' and 'dissolution') and to link those factors to firm performance at the moment of exit. Specifically, the analysis uses a longitudinal matched employer–employee database to test a typology of 'entrepreneurial exit', while addressing three key questions:

1. What are the factors associated with exit from entrepreneurship?
2. What distinguishes individuals who exit entrepreneurship by discontinuing the firm from those who exit entrepreneurship through sell-out?
3. How does the entrepreneur's individual decision to sell out or close the business relate to its performance in the market?

The article is structured as follows. The next section briefly describes the underlying theoretical contributions on entrepreneurial exit, defines the research goals and propositions of the present study and proposes a theoretical framework for the analysis. The third section presents the data, discusses in some detail the issues in construction of the variables and describes the empirical methods used. The fourth section displays the estimation results, and the final section provides some discussion and concluding remarks.

BACKGROUND LITERATURE AND HYPOTHESES

Modes of Entrepreneurial Exit

Many different types of exit are discussed in the literature. A large majority of the extant studies focus on the firm or industry level and explore different types of firm discontinuance, such as market exit or technological exit (Bowman and Singh, 1993; Burgelman, 1994; Argyres, 1996). However, as pointed out earlier, recent scholarship has been shifting attention towards the exit decisions of the entrepreneur, perceiving business dissolution and entrepreneurial failure as distinct phenomena.

In an early study in this vein, Schary (1991) considers that entrepreneurs can choose at any time to continue operations, sell the firm, voluntarily liquidate or declare bankruptcy. Additionally, this author considers that there are important economic differences between the different forms of exit, estimating models linking the form of exit to profitability, firm characteristics and decision-making processes. Watson and Everett (1993, 1996) introduce five categories for exit; namely, ceasing to exist (discontinuation for any reason), change in ownership, filing for bankruptcy, closing to limit losses, and failing to reach financial goals. Clark and Wrigley (1997) assert that exit can happen by means of closure, de-merger or divestment. Holmes and Schmitz's (1995, 1996) research on business turnover distinguishes small business discontinuity (failures) from sale (success). For the purpose of the present study, the following hypothesis is formulated:

H1: There exists significant heterogeneity across forms of exit involving individual and firm-level characteristics and performance.

Looking at individual-specific variables associated with exit, Holmes and Schmitz (1995, 1996), using a model matching the owner and the business as well as the characteristics of firms that survive beyond that match, find that the probability that a business manager changes jobs, in the case of the firm being sold, is the highest for those with the shortest tenure. Taylor (1999) finds that previous labour market experience is in general a strong predictor of the probability of exit from self-employment. This author finds that individuals who have work experience as paid employees and/or no previous unemployment experience are more likely to voluntarily exit (within the context of Taylor's research, voluntary exits are identified with sell-outs). On the basis of this result, a second hypothesis can be formulated in the present study:

H2:   The number of years of experience as a paid employee (entrepreneur or non-employed) is positively (negatively) associated with exit through sell-out.

The finding that firms' exit rates decline with age (Mata and Portugal, 1994; Carroll and Hannan, 2000) is only partially corroborated when looking at the modes of exit. Mitchell (1994) finds that while the dissolution rate declines with age for start-up firms, sell-out rates increase with age. This finding is corroborated by Holmes and Schmitz (1995, 1996), who claim that, among firms with managers who have the same tenure at their business, the probability that a firm is dissolved decreases with the age of the business. Drawing on these findings, the following hypothesis is proposed:

H3:   Exit through dissolution (sell-out) is negatively (positively) associated with firms' age.

Entrepreneurial Exit and Firm Performance

The literature in economics and business focusing on firm performance and entrepreneurial success uses a great variety of often disconnected measures, whether normative (such as firm survival, market share, sales revenue, productivity, profitability or growth) or subjective (such as entrepreneurial perceptions of failure).

Approaches such as those developed by Taylor (1999) or Van Praag (2003) differ from the traditional views on performance as measured by duration of the firm, such as Chopra's (2005) review of survival. While the former author estimates separate models distinguishing voluntary and involuntary terminations, the latter uses a competing risks model where success in business is defined as negative if the firm experiences compulsory exit (dissolution) and positive if exit results from a voluntary decision (sell-out) of the entrepreneur.

The literature presents mixed evidence regarding the relationship between firm performance (as measured by economic measures such as turnover or profitability) and exit. Mitchell (1994) stresses that dissolution declines with greater sales for start-ups, but sell-out rates are not significantly related with sales. Furthermore, sales levels have little effect on the divestiture rate. Wennberg and Wiklund (2006), using data on exit for both firms and entrepreneurs, distinguish between 'sell-off', 'closure' and 'full exit', characterizing the large majority of entrepreneurial exits as being 'exits by success'; that is, firms that are sold while outperforming other incumbent firms in the market (in terms of gross turnover). However, Schary (1991) finds no significant relation between exit and profitability. For the purpose of the present study, the following hypothesis is tested:

H4: Exit through dissolution (sell-out) is negatively (positively) associated with firms' sales revenue.

With regard to entrepreneurs' perceptions of success (or failure) when dissolving the business, Headd (2003) finds that about half of new firms survive beyond four years and about a third of closed businesses were successful at dissolution. This author also finds that firms with no start-up capital and relatively young owners were more frequently considered successful at dissolution, while entrepreneurs' race and gender played negligible roles in determining survivability and success at dissolution. Bates (2005) finds that successful dissolution is more likely to take place among highly educated owners running firms in skilled-service fields such as professional services; individuals with prior experience in the field where they set up their small business; and where there are strong owner human capital traits, namely college graduates with relevant prior work experience.

The failure of entrepreneurs in achieving their intangible goals (Headd, 2003; Bates, 2005) and the poor economic performance of firms (Gimeno et al., 1997) per se may not be sufficient to guarantee firm dissolution or entrepreneurial exit. In fact, many individuals re-enter or continue in entrepreneurship despite not having had success in their previous entrepreneurial efforts (Flores-Romero and Blackburn, 2006). Hence, along with the investigation of hypotheses resulting from the literature, the present study draws on the theoretical underpinnings of entrepreneurial exit seeking to match modes of exit (sell-out vs. dissolution) with firms' observed economic performance (sales revenue above or below the market average). For this purpose, four different modes of exit are proposed, identified and described empirically using the available data:

- *entrepreneurial failure* (dissolution with low economic performance);[1]
- *divestment choice* (dissolution with high economic performance);
- *managerial turnover* (sell-out with low economic performance);
- *planned exit strategy* (sell-out with high economic performance).

RESEARCH DESIGN

Data Description and Construction of the Variables

The present investigation uses detailed information on individuals' backgrounds, career paths, and flows between firms and sectors in the Portuguese economy. The main data source is the 'Quadros de Pessoal'

(QP), a unique database gathered from mandatory information submitted each year by Portuguese firms to the Ministry of Social Security and Labour. The longitudinal matched employer–employee data is available for the period 1986–2003. The sample under study covers the period 1986–2000 and, after data cleansing, accounts for about 340 000 exits from entrepreneurship out of nearly 1.2 million individual observations.

For the purpose of this research, a broad definition of 'entrepreneur' is used, incorporating all those individuals who are reported as business owners in the QP, regardless if they have full or partial ownership, and have started, acquired or inherited the business. The choice not to restrict the analysis to those individuals who started new businesses was deliberate, since it allows us to examine differences between starters and acquirers/inheritors in the empirical analysis.

The data allow disentangling continuance from discontinuance of firms.[2] The QP data result from a questionnaire that is mandatory for all private firms in the Portuguese economy. Hence, if at a certain period one firm stops being present in the data set and does not return in the following two years, we assume that it has been discontinued. For this reason, the analysis uses only individuals and firms that are present within the period 1986–2000, so that we can guarantee that only complete spells are being considered.[3]

Three major dimensions of variables are considered for the empirical analysis:

- Owner demographic traits and human capital: age; retirement (more than 65 years old); gender; university education; years of experience, as a paid employee, as an entrepreneur and as non-employed; experience in different firms, in different firms as an entrepreneur or in different sectors; the owner, who is the founder of the firm; number of business owners in the firm; earnings; exit from entrepreneurship; and modes of entrepreneurial exit.
- Firm-level characteristics: age of the firm; firm size; firm sales revenue; and sector of economic activity.
- Macroeconomic context: performance of the sector (average turnover) and unemployment rate.

Dependent Variables

The main variable of interest is 'entrepreneurial exit', which is defined as a binary dependent variable. An individual is considered to exit entrepreneurship if he or she leaves his or her current business to enter non-employment[4] or paid employment in another firm. Entrepreneurial exit excludes those cases of entrepreneurs who, despite exiting the firm, do not change their professional occupation. In other words, an individual who switches directly[5] to another firm but continues as an entrepreneur (business owner) in that firm is not considered to have exited entrepreneurship.[6] The binary dependent variable distinguishes 'entrepreneurial exit' (assuming value 1) from a control group for 'continuance in entrepreneurship' (assuming value 0).

The second main variable of interest is 'modes of entrepreneurial exit' and is defined as a categorical dependent variable. The multiple response distinguishes between a control group of individuals who 'continue in entrepreneurship' (assuming value 0); entrepreneurial exit with continuance of the firm; that is, through 'sell-out' (assuming value 1) and, finally, entrepreneurial exit with discontinuance of the firm; that is, through 'dissolution' (assuming value 2).

In order to account for exits with high or low performance in our descriptive analysis, a dummy variable was constructed based on information on average sales revenue per sector of economic activity, at the two-digit level of NACE. This variable equals 1 – 'high performance' – if, at the moment of exit, sales revenue per employee is equal to or higher than the sector average; and equals 0 – 'low performance' – if sales revenue per employee is lower than the sector average. This allows for the use of a variable that is the product of interaction of 'modes of entrepreneurial exit' and the 'performance' binary variable so that the four types of exit proposed in the last section can be empirically assessed.[7]

Independent Variables

Two variables are included in the models in a way that accounts for ownership status: number of business owners in the firm and a binary variable, distinguishing individuals who have started the firm from those who did not. We assume that entry into entrepreneurship occurs through a start-up if an individual enters a firm for the first time and that same firm is new in the market (i.e. the firm's date of foundation and the owner's date of admission in the firm are the same). Otherwise, we consider that an existing firm has been acquired by the entrepreneur.

In order to study the influence of specific and general experience in the labour market, different variables are built, accounting for the number of years individuals have spent in paid employment, entrepreneurship and non-employment. Moreover, a set of variables also measure the number of prior entrepreneurial experiences in different firms, and the number of prior experiences in different economic sectors.

In the original database, information on entrepreneurs' earnings is provided only for a negligible number of cases. As a way to overcome this limitation, the highest wage paid by the firm is used as a proxy for entrepreneurs' earnings. Hourly earnings are calculated by dividing the base wage plus regular payments by the number of hours worked per month, and deflated using the Consumer Price Index. Overtime payments are not included.

Control Variables

Several factors have been shown by the literature to impact on individuals' decisions to exit entrepreneurship. The more important of these factors are considered in the present study through the inclusion of control variables.

Estimations control for sector of economic activity because specific business environments may impact differently on firms' profitability and performance as well as on the individual choice to exit or continue in entrepreneurship. Dummy variables distinguish between primary sectors, manufacturing, energy and construction, services and community, social and personal services.

A measure of industry performance uses the yearly variation in average sales revenue per two digit sector. A control variable for macroeconomic environment is also included. This variable was constructed by calculating the unemployment rate variation[8] relative to the homologous last quarters in 1986–2000, based on official statistical information regarding unemployment rate, drawn from INE – Statistics Portugal.

It is important to acknowledge the inability of the data to provide evidence regarding some factors that inevitably play a role in determining entrepreneurial exit (e.g. ill health, death). In order to partially account for these issues a dummy variable is included to control for exits that may be a result of entrepreneurial retirement. This variable assumes the value 1 if the individual is aged 65 or more years, and 0 otherwise.

Empirical Methods

In order to investigate why individuals exit entrepreneurship and the different modes of such exit, the present study resorts to a form of the classic discrete choice model as reviewed by Parker (2004). In these models, occupational choice is determined by the expected utility from each different occupation. Given the type of response variable, the logit and the multinomial logit models are found to be a suitable empirical strategy (following similar approaches to entrepreneurial exit developed by, for example, Schary, 1991; Headd, 2003; Bates, 2005).

The model assumes that there are two entrepreneurial choices (j), here denoted by E (exit entrepreneurship) and C (continue in entrepreneurship). Each individual (i) has a vector X_i of observed characteristics and derives utility $U_{ij} = U(X_i, j) + u_{ij}$ if they work in a j specific situation (E or C), where $U(X_i, j)$ is observable utility and u_{ij} is idiosyncratic unobserved utility. The vector X_i comprises measures of individual demographic characteristics, human capital and experience, organizational features, and economic environment.

Expected utility is defined as $[E(U_{ij})]$. An individual will exit entrepreneurship if $E(U_{iE}) > E(U_{iC})$, and will continue as an entrepreneur if $E(U_{iE}) < E(U_{iC})$.

A logit specification was used to assess the factors affecting the decision to exit entrepreneurship. Hence, our model becomes:

$$Pr(z_i = 1) = \frac{e^{(\beta X_i)}}{1 + e^{(\beta X_i)}} \tag{8.1}$$

The initial logit model (8.1) is extended to estimate different modes of exit. Hence, we consider that individual i has J possible outcomes and let z_{ij} denote the jth observation for individual i, $j = 1, \ldots, J$. If there are J possible response states, then $Pr(z_{it} = j | X_{ij})$, $j = 1, \ldots, J$ is the probability that individual i has response j given X_{ij}, a column vector of explanatory variables for that observation.

The multinomial model is expressed as:

$$Pr(z_{ij} = j | X_{ij}) = \frac{e^{(\beta_{ij} X_{ij})}}{\sum_{j=1}^{J} e^{(\beta_{ij} X_{ij})}} \tag{8.2}$$

The model pairs each response category with an arbitrary baseline category. In our analysis the response has three states ($J = 3$): individuals who continue in entrepreneurship ($j = 0$), individuals who exit entrepreneurship through sell-out ($j = 1$) and individuals who exit entrepreneurship through dissolution ($j = 2$). The group of individuals who do not exit entrepreneurship is set as the reference category in order to facilitate interpretation of the results, so that $\beta_1 = 0$.

Two different models accounting for individual and firm-level factors associated with entrepreneurial exit are estimated:

- *Model I:* the probability of exiting entrepreneurship (a logit model reporting marginal effects).
- *Model II:* the probability of exiting entrepreneurship through different modes: sell-out versus dissolution (multinomial logit model reporting both log-odds and marginal effects).

RESULTS

Descriptive Statistics

Descriptive statistics (presented in Table 8.1) show female entrepreneurs are more likely to exit through dissolution than sell-out when compared to male entrepreneurs. On average, individuals exiting through sell-out are older than individuals exiting through dissolution (about 47 vs. about 44 years old). With regard to individuals of retirement age (over 65 years old), around 8 per cent leave entrepreneurship through sell-out, while only 6 per cent exit by closing their firms.

Descriptive statistics of individual experience in a given professional occupation show that a higher percentage of individuals who exit through dissolution have spent more time as paid employees or in non-employment before exiting, than individuals who exit through sell-out. Conversely, the frequency of individuals with more entrepreneurial experience is higher for the ones who exit through sell-out than for those who close the firm. Levels of education are similar for both sell-outs and dissolutions. However, there is a higher frequency of individuals with university education among sell-outs than among dissolutions. Average earnings per hour are two times higher for entrepreneurs who continue in entrepreneurship or exit by selling, than for those who exit through firm dissolution.

When distinguishing between firm founders or acquirers, the data reveal a higher frequency of founders who close the firm (23 per cent) than of sellers (10 per cent). This may be connected to the fact that there are, on average, more entrepreneurial partnerships among individuals who sell (1.7 owners) than among individuals who close their firms (1.4 owners).

Concerning individual experience across different firms, only 4.5 per cent of entrepreneurs who exit through sell-out have experience in two or more firms (regardless of their occupational attainment within those firms) comparing to the figure of around 9 per cent for dissolutions. However, when looking specifically at individuals' previous entrepreneurial experiences in different firms, there is a higher frequency of cases with two or more entrepreneurial events who exit entrepreneurship through dissolution, compared to the ones who sell out and even to those who do not exit. Individuals with experience in two or more sectors of activity more frequently dissolve than sell their firms.

The average age of the firm at the moment individuals decide to exit entrepreneurship is around 16 years for sell-out and 11 years for dissolution, while the average age for all firms in the dataset is 15 years. Firm size, measured in number of workers, is 14 people on average for all cases considered in the data set and also for those who continue in

Table 8.1 Descriptive statistics

Variable	All individuals		'Continue'		Entrepreneurial exit			
					Sell-out		Dissolution	
	Mean	SD	Mean	SD	Mean	SD	Mean	SD
1 if the individual is a female	0.252	0.434	0.251	0.434	0.247	0.431	0.275	0.446
Age of the individual	45.088	11.586	44.899	11.292	46.540	12.843	44.369	12.248
1 if the individual is 65 or more years old	0.048	0.215	0.043	0.202	0.081	0.273	0.055	0.227
Number of years of experience as non-employed	0.343	1.126	0.330	1.079	0.356	1.257	0.475	1.396
Number of years of experience as a paid employee	1.907	4.366	1.991	4.403	1.351	4.066	2.028	4.416
Number of years of experience as an entrepreneur	8.402	7.806	8.560	7.723	8.184	8.463	6.775	7.140
Total years of schooling	6.648	3.663	6.632	3.637	6.677	3.807	6.787	3.676
Schooling: university education	0.111	0.315	0.109	0.312	0.125	0.330	0.109	0.311
Individual's earnings per hour (in euros)	8.470	28.106	8.665	30.344	8.976	16.302	4.703	13.941
Age of the firm	14.914	15.096	14.943	15.073	16.437	16.150	11.109	11.979
Firm size, measured as number of people employed in the firm	14.483	77.439	14.536	73.869	16.367	98.001	9.531	71.518
Firm sales, measured in sales revenue per worker/1000 (€)	58	1910	59	2110	56	744	55	413
Firm's sales revenue/1000	741	11500	743	11300	864	14400	436	5090
Average sales variation in the sector	0.352	2.904	0.336	3.040	0.441	2.358	0.361	1.982
1 if Primary sector	0.018	0.135	0.018	0.133	0.021	0.142	0.021	0.145
1 if Manufacturing	0.245	0.430	0.248	0.432	0.232	0.422	0.233	0.423
1 if Energy and Construction	0.113	0.316	0.115	0.319	0.098	0.297	0.119	0.323
1 if Services	0.575	0.494	0.571	0.495	0.597	0.490	0.581	0.493
Number of business owners in the firm	1.690	1.331	1.703	1.326	1.720	1.497	1.437	0.911
1 if the individual is the founder of the firm	0.169	0.375	0.177	0.381	0.095	0.293	0.236	0.425
1 if the individual has experience in two or more firms	0.068	0.251	0.070	0.255	0.045	0.206	0.094	0.292

Table 8.1   (continued)

Variable	All individuals		'Continue'		Entrepreneurial exit			
					Sell-out		Dissolution	
	Mean	SD	Mean	SD	Mean	SD	Mean	SD
1 if the individual has experience as an entrepreneur in two or more firms	0.006	0.077	0.006	0.079	0.004	0.060	0.006	0.080
1 if the individual has experience in two or more sectors of activity	0.030	0.171	0.031	0.173	0.021	0.144	0.040	0.195
Unemployment rate variation	−0.040	0.141	−0.042	0.138	−0.027	0.154	−0.033	0.150
Number of observations	1 173 241		944 932		158 070		70 239	

entrepreneurship. Looking at firm size figures for entrepreneurial exits and distinguishing between sell-outs and dissolutions, the data show that at the moment individuals leave entrepreneurship through sell-out, their firms are, on average, larger (16 workers) than the ones belonging to those individuals who exit through dissolution (9 workers).

Sales revenue per worker is higher for those who continue in entrepreneurship than for those who exit. Among individuals who exit, sell-outs exhibit higher sales per worker than dissolutions. Firms' average sales revenue is higher for sell-outs than for dissolutions (more than double).

In order to further explore the relationship between the mode of entrepreneurial exit and firm performance, Table 8.2 presents additional descriptive statistics focusing mainly on firm characteristics and performance-related indicators. Four groups are distinguished, combining the mode of exit (sell vs. close) with firms' sales revenue – above or below the sector average – in the exit event (high-performance vs. low-performance).

Table 8.2 shows that, in accordance with Table 8.1, firm average age is around 16 years for sell-outs. However, it is possible to observe that entrepreneurial exits through dissolution with high performance happen more frequently in firms that live longer than dissolutions with low performance. Firm size is higher for firms that perform better at the moment of dissolution than for firms that perform below the market average.

Sales revenue per worker is lower for sell-out with low performance than for sell-out with high performance. Entrepreneurs' earnings per hour are, on average, higher for those who exit through sell-out rather than

Table 8.2 Descriptive statistics (firm performance at the exit moment)

Variable	Continue in Entrepreneurship		Sell-out with high performance (Planned exit strategy)		Sell-out with low performance (Managerial turnover)		Dissolution with high performance (Divestment choice)		Dissolution with low performance (Entrepreneurial failure)	
	Mean	SD	Mean	SD	Mean	SD	Mean	SD	Mean	SD
Age of the firm	14.943	15.073	22.734	18.049	14.797	15.195	16.051	15.335	10.508	11.359
Firm size (no. of people employed in the firm)	14.536	73.869	48.815	207.798	7.916	22.668	40.651	213.123	5.747	9.108
Firm sales revenue per worker/1000 (€)	58.9	2110	154	1630	31	40.9	230	1230	33.4	53.9
Firm sales revenue/1000 (€)	743	11300	3440	31500	193	444	2840	15200	144	232
Average sales variation in the sector	0.336	3.040	0.070	1.140	0.538	2.573	0.044	0.478	0.399	2.089
Individual's earnings per hour (€)	8.665	30.344	16.996	27.649	6.887	10.712	9.889	15.854	4.072	13.556
Number of observations	944932		32663		125407		7614		62625	

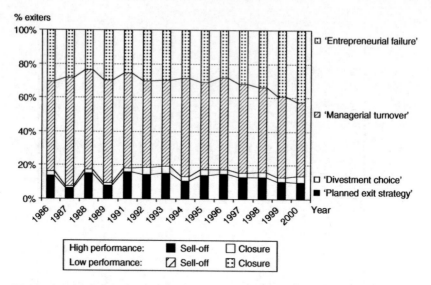

Figure 8.1   Percentage of entrepreneurs selling or discontinuing 'high' or 'low performance' businesses in 1986–2000

for those entrepreneurs who dissolve the business. Comparing different modes of exit combined with the firm performance measure, our typology shows that within sell-out and dissolution groups, those who exit high-performing firms earn more than those who exit low-performing firms.

In opposition to the common perception that individuals leave entrepreneurship through dissolution – which is often associated with poor firm performance (bankruptcy or insolvency) – our descriptive analysis shows a large percentage of entrepreneurs exiting their firms through sell-out (about 70 per cent) instead of dissolution; that is, leaving the business does not imply the extinction of the firm.

Hence, it can be argued that, notwithstanding being interdependent entities, the firm and the entrepreneur(s) can be analysed separately. In particular, the performance thresholds that lead to entrepreneurs' exit from a firm are not necessarily the same as those that lead to firm exit from the market.

As shown in Figure 8.1, about 80 per cent of exits from entrepreneurship are associated with low performance of the firm when compared with the average performance of the industry. The fact that a considerable number of entrepreneurial exits take place despite firm success in the market (the remaining 20 per cent of exits occur when firms are performing above the industry average) is in line with hypothesis H1 and suggests that exit should be dissociated from failure.

Estimations on Entrepreneurial Exit (Logit Regression Reporting Marginal Effects)

In order to fit the final model, several estimations were analysed and compared. Specifically, a simple logit model including only individuals' characteristics was extended to a subsequent model including non-linear independent variables for age and years of occupational experience. Firm-level, sector-specific and macroeconomic variables were also included in the estimations and fit was assessed considering the conceptual background discussed in the introductory section of this chapter. The assessment of diverse measures of fit provided additional empirical support for the variables included in the final models.

Results presented in Table 8.3 show marginal effects estimated around mean points and the log-odds. The predicted probability of entrepreneurial exit is lower for females than for males, for someone who is average in the remaining variables. The marginal effect of age on the likelihood of exit is negative. Being 65 (or more) years old does not impact on entrepreneurial exit and this may suggest that a significant percentage of the entrepreneurs remain active instead of exiting once they reach retirement age or that, otherwise, individuals leave entrepreneurship before they reach retirement age.

Professional experience in different occupations is negative, thus deterring the likelihood of exiting entrepreneurship. Comparing different magnitudes across occupations, it is possible to observe that the more years an individual had previously remained in paid employment, the lower the likelihood of exiting entrepreneurship. The effect is less negative for years of previous experience as an entrepreneur and very small for years of previous experience as non-employed (i.e. out of the database). Nevertheless, it is important to note that when analysing non-linear terms for occupational experience variables, the estimation reports positive coefficients.

Individuals' previous professional experience can also be assessed by considering the number of firms they were engaged with. The fact that individuals have been previously present in two or more different firms is negatively associated with the decision to exit entrepreneurship. This negative effect on entrepreneurial exit is considerably stronger when considering previous experience in two or more different firms as entrepreneurs. Having prior professional experience in diverse sectors of economic activity does not impact significantly on exit.

Results show that the higher the entrepreneurs' earnings per hour, the lower the likelihood of exiting entrepreneurial activity. Being a firm founder also impacts negatively on the decision to exit entrepreneurship. The number of entrepreneurs in the same firm has a small negative

Table 8.3 Logit regressions on entrepreneurial exit

Variable	Marginal effects	Log-odds
1 if the individual is a female	−0.005***	−0.036***
	[0.001]	[0.006]
Age of the individual	−0.008***	−0.051***
	[0.000]	[0.001]
Squared age of the individual (divided by 1000)	0.104***	0.690***
	[0.002]	[0.017]
1 if the individual is 65 or more years old	−0.002	−0.013
	[0.002]	[0.015]
Years of experience as non-employed	−0.003***	−0.021***
	[0.001]	[0.005]
Squared years of experience as non-employed (/ 1000)	1.372***	9.079***
	[0.087]	[0.577]
Years of experience as a paid employee	−0.013***	−0.087***
	[0.000]	[0.002]
Squared years of experience as a paid employee (/ 1000)	0.393***	2.604***
	[0.010]	[0.065]
Years of experience as an entrepreneur	−0.010***	−0.063***
	[0.000]	[0.001]
Squared years of experience as an entrepreneur (/ 1000)	0.180***	1.194***
	[0.003]	[0.021]
1 if the individual has university education	0.022***	0.145***
	[0.001]	[0.008]
Logarithm of firm age (in years)	−0.012***	−0.077***
	[0.001]	[0.004]
Logarithm of the individual's earnings per hour	−0.027***	−0.182***
	[0.001]	[0.004]
1 if the individual has experience in two or more firms	−0.016***	−0.105***
	[0.002]	[0.011]
1 if the individual has experience as an entrepreneur in two or more firms	−0.054***	−0.359***
	[0.002]	[0.014]
1 if the individual has experience in two or more sectors of activity	0.002	0.012
	[0.001]	[0.008]
Logarithm of firm size (people employed in the firm)	−0.004***	−0.029***
	[0.001]	[0.003]
Logarithm of firm sales (sales revenue per worker)	−0.010***	−0.068***
	[0.000]	[0.002]
Average sales variation in the sector	0.001***	0.004***
	[0.000]	[0.001]
Number of business owners in the firm	−0.002***	−0.012***
	[0.000]	[0.002]
1 if the individual is the founder of the firm	−0.066***	−0.436***
	[0.001]	[0.008]

Table 8.3   (continued)

Variable	Marginal effects	Log-odds
Unemployment rate variation	0.097***	0.639***
	[0.002]	[0.016]
Constant	0.168***	1.109***
	[0.006]	[0.040]
Number of observations	1 173 241	1 173 241
Log likelihood	− 560 338.47	− 560 338.47
Wald chi²	35 944.38	35 716.81
Pseudo R²	0.0309	0.0309

Notes: * Significant at 10%; ** significant at 5%; *** significant at 1%; standard errors in brackets. We use the highest wage paid within the firm as a proxy for entrepreneurs' earnings. *Hourly earnings* is calculated by dividing base wage plus regular payments by the number of hours worked per month and deflated with the Consumer Price Index. *Age, experience as entrepreneur, experience as paid employee,* and *experience as non-employed* are measured in years. *University education* is defined as a dummy variable. A dummy variable accounting for the individual being the *founder of the firm* is included since the analysis follows a broad concept of entrepreneurship where individuals can start up or acquire/ inherit a business. All specifications control for the business cycle by using dummy variables for industry, as well as *national unemployment rate variations* in 1986–2000.

marginal effect on exit; which means that, the more partners in a firm, the higher the probability of them continuing in the same occupational status as entrepreneurs.

Estimations on the Modes of Entrepreneurial Exit (Multinomial Logit Model Reporting Marginal Effects and the Log-odds)

Table 8.4 provides results for entrepreneurial exit distinguishing between individuals who do not exit entrepreneurship (continue), those who exit and sell the firm (sell-out) and the ones who exit and extinguish the firm (dissolution).[9] Both the coefficients (log-odds) and marginal effects of the independent variables on the probability of observing a particular mode of exit are reported.

With regard to entrepreneurs' demographic variables, results show that, for individuals with average values for all variables, the predicted probability of selling the firm is slightly lower for females than for males. Moreover, there is a higher marginal probability of continuing in business or exit through dissolution if the entrepreneur is a female.

The probability of exit through sell-out and dissolution is significantly reduced by an increase in the entrepreneur's age, which means that the probability of continuing in entrepreneurship increases with age.

Table 8.4   Multinomial logit on the modes of entrepreneurial exit

Variables	Model III - Multinomial logit				
	Continue (Z = 0)	Sell-out (Z = 1)		Dissolution (Z = 2)	
	Marginal effects	Marginal effects	Log odds	Marginal effects	Log odds
1 if the individual is a female [(d)]	0.007*** [0.001]	−0.009*** [0.001]	−0.079*** [0.007]	0.002*** [0.000]	0.046*** [0.009]
Age of the individual	0.007*** [0.000]	−0.006*** [0.000]	−0.053*** [0.002]	−0.001*** [0.000]	−0.043*** [0.002]
Squared age of the individual (divided by 1000)	−0.096*** [0.002]	0.075*** [0.002]	0.706*** [0.019]	0.021*** [0.001]	0.603*** [0.028]
1 if the individual is 65 or more years old[(d)]	0.002 [0.002]	−0.005** [0.002]	−0.040** [0.017]	0.002** [0.001]	0.049* [0.028]
Years of experience as non-employed	0.005*** [0.001]	−0.008*** [0.001]	−0.065*** [0.006]	0.002*** [0.000]	0.051*** [0.007]
Squared years of experience as non-employed (divided by 1000)	−1.509*** [0.082]	1.610*** [0.074]	14.472*** [0.670]	−0.101*** [0.037]	−0.552 [0.924]
Years of experience as a paid employee	0.013*** [0.000]	−0.011*** [0.000]	−0.103*** [0.002]	−0.002*** [0.000]	−0.055*** [0.003]
Squared years of experience as a paid employee (divided by 1000)	−0.387*** [0.009]	0.344*** [0.008]	3.167*** [0.074]	0.043*** [0.004]	1.489*** [0.109]
Years of experience as an entrepreneur	0.009*** [0.000]	−0.008*** [0.000]	−0.074*** [0.001]	−0.001*** [0.000]	−0.027*** [0.002]
Squared years of experience as an entrepreneur (divided by 1000)	−0.164*** [0.003]	0.144*** [0.002]	1.326*** [0.022]	0.020*** [0.002]	0.675*** [0.038]
1 if the individual has university education[(d)]	−0.019*** [0.001]	0.008*** [0.001]	0.084*** [0.009]	0.012*** [0.001]	0.299*** [0.013]
Logarithm of firm age (in years)	0.010*** [0.001]	0.000 [0.000]	−0.010** [0.004]	−0.011*** [0.000]	−0.262*** [0.006]
Logarithm of the individual's earnings per hour	0.032*** [0.001]	0.010*** [0.000]	0.040*** [0.004]	−0.042*** [0.000]	−1.035*** [0.009]
1 if the individual has experience in two or more firms[(d)]	0.016*** [0.002]	−0.019*** [0.002]	−0.171*** [0.014]	0.003*** [0.001]	0.063*** [0.018]

Table 8.4 (continued)

Variables	Model III - Multinomial logit				
	Continue (Z = 0)	Sell-out (Z = 1)		Dissolution (Z = 2)	
	Marginal effects	Marginal effects	Log odds	Marginal effects	Log odds
1 if the individual has experience as entrepreneur in two or more firms[(d)]	0.055*** [0.002]	−0.047*** [0.002]	−0.432*** [0.017]	−0.008*** [0.001]	−0.258*** [0.020]
1 if the individual has experience in two or more sectors of activity[(d)]	0.001 [0.001]	−0.006*** [0.001]	−0.048*** [0.010]	0.005*** [0.001]	0.127*** [0.013]
Logarithm of firm size (people employed in the firm)	0.004*** [0.000]	0.000 [0.000]	−0.003 [0.004]	−0.004*** [0.000]	−0.097*** [0.006]
Logarithm of firm sales (sales revenue per worker)	0.008*** [0.000]	−0.009*** [0.000]	−0.077*** [0.003]	0.000 [0.000]	−0.009** [0.004]
Average sales' variation in the sector	−0.000*** [0.000]	0.000*** [0.000]	0.003*** [0.001]	0.000** [0.000]	0.003** [0.001]
Number of business owners in the firm	0.004*** [0.000]	0.001*** [0.000]	0.006*** [0.002]	−0.006*** [0.000]	−0.138*** [0.005]
1 if the individual is the founder of the firm[(d)]	0.079*** [0.001]	−0.077*** [0.001]	−0.703*** [0.011]	−0.001** [0.000]	−0.121*** [0.012]
Unemployment rate variation	−0.090*** [0.002]	0.069*** [0.002]	0.654*** [0.018]	0.020*** [0.001]	0.586*** [0.027]
Constant	−0.069*** [0.006]	0.058*** [0.005]	0.539*** [0.046]	0.011*** [0.003]	0.342*** [0.066]
Observations				1 173 241	
Log likelihood				−681 457.05	
chi²				86 874.65	

Notes: * Significant at 10%; ** significant at 5%; *** significant at 1%. Standard errors in brackets. For dummy variables – indicated by superscript (d) – the result expresses the impact of a discrete change of the variable from 0 to 1. For results reports in log-odds, the base outcome is the alternative 'Continue'. See notes on Table 8.3.

Individuals at retirement age (65, or more, years old) have a lower likelihood of exit and selling their firms rather than entrepreneurs younger than 65 years old. The opposite effect happens for dissolutions; that is, the probability of people at retirement age exiting through dissolution is higher than for sell-out. Retirement age does not impact significantly on the probability of continuing rather than exiting entrepreneurship.

Regarding human capital and experience, it is possible to observe that having a university education increases the likelihood of entrepreneurs exiting businesses, whether through selling or closing the firm. Results for previous occupational experience show that for non-employment, there are different impacts across modes of exit. The more years that entrepreneurs have experienced non-employment the lower the probability of exiting through sell-out, with the probability of closing or continuing being increased by the number of previous spells out of the private labour market. Both previous experiences as an entrepreneur or as a paid employee seem to deter the marginal probability of exit, whether selling or closing the firm.

Results report differences between the signs of the marginal probabilities for entrepreneurs' previous experience across different firms (regardless of their occupation within those firms) and across different economic sectors. Evidence shows that these two types of experience impact negatively on exit through sell-out and positively on exit through firm dissolution; that is, entrepreneurs are likely to choose to continue or close their business and exit, rather than sell and exit. However, when considering the specific case of experience in different firms as an entrepreneur, there is a higher probability that individuals continue in entrepreneurship rather than exit indistinctly through sell-out or dissolution.

Individuals with higher earnings per hour are more likely to continue as entrepreneurs and if they decide to exit, higher earnings will be associated with a higher marginal probability of exiting through sell-out rather than through dissolution.

Variables controlling for firm-level characteristics report that the older the firm, the lower the probability of exiting and selling compared to the probability of continuing as an entrepreneur. The same reasoning applies for exit and closing compared to continuing. Additionally, while increasing the number of employees reduces the marginal probability of exiting through dissolution, firm size is not significant for the sell-out alternative. Each additional entrepreneur owning a share of the firm will marginally increase the probability of entrepreneurial exit through selling (or continuing) and decrease the probability of exiting and closing for all the entrepreneurial team.

Results on our proxy for firm productivity (sales revenue) show that, as expected, higher sales revenue per worker will impact positively on the entrepreneur's decision to continue in business rather than to sell or close the firm and abandon entrepreneurship. Entrepreneurs' decisions to continue in business are strongly and positively associated with the fact they have started the business instead of having acquired it.

Unemployment rate variation is used as a proxy for the macroeconomic cycle, and evidence suggests that in contexts of high unemployment, individuals' probability of exiting entrepreneurship is significant and high, particularly for sell-outs.

DISCUSSION AND CONCLUDING REMARKS

Results from estimations on the two different modes of entrepreneurial exit – sell-out and dissolution – provide support for the initial claim that heterogeneity exists across forms of exit, involving individual and firm-level characteristics (H1). In effect, some of the factors associated with entrepreneurial exit through sell-out contrast with the characteristics that make individuals more likely to exit entrepreneurship through firm dissolution. Some of those factors are related to demographic variables such as gender, entrepreneur's age of retirement, earnings, professional experience and composition of the entrepreneurial team. The fact that females are less likely to sell than to exit may help in explaining the lower incidence of female entrepreneurship in the Portuguese context where, to a great extent, entrepreneurial activity results from businesses acquisition rather than start-up. Retirement age is negatively associated with exit in general. It might be that the positive effect of age found in the literature regarding entrepreneurial entry (Van Praag and Van Ophem, 1995) and learning processes allowing older people to build better networks for creating and exploiting opportunities (Calvo and Wellisz, 1980) may also hold for individuals' persistence in entrepreneurship. However, the results are not conclusive regarding the reasons underlying the positive effect of retirement age on firm dissolution contrasting with a negative effect for sell-out. Entrepreneurs' earnings also appear to be a relevant variable associated with heterogeneity between modes of exit. In fact, results for earnings are in line with the descriptive statistics presented in Table 8.2 and the higher an individual's earnings, the higher the probability of continuing in entrepreneurship. Nevertheless, if exiting, they are likely to sell out rather than dissolve the business.

Results on the number of business owners within the same firm impact negatively on exit in general and differ between sell-out (positive effect) and dissolution (negative effect). This suggests that having partial ownership of a firm implies a shared responsibility and strategic decision-making.

Thus, for instance, if the firm fails to continue in the market it does not necessarily jeopardize each of the owners' continuance in the occupation of entrepreneur (e.g. they can immediately start or acquire a different firm). Furthermore, different impacts of this variable among modes of exit might be explained by the fact that if one business owner decides to exit entrepreneurship, it does not necessarily imply that all the remaining partners will do so and dissolve the business.

The data reveal different categories of exit that fit our proposed typology in the following way: 27 per cent of dissolutions with low performance ('entrepreneurial failure'); 3 per cent of dissolutions with high performance ('divestment choice'); 48 per cent of sell-outs with low performance ('managerial turnover') and 22 per cent of sell-outs with high performance ('planned exit strategy'). The high proportion of sell-outs and, in particular, the fact that a majority of firm sell-outs are of low-performing firms, deserves further discussion. Results show that being the founder of the firm impacts negatively on the decision to leave the firm and exit entrepreneurship, which suggests that founders may be more intrinsically involved with their venture and possess relevant knowledge about the specificities of the business and the market where they operate. This may represent an important asset facilitating entrepreneurial persistence. In a context of high firm turbulence (entries and exits from the market) such as the Portuguese one, the relative scarcity of starters implies that high turbulence happens also at the occupational mobility level into, and out of, entrepreneurship.

The high proportion of individuals who become entrepreneurs through acquisition is a distinguishing characteristic of the Portuguese economy; that is, one with high rates of business ownership but with relatively low start-up rates (Baptista and Thurik, 2007; Baptista et al., 2008), and is probably associated with high start-up costs and bureaucracy. However, the proportion of sell-outs of low-performance firms indicates that entrepreneurs have significantly different preferences and performance thresholds with regard to the businesses they wish to own. The study of the determinants of these performance thresholds is therefore an important avenue of research for future exploration.

Drawing on the literature, H2 proposes that years of experience as an entrepreneur or paid employee (unemployed) is positively (negatively) associated with exit through sell-out. The results partially support this hypothesis since a negative effect on sell-out was found for individuals with non-employment experiences. The effect is also negative for years of experience in the two remaining occupations, namely paid employment and entrepreneurship. When considering dummy variables for assessing experience in different firms, in different firms as an entrepreneur or in different economic sectors, the effect still negatively influences the likelihood of exit through sell-out.

Results confirm that exit through dissolution (sell-out) is negatively (positively) associated with firms' age (H3). The effect of firm age on entrepreneurial exit is, in general, negative. Moreover, it is possible to observe that the influence of firm age is significantly stronger for dissolution rather than for sell-out. Multinomial estimations validate the proposition that exit through dissolution is negatively associated with firms' sales revenue (H4), although the positive influence of sales revenue over the decision to exit through sell-out is not confirmed. Sales revenue per worker seems to have a general negative influence on entrepreneurial exit, regardless of the mode of that exit. Although the fact that exit through dissolution (sell-out) does not necessarily associate with firms' negative (positive) economic performance (H4) can be derived intuitively from the descriptive statistics, additional empirical research should focus on the different modes of exit proposed in this chapter, namely 'entrepreneurial failure', 'divestment choice', 'managerial turnover' and 'planned exit strategy'. Hence, further research work drawing on this exploratory study should seek to answer the specific question of how firms' observed threshold of performance in the market influences individuals' decisions to sell-out or close the business. One possible methodological approach may be to model simultaneously firm performance (measured as firm sales revenue above or below the sector average) and individuals' decision to exit entrepreneurship through sell-out or dissolution. This methodological choice has to do with the fact that the relation between entrepreneurial exit and firm performance cannot be studied using a single logit equation framework as the entrepreneur's decision to exit may not be independent of the firm's observable performance. In such a framework, it is admitted there is a possibility that the disturbances in the firm performance equation are correlated with those in the exit decision equation, and therefore assume the existence of unobservable characteristics that affect the decisions under study. Finally, the use of discrete choice duration models with 'frailty' may also be a suitable strategy to deal with transitions to different occupations after entrepreneurial exit.

This study has provided an exploratory investigation of the modes and determinants of entrepreneurial exit using a large longitudinal dataset linking firms and individuals. More specifically, the analysis examines the characteristics and backgrounds of individuals who exit entrepreneurship towards non-employment or paid-employment. Determinants of entrepreneurial exit are examined in the framework of an occupational choice model using a wide array of variables, including individuals' demographics, general human capital (formal education), specific human capital (labour market and entrepreneurial experience), firm-level characteristics and macroeconomic context. This investigation also proposes and tests a typology consisting of four different modes of exit: 'entrepreneurial failure', 'divestment choice', 'managerial turnover' and 'planned exit strategy'. Several hypotheses based on the literature were explored, unveiling new evidence for entrepreneurial dynamics in the Portuguese context, as well as for the advance of research in the field of entrepreneurial dynamics.

NOTES

1. We consider that, among these four typologies, only entrepreneurial failure is associated with involuntary exit. For the purpose of this study, the remaining forms of exit are deemed voluntary.
2. In the present study the concept of firm dissolution is adopted for the cases when the firm ceases to exist when the entrepreneur leaves; as opposed to sell-out, when the firm continues operating in the market after the entrepreneur leaves, being run by someone else. However, as the literature often uses diverse terms such as firm exit, liquidation, dissolution, discontinuance or closure, they are hereafter used interchangeably.
3. We forward-track firms' lifecycle after the entrepreneur exits and only those firms that remain out of the data set in the following three years after entrepreneurial exit are deemed not to have survived. Additionally, we estimate a proxy for merger accounting for dissolutions, by looking at the extent to which a sizeable part of the workforce of each firm moves to a different one in the QP database. We reach the conclusion that less than 1 per cent of the total number of dissolutions is due to merger within the Portuguese private sector, which suggests that an inability to track mergers is not likely to impact significantly on results.
4. In this study, 'non-employed' is defined as individuals who are disengaged from any firm (i.e. exit the database) for two or more years, either because they are unemployed or because they exited the job market.
5. In the context of the present study, 'switching directly' refers to the cases where entrepreneurs leave their firms to re-enter entrepreneurship in another firm immediately in the next year.
6. We acknowledge the fact that these entrepreneurs – known in the literature as serial entrepreneurs (Westhead and Wright, 1998) – despite not changing their occupation, have to face a sell or liquidate decision. However, since they change firm but do not leave entrepreneurship, we treat them as part of the counterfactual group in our empirical analysis.
7. The choice of exploring performance as an economic outcome was contingent on the information available in our data set (data do not provide information on owners' perceptions). However, despite its significance for entrepreneurship research, subjective measures of success (overlooking economic indicators) may be associated with a sort of 'choice-supportive bias', where after exit entrepreneurs have the tendency to remember their choices as better than they actually were and overestimate firm performance. In fact, the literature provides evidence that entrepreneurs may suffer from unrealistic optimism in anticipating high entrepreneurial performance in the start-up process (Cooper et al., 1988; De Meza and Southey, 1996) or during the development process (Lowe and Ziedonis, 2006). Overoptimism can also be viewed as one possible explanation for the high rate of new business failures (Camerer and Lovallo, 1999).
8. In order to calculate the unemployment rate variation, we employ the formula

$(UN_t - UN_{t-1}) / UN_{t-1}$, where UN refers to the unemployment rate at year t, or at the previous year $t - 1$.

9. Multinomial logit estimation imposes the Independence of Irrelevant Alternative (IIA) assumption. This assumption requires that for any two alternatives, the ratio of their choice probabilities is independent of the specification of any alternative in the choice set (i.e. any combination of continue, sell-out and dissolution). Specific tests were used in order to account for the IIA. Specifically, the Hausman and McFadden (1984) test and the Small and Hsiao (1985) test were computed, providing positive support for IIA, therefore validating the use of a multinomial model (see Long and Freese, 2005 for operational issues).

REFERENCES

Argyres, N. (1996), 'Capabilities, technological diversification, and divisionalization', *Strategic Management Journal*, **17**, 395–410.

Baptista, R. and A.R. Thurik (2007), 'The relationship between entrepreneurship and unemployment: is Portugal an outlier?', *Technological Forecasting and Social Change*, **74** (1), 75–89.

Baptista, R., V. Escária and P. Madruga (2008), 'Entrepreneurship, regional development and job creation: the case of Portugal', *Small Business Economics*, **30** (1), 49–58.

Bates, T. (1999), 'Exiting self-employment: an analysis of Asian immigrant-owned small businesses', *Small Business Economics*, **13** (3), 171–83.

Bates, T. (2005), 'Analysis of young, small firms that have closed: delineating successful from unsuccessful closures', *Journal of Business Venturing*, **20** (3), 343–58.

Bowman, E.H. and H. Singh (1993), 'Corporate restructuring: reconfiguring the firm', *Strategic Management Journal*, **14**, 5–14.

Burgelman, R. (1994), 'Fading memories: a process theory of strategic business exit in dynamic environments', *Administrative Science Quarterly*, **39**, 24–56.

Calvo, G.A. and S. Wellisz (1980), 'Technology, entrepreneurs and firm size', *Quarterly Journal of Economics*, **95** (4), 663–77.

Camerer, C.F. and D. Lovallo (1999), 'Overconfidence and excess entry: an experimental approach', *American Economic Review*, **89** (1), 306–18.

Carroll, G.R. and M.T. Hannan (2000), *The Demography of Corporations and Industries*, Princeton, NJ: Princeton University Press.

Caves, R.E. (1998), 'Industrial organization and new findings on the turnover and mobility of firms', *Journal of Economic Literature*, **XXXVI**, 1947–82.

Chopra, A. (2005), 'Survival', paper presented at the Academy of Management Meeting, Hawaii, 5–8 August.

Chrisman, J.J. and W.E. McMullan (2000), 'A preliminary assessment of outsider assistance as a knowledge resource: the longer-term impact of new venture counselling', *Entrepreneurship Theory and Practice*, **24** (3), 37–54.

Clark, G.L. and N. Wrigley (1997), 'Exit, the firm and sunk costs: reconceptualizing the corporate geography of disinvestment and plant closure', *Progress in Human Geography*, **21** (3), 338–58.

Cooper, A.C., C.J. Woo and W.C. Dunkelberg (1988), 'Entrepreneurs' perceived chances for success', *Journal of Business Venturing*, **2**, 97–108.

De Meza, D. and C. Southey (1996), 'The borrower's curse: optimism, finance and entrepreneurship', *Economic Journal*, **106** (435), 375–86.

Flores-Romero, M. and R. Blackburn (2006), 'Is entrepreneurship more about sticking with a firm, or about running several of them? Evidence from novice and serial entrepreneurs', paper presented at the Workshop on Firm Exit and Serial Entrepreneurship, Max Planck Institute of Economics, Jena, 4 January.

Gimeno, J., T.B. Folta, A.C. Cooper and C.Y. Woo (1997), 'Survival of the fittest? Entrepreneurial human capital and the persistence of underperforming firms', *Administrative Science Quarterly*, **42** (4), 750–83.

Hausman, J. and D. McFadden (1984), 'Specification tests for the multinomial logit model', *Econometrica*, **52** (5), 1219–40.

Headd, B. (2003), 'Redefining business success: distinguishing between closure and failure', *Small Business Economics*, **21**, 51–61.

Holmes, T.J. and J.A. Schmitz Jr (1995), 'On the turnover of business firms and business managers', *Journal of Political Economy*, **103** (5), 1005–38.

Holmes, T.J. and J.A. Schmitz Jr (1996), 'Managerial tenure, business age, and small business turnover', *Journal of Labor Economics*, **14**, 79–99.

Long, J.S. and J. Freese (2005), *Regression Models for Categorical Outcomes Using Stata*, 2nd edn, College Station, TX: Stata Press.

Lowe, R.A. and A.A Ziedonis (2006), 'Overoptimism and the performance of entrepreneurial firms', *Management Science*, **52** (2), 173–86.

McGrath, R.G. (1999), 'Falling forward: real options reasoning and entrepreneurial failure', *Academy of Management Review*, **24** (1), 13–30.

McGrath, R.G. and I. Macmillan (2000), *The Entrepreneurial Mindset*, Boston, MA: Harvard Business School Press.

Mata, J. and P. Portugal (1994), 'Life duration of new firms', *Journal of Industrial Economics*, **42**, 227–46.

Mitchell, W. (1994), 'The dynamics of evolving markets: the effects of business sales and age on dissolutions and divestitures', *Administrative Science Quarterly*, **39** (4), 575–602.

Parker, S. (2004), *The Economics of Self-employment and Entrepreneurship*, Cambridge: Cambridge University Press.

Santarelli, E. and M. Vivarelli (2006), 'Entrepreneurship and the process of firms' entry, Survival and Growth', IZA Discussion Paper No. 2475, December.

Schary, M.A. (1991), 'The probability of exit', *RAND Journal of Economics*, **22** (3), 339–53.

Shane, S. (2000), 'Prior knowledge and the discovery of entrepreneurial opportunities', *Organization Science*, **11**, 448–69.

Small, K.A. and C. Hsiao (1985), 'Multinomial logit specification tests', *International Economic Review*, **26**, 619–27.

Taylor, M.P. (1999), 'Survival of the fittest? An analysis of self-employment durations in Britain', *Economic Journal*, **109** (454), C140–C155.

Van Praag, C.M. (2003), 'Business survival and success of young small business owners', *Small Business Economics*, **21**, 1–17.

Van Praag, C.M. and H. Van Ophem (1995), 'Determinants of willingness and opportunity to start as an entrepreneur', *Kyklos*, **48** (4), 513–40.

Watson, J. and J. Everett (1993), 'Defining small business failure', *International Small Business Journal*, **11** (3), 35–48.

Watson, J. and J. Everett (1996), 'Do small businesses have high failure rates?', *Journal of Small Business Management*, **34** (4), 45–62.

Wennberg, K. and J. Wiklund (2006), 'Entrepreneurial exit', paper presented at the Academy of Management Meeting, Atlanta, 11–16 August.

Westhead, P. and M. Wright (1998), 'Novice, portfolio, and serial founders: are they different?', *Journal of Business Venturing*, **13** (3), 173–204.

9. The entrepreneur in 'risk society': the personal consequences of business failure

Colin Mason, Sara Carter and Stephen Tagg

INTRODUCTION

Ulrich Beck is one of a number of theorists to have argued that advanced societies are experiencing a structural break with the past that is producing a new kind of capitalism, a new kind of labour, a new kind of social order and a new kind of society (Beck, 2003). However, Beck's distinctive perspective is to argue that, as a consequence of these discontinuities, risk has become a pervasive and integral part of the modern condition, permeating through social life. His risk society perspective has been applied in a variety of contexts but most notably in terms of employment. Indeed, Beck (2000) 'singles out labour market change as a decisive factor in the development of uncertain and insecure forms of lived experience' (Mythen, 2005, p. 130). Work has become de-standardized. Firms have sought to become more flexible in how they use their employees so as to more closely match their labour needs with demand cycles and more generally to reduce their costs. This has involved a shift from a system of full-time employment to non-standard labour, including greater use of part-time, temporary and contract labour, greater utilization of sub-contracting to independent businesses and the growth of project work involving freelance labour (Ekinsmyth, 2002). Jobs are based on less secure, individualized employment contracts and organizations have become more fragmented. This has provided flexibility for employers but created a 'risk fraught system of employment' (Reimer, 1998) for the employee. Workers face new sets of uncertainties that in turn have fashioned a 'new form of individualism' in which they are forced to fall back on their own resources to navigate their own individual paths through life, with all its hazards and inherent insecurities (Beck, 1992; Allen and Henry, 1997; Ekinsmyth, 1999, 2002). Moreover employment risk and uncertainties have permeated more deeply into the workforce, impacting on a wider section of society than in previous eras of restructuring (Mythen, 2005).

The consequences of this growth of 'de-standardized labour' are both ambivalent and contradictory. On the one hand they have transferred risk from employer to worker, creating greater insecurity for individuals. Accompanying this greater uncertainty is a new form of individualism that has forced workers to accept a higher level of personal responsibility for their individual destinies (e.g. upgrading skills, pension provision), to be pro-active in seeking opportunities (whether career or business) and to place increased reliance on private experts for health, pension, legal and accountancy needs. On the other hand, these changes provide certain freedoms from old regimes and structures of work, flexibility (e.g. in terms of hours worked) and choice (e.g. to 'be one's own boss'), but at the risk of increased self-exploitation. The risks and the benefits in this new condition are differentiated by such factors as social class and gender, creating new opportunities for those with tradable skills and knowledge. For some people, the benefits therefore outweigh the risks (Reimer, 1998; Ekinsmyth, 1999, 2002).

Our focus in this chapter is on the position of the small business owner in risk society, a group that has been largely ignored in the literature on economic uncertainty and insecurity. There are a variety of ways in which risk in a small business context can be defined and measured. Because of the nature of the data available to us, we equate risk with the personal financial consequences for the small business owner of the failure of their business. The chapter addresses two questions. First, what proportion of small business owners are highly exposed to personal financial risk? Second, how is this risk distributed across different types of small business owners?

SMALL BUSINESS OWNERSHIP AND RISK

Risk is fundamental to entrepreneurship. Indeed, one influential view of the entrepreneur is 'someone who is prepared to undertake risk in an uncertain world' in return for the prospect of reward (Deakins and Freel, 2006, p. 6). However, risk is a multi-faceted concept. There are gambling-type risks where there is no control over the outcome. There are also insurable risks, where potential losses can be protected on the basis of actuarial calculations of the statistical probability of specific outcomes. 'Entrepreneurial risk', in contrast, arises from uncertainty that, in turn, stems from imperfect information. An entrepreneur is someone who is able to manage this uncertainty-related risk in a way that gets the odds in their favour. But clearly, by no means all small business owners are able to successfully manage risk. So, what is the risk that a small business will fail?

Various definitional and measurement problems are encountered in attempting to answer this question. First, in terms of definitions, businesses that cease trading (often termed business dissolutions or exits) do so for a variety of reasons. Many do so for voluntary reasons. The business may be sold and its activities absorbed into the acquirer's operations, so its separate legal identity is lost. The retirement of the owner is another reason for voluntary closure. The owner may take up a better opportunity as an employee. One study of closures reported that 29 per cent of owners considered that their firm was successful at the time of closure (Headd, 2003). At the other extreme are businesses that fail. These businesses typically leave customers unpaid and may result in the personal bankruptcy of the owner, especially if they are self-employed or in a partnership, if creditors pursue their debts through the courts by claiming the owner's personal assets. In the case of limited companies, the inability to pay creditors can lead to insolvency, then receivership, with a receiver appointed to dispose of the assets with their value going to the creditors. This is also likely to lead to personal financial loss on the part of the entrepreneur, and even personal bankruptcy, if they have invested a significant proportion of their own wealth in the business or have given personal guarantees to their bank or landlord. However, some businesses are closed voluntarily by their owners in the knowledge that they are financially unsuccessful and to avoid further losses. Such businesses are unlikely to get to the point where they are put into receivership and the owners face personal bankruptcy. These business owners who have 'failed to make a go of it' confuse the apparent sharp distinction between voluntary closures and failed businesses.

Measuring business failure is also fraught with difficulty. First, it is clear from the preceding discussion that business closure is not the same as business failure – even though many commentators fail to make this critical distinction. Second, some statistics (including the UK's VAT database) classify a change of ownership of an existing business as an exit and entry (Johnson and Conway, 1997). Third, official statistics on bankruptcy, receiverships and liquidations underestimate the extent of business failures, as by no means all failing businesses will end up in any of these categories. However, the consensus view is that only a small proportion of firms that cease to trade represent financial failures. In the USA, failures account for less than 10 per cent of all closures. To put it another way, eight times as many firms stop operations voluntarily than fail (Phillips, 1993). The same point is made by Watson and Everett

(1996) in a study of Australian retailers: the ten-year rate of business discontinuance was 64.2 per cent, whereas the equivalent rate for bankruptcy was just 5.3 per cent.

SMALL BUSINESS AND FAILURE

The literature on business failure is surprisingly limited, especially in comparison with the attention that has been given to business start-up. Four strands can be recognized. The first, and largest, strand comprises studies of the types of businesses most at risk of failure. This is fairly consistent in highlighting a strong link between failure and the age of the business. For example, Cressy (2006) notes that failure rates rise steeply after start-up to peak at 18–24 months, and then fall gradually with increased longevity. There are also strong links between failure and the size of the business (larger businesses being less at risk of failure) and past growth (businesses that have been growing are less at risk of failure) (Storey, 1994). Some studies also identify sectoral effects (higher failure in retailing) and ownership effects (higher failure among sole proprietors and partnerships) (Carter and Van Auken, 2006). It is argued that technology firms are less likely to fail because even failing firms are likely to have assets (e.g. intellectual property) that are attractive to a trade buyer (Bruno et al., 1992). There is also a debate about whether franchisees are at a lower risk of failure (Stanworth and Purdy, 2006).

A second, and much smaller, strand focuses on links between failure and owner characteristics. It might be expected that various dimensions of the business owner's human capital (e.g. education, prior management experience, nature of prior work experience, prior experience as a business owner, etc.) would influence the probability of business survival and failure. However, research has failed to identify any strong links (e.g. see Van Praag, 2003). Hayward et al.'s (2006) hubris theory of entrepreneurship links overconfidence of the entrepreneur, a cognitive attribute, to failure.

A third strand of literature looks at the reasons why businesses fail. These studies are of two types. The first type are quantitative studies, based on company accounts, which have sought to identify failures based on financial ratios and thereby develop predictive models (e.g. Storey et al., 1987; Pompa and Bilderbeek, 2005). The second type comprises qualitative studies that have sought to attribute the causes of business failure (e.g. Berryman, 1983). These studies typically focus on the perceptions of the owner-manager, but some have extended this perspective by comparing the views of the owner-manager with those of other actors, such as the official receiver (Hall and Young, 1991; Hall, 1992, 1995), and venture capital investors (Zacharakis et al., 1999). However, as Fredland and Morris (1976, p. 8) note, 'pinpointing the causes of failure is largely a matter of definition'. It is very easy to attribute the causes of business failure to 'poor management' (Berryman, 1983). 'The causes of failure may always be said to be poor management. No matter what disaster befalls a firm in the marketplace, sufficient management foresight could by definition have avoided it' (Fredland and Morris, 1976, p. 8). Equally, 'the cause of failure may always be said to be lack of funds, for if the firm had sufficient funds to pay its obligations there would be no losses to creditors' (Fredland and Morris, 1976, p. 8). Nevertheless, there is considerable evidence from these studies that failure is largely attributable to weaknesses in operational management and under-capitalization. Carter and Van Auken (2006) also noted that bankrupt firms were more likely to exhibit cash flow and financing problems than surviving firms. Perry (2001) observes that failed firms do less planning (in the form of producing written documents) than similar surviving firms.

However, it is likely to be an over-simplification to attribute failure to a single cause. Burns (2007, p. 329) suggests that 'it is a coincidence of a number of factors that is likely to lead to failure'. He identifies four main ingredients of business failure:

- Entrepreneurial character: negative characteristics of the entrepreneur (e.g. delusional optimism and self-confidence).
- Business decisions: this includes decisions made with a lack of information or unwillingness to understand the information available, limited management team, lack of delegation and 'betting the ranch' decisions.
- Company weaknesses: which may reflect bad management decisions in the past, such as poor financial control and over-dependence on a small number of customers.
- The external environment: macroeconomic changes (e.g. demand, interest rates) and 'Acts of God' (e.g. illness, strikes, fire).

These factors interact. Some may be latent in a small business but only become significant when there is a trigger event, often linked to an outside factor, and may lead to further bad decisions being made.

The final strand in the research literature comprises a handful of studies that have explored the impact of failure on the entrepreneur. Brockhaus (1985) looks at how failure affects owner-managers and their ability to resume life. Shepherd and Wiklund (2005) suggest that failed entrepreneurs go through a grieving process. Ronstadt (1985) and Stokes and

Blackburn (2001) have explored what happens to business owners after the failure. An emerging theme is that failure can be a learning experience for business owners (Cope, 2005).

This chapter takes a distinctive perspective on small business failure that cuts across these four strands. Its focus is on a subset of business failures, namely those that would have a profound negative financial impact on the entrepreneur and their households. It links with the literature on the impact of business failure by exploring effects of business failure – or, strictly speaking, the *prospect* of business failure – on the entrepreneur's personal finances and lifestyle. However, it also links with the first and second strands by considering which characteristics of the businesses and owner-managers are associated with those failures that have a severe negative impact on the owner's personal financial position.

METHODOLOGY

Data for this study were drawn from a large-scale biennial survey of small business attitudes and opinions undertaken on behalf of the Federation of Small Businesses (FSB), a voluntary membership association of independent business owners in the UK. The sampling frame consisted of the FSB membership list. Questionnaires designed to elicit small business attitudes and opinions on a wide range of contemporary issues were distributed to 169 418 FSB members in September 2005 (Carter et al., 2006). By the November 2005 cut-off date, 18 939 responses were received, a usable response rate of 11.17 per cent. Cost restrictions prevented follow-up mailings to boost response rates, and data protection restrictions on the mailing list prevented the research team from identifying and contacting non-respondents in order to investigate response bias. Without the option of conventional non-response bias tests, a comparison of early and late responses was used to test response bias. No significant differences were found between early and late responses across any of the variables typically used to describe the owners and the firms (age of owner, business entry mode, age of business, sales volume and VAT registration). An analysis of respondents with regard to their sectoral and regional distribution suggested a sample with close similarities to that of the total population of UK VAT registered SMEs (Office for National Statistics, 2005; Small Business Service, 2005)

The dependent variable was a self-assessed measure of the consequence of business insolvency using a nominal scale. There were four alternative response categories relating to the consequences of insolvency offered within the questionnaire:

1. 'My standard of living would be unaffected';
2. 'I would have to scale down my lifestyle';
3. 'My basic survival and home would be under threat'; and
4. 'I would lose everything, become bankrupt'.

Responses to this question were received from 18332 respondents; 607 (3.2 per cent) respondents failed to complete this question and were excluded from the analysis.

The research questions required both univariate and multivariate analysis. As an exploratory study, the initial analysis comprised cross-tabulations of the dependent variable against a selection of measures in order to provide a broad indication of patterns. Following this, multinomial logistic regression was undertaken to explore the possibility of predicting respondents' levels of financial risk as a consequence of business insolvency. Given the generalist nature of the FSB survey and the resulting wide range of topics covered, the choice of independent variables was constrained by the nature of the questions asked. Nevertheless, information was available on a wide range of business and owner characteristics that have been used in previous studies of firm failure.

PROFILE OF RESPONDENTS

The respondents can be profiled in terms of both their business characteristics and the characteristics of their owner-managers (see Carter et al., 2006 for further details). In terms of business characteristics, respondents were concentrated in just four industry sectors: retail, wholesale and motor trades (25 per cent), business services (18 per cent), construction (12 per cent) and manufacturing (11 per cent). The majority were small. In terms of turnover, 42 per cent had sales of £100,000 or less and 80 per cent had sales of £500,000 or less. Measured by number of employees, 42 per cent had fewer than five workers and 66 per cent fewer than ten employees (including owners). Just over three-quarters were registered for VAT. Just over half (54 per cent) had increased sales in the previous year and 59 per cent were seeking to grow over the next two years, with 10 per cent seeking to grow rapidly.

Turning to the characteristics of the owners, there was a wide spread in terms of their age, with just 7 per cent under 35 years old, 55 per cent between 35 and 54 years old, 31 per cent in the 55–64 age band and 7 per cent were aged 65 years and over. This diversity was also reflected in the length of time that the present owner had owned the business, ranging from less than three years (24 per cent) to over 20 years (19 per cent). In 38 per cent of cases the business was co-owned with other family members, but in only 26 per cent of cases did family members, typically the spouse, play a management role. However, male ownership dominated: males were the exclusive or majority owners of 53 per cent of businesses; 33 per cent of businesses had equal male–female ownership, and only 14 per cent had female majority or exclusive ownership. In terms of their education 28 per cent of business owners had a degree and 26 per cent had non-degree professional qualifications. Only 13 per cent had no qualifications. A remarkably high proportion of respondents were habitual entrepreneurs: 46 per cent had owned one or more businesses previously (serial entrepreneurs) and 26 per cent currently owned another business (portfolio entrepreneurs). The vast majority of the respondents worked full-time in the business: only 7 per cent worked less than 30 hours and 6 per cent worked 30–40 hours. For two-thirds of the respondents this business was their only source of income; for 80 per cent of respondents their only income came from this and their other businesses.

RESULTS

Exposure to Financial Risk as a Consequence of Business Insolvency

The first research question concerned identifying the proportion of small business owners who believe that they are highly exposed to financial risk if their business becomes insolvent. This question is most simply answered by an analysis of the responses to the basic survey question: What would be the personal consequences of the business becoming insolvent? Only a minority (11 per cent) of business owners reported that their standard of living would be unaffected by insolvency and a further 44 per cent of respondents, the largest proportion, reported that, following insolvency, they would have to scale down their lifestyle. The remaining respondents reported more severe consequences of insolvency. Just over one-third (34 per cent) reported that their basic survival and home would be under threat and a further 11 per cent reported that they would lose everything and become bankrupt (Table 9.1).

These results demonstrate that the consequences of business insolvency vary quite markedly. At the extremes, roughly 10 per cent of business owners would be unaffected and 10 per cent risk losing everything. However, for the majority of business owners, the consequences of insolvency lie somewhere between a more restrained lifestyle and more severe effects.

Table 9.1   Consequence of business insolvency

What would be the consequence of the business becoming insolvent?	No.	%
My standard of living would remain unaffected	1 961	10.7
I would have to scale down my lifestyle	8 131	44.4
My basic survival and home would be under threat	6 253	34.1
I would lose everything, become bankrupt	1 987	10.8
Total	18 332	100

Financial Risk and Owner Characteristics

Given such variability in the perceived effects of business insolvency across this large sample of small business owners, it is appropriate to consider whether business owners who perceive themselves to be at extreme financial risk following insolvency share any discernible characteristics. Univariate analysis revealed 14 owner characteristics significantly associated with perceptions of financial risk as a consequence of insolvency (Table 9.2).

The first group of characteristics relate to the prior entrepreneurial experience of the owner-manager. Respondents most likely to perceive personal financial risk are those whose business is relatively newly established (<5 years). Reflecting the variability of personal resource usage at start-up, owners of very new businesses (1–3 years) are significantly more likely to report extreme responses: either that their standard of living would be unaffected or that they would 'lose everything, become bankrupt'. Owners of mature businesses (≥11 years) are significantly less likely to report extreme financial risk as a consequence of insolvency. While portfolio entrepreneurship appears to shield business owners from the most extreme effects of insolvency, serial entrepreneurship appears to have a contrary effect. Respondents who had previously owned one or more businesses before starting their current enterprise are significantly more likely to report financial exposure, perhaps as a consequence of transferring potential liabilities and stale resources from the earlier venture (Starr and Bygrave, 1992; Alsos and Carter, 2006).

Differences in the perceived consequences of business insolvency were found between those entrepreneurs for whom the business constituted their sole income, who were most likely to report extreme financial exposure, and those with multiple income sources, who were more likely to report that their standard of living would be unaffected. Similarly, extreme

Table 9.2　Owner characteristics associated with financial risk

Owner characteristics	χ^2	df	Sig.
Currently own >1 business	9.063	3	.028*
Previously owned ≥1 business	14.279	3	.003*
Years owned this business	252.763	24	.000*
Status prior to start-up	183.411	28	.000*
Multiple income sources	62.076	3	.000*
Proportion household wealth in business	3967.190	12	.000*
Education level	201.517	20	.000*
Time between education and start-up	44.234	20	.001*
Number of jobs before start-up	90.772	20	.000*
Comparative financial status	535.881	16	.000*
Comparative quality of life	613.693	16	.000*
Hours worked by owner	1660.411	16	.000*
Sex of owner	168.919	16	.000*
Age of owner	519.549	20	.000*

Note:　* χ^2 significant at the 0.05 level.

financial risk was significantly higher among respondents who had invested a very high proportion (≥ 76 per cent) of total household wealth in the business. Indeed, half of all respondents reporting extreme financial risk had invested over three-quarters of total household wealth in the business. The contrast between these respondents and those who had invested a lesser proportion of household wealth (≤ 25 per cent) was marked. Of the respondents who invested only a small proportion of household wealth in the business, more than 80 per cent reported that their standard of living would be unaffected as a consequence of business insolvency.

It may be speculated that exposure to financial risk is related to levels of human capital among owner-managers, for example, their educational achievements and prior labour market experience (Becker, 1964). As Table 9.2 demonstrates, educational level was found to be significantly associated with exposure to financial risk. Respondents with tertiary education (bachelors degree and above) are least likely to report high exposure to financial risk, while those with primary or secondary education (up to age 16) are more likely to report exposure to financial risk.

Respondents' perceptions of their comparative quality of life and financial status as a business owner are significantly associated with their exposure to financial risk as a consequence of insolvency. Those agreeing that their financial status as a business owner is 'a lot better' than as an employee, are more likely to report being 'unaffected' by business insolvency. In contrast, those who believe their financial status to be 'a lot worse' as a business owner are twice as likely to be highly exposed to financial risk. Similar results were seen with regard to respondents' comparative quality of life as a business owner. Those who believe their quality of life to be 'a lot better' as a business owner are least exposed to personal financial risk, while those for whom quality of life had deteriorated by becoming a business owner ('a lot worse') are significantly more likely to be highly exposed to personal financial risk in the event of insolvency.

Finally, three further owner characteristics (age, sex, hours worked) are significantly associated with financial risk. The age groups most likely to report extreme financial exposure are the median age ranges (35–44 years and 45–54 years), while those in the older age groups (55–64 years and over 65 years) are more likely to be unaffected by the consequences of business insolvency. Owners of businesses equally co-owned by men and women, usually matrimonial partnerships, are significantly more likely to be financially exposed, while the owners of businesses wholly owned by women are more likely to be unaffected by business insolvency. As expected, business owners operating businesses on a part-time basis, or which occupied less than 30 hours per week of owners' time, are more likely to report being unaffected, while those running businesses that occupied more than 60 hours of owners' time per week are the most likely to report financial exposure to business insolvency.

Financial Risk and Firm-level Characteristics

Univariate analysis also identifies 15 separate firm level characteristics that are significantly associated with exposure to financial risk following business insolvency (Table 9.3). Respondents owning VAT registered businesses (77 per cent of all respondents) are significantly more likely to report extreme financial exposure, as are those operating partnerships (17 per cent) and sole traderships (33 per cent). Industry sectors that demonstrate the greatest financial exposure as a consequence of insolvency are the hotels & catering and the wholesale & retail sectors. In contrast, owners of business services ventures are significantly less likely to report that they would 'lose everything' through insolvency. Demonstrating their capacity to shield themselves from financial risk by their relatively low cost base, owners of home-based businesses (36 per cent of all respondents) are more likely to report being 'unaffected' by insolvency. A strong relationship between entry mode and financial risk was also revealed. The insolvency of businesses started from scratch is less likely to result in financial risk to the owners, while the insolvency of businesses bought as a going concern is significantly more likely to result in owner bankruptcy.

Table 9.3   Firm characteristics associated with financial risk

Firm characteristics	χ^2	df	Sig.
VAT registered	169.980	8	.000*
Legal form of business	297.266	16	.000*
Industry sector	381.853	18	.000*
Home-based business	95.087	4	.000*
Start-up entry mode	254.647	20	.000*
Family-owned	112.193	20	.000*
Family-managed	56.713	20	.000*
Growth objective	228.876	24	.000*
Applied for ≥ 1 bank loan in last 2 years	626.332	8	.000*
Bank loan rejection in last 2 years	113.032	4	.000*
Fear of rejection deterred loan application	784.624	4	.000*
Sales turnover	562.868	18	.000*
Full-time employees	341.888	24	.000*
Total FTE employment	372.846	24	.000*
Anticipated employment change	127.429	16	.000*

Note: * χ^2 significant at the 0.05 level.

Sharing the ownership or management of the firm with a family member has a complex effect on the likely consequences of insolvency. Owners of businesses that are co-owned with their spouse are less likely to be 'unaffected', while owners of businesses co-owned with adult children (who comprised 6 per cent of respondents) are more likely to be 'unaffected' by insolvency. Owners of businesses in which the management is shared with a family member produced similarly complex results. Those owners who co-manage their business with a spouse are less likely to be 'unaffected' and more likely to report that their 'basic survival and home would be under threat'. Owners of businesses that they co-manage with their children (8 per cent) or siblings (2 per cent) are more likely to be 'unaffected' by business insolvency.

The consequences of insolvency are also associated with the business's growth objective. Owners of businesses with an objective of rapid growth (10 per cent of respondents) are significantly more likely to be highly exposed to financial risk, whereas owners of businesses pursuing an objective of moderate growth are less likely to be 'unaffected' by insolvency and more likely to report that the owner's 'basic survival and home under threat'. Owners of businesses with a static growth objective ('stay the same size') are significantly less likely to report that business insolvency would lead to bankruptcy.

Owners of businesses that had applied for a bank loan within the previous two years (29 per cent of all respondents) are significantly more likely to be highly exposed to financial risk. Financial risk was greater for those that had applied for more than one bank loan in this period (5 per cent of all respondents). In contrast, owners of businesses that had not applied for bank debt were significantly more likely to report that their standard of living would be 'unaffected' by business insolvency. Owners of businesses that had been successful in their bank loan application (91 per cent of applicants) were more likely to report that bankruptcy would lead to them 'scaling down their lifestyle', while those that had failed to secure bank debt, or had been deterred from applying because of fear of rejection (10 per cent of all respondents), were more likely to report that insolvency would lead them to 'lose everything'.

Size of firm, measured by sales turnover, is significantly associated with financial exposure. Owners of the smallest businesses ($\leq$ £50 000) are least likely to be affected by business insolvency, while owners of median-size businesses (£100 001–£250 000) are the most likely to report extreme financial risk. Interestingly, the owners of businesses with the highest sales turnover (over £1 million) appear relatively cushioned from the financial risks associated with bankruptcy. Employment size, an alternative measure of business size, is also significantly associated with financial risk. The employment size of businesses whose owners face most extreme financial risk following insolvency are those in the 5–9 full-time equivalent (FTE) employment size band. Owners of businesses with 1 FTE are most likely to report that their standard of living would be unaffected by insolvency. Anticipated employment change is also significantly associated with financial exposure. Those anticipating definite increases in employment numbers within the next year (11 per cent) are more likely to report extreme financial exposure to insolvency. Similarly, business owners anticipating definite (3 per cent) or possible (6 per cent) decreases in employment numbers are also more likely to report being highly exposed.

Predicting Exposure to Financial Risk

While univariate analysis provides a descriptive insight into the range of characteristics associated with exposure to financial risk, the use of the chi-square statistic at a univariate level with a large number of cases is likely to be over-sensitive. Understanding the more powerful relationships that underpin exposure to financial risk requires an overall analysis. As the dependent variable was a nominal variable, stepwise multinomial logistic regression was selected as the appropriate analysis procedure, both to predict which cases would be allocated to a particular response category, and to identify the potential predictor variables associated with category membership. The alternative analytic approach, ordinal regression, was rejected as it can only model the relationships assuming effects increase across the four categories in Table 9.1. However, it was expected that some effects would relate to the middle categories. Multinomial logistic regression also allows the use of a mixture of predictor variables at various levels of measurement in the same analysis.

The initial analysis was conducted with a large range of potential predictors, but the results proved unstable. In order to stabilize the results, non-significant variables were removed from the analysis. While univariate cross-tabulations had shown relationships with most of the initial large range of variables, only a sub-set of variables remained significant in the presence of other predictors. This was probably because of the overlap between the predictor variables. The likelihood ratio test was used to assess the extent of error not explained by model fitting. The chi-square was 4076, df $= 120$ $p < .001$, which showed that there was a considerable amount of unexplained variation in the dependent variable with the sub-set model in Table 9.4. This shows that the predictive element of the multinomial analysis was incomplete.

Despite this, the model allows an insight into the large number of potential predictors associated with response category membership. Table 9.4 shows the multinomial parameters (with the reference category 'I would have to scale down my lifestyle') in the sub-set model. Several category distinctions are significant without being significant overall. The table gives a note-form for interpreting the direction of the significant relationships.

Individual level variables significant at the overall level include a range of investment, human capital and perceptual factors. Notably, the model demonstrates the strength of the relationship between the proportion of household wealth invested in the venture and exposure to financial risk following insolvency. Similarly, it appears that high levels of investment in the form of owner-manager time (hours worked by owner) are also significantly related to financial risk. Multiple business ownership is strongly related to financial risk, though the model shows that this will lead to portfolio entrepreneurs being both less likely to 'remain unaffected' and more likely to anticipate bankruptcy.

Human capital variables, including number of jobs prior to start-up and educational level, are also related to financial risk. The greater the number of jobs held prior to start-up, the more likely respondents are to be 'under threat' or to face bankruptcy following insolvency. The relationship between education level and risk of financial exposure is modest; this

Table 9.4   Multinomial B parameters: versus group 2 (scale down lifestyle)

Variable	Overall	Group 1 unaffected	Group 3 under threat	Group 4 bankrupt	Interpretation
Years owned this business	*	−.021	.050*	−.018	More years = more under threat
Years as business owner	*	−.078*	−.056*	−.004	More years = − unaffected − under threat
Sales turnover	***	−.248***	−.033*	−.042	Higher = − unaffected − under threat
Proportion household wealth in business	***	−.378***	.510***	1.130***	Higher = − unaffected + under threat + bankrupt
Number of jobs before start up	***	−.028	.069***	.089**	More jobs = + under threat + bankrupt
Comparative financial status as owner	***	−.031	−.112***	−.171***	Better off = − under threat − less bankrupt
Comparative quality of life as owner	***	−.005	−.069***	−.089**	Better off = − under threat − less bankrupt
Hours worked by owner	***	−.150***	.194***	.345***	More hours = − unaffected + under threat + bankrupt
Age of owner	***	.119**	−.249***	−.300***	Older age = + unaffected − under threat − bankrupt
Currently own >1 business	***	−.371***	.221	.178*	Own >1 business = − unaffected + bankrupt
Previously owned >1 business		.025	.085	−.006	
Legal status (compared to LLP)	***	−.095	−.015	−.403	
Sex of owner(s) (compared to 100% female)	***	.007	−.181	−.403*	Male majority = − less fear of bankruptcy
Equal male/female		−.008	−.103	.143*	+ more bankruptcy fear
Share owner /spouse	***	.218*	−.003	.133	+ unaffected

Table 9.4 (continued)

Variable	Overall	Group 1 unaffected	Group 3 under threat	Group 4 bankrupt	Interpretation
Share management/ spouse	**	.096	−.106*	.212	− under threat
Share owner / child	*	−.347*	.013	.176	− unaffected
Share owner / sibling	*	−.420*	.229	.300	− unaffected
Industry sector (compared /'other')	***	−.296*	.054	.169	Manufacture = − unaffected
Postal services		−.581***	.209**	−.042	Postal services = − unaffected + survival under threat
Personal services		−.523***	.171	.020	Personal services = − unaffected
Applied bank loan in past 2 years (vs. > once)	***	−.172	−.528***	−1.004***	None = − under threat − bankrupt
Once		−.313	−.134	−.422**	Applied once = − bankrupt
Fear rejection prevented bank loan application	***	−.204	.713***	1.379***	+ under threat + bankrupt
Education: higher/A	*	−.021	−.148*	.096	No A levels = − under threat
Employment pre-start-up (compared / school)	**	−.127	−.710*	−1.149*	Retired = − under threat & − bankrupt

Notes:
Rows of multi-category predictors where more no parameters are significant have been omitted from the table.
The classification summary showed only 53.6% correctly predicted. The prediction of the multinomial analysis was incomplete and there was a lot of overlap between variables.
χ^2 test significance levels: * < 0.05; ** < 0.01; *** < 0.001.

analysis shows only that completing secondary education (getting A levels or higher) leads a business owner to be less 'under threat'.

Variables that capture perceived financial status and quality of life as an entrepreneur compared with employment were more strongly related to financial risk. When respondents perceive themselves to be financially better off as an entrepreneur, they are less likely to be either 'under threat' or exposed to bankruptcy. The quality of life perceptions have a similar effect on impact.

Two personal characteristics are significantly related at the overall level to financial risk. The older the owners, the more likely they are to be 'unaffected' by insolvency, and the less likely they are to be exposed to extreme financial risk, either 'under threat' or facing bankruptcy following insolvency. Sex of ownership also emerges as significant at the overall level. Firms that are wholly male owned are less likely to anticipate bankruptcy, and equal male–female owned firms – usually matrimonial partnerships – are more likely to anticipate bankruptcy.

Firm level variables that are significant at the overall level include a measure of size, legal status, sector, shared ownership and management and recent application for bank debt. The larger the firm's sales turnover, the less likely respondents are to be 'unaffected' by insolvency and the less likely they are to be under threat. Legal status is also significant at the overall level: it suggests that non limited liability firms are more likely to have to scale down their lifestyle.

Sharing the ownership of the firm with a spouse is significantly likely to increase the likelihood of being unaffected by the failure of the business. (The apparent contradiction with the earlier finding for equal male–female owned firms needs further investigation.) Sharing management, but not necessarily ownership, with a spouse reduces the risk of being under threat. In contrast, owners who share ownership with siblings are less likely to be unaffected.

Finally, recent application for bank debt is strongly related to financial risk following insolvency. Respondents who have not applied for bank debt in the previous two years are significantly less likely to be 'under threat' or face bankruptcy as a consequence of insolvency. Respondents who have made only one recent application for bank debt are also less likely to be exposed to extreme financial risk. In contrast, entrepreneurs who have been constrained in applying for bank debt because of a fear of rejection are significantly more likely to be 'under threat' and face bankruptcy as a consequence of insolvency.

Discussion

Two clear themes run through this analysis. The first is that small business owners who are seeking to grow rapidly, and who have made significant commitments of time and financial resources in their businesses, are potentially vulnerable to increased personal financial risk in the event that their business fails. Those business owners who anticipate severe personal financial implications in the event that their business becomes insolvent are seeking the rapid growth of their business, have made significant financial investment (in the form of personal investment in the business and raising bank loans) and work long hours. The businesses are typically relatively new and small, often co-owned with a spouse, and are seeking to expand from just a handful of employees. It is the owners of these businesses who are exposed to the greatest personal financial risk should the business fail. On the other hand, this risk may be worthwhile given the evidence that owners of larger businesses and owners who perceive themselves to be financially better off compared with their likely situation as an employee (suggesting that their business has been financially successful) perceive themselves to be at little or no personal financial risk should their business fail.

The second theme is reflects the opposite situation. Owners of businesses requiring little or no personal investment by the owner, and those that have low capital intensity, and older owners, are at little or no personal financial risk should their business fail. Owners who are least exposed to personal financial risk should their business fail have little or none of their household wealth invested in their business, operate from home and are in service industries (which typically have low capital intensity). This supports Bhidé's (2001) thesis that owners who bootstrap their business at start-up, either from choice or because they are forced to, do not face much personal financial risk.

The chapter is not concerned with actual business failures. Nevertheless, it can observed that the characteristics of the businesses and owners identified in the literature associated with business failure are only an imperfect match with those of the businesses whose owners are personally the most financially vulnerable to failure. Specifically, whereas the age and size of the business are associated with the risk of business failure, growth is not featured in the literature as being statistically associated with a high risk of business failure: if anything, growth has the effect of reducing failure (Storey, 1994). Moreover, there are few human capital variables that link business failure to personal financial risk, whereas they are somewhat more strongly associated with the risk of business failure.

CONCLUSION

This chapter has taken a distinctive perspective on business failure. Starting with the notion that individuals are exposed to greater economic risks than in the past, we offer an initial exploration of the vulnerability of small business owners to personal financial risk in the event that their business should fail. It reveals that exposure to risk is differentiated across the small business sector. Only a minority of small business owners face extreme risk (10 per cent state that they would lose everything and become bankrupt), but a substantial minority (a further 33 per cent) face some risk, stating that their basic survival and home would be 'under threat'. Just over half of respondents report being relatively unaffected by business insolvency, and of these, 10 per cent report that their standard of living would be unaffected.

Exposure to risk is most associated with personal financial investment in the business, the recent use of bank debt and growth from a small base (scaling up). The greatest risk appears to be associated with growth businesses, especially those growing from micro to small (5–9 employees). However, personal financial risk is likely to be reduced if growth is successfully achieved. Owners who have little or no personal financial exposure in the event of business failure are likely to own larger businesses and perceive themselves to have a higher financial status than if they had been employees.

The evidence presented here on the types of business owners who are most exposed to personal financial risk should be a source of disquiet for policy makers. There is a general concern, both in the UK and elsewhere, that although enterprise policies have resulted in the creation of considerable numbers of micro businesses, there are insufficient businesses that create jobs for more than just the owner and their immediate family. Removing impediments to growth should therefore be a key focus for policy. The case for intervention requires evidence on two key issues. First, does the recognition of the considerable personal financial risk that is involved in growing a business encourage business owners to remain small? Second, does it prompt forms of 'loss aversion behaviour' (Bhidé, 2001), such as selling the business at the earliest opportunity to capture the value that has been created, or consolidating rather than going on to build a large business? If further research reveals evidence of these outcomes then two further questions arise. First, can policy makers design forms of intervention that can change such behaviour? Second, is this a legitimate focus for intervention? There are many other issues where evidence is required. What are the actual risks of failing of businesses that are seeking to scale up from a handful of employees? Is the failure experience of the owners of these businesses distinctive? For example, are they less willing, or less able (for financial or emotional reasons), to start another business? Do the owner-managers recognize their exposure to these personal financial risks? In short, this points to the need for the business failure literature to broaden out from its present focus on what types of firms fail to consider in much more detail the impacts of failure on the business owner, whether the impacts of failure are differentiated across the small business population, and the impact of the perception of the risk and effects of failure on the behaviour of business owners.

REFERENCES

Allen, J. and N. Henry (1997), 'Ulrich Beck's "risk society" at work: labour and employment in the contract service industries', *Transactions of the Institute of British Geographers*, **22** (2), 180–96.

Alsos, G. and S. Carter (2006), 'Multiple business ownership in the Norwegian farm sector: resource transfer and performance consequences', *Journal of Rural Studies*, **22** (3), 313–22.

Beck, U. (1992), *Risk Society: Towards a New Modernity*, London: Sage.

Beck, U. (2000), *The Brave New World of Work*, Cambridge: Polity Press.

Beck, U. (2003), 'The theory of reflexive modernization: problematic, hypothesis and research programme', *Theory, Culture and Society*, **20** (2), 1–33.

Becker, G. (1964), *Human Capital: A Theoretical and Empirical Analysis, with Special Reference to Education*, New York: Columbia University Press for National Bureau of Economic Research.

Berryman, J. (1983), 'Small business failure and bankruptcy: a survey of the literature', *European Small Business Journal*, **1** (4) 47–59.

Bhidé, A.V. (2001), *The Origin and Evolution of New Businesses*, New York: Oxford University Press.

Brockhaus, R.H. (1985), 'Is there life after death: the impact of unsuccessful entrepreneurial endeavours on the life of the entrepreneur', in *Frontiers of Entrepreneurship Research 1985*, Wellesley, MA: Center for Entrepreneurial Studies, Babson College, pp. 468–81.

Bruno, A., E. McQuarrie and C. Torgrimson (1992), 'The evolution of high technology companies: a twenty-year perspective', *Journal of Business Venturing*, **7** (4), 291–302.

Burns, P. (2007), *Entrepreneurship and Small Business*, 2nd edn, Basingstoke: Palgrave.

Carter, R. and H. Van Auken (2006), 'Small firm bankruptcy', *Journal of Small Business Management*, **44** (4), 493–512.

Carter, S., C. Mason and S. Tagg (2006), *Lifting the Barriers to Growth in UK Small Businesses: The FSB Biennial Membership Survey 2006*, London: FSB.

Cope, J. (2005), 'Towards a dynamic learning perspective of entrepreneurship', *Entrepreneurship Theory and Practice*, **29**, 373–98.

Cressy, R. (2006), 'Why do most firms die young?', *Small Business Economics*, **26**, 103–16.

Deakins, D. and M. Freel (2006), *Entrepreneurship and Small Firms*, 4th edn, Maidenhead: McGraw-Hill.

Ekinsmyth, C. (1999), 'Professional workers in a risk society', *Transactions of the Institute of British Geographers*, **24** (3), 353–66.

Ekinsmyth, C. (2002), 'Project organisation, embeddedness and risk in magazine publishing', *Regional Studies*, **36** (3), 229–43.

Fredland, J.E. and C.E. Morris (1976), 'A cross section analysis of small business failure', *American Journal of Small Business*, **1**, 7–18.

Hall, G. (1992), 'Reasons for insolvency amongst small firms – a review and fresh evidence', *Small Business Economics*, **4** (3), 237–50.

Hall, G. (1995), *Surviving and Prospering in the Small Firm Sector*, London: Routledge.

Hall, G. and B. Young (1991), 'Factors associated with insolvency amongst small firms', *International Small Business Journal*, **9** (2) 54–63.

Hayward, M.L.A., D.A. Shepherd and D. Griffin (2006), 'A hubris theory of entrepreneurship', *Strategic Management Journal*, **52**, 160–72.

Headd, B. (2003), 'Redefining business success: distinguishing between closure and failure', *Small Business Economics*, **21**, 51–61.

Johnson, P. and C. Conway (1997), 'How good are the UK VAT registration data at measuring firm births?', *Small Business Economics*, **9**, 403–9.

Mythen, G. (2005), 'Employment, individualisation and insecurity: rethinking the risk society perspective', *Sociological Review*, **53**, 129–49.

Office for National Statistics (2005), *UK Business: Activity, Size and Location – 2005*, London: Office for National Statistics.

Perry, S.C. (2001), 'The relationship between written business plans and the failure of small businesses in the US', *Journal of Small Business Management*, **39**, 201–8.

Phillips, B.D. (1993), 'The influence of industry and location on small business failure rates', paper presented to the Babson Entrepreneurship Research Conference, Houston, Texas.

Pompa, P.P.M. and J. Bilderbeek (2005), 'The prediction of bankruptcy of small and medium-sized industrial firms', *Journal of Business Venturing*, **20**, 847–68.

Reimer, S. (1998), 'Working in a risk society', *Transactions of the Institute of British Geographers*, **23** (1), 116–27.

Ronstadt, R. (1985), 'Every entrepreneur's nightmare: the decision to become an ex-entrepreneur and work for someone else', in *Frontiers of Entrepreneurship Research 1985*, Wellesley, MA: Center for Entrepreneurial Studies, Babson College, pp. 409–34.

Shepherd, D.A. and J. Wiklund (2005), *Entrepreneurial Small Businesses*, Cheltenham, UK and Northampton, MA, USA: Edward Elgar.

Small Business Service (2005), *Business Start-ups and Closures: VAT Registrations and Deregistrations in 2004*, Statistical Press Release URN 05/11 12 October 2005, London: Small Business Service.

Stanworth, J. and D. Purdy (2006), 'Franchising and the small business', in S. Carter and D. Jones-Evans (eds), *Enterprise and Small Business*, Harlow, Essex: FT Prentice Hall; pp. 441–64.

Starr, J.A. and W.D. Bygrave (1992), 'The second time around: the outcomes, assets and liabilities of prior start-up experience', in S. Birley and I.C. MacMillan (eds), *International Perspectives on Entrepreneurship Research*, Amsterdam: Elsevier, pp. 340–63.

Stokes, D. and R. Blackburn (2001), 'Opening up business closures: a study of businesses that close and owners' exit routes', A Research Report for HSBC, Kingston University Small Business Research Centre.

Storey, D. (1994), *Understanding the Small Business Sector*, London: Routledge.

Storey, D.J., K. Keasey, R. Watson and P. Wynarczyk (1987), *The Performance of Small Firms: Profits, Jobs and Failures*, London: Croom-Helm.

Van Praag, C.M. (2003), 'Business survival and success of young small business owners', *Small Business Economics*, **21**, 1–17.

Watson, J. and J.E. Everett (1996), 'Do small businesses have high failure rates?', *Journal of Small Business Management*, **34**, 45–62.

Zacharakis, A.L., G.D. Mayer and J. DeCastro (1999), 'Differing perceptions of new venture failure: a matched exploratory study of venture capitalists and entrepreneurs', *Journal of Small Business Management*, **37** (3), 1–14.

PART V

Knowledge-based Entrepreneurship

10. The creation of higher education institutions and firm entry: a policy evaluation

Joana Mendonça, Rui Baptista and Francisco Lima

INTRODUCTION

Various studies have examined the role played by universities in promoting entrepreneurship in nearby regions. Results obtained by Audretsch et al. (2005) suggest that, in general, new knowledge-based firms have a high propensity to locate close to universities. In addition, academic research and development expenditure has been found to be significantly associated with rates of new firm formation across regions (Lee et al., 2004). There is also strong evidence from the United States of a growth effect of clusters influenced by research-active universities (Feldman, 2000).

In a modern economy, universities are generators of a steady flow of novel technical ideas, and the system of public research and higher education is largely responsible for the capability in modern technologies (Mazzoneli and Nelson, 2007). In addition to their traditional role as sources of ideas, knowledge and intellectual capital, universities have become agents of innovations through the development and commercialization of new ideas generated by academic research and development (R&D). Entrepreneurial universities enhance regional development and international competitiveness and their role is especially important in structurally weak and peripheral regions, where universities tend to have a monopoly over the production of intellectual capital.

The local presence of universities can generate positive externalities through both the performance of knowledge-generating R&D activities and the education of specialized human capital, capable of absorbing such knowledge. Firms can cultivate relationships with universities, participating in research consortia and partnering with academics who do related scientific work (Audretsch and Feldman, 2004). For instance, personal networks of academics and industrial researchers facilitate the commercial exploitation of knowledge generated at universities by existing firms or university spin-off start-ups. Moreover, fresh graduates may be important channels for disseminating the latest knowledge from academia to the local high-technology industry (Varga, 2000). Empirical studies have found that new firms are highly likely to start in the home region of their founders (Klepper, 2002) and, as a result, universities and other research institutions can become important focal points for regional economic development.

The presence of a university in a region is an additional factor influencing the location decision made by new firms. This influence should be greater in industries where new knowledge plays a more important role. The transmission of new, as yet uncodified, knowledge tends to occur only within limited geographic areas, embedding economic activity based on this knowledge within the region (Baptista and Swann, 1999). As a result, it is expected that access to local knowledge sources is particularly significant for high-technology and knowledge-based manufacturing and services.

In Portugal, there was a revolution in 1974 ending the dictatorship. Until then, the higher university education system was made for the elite and characterized by a low number of students. After the revolution education was democratized, and the higher education system was expanded. In the 1980s, there was political support for the growth of the private university higher education sector (Correia et al., 2002) and, as a result of this political context, several new private and public schools emerged. In this chapter, we examine the effect of the creation of these new higher education institutions on subsequent regional levels of entry by knowledge-based firms. We apply a procedure based on propensity score matching methods because with this methodology we can identify the shift in the distribution of firm entry rates for regions with new universities as compared with regions that maintain the same number of universities but otherwise share similar characteristics.

Our results indicate that the creation of new higher education school in a region has a positive impact on the lagged share of new firm entry in knowledge-intensive sectors, which is followed by a significant decrease in the entry of firms in low-technology sectors. In general, our results illustrate that universities effectively contribute to the regional development of knowledge-related activities.

The chapter is organized as follows. The next section presents some background literature on the role of universities in regional development, presenting the research questions addressed. The third section presents the data and methodological approach used in the present study, while the fourth section reports and discusses the results obtained. The final section presents our main conclusions, and highlights avenues for improving and broadening this research.

UNIVERSITIES AND NEW FIRM CREATION

Universities and Location

One of the major socio-economic trends observed in the last decades is the rise of entrepreneurship as a driver of innovation, competitiveness and economic development. Both academics and policy makers have claimed that entrepreneurial activity is vital to economic progress. As a result, government policies fostering new firm creation have been adopted by many countries. Empirical research has suggested that the entrepreneurial efforts most likely to impact on subsequent economic development and employment growth are knowledge-based firms (Baptista and Preto, 2006). Knowledge-based entrepreneurial activity requires a steady flow of novel ideas in order to flourish. The existence of human capital with the technological knowledge required to recognize and implement entrepreneurial opportunities arising from novel ideas is essential for successful technology commercialization. Universities and R&D laboratories are fundamental sources of technical knowledge that can be commercialized. Universities and polytechnic institutes also play a major role in educating human capital capable of recognizing and implementing technological opportunities.

Recent research has addressed the issue of 'technology transfer and commercialization', referring to the mechanisms and incentives through which universities can bring knowledge developed in R&D activities to the market. Fewer works have addressed the regional dimension of university knowledge transfer. A variety of research streams have demonstrated the importance of geographical proximity for the transmission of new knowledge, and it is therefore reasonable to expect that the economic exploitation of such knowledge will occur close to the sources generating it.

Complex technological knowledge, seemingly the most valuable type of knowledge, usually contains a strong element of tacitness, meaning its flow and diffusion are constrained by the geographic proximity and extent of interaction among individuals within whom the tacit component resides. Considering tacit knowledge as an important element for new innovative firms, access to this type of knowledge can become a major determinant in the competitiveness of regions and the location of these firms (Audrestch et al., 2004). A host of recent empirical studies have confirmed that knowledge spillovers are geographically bounded (Jaffe, 1989, Anselin et al., 1997). Accordingly, the location decision of new firms should be influenced significantly by access to the sources of knowledge spillovers, including specialized human capital and institutions performing R&D activities (Audretsch et al., 2005). In addition, the propensity to cluster geographically should be higher in industries where new knowledge plays a more important role as such knowledge is less likely to be codified and easy to transmit over great distances, with no need for personal contact (Baptista and Swann, 1999).

Recent literature has advocated that knowledge spillovers play an important role in fostering entrepreneurship and innovative activity (Sorenson and Audia, 2000; Baum and Sorenson, 2003). Companies in innovative sectors tend to choose locations where significant knowledge-generating activities associated with these sectors occur (Zucker et al., 1998, 2002; Audretsch and Stephan, 1996) and these activities may be performed by universities or other firms, and implies the presence of world class scientific research and human capital. Spillovers from universities, as well as from private firms, have been recognized as key sources promoting firm innovation and performance (Stuart and Sorenson, 2003). Stahlecker and Koschatzky (2004) indicate that spatial proximity matters for the founding and early performance of firms in the knowledge-intensive business services sectors. Also, Capello (2002) has found that high-technology industries display high spatial concentration and, in contrast to start-ups with traditional products and processes, knowledge-based firms tend to offer new or improved products, operating in markets in early development stages. Thus, access to knowledge sources should be particularly significant for high-technology and knowledge-based industries and services.

Universities as Knowledge Sources

Modern universities have had a role in the dissemination and transmission of knowledge since their creation (Caraça et al., 2000). In particular, university research contributes to the basic stock of scientific knowledge available in any country or region, and it appears to have the potential to improve national competitiveness (Spencer, 2001). In addition, research has identified the important role that universities play in generating knowledge spillovers (Audretsch et al., 2004). Studies have also found that academic research can be linked to the development of a high percentage of product innovations, and that the development of certain sectors happened in countries where there were strong university research programmes in related areas. Public research is used not only to help generate ideas, but also to help complete existing R&D projects in firms (Laursen and Salter, 2004). Start-ups, in particular, can be a vehicle to transfer university research into commercial innovation, especially in science-based sectors (Laursen and Salter, 2004). Geographical proximity of an academic institution to a knowledge-intensive industry may be a source of positive knowledge externalities, since firms can cultivate relationships with universities, establishing partnerships with academics who do related scientific work, thus allowing the sharing and exchange of tacit knowledge (Audretsch and Feldman, 2004). Cooperative relationships can be considered as a channel for knowledge spillovers, and the establishment of such cooperation is favoured by location proximity (Fritsch, 2001). For instance, personal networks of academics and industrial researchers may lead to the commercial exploitation of knowledge generated at universities by existing firms or university spin-off start-ups. The possibility of developing research partnerships with academic institutions may also positively affect the absorptive capacity of firms (Scott, 2003). Fresh graduates may be important channels for disseminating the latest knowledge from academia to the local high-technology industry (Varga, 2000). Students can also provide a channel to transmit knowledge from the university where it is created to the firm where it can be commercialized (Audretsch et al., 2004). In addition, the establishment of new firms can also be advantageous to the universities, since they can make the institutions more attractive to students, faculty and other partners. By creating new knowledge and training people, universities can support the formation of new firms, and therefore have been considered as an important source of investment ideas by venture capitalist (Lerner, 2005).

Given that the commercialization of knowledge depends on knowledge generation by universities and public R&D laboratories, as well as R&D activities by firms, a low level of new business formation in knowledge-dependent sectors should be associated with a lack of knowledge-generating sources (Cohen and Levinthal, 1989). Acs et al. (1994) find that small firms are recipients of R&D spillovers generated both in universities and in the R&D centres of their larger counterparts, and such spillovers are apparently more significant in stimulating innovative activity by small firms than by large corporations. Anselin et al. (1997) find evidence of local spatial externalities between university research and high-technology innovative activity. Feldman (2000) reports strong evidence in favour of a growth effect of geographical clusters influenced by active research universities for the United States. Fisher and Varga (2003) provide evidence of the importance of geographically mediated knowledge spillovers from university research activities to regional knowledge production in high-tech industries in Austria. Other studies, such as Bania et al. (1993), find that the relationship between university research and firm births varies across industrial sectors. Furthermore, the role of universities in the commercialization of knowledge has increased over time; Henderson et al. (1998) have found an increase in the rate of technology transfer to the private sector.

HYPOTHESIS FORMULATION

On 25 April 1974, there was a revolution in Portugal leading to the fall of the government of Marcelo Caetano and ending the authoritarian regime that had lasted for almost half a century. During the regime, there was extensive state regulation and predominantly private ownership of the means of production. The state exercised extensive authority regarding private investment decisions and the level of wages. After the revolution, there was a time of political uncertainty and turbulence. Following the revolution, the Portuguese higher education system grew very significantly as a consequence of a political effort to democratize and facilitate access to universities and an associated increase in the demand for higher education. Since then, several public and private higher education institutions have been created across the country, giving rise to a private higher education sector and to a network of polytechnic institutions supported by the government. This growth is reflected in the number of enrolled students, which increased from an average of 30000 in the 1960s to 400000 in the 1990s (Horta, 2008; Correia et al., 2002). The emergence of these institutions represented an attempt to offer new degrees and to address specific local or regional needs. In particular, new private higher education institutions tried to explore market niches that remained untouched (Correia et al., 2002). This policy development enables us to recognize the creation of new higher education institutions in specific regions and to address their effects.

Observing this phenomenon allows us to identify the impact of these institutions in the regions where they are located. If universities do have a role in fostering entrepreneurial activity, we can assume that the creation of universities in regions will have an impact on the number of start-ups in the same region. In this mindset, we wish to address the following research question: What is the impact of the creation of a new university on the levels of firm entry in a region? We address this research question by testing the following hypothesis:

H1:   The creation of a new higher education institution in a municipality has a positive effect on subsequent levels of new firm entry in that municipality.

Furthermore, it is not clear if universities will affect entrepreneurial activity across industries, or if this effect will be more pronounced in knowledge-related sectors. Firms in high-technology industries often seek to increase levels of intellectual capital through the use of external sources, making proximity to a university more important. Thus, we test a second hypothesis:

H2: The impact of a new higher education institution in a municipality will vary according to the sector considered.

In particular, we assume that there should be a more short-term immediate impact on the entry of new firms, focused on supplying the new higher education institutions with services and technology. We also expect that there will be a gradual effect, more long term, which can take some years to reach a peak, whereby new firms are started by faculty and graduates of these institutions, and as a consequence of knowledge spillovers generated by education and research activities. In addition, we assume that activities in knowledge-based industry and services will benefit more from locating in the proximity of higher education institutions and we expect these new institutions to have a bigger impact in knowledge-dependent sectors.

DATA AND METHODOLOGY

The Data

Data on firm dynamics and levels of human capital were drawn from the Portuguese *Quadros de Pessoal* database. This is a longitudinal employer–employee matched database built from mandatory information submitted by firms to the Ministry for Employment and Social Security. It includes extensive information on all private firms, establishments, workers and business owners in the Portuguese economy. There are on average over 145 000 firms, 170 000 establishments and two million workers in each annual return, which are fully linked through the use of a unique identification number, thus allowing for the recognition of new entrants and exiting firms, as well as the opening and closure of subsidiary establishments. For each firm, data are available for size, age, location, sector and number of establishments. Data on business owners and employees for each firm and establishment include gender, age, function, tenure, schooling and skill levels.[1] The present study focuses on firms in manufacturing sectors and in knowledge-intensive business services, making use of the OECD classification (OECD, 2002) (see the Appendix for detailed sector descriptions). We identified entry by observing the appearance of a new firm identifier in the data set and comparing this entry with the earliest employee admission date. We considered entry if the worker's admission date did not differ by more than two years from the firm's entry date identified. Firms for which entry year was not identified were not included in the analysis. A data set was built containing all new firms starting their activity in the period 1992–2002 in the considered sectors. Data were aggregated at the municipality level, considering the 275 Portuguese continental municipalities.

Data concerning higher education institutions were obtained from the Portuguese Ministry for Science, Technology and Higher Education. The available data set includes information on every higher education institution in Portugal from 1992 to 2002, private and public institutions and polytechnic schools. For each year there is information on the number of students, number of graduates and the degrees provided by each school. This information was collected and aggregated at the municipality level.

Table 10.1 presents the descriptive statistics of the variables used. As can be observed, Portuguese municipalities display a high dispersion in terms of number of start-ups (Baptista and Mendonça, 2007). There is also significant demographic dispersion; municipalities on the coast and surrounding the main cities display higher population densities, while those in the inner regions have experienced population reductions. This regional asymmetry is reflected in the demography of new firms; indeed, previous research indicates that Portuguese entrepreneurs tend to start firms in the region where they live, and they do not often choose to locate their business elsewhere (Figueiredo et al., 2000).

In this chapter we are evaluating the policy aimed at creating new higher

Table 10.1 Descriptive statistics

	Mean	Std. Dev.	Min.	Max.
Pop. density (inhabitants per km²)	252.577	809.145	6.240	7835.059
Work force education (no. of years)	6.056	0.857	1.813	9.609
No. of workers in the region	8115.832	32343.93	52	564964
Share of micro firms in the region (proportion of firms with less than 10 employees)	85.083	5.909	46.667	100
Entry (no. of new firms)	23.534	52.746	0	911
Distance to Lisbon (km)	198.106	99.041	6.5	396
Distance to Oporto (km)	174.104	116.574	3.5	463.5

Note: Data for 275 regions (municipalities), pooled 1992–2002.

education institutions by measuring its impact on the formation of new firms. Thus, we compare levels of firm entry in municipalities where new higher education institutions were created, with firm entry in municipalities where there were no new institutions. This will check whether or not the creation of a new institution significantly affects subsequent rates of new business formation, and how if this effect varies in different sectors. As such, we consider the creation of a new institution to be a treatment variable and evaluate the impact of this treatment by comparing municipalities where the treatment variable is equal to one with those where the treatment variable is equal to zero (i.e. municipalities where no new higher education institutions were created in that same period). We compare the group of municipalities where a new higher education institution was created with two control groups, namely municipalities where the number of institutions is zero and remains zero during the entire time of the study (group A); and municipalities where the number of institutions is different from zero and remains constant (group B). We have excluded the municipalities for which there was a decrease in the number of institutions, because there may be effects of this decrease that we were unable to control. We also excluded municipalities where new institutions were created outside the time span of our analysis, since these new institutions may have impacts that we could not distinguish, and to make sure that we were observing the effect of only new institutions.

From 1992 to 2002, we can identify 46 municipalities where a new institution was created, and 14 municipalities where more than one institution appeared during this time. There are 204 municipalities that remain with no institution in the same period (group A), and 17 municipalities for which the number of institutions is different from zero and remains the same throughout the period (group B).

In this analysis, we have chosen to observe the treatment for the years 1993 and 1994, so that we would have at least two years before treatment to control for pre-treatment characteristics. As we are comparing municipalities in the different groups, we need to be able to observe the municipalities at least two years before the treatment, to make sure we compare municipalities with similar characteristics regardless of the creation of the new institution. In addition, we wish to have a considerable number of years after the treatment in order to distinguish short-term, indirect effects and long-term effects. Furthermore, using two adjacent years avoids comparing the treatment in different environmental conditions.

In 1993 and 1994, we have identified 17 new institutions in 17 different municipalities. From these new institutions, we have identified six private schools, eight polytechnics, five that have active research centres and develop research activities, and four that provide technology-related

Table 10.2   Pre-treatment characteristics of regions

$t = -2$	Pop. density	No. of workers	Workforce education	Share of micro firms	Distance to Lisbon	Distance to Oporto
Treated group	1132.329	6.020	80.749	178.031	167.062	1132.329
	(2447.756)	(0.956)	(5.201)	(110.592)	(104.297)	(2447.756)
Group A	117.909	4.764	82.823	197.362	179.593	117.909
	(247.854)	(0.816)	(8.128)	(96.985)	(113.731)	(247.854)
Group B	863.055	5.151	78.901	177.529	119.088	863.055
	(1847.325)	(0.748)	(7.280)	(98.376)	(97.360)	(1847.325)

Notes:
Standard errors in brackets.
Treated group = municipalities where there was a new higher education institution between 1993 and 1994 ($t = 0$).
Group A = municipalities with number of institutions equal to zero.
Group B = municipalities with number of institutions constant and different from zero.

degrees. There are 204 municipalities that remain with no higher education institutions throughout the period of analysis (control group A), and 17 which already had at least one higher education institution and where no new institutions were created in the period of analysis (control group B). The time scale is used with reference to the treatment period: for municipalities where a new higher education institution was created, the time zero ($t = 0$) corresponds to the year of creation (i.e. of treatment, 1993 or 1994); for municipalities where no higher education institutions were created, the time $t = 0$ is set to the first year of treatment (1993).

Table 10.2 displays the relevant characteristics two years before treatment ($t = -2$) across the groups of municipalities considered. Control group A, which has no universities or polytechnics throughout the whole period of analysis, shows lower average levels of education, population density and number of workers, and the firms in these municipalities are smaller. In addition, group A represents municipalities that are further away from the main urban centres (Lisbon and Oporto). In contrast, municipalities in the treated group display higher average levels of education of the workforce, higher population density, and a higher number of employed workers. In our analysis we control for these pre-treatment differences so we can match municipalities within each group that have similar pre-treatment conditions. Without such a process of matching, it is evident that it is impossible to compare the two groups as shown by the figures presented in Table 10.2. The same pattern of differences in the pre-treatment variables is observed for group B (municipalities with number of institutions constant and different from zero). The municipalities in this group are larger than those in group A, but smaller than those treated, as measured by population density and number of workers. The same type of relationship is found for average years of education for the workforce. As expected, these municipalities are closer to the two main urban centres (measured in km). Moreover, the share of small firms is smaller than in municipalities belonging to the other two groups.

EMPIRICAL ANALYSIS

First-differences Method

We start by applying a first-differences method to determine the effect of the creation of a new higher education institution on the entry rates of new firms. This methodology is often used with data obtained from a natural experiment, which occurs when some exogenous event, such as a change in government policy, changes the environment. A natural experiment always has a control group, which is not subject to any change, and a treatment group, which is affected by the policy change. In this case, the exogenous event is the creation of higher education institutions, which were created during the 1990s as a consequence of government policies to change the structure of the higher education sector, and increase the number of graduates in Portugal. Accordingly, the control group consists of municipalities that have experienced no change in the number of higher education institutions (in the entire period from 1992 to 2002) while the treatment group consists of those municipalities where a new higher education was created in the period 1993–94.

A first-differenced equation of the entry rates of firms is estimated by ordinary least squares (OLS) distinguishing the control group from the treated. The treatment is introduced using a dummy variable that assumes the value one for treated regions, and zero otherwise. The treatment effect is captured in the municipality entry rates. We differentiate the entry rates across time for the same cross-sectional units, and differentiating adjacent time periods. We control for differences between municipalities by including a set of control factors, which are also differentiated over time, such as population density; the share of micro firms; number of employees (log); the distances to the main urban centres, Oporto and Lisbon; and year dummies to capture time/business cycle effects. We use these variables to control for the probability that new firms will locate in each municipality regardless of the existence of higher education institutions (Figueiredo et al., 2000).

The first-differences estimator on the treatment variable is not statistically significant, which means that we were unable to capture the effect of a new university on the one year lag of regional rates of entry of firms.[2] The first-differences estimator compares the group of treated regions with the group of non-treated regions, regardless of individual characteristics within the two groups. Since we have very heterogeneous groups of municipalities, which cannot be directly compared, we are unable to isolate the effect of the creation of new higher education institutions. Another reason for these results is that one year differences are not enough to observe any effects of the new institutions on the regional levels of new firm formation. It is reasonable to assume that a new institution will take more than one year to affect new firm creation in the region. This may be even more significant in knowledge-intensive activities that can be generated through knowledge spillovers resulting from university R&D, or from companies started from graduates coming out from these institutions.

In order to observe the treatment effect more exactly, we used a different matching technique, allowing for a more accurate comparison between municipalities. We therefore make use of the propensity score matching estimator, which will allow us to match municipalities according to their characteristics, and observe the effect more than one year after the creation of new institutions.

Propensity Score Matching Method

The propensity score matching method is a matching technique that makes the distribution of observable characteristics of treatment and control groups similar (Rosenbaum and Rubin, 1983). The difference is that we now compare treated municipalities with non-treated municipalities that are similar in a number of characteristics, controlling for the heterogeneity of the treated group. This is the advantage of propensity scores matching methods, since they correct for sample selection bias resulting from observable differences between the treatment and comparison groups (Dehejia and Wahba, 2002).

The propensity score is the conditional probability of receiving a particular treatment (in this case, having a new higher education institution) given a vector of observed covariates (pre-treatment characteristics):

$$p(X) \equiv Pr\{D = 1|X\} = E\{D|X\} \tag{10.1}$$

Where $D = \{0, 1\}$ is the indicator of exposure to treatment and X is the multidimensional vector of pre-treatment characteristics (Becker and Ichino, 2002).

We estimate the propensity score of the treatment on the control variables using a probit model and stratify individuals in blocks according to the estimated score. We estimate the probability of having an increase in the number of universities, given the municipalities' characteristics from period $t = -2$ (pre-treatment variables). The propensity score is estimated and the balancing property is tested. The balancing property ensures that the means of each characteristic do not differ significantly between treated and control municipalities, which allows us to compare municipalities of the different groups that are similar in terms of their pre-treatment characteristics. This estimated probability of another institution conditional on the full set of covariates included in the regression is used to match treated and control individuals. The matching involves pairing treatment and comparison units that are similar in terms of their observable characteristics (Dehejia and Wahba, 2002).

The matching between municipalities to create the blocks was carried out using variables that reflect the municipalities' size and industry structure: number of employees (log); share of small firms; and the distances to the main cities, Oporto and Lisbon. These variables control for the probability that new firms will locate in each municipality regardless of the existence of higher education institutions (Figueiredo et al., 2000). The results for this estimation are presented in Table 10.3.

Afterwards, we use the stratification method to match the treated group and the control groups' observations and to estimate the average effect

Table 10.3   Propensity scores estimation – probit regression

In $t = -2$	Dummy for treatment
Distance to Oporto	−0.002
	[0.001]
Distance to Lisbon	−0.001
	[0.001]
Number of workers (ln)	0.544***
	[0.125]
Share of micro firms	0.071**
	[0.031]
Constant	−11.750***
	[3.279]
Observations	530

Notes:
Dummy for treatment equals 1 for treated regions at the time of treatment.
Standard errors in parentheses.
* Significant at 10%; ** significant at 5%; *** significant at 1%.

of treatment on the treated (ATT). With the stratification matching, the range of variation of the propensity score is divided in intervals such that within each interval, treated and control units have on average the same propensity score (Becker and Ichino, 2002). The ATT is then estimated within each block:

$$\tau_q^s = \frac{\sum_{i \in I(q)} Y_i^T}{N_q^T} - \frac{\sum_{j \in I(q)} Y_j^C}{N_q^C} \tag{10.2}$$

Where $I(q)$ is the set of units in block q while N_q^T and N_q^C are the numbers of treated and control units in block q, and Y represents the outcome variable. The estimator of the ATT based on this method is then computed with expression (10.3):

$$\tau^s = \sum_{q=1}^{Q} \tau_q^s \frac{\sum_{i \in I(q)} D_i}{\sum_{\forall_i} D_i} \tag{10.3}$$

Where the weight for each block is given by the corresponding fraction of treated units, and Q is the total number of blocks. The matching estimator computes the average difference in the outcome of interest (share of new firms) between the treatment and control group.

We observe the effect of the treatment in the variation in the share of new firms in the region from pre-treatment ($t = -2$) to post-treatment ($t = 3$, $t = 5$ and $t = 7$). The main argument for this time difference is that we need at least three years to observe any effect of a new school on new firm formation, since it takes at least three years for a graduate student to leave the school with a bachelor degree. There is a chance of spin-off created by results of R&D performed in these institutions, for which a time period is also required.

We compare municipalities where there was a new institution with two control groups: group A is municipalities where the number of institutions is zero and remains zero during the entire time of the study; group B is municipalities where the number of institutions is different from zero and remains constant. We then distinguish these effects in several sectors: knowledge-based firms and low-technology manufacturing. In addition, we try to separate out the effect on high-technology manufacturing, ICT and knowledge-intensive services. The results are presented in Tables 10.4 to 10.7.

In Table 10.4, we have used as outcome variables the difference in share of new firms in the sample. We observe positive coefficients five years after the treatment when we compare the treated group with the control group

Table 10.4 *Effect of a new higher education institution on firm entry in regions – ATT estimation with the stratification matching method*

	No. treated	No. control	ATT	Std. error
Difference in the share of new firms between $t = 3$ and $t = -2$				
Control group A+B	15	441	−2.176	1.448
Control group A	13	406	−2.806	2.125
Control group B	13	37	0.087	2.185
Difference in the share of new firms between $t = 5$ and $t = -2$				
Control group A+B	15	441	0.115	1.799
Control group A	13	406	−1.247	1.995
Control group B	13	37	6.511*	2.036
Difference in the share of new firms between $t = 7$ and $t = -2$				
Control group A+B	15	441	−1.489	2.146
Control group A	13	406	−2.712	2.593
Control group B	13	37	2.436	2.319

Notes:
ATT = average treatment effect on the treated.
* Significant at 10%; ** significant at 5%; *** significant at 1%.
Group A = municipalities with number of institutions equal to zero.
Group B = municipalities with number of institutions constant and different from zero.

B (group with constant and positive number of universities). This means that for general manufacturing firms, the creation of a new university in a region generated an increase of 6.5 per cent in the share of new firms five years after the entrance of a new higher education institution. All other estimations provided insignificant results. These results mean that there is no significant difference in the rates of new firm entry between treated municipalities and the control groups, when considering the manufacturing sectors.

In Table 10.5, we present the results for knowledge-based firms. We observe that the creation of new universities has a positive impact on the entry of firms in knowledge-related activities. This positive effect is observed in the differences in the share of new firms three and five years after the treatment. When we use both control groups together, we obtain an effect of 21 and 24 per cent, which increases when we compare only with group A (with no universities), where the effect rises to 30 per cent and 33 per cent. Comparing with control group B provided insignificant results. For the difference in the share of new knowledge-based firms seven years after treatment, we observe an increase of 27 per cent when using both control groups, but this impact is not visible when comparing separately

Table 10.5   Effect of a new higher education institution on the entry of knowledge-based firms in regions – ATT estimation with the stratification matching method

	No. treated	No. control	ATT	Std. error
Difference in the share of new firms between $t = 3$ and $t = -2$				
Control group A+B	15	441	23.862*	13.069
Control group A	13	406	30.338*	17.132
Control group B	15	35	166.945	120.570
Difference in the share of new firms between $t = 5$ and $t = -2$				
Control group A+B	15	441	26.739**	13.286
Control group A	13	406	33.068**	15.715
Control group B	15	35	172.001	118.146
Difference in the share of new firms between $t = 7$ and $t = -2$				
Control group A+B	15	441	27.014*	16.047
Control group A	13	406	–	–
Control group B	13	37	321.946	225.462

Notes:
ATT = average treatment effect on the treated.
* Significant at 10%; ** significant at 5%; *** significant at 1%.
Group A = municipalities with number of institutions equal to zero.
Group B = municipalities with number of institutions constant and different from zero.

with control groups A and B. Access to external knowledge sources is important for firms' innovative activity. Thus we would expect sectors that are more dependent on new knowledge to benefit more from locating near a university. According to Audretsch et al. (2004), younger firms are more likely to locate closer to universities with a high number of students. These results reflect this tendency and provide evidence of the role of higher education institutions in the shift towards knowledge-based sectors, visible in municipalities where a new university was created. This result is strengthened when we compare the treated group with municipalities that have no higher education institutions, suggesting once more that universities do make a difference to make this shift to knowledge-based sectors.

The opposite effect is observed when we focus only on low-technology firms, as can be seen in Table 10.6. All estimations revealed a negative and significant coefficient, showing a negative impact of new higher education institutions on entry of firms in these sectors. There is evidence that low-technology sectors benefit less from locating close to a university, since they are less likely to use it as a source of knowledge and as a cooperation partner (Faria et al., 2007). These results are also in agreement with a transfer towards the 'new economy'. The decrease of entry in low-

Table 10.6   *Effect of a new higher education institution on the entry of low-technology firms in regions – ATT estimation with the stratification matching method*

	No. treated	No. control	ATT	Std. error
Difference in the share of new firms between $t = 3$ and $t = -2$				
Control group A+B	15	441	−3.989***	1.010
Control group A	15	407	−3.484***	1.071
Control group B	15	35	−4.723***	1.461
Difference in the share of new firms between $t = 5$ and $t = -2$				
Control group A+B	15	441	−3.190**	1.574
Control group A	15	407	−3.725**	1.599
Control group B	15	35	0.792	1.620
Difference in the share of new firms between $t = 7$ and $t = -2$				
Control group A+B	15	441	−4.589***	1.914
Control group A	15	407	−4.502**	2.106
Control group B	13	37	−2.788	2.230

Notes:
ATT = average treatment effect on the treated.
* Significant at 10%; ** significant at 5%; *** significant at 1%.
Group A = municipalities with number of institutions equal to zero.
Group B = municipalities with number of institutions constant and different from zero.

technology sectors is stronger in regions where a new university is created, when compared with others. Again, these results suggest that higher education institutions have a role in the change of economic activity in municipalities.

We try to distinguish if entry of knowledge-based firms is more focused on high technology activities, ICT, or knowledge-intensive services, by dividing our sample into these three sectors. The results obtained are illustrated in Table 10.7. In the knowledge-intensive services sample, we obtain a positive effect in the difference of the share of new firms between $t = 5$ and $t = -2$, when comparing the treated group with control group B. Thus, we observe a 9 per cent increase in the entry of firms in knowledge-intensive services for the treated group five years after treatment, when compared with regions with a constant number of universities. This may be a combination of short- and long-term effects, on the one hand a consequence of firms in services sectors starting their activity to serve the needs of a new institution in the municipality, and on the other hand some firms in consulting businesses coming out of faculty members and/or students from the institutions. All the other estimations lead to insignificant results. These results are unexpected; we were expecting an effect on entry of ICT firms,

Table 10.7   Effect of a new higher education institution on the entry of different knowledge-based sectors – ATT estimation with the stratification matching method

	No. treated	No. control	ATT	Std. error
High-tech firms				
Difference in the share of new firms between $t = 3$ and $t = -2$				
Control group A+B	15	441	−0.138	17.746
Control group A	15	407	2.997	20.439
Control group B	15	35	−	−
Difference in the share of new firms between $t = 5$ and $t = -2$				
Control group A+B	15	441	−4.219	19.251
Control group A	15	407	−3.649	13.738
Control group B	15	35	−	−
Difference in the share of new firms between $t = 7$ and $t = -2$				
Control group A+B	15	441	−13.088	20.797
Control group A	15	407	−13.080	22.898
Control group B	15	35	−	−
ICT firms				
Difference in the share of new firms between $t = 3$ and $t = -2$				
Control group A+B	15	441	2.857	13.507
Control group A	15	407	5.983	13.647
Control group B	15	35	−	−
Difference in the share of new firms between $t = 5$ and $t = -2$				
Control group A+B	15	441	−3.271	9.999
Control group A	15	407	0.146	11.467
Control group B	15	35		
Difference in the share of new firms between $t = 7$ and $t = -2$				
Control group A+B	15	441	−7.626	9.507
Control group A	15	407	−3.842	11.139
Control group B	13	37	−	−
Knowledge-intensive service firms				
Difference in the share of new firms between $t = 3$ and $t = -2$				
Control group A+B	15	441	−0.997	2.697
Control group A	15	407	1.143	3.239
Control group B	15	35	3.459	6.148
Difference in the share of new firms between $t = 5$ and $t = -2$				
Control group A+B	15	441	2.778	2.879
Control group A	15	407	5.396	3.388
Control group B	13	37	9.942***	3.868
Difference in the share of new firms between $t = 7$ and $t = -2$				
Control group A+B	15	441	0.785	3.135
Control group A	15	407	1.558	3.272
Control group B	13	37	8.489	7.675

Table 10.7   (continued)

Notes:
ATT = average treatment effect on the treated.
* Significant at 10%; ** significant at 5%; *** significant at 1%.
Group A = municipalities with number of institutions equal to zero.
Group B = municipalities with number of institutions constant and different from zero.

at least in the short run, entering by using the opportunity to serve the needs of the new institutions in the municipality. One of the explanations for this is that we decrease the number of firms entering, the number of observations in the sample, which does not allow us to observe any effect.

The results give partial support for hypothesis 1, since the impact of a new higher education institution will affect new firm entry only in certain sectors, and provide support for hypothesis 2, given that we obtained different results when differentiating the sector.

CONCLUDING REMARKS

In this chapter we determined the impact of the creation of new higher education institutions in municipalities on the subsequent levels of new firm entry. We studied this effect making use of the first-differences and propensity score matching, appropriate to the study of policy analysis, to capture the effect of an increase in the number of universities in a municipality on the levels of new firm entry, and explain differences between the treatment and the control groups. We compare municipalities where there was an increase in the number of universities with municipalities that have no universities throughout the entire time period and with municipalities with a constant number of universities. We find that these three groups (the treatment and two control groups) have different patterns of new firm entry throughout time. Estimations of the averaged treatment effect reveal a positive impact of the creation of new universities in the lagged share of new firm entry in knowledge-intensive sectors. There is a significant decrease in the entry of firms in low-technology industries in regions where a new higher education institution was created. We also observe an increase in the entry of firms in knowledge-intensive services, five years after treatment. We cannot observe any other effects when distinguishing knowledge-based activities in high-tech manufacturing, ICT and knowledge-related services, probably because of the small number of entries observed in these sectors using the municipality as the regional unit of analysis. The overall results indicate that the creation of a new higher education school in a region will contribute to the shift to a knowledge-based economy.

Our analysis contributes to the literature on the role played by universities and the regional knowledge base as sources of entrepreneurial opportunities, through the use of data allowing the application of econometric techniques for the analysis of policy and treatment effects. The identification of the structural determinants that have an impact on the growth of start-up rates, at a regional level, is useful to formulate public policies that have as objective influence the start-up activity by region. Many governments have created initiatives to foster technological commercialization, and with that purpose in mind have supported the interaction between universities and regions (Laursen and Salter, 2004). However, even without establishing formal relationships, firms and regions can benefit from the presence of a university. Our results indicate that universities enhance regional development and that less favoured regions would benefit from the establishment of a new institution. These regions can benefit not only from knowledge spillovers from the institutions, but also from the availability of more highly educated people.

NOTES

1. See Cabral and Mata (2003) for a description of the quality and coverage of the data.
2. Results available from the authors.

REFERENCES

Acs, Z., D.B. Audretsch and M.P. Feldman (1994), 'R&D spillovers and recipient firm size', *Review of Economics and Statistics*, **76** (2), 336–40.

Anselin, L., A. Varga and Z. Acs (1997), 'Local geographic spillovers between university research and high technology innovations', *Journal of Urban Economics*, **42** (3), 422–48.

Audretsch, D.B. and M.P. Feldman (2004), Knowledge spillovers and the geography of innovation, in *Handbook of Regional and Urban Economics*, Vol. 4, Amsterdam: Elsevier, pp. 2713–39.

Audretsch, D.B., E. Lehmann and S. Warning (2004), 'University spillovers: does the kind of science matter?', *Industry and Innovation*, **11** (3), 193–205.

Audretsch, D.B., E. Lehmann and S. Warning (2005), 'University spillovers and new firm location', *Research Policy*, **34** (7), 1113–22.

Audretsch, D.B. and P.E. Stephan (1996), 'Company-scientist locational links: the case of biotechnology', *The American Economic Review*, **86** (3), 641–52.

Bania, N., R.W. Eberts and M.S. Fogarty (1993), 'Universities and the start-up of new companies: can we generalise from Route 128 and Silicon Valley?', *The Review of Economics and Statistics*, **75**, 761–66.

Baptista, R. and J. Mendonça (2007), 'Proximity to knowledge sources and the location of knowledge based start-ups', Workshop on Agglomeration and Growth in Knowledge-based Societies, Kiel Institute for the World Economy, Kiel, Germany.

Baptista, R. and M.T. Preto (2006), 'Entrepreneurship and industrial re-structuring: what kinds of start-ups matter most for job creation?', Discussion Paper 06/06, Centre for Innovation, Technology and Policy Research, IN+, Instituto Superior Técnico, Technical University of Lisbon, Portugal.

Baptista R. and P. Swann (1999), 'A comparison of clustering dynamics in the US and UK computer industries', *Journal of Evolutionary Economics*, **9** (3), 373–99.

Baum, J.A.C. and O. Sorenson (eds) (2003), *Advances in Strategic Management: Geography and Strategy*, Vol. 20, Greenwich, CT: JAI Press.

Becker, S.O. and A. Ichino (2002), 'Estimation of average treatment effects based in propensity scores', *Stata Journal*, **2** (4), 358–77.

Cabral, L.M.B. and J. Mata (2003), 'On the evolution of the firm size distribution: facts and theory', *American Economic Review*, **93** (4), 1075–90.

Capello, R. (2002), 'Entrepreneurship and spatial externalities: theory and measurement', *The Annals of Regional Science*, **36** (3), 387–402.

Caraça, J., P. Conceição and M.V. Heitor (2000), 'Towards a public policy for the research university in Portugal', *Higher Education Policy*, **13** (2), 181–201.

Cohen, W.M. and D.A. Levinthal (1989), 'Innovation and learning: the two faces of R&D', *The Economic Journal*, **99** (397), 569–96.

Correia, F., A. Amaral and A. Magalhães (2002), 'Public and private higher education in Portugal: unintended effects of deregulation', *European Journal of Education*, **37** (4), 457–72.

Dehejia, R.H. and S. Wahba (2002), 'Propensity score-matching methods for nonexperimental causal studies', *The Review of Economics and Statistics*, **84** (1), 151–61.

Faria, P., F. Lima and R. Santos (2007), 'Cooperation in innovation: empirical evidence from an innovation survey', *Academy of Management, Annual Meeting*, Philadelphia, USA.

Feldman, M.P. (2000), 'Location and innovation: the new economic geography of innovation', in G. Clark, M.P. Feldman and M. Gertler (eds), *Oxford Handbook of Economic Geography*, Oxford: Oxford University Press.

Figueiredo, O., P. Guimarães and D. Woodward (2000), 'Home-field advantage: location decisions of Portuguese entrepreneurs', *Journal of Urban Economies*, **52** (2), 341–61.

Fisher, M.M. and A. Varga (2003), 'Spatial knowledge spillovers and university research: evidence from Austria', *The Annals of Regional Science*, **37** (2), 303–22.

Fritsch, M. (2001), 'Cooperation in regional innovation systems', *Regional Studies*, **35** (4), 297–307.

Henderson, R., A.B. Jaffe and M. Trajtenberg (1998), 'Universities as a source of commercial technology: a detailed analysis of university patenting, 1965–1988', *Review of Economics and Statistics*, **80** (1), 119–27.

Horta, H. (2008), 'On improving the university research base: the Technical University of Lisbon case in perspective', *Higher Education Policy*, **21** (1) 123–46.

Jaffe, A. (1989), 'Real effects of academic research', *The American Economic Review*, **79** (5), 957–69.

Klepper, S. (2002), 'The capabilities of new firms and the evolution of the US auto-mobile industry', *Industrial and Corporate Change*, **11** (4), 645–66.

Laursen, K. and A. Salter (2004), 'Searching high and low: what types of firms use universities as a source of innovation?', *Research Policy*, **33** (8), 1201–15.

Lee, S., R. Florida and Z. Acs (2004), 'Creativity and entrepreneurship: a regional analysis of new firm formation', MPI, Discussion Papers on Entrepreneurship, Growth and Public Policy 1704.

Lerner, J. (2005), 'The universities and the start-up: lessons from the past two decades', *Journal of Technology Transfer*, **30** (1/2), 49–56.

Mazzoneli, R. and R.R. Nelson (2007), 'Public research institutions and economic catch-up', *Research Policy*, **36** (10), 1512–28.

OECD (2002), *Science, Technology and Industry*, Paris: Organisation for Economic Co-operation and Development.

Rosenbaum, P. and D. Rubin (1983), 'The central role of the propensity score in observational studies for causal effects', *Biometrika*, **70** (1), 41–55.

Scott, J.T. (2003), 'Absorptive capacity and the efficiency of research partnerships', *Technology Analysis and Strategic Management*, **15** (2), 247–53.

Sorenson, O. and G. Audia (2000), 'The social structure of entrepreneurial activity: geographic concentration of footwear production in the U.S., 1940–1989', *American Journal of Sociology*, **106** (2), 324–62.

Spencer, J.W. (2001), 'How relevant is university-based scientific research to private high-technology firms? a United States–Japan comparison', *Academy of Management Journal*, **44** (2), 432–40.

Stahlecker, T. and K. Koschatzky (2004), 'On the significance of geographical proximity for the structure and development of newly founded knowledge inten-sive business service firms', Working Papers Firms and Regions, No. R2/2004, Fraunhofer Institute.

Stuart, T.E. and O. Sorenson (2003), 'The geography of opportunity: spatial heterogeneity in founding rates and the performance of biotechnology firms', *Research Policy*, **32** (2), 229–53.

Varga, A. (2000), 'Local academic knowledge transfers and the concentration of economic activity', *Journal of Regional Science*, **40** (2), 289–309.

Zucker, L., M.R. Darby and J. Armstrong (1998), 'Intellectual human capital and the birth of U.S. biotechnology enterprises', *The American Economic Review*, **88** (1), 290–306.

Zucker, L., M.R. Darby and J. Armstrong (2002), 'Commercializing knowledge: university science, knowledge capture and firm performance in biotechnology', *Management Science*, **48** (1), 138–53.

APPENDIX: SECTORS CONSIDERED (OECD, 2002)

High-technology Industries

- Aircraft and spacecraft (35.3)
- Pharmaceuticals (24.4)
- Office and computing machinery (30)
- Radio, TV and communication equipment (32)
- Medical, precision and optical equipment (33)

Medium-high-technology Industries

- Chemicals excluding pharmaceuticals (24 excp. 24.4)
- Machinery and equipment (29)
- Electrical machinery and apparatus (34)
- Motor vehicles and trailers (34)
- Railroad and transport equipment (352 + 359)

Medium-low-technology Industries

- Coke, refined petroleum products and nuclear fuel (23)
- Rubber and plastic services (25)
- Other non-metallic mineral products (26)
- Basic metals (27)
- Fabricated metal products except machinery and equipment (28)
- Building and repairing of ships and boats (351)

Low-technology Industries

- Food products, beverages and tobacco (15–16)
- Textile, textile products, leather and footware (17–19)
- Wood, pulp, paper, paper products, printing and publishing (21–22)
- Manufacturing and recycling (21–22)

Information and Communication Technologies Industries (ICT)

- Office and computing machinery (30)
- Radio, TV and communication equipment (32)
- Medical, precision and optical equipment (33)
- Post and Communication (64)
- Computer and related activities (72)

Knowledge-based industries (KBE)

- High-technology industries: Aircraft and spacecraft (35.3) + pharmaceuticals (24.4) + Office and computing machinery (30) + Radio, TV and communication equipment (32) + Medical, precision and optical equipment (33)
- Medium-high-technology: Chemicals excluding pharmaceuticals (24 excp. 24.4) + Machinery and equipment (29) + Electrical machinery and apparatus (34) + motor vehicles and trailers (34) + Railroad and transport equipment (352 + 359)
- Post and communication (64)
- Finance and insurance (65–67)
- Business services (71–74)

11. Cooperation with universities and research institutions for corporate entrepreneurship activities: the influence of the technological intensity of the environment

Ángela González-Moreno and
Francisco J. Sáez-Martínez

INTRODUCTION

Entrepreneurship research has primarily been concerned with the start-up of new firms, being traditionally viewed as an individual-level activity related to the creation of new organizations. However, entrepreneurship has recently become accepted as a firm-level phenomenon (Teng, 2007), which is of relevance to managers regardless of the size and age of their organization. The notion of corporate entrepreneurship (CE) extends the idea of being bold, proactive and aggressive to established firms and can be defined as 'the sum of a company's innovation, renewal and venturing efforts' (Zahra, 1995, p. 227). CE is therefore defined as entrepreneurship activities within an existing organization.

Innovation is the most common and important aspect of CE (Covin and Miles, 1999). Innovation activities have often emphasized research and development (R&D) work leading to technological novelties, with academics traditionally paying attention to high-technology sectors, while largely neglecting or underestimating innovations in low- and medium-technology industries. CE activities have a high degree of risk, and firms try to improve the odds of innovation through various approaches, with one example being the formation of R&D alliances to carry out joint research (Hagedoorn, 1993). In R&D alliances, firms can share costs and risks, as well as achieve economies of scale in research (Deeds and Hill, 1996). There is growing interest in cooperative arrangements for innovation in the literature, and innovation is seen as becoming increasingly distributed as fewer firms are able to 'go it alone' in technological development

(Tether, 2002, p. 947). This is particularly important for firms located in low- and medium-technology industries who look for cooperation in the absence of formal R&D activities on their own part.

High-technology sectors are associated with high technological opportunities and firms in these types of industries are expected to be more frequent innovators than those in low-technology sectors. Tether (2002) found that high-technology firms are more likely than other firms to cooperate with regard to innovation. However, the relationship between the sector and the motivation of firms for cooperation still remains unclear. One open question is whether the firm's innovation strategy influences its proclivity to pursue external alliances, and whether there is a different pattern of cooperation regarding the technological intensity of the industry in which the firm operates. This chapter intends to fill this gap in the literature.

Firms benefit from entering into cooperative arrangements regarding innovation with different types of organizations. However, there is a risk in losing one's distinctive competencies through collaboration, as partners can appropriate firm-specific knowledge (Hamel, 1991). Bercovitz and Feldman (2007) suggest that universities are preferred partners when there are concerns about the perceived ability to fully appropriate the results of R&D investments. For the purpose of this chapter, we analyse the cooperation arrangements with universities and research institutions (U&RI), as both are important contributors to the supply of new technological knowledge. The growing level of activity at the university–industry interface makes it imperative that we increase our understanding of this relationship. Although firm–university cooperative relationships have been analysed in several papers (Acosta and Modrego, 2001; Bayona et al., 2002), it has been mainly done from the university point of view (Jones-Evans and Klofsten, 1998; Azagra-Caro et al., 2006). A remaining question is if, or how, the balance a firm maintains with the R&D conducted in-house influences the firm's proclivity to pursue U&RI cooperation (Bercovitz and Feldman, 2007) and whether there is a different pattern of cooperation in low- and medium-technology sectors compared to high-technology industries. This chapter contributes to the literature by answering this question. The objective is to investigate how a firm's innovation strategy, in terms of internal focus and internal organization, influences the decision to engage in R&D cooperation with U&RI, and to analyse the main motivation for these arrangements. We also analyse whether a firm's motivation to cooperate with U&RI and its innovation strategy is different in the case of high-tech industries than in firms in low- and medium-technology sectors. In doing so, we investigate the determinants of cooperative arrangements with U&RI in Spain during the period between 1998 and 2000.

The chapter is organized as follows. In the next section, we present the main motivations to cooperate with U&RI identified in the literature. Next, we consider the characteristics of low- and medium-technology sectors and their relationship with R&D cooperation with U&RI. Then we present the theoretical framework used to examine the connections between a firm's innovation strategy and its cooperation with U&RI, followed by presentation of the data and the methodology. Finally, we show the results of our empirical analysis and the main conclusions that can be extracted.

LITERATURE REVIEW

Why Cooperate with Universities and Research Institutions?

A common thread throughout the literature on firm strategy and performance is the widespread use of collaboration at all stages of the innovation process in order to accelerate innovative activities (Hall and Bagchi-Sen, 2007; Terziosvki and Morgan, 2006). Furthermore, the circular or interactive model of innovation process in which multiple relationships must be established between all the departments of the firm, as well as with external agents, means that cooperative R&D is a necessary condition for a firm to survive (Häusler et al., 1994).

Hagedoorn et al. (2000) describe the literature that attempts to explain, from a theoretical point of view, why firms enter into cooperative arrangements. They point out three broad categories of literature, namely transaction costs, strategic management and industrial organization theory. Industrial organization theory typically examines the effects of firms' actions on industrial structure, social welfare and economic efficiency, whereas management theory focuses on the firm and the internal organization of its activities. Transaction costs also attempts to explain the reasons for firms to organize internally. As we have already mentioned, the objective of this chapter is to study how a firm's innovation strategy, in terms of internal focus and internal organization, influences its decision to engage in R&D cooperation with U&RI. Our focus is on the firm's organization of R&D activities, and following Combs (1999), we use the strategic management approach with transactions costs as a framework to analyse the main reasons that lead a firm to cooperate with U&RI (Table 11.1). Rather than mutually exclusive, these approaches are complementary.

Transaction costs economics (Williamson, 1985) considers cooperation agreements as a hybrid form of organization between the market and the hierarchy that facilitates carrying out R&D activities. From this theoretical point of view, firms would engage in cooperation with U&RI to

Table 11.1   Motives to cooperate with U&RI

Theoretical perspective	Motivations to cooperate with U&RI	Authors
Transaction costs	Minimize transactions costs	Williamson, 1985
	Reduce uncertainty in R&D	Hagedoorn et al., 2000
	Control of partner's opportunistic behaviour	Bercovitz and Feldman, 2007
Strategic management	Share R&D risk and cost	Hagedoorn et al., 2000 Tether, 2002 Tsang, 1998
	Access to networks	Jarillo, 1988 Bayona et al., 2002 Jones-Evans et al., 1999 Okubo and Sjöberg, 2000
	Response to innovation barriers	Greis et al., 1995
	Access to external complementary resources	Teece, 1986
		Tsang, 1998

minimize the cost of transactions involving intangible assets such as technical knowledge and to reduce and share uncertainty in R&D (Hagedoorn et al., 2000). Moreover, cooperation with U&RI reduces the risk of losing control over the results of R&D projects. R&D cooperation may enhance the potential for discovery as well as the potential for loss of control over the intellectual property generated. The outcome of joint research is often known to, and claimed by, both parties. However, universities have limited incentives to act opportunistically; therefore, they may be preferred as research partners when firms face appropriability concerns (Bercovitz and Feldman, 2007).

From a strategic management perspective, firms would cooperate with U&RI to share R&D costs and risks (Hagedoorn, 1993; Tether, 2002). Innovation activities are considered risky and costly. The risk of innovation lies in the expected result not being obtained and/or in the necessity of more financial and technological funds being required (Tsang, 1998). Firms collaborating with U&RI can also increase efficiency, power and synergy by gaining access to networks (Jarillo, 1988; Bayona et al., 2002). Collaboration with universities provides access to national and international knowledge networks. Firms can gain access to knowledge networks in which their public partners are included (Jones-Evans et al., 1999; Okubo and Sjöberg, 2000).

Another explanation from this theoretical point of view is that firms cooperating with U&RI gain access to external complementary resources such as financial, personnel and knowledge resources (Teece, 1986; Tsang, 1998). Firms seek cooperation and external partnering as a response to innovation barriers (Greis et al., 1995). These barriers usually reflect a lack of resources and the impact of regulations and other factors that make innovation difficult. In summary, from the perspective of transaction costs and strategic management, we can affirm that firms will cooperate with U&RI in order to gain access to resources (financial, organizational, etc.) that without them make innovation difficult. Firms cooperate for innovation because they do not have all the necessary resources internally. Formally, we propose:

H1:   The probability of cooperating with U&RI for CE activities is positively related to the perception of factors hampering innovation.

Innovation Strategy and Cooperation with U&RI

Innovation strategy is strongly related to cooperation, and research has found that firms that undertake R&D are more rather than less likely to enter into cooperation agreements (Fritsch and Lukas, 2001; Tether, 2002). Firms carry on R&D partly to raise their absorptive capacity; that is, their ability to learn from their environment and from the work of others (Cohen and Levinthal, 1990). The greater the importance the company gives to R&D, the greater its propensity to cooperate.

Collaboration as an innovation strategy allows individual firms lacking the specific resources or expertise to advance scientific discoveries. However, internal capability and external cooperation have been found to be complementary to each other rather than substitutes (Rothaermel, 2001). Some studies have found that higher levels of R&D spending and technological sophistication are positively associated with higher levels of cooperation (Hagedoorn, 1995). Firms with strong R&D possess the resources and technological base to offer potential partners, and, hence, are more likely to be presented with opportunities to cooperate (Rothaermel, 2001).

A firm's investment in internal R&D builds absorptive capacity that positions the firm to take advantage of external cooperation. Absorptive capacity is particularly acute when tapping university-based resources:

> When outside knowledge is less targeted to the firm's particular needs and concerns, a firm's own R&D becomes more important in permitting it to recognize the value of knowledge and to assimilate and exploit it. Sources that

produce less targeted knowledge would include university labs involved in basic research. (Cohen and Levinthal, 1990, p. 140)

Following this argument, some authors (e.g. Fontana et al., 2006; Schartinger et al., 2001) incorporate the level of R&D expenditure when analysing firm–university relationships.[1] Firms that invest heavily in R&D are likely to possess high technological capability. This capability also allows them to absorb the knowledge developed outside the firm. According to the notion of absorptive capacity, the higher the firm's internal R&D, the higher the probability of cooperation with U&RI. R&D-intensive firms might be more likely to establish cooperation with U&RI, as they are active at the technological cutting edge and thus are more dependent on innovation developments than other firms. Firms with little internal exploration will be poorly positioned to either recognize or assimilate knowledge generated externally compared with firms that are actively generating new and diverse knowledge internally (Cohen and Levinthal, 1990).

Recently, Hall and Bagchi-Sen (2007) have found that firms with high levels of R&D intensity placed significantly more importance on their own research capability, their access to university research, and their ability to enter into cooperation with universities. Similarly, Tether (2002) showed that firms engaged in R&D were more likely to have cooperative arrangements with universities. Moreover, the intensity of R&D also had an impact. Firms that undertook R&D on a continuous basis, and also spent especially highly on R&D, were more likely to cooperate with universities for innovation purposes. Therefore, we would expect the higher a firm's internal R&D, the higher its propensity to cooperate with U&RI. Based on the concept of absorptive capacity and the mentioned empirical findings, we postulate:

H2: The probability of cooperating with U&RI for CE activities is positively related to the firm's internal R&D expenses.

Laursen and Salter (2004) found that a firm's 'open' searching activity is an important determinant of university–industry collaborations. Following this line, but with a broader perspective, Fontana et al. (2006)[2] found that openness impacted on the probability of a firm to develop a research project with U&RI, as well as on the number of research agreements developed. The percentage of external expenditure of independent organizations in total firm R&D expenditure is used as a proxy for the 'openness of the firm'. Firms with a higher propensity to establish R&D collaboration with external organizations may have a greater propensity to cooperate with U&RI. This could be explained by saying that once firms have developed the skills needed to manage cross-boundary relationships, they are likely to be more willing to cooperate with other external partners (U&RI) in the development of innovation activities. We would then expect that the greater the firm's external expenses in R&D the greater its propensity to cooperate with U&RI. Formally, we propose:

H3:   The probability of cooperating with U&RI for CE activities is positively related to the firm's external R&D expenses.

Finally, other elements of innovation strategy such as the acquisition of machinery and equipment, other external knowledge (licences and patents), internal and external training for personnel, and marketing activities aimed at the introduction of the firm's innovation may also affect its propensity to cooperate with U&RI for innovation. However, we do not make any a priori hypothesis about their influence.

Technology Intensity of the Environment and R&D Cooperation with U&RI

Companies innovate and take risks in anticipation of, or in response to, their environment, which poses challenges and offers new opportunities to which organizations must respond creatively through CE (Zahra, 1993). The environment also serves as a source of ideas for innovations, and suppliers, competitors and customers provide incentives for firms' innovation and risk taking. Firms in turbulent rather than stable environments tend to be more innovative and proactive (Naman and Slevin, 1993).

Dynamic environments have been found to encourage CE behaviour (Miller et al., 1988) and organizations often respond to challenging environments, such as dynamic environments, by taking risks, innovating and exhibiting proactive behaviours (Khandwalla, 1987). According to Miller and Friesen (1982, p. 6):

> entrepreneurial firms are often found in dynamic environments [. . .] Such firms may even be partly responsible for making the environment dynamic [. . .] Because innovation prompts imitation, the more innovative the firms, the more dynamic their environments can become.

These arguments suggest a bi-directional relationship between environmental conditions and CE, which makes the latter a necessary condition to survive in dynamic environments. There are several sources of environmental dynamism, such as technological intensity (Sarkar et al., 2001).

Sectors with high technological opportunity are associated with high-technology activities, and firms in these sectors are expected to be more frequent innovators than those with low-technology activities.

Industries with greater aggregate levels of R&D intensity tend to support higher rates of firm-level innovative activity (Thornhill, 2006). The technological intensity of the environment affects innovation strategies, such as cooperative R&D. Empirically, Bayona et al. (2001) found that high-technology firms have a higher propensity to cooperate with clients. In the service industry, Tether (2002) found that high-technology firms were more likely to cooperate in innovation, as suggested in existing literature on knowledge-intensive and technology-based services (Sundbo and Gallouj, 2000). Regarding cooperation with universities, Tether (2002) found that high-technology manufacturers were more likely to have cooperation with universities than low-technology ones were. Technological intensity of the environment affects R&D cooperation in three ways. It affects partner identification, motivation for cooperative arrangements and the intensity of the relationship. For the purpose of this chapter, we focus on the motivation for cooperative arrangements with U&RI.

In the majority of cooperative partnerships, acquiring complementary knowledge is one of the main reasons to engage in these arrangements. Firms cooperate with U&RI as part of a demand for basic knowledge and for generic information, which U&RI are able to offer. Collaboration with U&RI is more focused on basic or generic knowledge (Bonaccorsi and Piccaluga, 1994; Vonortas, 1997). However, there is growing demand for applied knowledge (Gonard, 1999) and universities are modifying their approach by developing more applied research that is closely geared to the needs of business world (Santoro and Chakrabarti, 1999). Basic knowledge is always associated with high-technology industries, and in sectors with a higher complexity of technology, R&D cooperation with U&RI will be more frequent than in sectors with a lower complexity of technology (Santangelo, 2000; Orsenigo et al., 2001; Hagedoorn, 2002). Therefore, we can expect high-technology firms to have a higher propensity to cooperate with U&RI. Formally, we propose:

H4: High-technology firms will have a higher propensity to cooperate with U&RI than low- and medium-technology firms.

However, a remaining question is whether the profile of the firm that cooperates with U&RI and its motivation are different depending on the industry in which the firm operates. Increased complexity of technology and the inter-industrial nature of new technologies are motivations for strategic alliances. According to Hagedoorn (1993) the technological intensity of different sectors of industry can be expected to affect the motivation of companies to participate in strategic alliances. Strategic technology partnering in high-technology industries is strongly related to R&D cooperation, whereas in low- and medium-technology sectors, research is not a dominant feature of partnering and market access objectives prevail. Firms in low- and medium-technology industries seek cooperation in the absence of formal R&D activities on their own part. Therefore, we would expect that the motivations for cooperating with U&RI will be different regarding the technology intensity of the industry. Formally, we propose:

H5: The motivations for cooperating with U&RI for CE activities of firms located in low- and medium-technology industries are different from those of firms located in high-technology sectors.

In order to test our hypotheses, we investigate the determinants of cooperative arrangements with U&RI in Spain during the period 1998 to 2000. In the next section, we briefly explain the data and the measures of variables.

DATA – THE SPANISH CONTEXT

The Spanish innovation system is characterized by reducing expenditures on R&D and a reduction of the importance of the public sector. Spain spends about 1.07 per cent of its GDP on R&D, which is little more than half the European average of 1.86 per cent (INE, 2005). Moreover, about 80 per cent of researchers belong to public institutions, compared with an average of 50 per cent in the European Union as a whole. Only 11 per cent of Spanish firms are innovative, compared with 25 per cent in the European Union. Private R&D accounts for 0.4 per cent of Spanish GDP, while in Europe it is about 1.2 per cent (Azagra-Caro et al., 2006).

In the USA and Japan, alliances with university partners are surprisingly common. As an example, Cohen et al. (2002a) found that more than one-third of their respondent firms used public research to address existing problems. On the contrary, in Europe, and particularly in Spain, this type of collaboration is less common. Spanish U&RI have been under pressure to move closer to industry, with government seeking to encourage these institutions to undertake more industrially relevant research and to increase the competitiveness of Spanish industry through U&RI's assistance. However, there is no tradition of these types of collaboration in the Spanish economy. In 1998, 7.8 per cent of innovating firms had cooperation agreements with U&RI (INE, 1998); in 2005 only 6.12 per cent of innovating firms were cooperating with U&RI (INE, 2005).

In this chapter, information regarding the firm's innovation and cooperation activities was drawn from the Third Community Innovation Survey (CIS3) carried out by the Spanish Statistical Institute (INE) in 2000. The unit of analysis is the firm and the sampling covered both manufacturing and services, excluding firms with fewer than ten employees. Our final sample consisted of 11 778 firms: 9684 firms in low- and medium-technology industries and 2094 firms in high-technology industries. Of these, 21.7 per cent of the former and 46 per cent of the latter carried out some innovation activity.[3]

The CIS3 survey explicitly defines cooperation as active participation in joint innovation projects (including R&D) with other organizations. It does not necessarily imply that either partner derives immediate commercial benefit from the venture. Pure contracting out of work, where there is no active collaboration, is not defined as cooperation in this survey. In our sample, 2.3 per cent of low-technology firms had a cooperation arrangement with U&RI during the period 1998–2000, whereas 11.2 per cent of high-technology firms had this type of arrangement

METHODOLOGY

In this chapter, we study how the firm's innovation strategy and its motivations affect the likelihood of a firm cooperating in innovation with U&RI. Table 11.2 describes the definition of variables. Cooperation with U&RI is measured using a dummy variable that takes the value one if a firm reports that it cooperates with any university within Spain, and zero otherwise.

Regarding motivations for cooperating, we included a range of economic and internal factors that hamper innovation. The variables measure, in a Likert-type scale, the perceptions of the importance of these factors hampering innovation activities. These factors are: the economic risk of innovation, the availability and cost of finance for innovation, organizational rigidities, lack of qualified personnel, lack of information on technology and/or markets, difficulties with regulations or standards, and lack of customers' responsiveness to innovation.[4]

As we have mentioned in the theoretical foundations, both the strategic management and transaction cost economics literature consider the reduction and sharing of risk and costs as one of the main motivations for cooperating with U&RI (Hagedoorn et al., 2000; Tether, 2002). Following the literature, we also consider the lack of resources such as

Table 11.2   Definition of variables

Motivations	*Factors hampering innovations*
Risk	Importance of excessive perceived risks of innovations
Cost	Importance of costs of innovations
Financing	Importance of lack of finance for innovation
Organization	Organizational rigidity as a factor that makes innovation difficult
Personnel	Lack of qualified personnel
Technology	Lack of information on technology
Market	Lack of information on markets
Regulations	Impact of regulations or standards
Customer	Lack of customer responsiveness to new goods or services
Innovation strategy	*Distribution of innovation-related expenditure*
Internal R&D	Percentage of internal R&D
External R&D	Percentage of external R&D
Machinery	Acquisition of machinery and equipment
External knowledge	Acquisition of external knowledge such as licences, patents.
Specifications	Design functions and specifications for production or delivery
Training	Training for personnel directly related to innovation activity
Marketing	Marketing activities aimed at the introduction of firm's innovation
Size	Log of number of employees
Cooperation with U&RI	Dummy variable (1 if firm cooperates with any university or public research centre within Spain; 0 otherwise)

economic (finance) and organizational resources, qualified personnel, and information on technology and markets (Greis et al., 1995; Tsang, 1998). Additionally, we include two other factors that can motivate a firm to cooperate with U&RI: these are the negative impact of regulations or standards on innovation, and the lack of customer responsiveness to new goods or services. These two factors may inhibit a firm's capacity to innovate and, therefore, may lead them to seek cooperation with U&RI. Empirical studies have found that firms that have encountered difficulties with customers' responsiveness to innovation are more likely to engage in cooperation agreements (Tether, 2002).

Our consideration of innovation strategy, as measured in the CIS3, is operationalized by using the distribution of R&D expenses – internal versus external – including acquisition of machinery and equipment, licences and patents, training for personnel, and marketing activities aimed at the introduction of the firm's innovation. Finally, we have also included the size of the firm in our empirical analysis. Size is measured using the log of number of employees. Although there is no consensus in the literature on the relationship between organizational size and cooperation (Robertson and Gatignon, 1998), size has been considered in the literature as a factor affecting firm–U&RI relationships (Cohen et al., 2002b; Fontana et al., 2006). Larger firms are considered to have more resources to establish relationships with U&RI and we have included size in our analysis.

In order to analyse the influence of the technological intensity of the environment, we divided the sample into two sub-samples following Organisation for Economic Co-operation and Development (OECD) criteria: high-technology firms and low- and medium-technology firms. Next, the non-parametric Mann–Whitney U-test was applied. This enables us to see whether, when industry is taken as a group variable, the two resulting samples show an equal distribution with respect to the remaining variables. We compared both types of industries (high-technology and low- and medium-technology) in terms of cooperation with U&RI, motivations for cooperating and innovation strategy. This technique also enables us to test our fourth hypothesis.

Finally, three logistic regression models for cooperation with U&RI were tested, one for each type of industry and one for the whole sample. These models aim to explain the motivations of a firm for engaging in R&D cooperation with U&RI – H1 and H5 – and the impact of the firm's innovation strategy – H2 and H3. The propensity of a firm to cooperate with U&RI is then explained by its size, its motivations and its innovation strategy.

RESULTS

Table 11.3 contains the descriptive statistics: mean, standard deviation, and correlations of the whole sample.

Table 11.4 reflects the results of the Mann–Whitney U-test, which allow us to determine whether the two sub-samples are equally distributed with respect to the variables. The data reveal that among high-technology firms there is a significant presence of larger firms. Furthermore, these firms have a greater R&D capacity, as reflected by the mean values of the variables that represent their innovation strategy. High-technology firms spend more on internal R&D, external R&D, machinery and equipment, training

Table 11.3 Descriptive statistics

	Size	Risk	Cost	Financing	Organization	Personnel	Technology	Market	Regulation	Customer	Internal R&D	External R&D	Machinery	External knowledge	Specification	Training	Marketing	Cooperation U&RI
Size	1																	
Risk	-.050	1																
Cost	-.026	.704	1															
Financing	-.038	.620	.652	1														
Organization	.049	.470	.464	.432	1													
Personnel	-.024	.511	.545	.500	.565	1												
Technology	-.026	.510	.542	.501	.530	.647	1											
Market	-.033	.534	.535	.536	.517	.593	.738	1										
Regulations	.034	.475	.464	.457	.454	.467	.476	.512	1									
Customer	.013	.472	.464	.415	.430	.445	.466	.512	.498	1								
Internal R&D	.146	.155	.178	.160	.095	.116	.106	.140	.131	.132	1							
External R&D	.103	.061	.083	.047	.075	.061	.048	.062	.057	.039	.070	1						
Machinery	.025	.124	.169	.105	.089	.125	.097	.101	.087	.072	-.045	.004	1					
External knowledge	.051	.020	.033	.012	.032	.027	.008	.007	.012	.031	-.003	.009	.025	1				
Specifications	.000	.054	.068	.048	.035	.053	.045	.051	.043	.047	-.006	.001	-.009	.002	1			
Training	.043	.053	.072	.057	.066	.069	.058	.054	.048	.049	.052	.034	-.058	.047	.055	1		
Marketing	.033	.071	.088	.052	.043	.060	.055	.068	.064	.095	.054	.025	.021	.037	.060	.070	1	
Cooperation U&RI	.155	.120	.120	.127	.079	.072	.067	.101	.100	.077	.375	.185	.042	.040	.016	.029	.063	1
Mean	4.672	.928	1.151	.821	.566	.773	.642	.618	.608	.695	10.305	2.114	12.580	2.250	1.794	1.337	1.897	.213
Sd	.708	1.167	1.277	1.128	.912	1.059	.953	.941	.989	1.016	26.323	10.712	29.280	2.250	10.592	7.222	9.617	.048

Table 11.4 Mann–Whitney U-test

Variable	High (2094)	Low and Medium (9684)	Z
Cooperation U&RI	0.133 (0.340)	0.029 (0.169)	−20.247***
Size	4.789 (0.700)	4.647 (0.707)	−8.931***
Risk	1.101 (1.179)	0.890 (1.161)	−8.011***
Cost	1.355 (1.271)	1.107 (1.275)	−8.143***
Financing	0.976 (1.153)	0.788 (1.120)	−7.829***
Organization	0.603 (0.874)	0.558 (0.920)	−4.172***
Personnel	0.832 (1.032)	0.760 (1.065)	−4.254***
Technology	0.674 (0.911)	0.635 (0.962)	−3.625***
Market	0.723 (0.943)	0.595 (0.939)	−7.366***
Regulations	0.706 (0.994)	0.587 (0.986)	−6.857***
Customers	0.786 (1.010)	0.676 (1.016)	−5.987***
Internal R&D	28.534 (38.549)	6.363 (20.836)	−34.335***
External R&D	3.852 (13.262)	1.738 (10.038)	−15.695***
Machinery	12.640 (26.968)	12.567 (29.758)	−9.708***
External knowledge	0.303 (2.526)	0.247 (2.186)	−4.413***
Specifications	2.519 (11.628)	1.637 (10.348)	−10.197***
Training	2.043 (8.197)	1.184 (6.984)	−16.634***
Marketing	2.891 (10.643)	1.682 (9.367)	−15.364***

Note: *** $p < 0.001$; standard deviations appear in parentheses.

personnel for innovation activities and marketing activities directly aimed at the introduction of firms' innovations on the market. These findings reveal that firms in high-technology industries have a greater commitment to innovation.

As we can see in Table 11.4, cooperation with U&RI has a different presence in both sub-samples. Cooperation with U&RI is significantly higher in high-technology industries. This finding is consistent with the literature (Tether, 2002) and shows that dynamic, high-technology environments encourage CE behaviour (Miller et al., 1988), with organizations often responding to challenging environments, such as dynamic environments, by taking risks, innovating and exhibiting proactive behaviours such as R&D cooperation. Sectors with high technological opportunity are associated with high-technology activities and firms in these sectors are more frequent innovators than those in low-technology activities. This finding corroborates H4. Hence, we can affirm that high-technology firms have a higher propensity to cooperate with U&RI than low- and medium-technology firms.

Table 11.5   Results of the logistic regressions for cooperation with U&RI

	Model 1 TOTAL (n = 11.778)	Model 2 HIGH (n = 2.094)	Model 3 LOW & MED (n = 9.684)
	β	β	β
RISK	0.180**	0.222**	0.150*
COST	−0.034	−0.106	0.015
FINANCING	0.291***	0.234**	0.331***
ORGANIZATION	−0.022	−0.129	0.086
PERSONNEL	−0.031	−0.047	−0.023
TECHNOLOGY	−0.113	−0.066	−0.137
MARKET	0.177**	0.272**	0.108
REGULATIONS	0.055	0.014	0.069
CUSTOMER	−0.075	−0.112	−0.055
INTERNAL R&D	0.045***	0.041***	0.044***
EXTERNAL R&D	0.046***	0.042***	0.046***
MACHINERY	0.026***	0.028***	0.025***
EXTERNAL KNOWLEDGE	0.057***	0.055**	0.058***
SPECIFICATIONS	0.023***	0.020**	0.023***
TRAINING	0.016**	0.016	0.014*
MARKETING	0.032***	0.036***	0.029***
SIZE	0.960***	0.747***	1.120***
Constant	−10.682***	−8.925***	−11.741***
χ^2 model	1649.930***	466.566***	907.830***
Nagelkerke R^2	0.409	0.367	0.384
% correctly predicted	95.2	86.1	97.1

*Note: *** $p < 0.01$; ** $p < 0.05$; * $p < 0.1$.

In general, the average values of the variables that represent motivations for cooperating with U&RI (obstacles faced by firms when seeking to innovate) are greater among those firms in high-technology industries. These findings suggest that firms in high-technology sectors have a stronger motivation to cooperate with U&RI, as they have greater mean values in all the factors analysed. In summary, the two sub-samples behave differently regarding size, innovation strategy and their motivation for cooperating with U&RI, suggesting that the analysis of the effect of innovation strategy and motivation on the propensity to cooperate with U&RI should be undertaken separately.

Table 11.5 shows the results of the logistic regression for the entire sample and for both sub-samples. It shows the values of the coefficients, their levels of significance, the value of the χ^2 statistic, Nagelkerke R^2, and the percentage of cases correctly forecast. If we focus on model 1 in Table 11.5, we can observe that all the innovation strategy variables positively and significantly affect a firm's propensity to cooperate with U&RI. These results hold true for both types of industries. Moreover, models 2 and 3 show a positive and significant relationship between the firm's internal R&D expenses and its propensity to cooperate with U&RI for CE activities. Therefore, we can corroborate H2 and affirm that the probability of cooperating with U&RI for CE activities is positively related with the firm's internal R&D expenses. This finding is consistent with Cohen and Levinthal's (1990) absorptive capacity, since, in order to absorb the basic knowledge generated by U&RI, firms need to have some internal R&D initiative.

From innovation strategy variables, external R&D (β = 0.046; $p <$ 0.01), and acquisition of other external knowledge (β = 0.057; $p < 0.01$), are the factors with a higher effect on firm's propensity to cooperate with U&RI. These variables show the degree of openness of the firms regarding innovation.[5] This finding lets us confirm H3, and affirm that the probability of cooperating with U&RI for CE activities is positively related with the firm's external R&D expenses. The greater a firm's openness to innovation, the greater its probability of cooperating with U&RI. Fontana et al. (2006) also found that openness impacts the probability of a firm developing a research project with universities.

Regarding the motivations for cooperating, our results show that a lack of financial resources seems to be positively correlated with the propensity to engage in cooperation for innovation with U&RI (β = 0.291; $p < 0.01$). This finding suggests that one motive that encourages firms to cooperate with U&RI is that it is a way of obtaining funds to conduct research. This is consistent with previous literature (Bayona et al., 2002; Bonaccorsi and Piccaluga, 1994) and the result holds for both types of industries. Firms cooperate for innovations because they do not have all the necessary resources internally. Firms that have encountered difficulties in financing innovations are more likely to engage in cooperative agreements with U&RI. Moreover, U&RI also need funds to finance research, and so turn to the business world as state budgets continue to reduce.

Motivations differ if we compare both industries, which partially supports H5. In low- and medium-technology industries, finance is the main factor (β = 0.331; $p < 0.01$) that significantly affects cooperation with U&RI, and risk perception has a marginal effect (β = 0.150; $p < 0.1$). By contrast, in high-technology industries, a lack of information about the market is the factor that has a greater effect on the propensity to cooperate with U&RI (β = 0.272; $p < 0.05$). Lack of finance (β = 0.234; $p < 0.05$) and perceived risk of innovation ($\beta = 0.222$; $p < 0.05$) also have a significant and positive effect. Surprisingly, lack of information on the market is the factor with a greater effect on cooperation with U&RI in high-technology sectors. This could be explained by the fact that universities are developing more applied research nowadays, such as market research, and firms in high-tech industries are aware of this. Another possible explanation comes from the network perspective. Firms are also aware that they can gain access to the knowledge networks in which their U&RI partners are included (Jones-Evans et al., 1999). Access to these networks would also provide them with information on different markets.

In Table 11.5, we can observe that only two factors hampering innovation have a different effect in high-technology industries than in low- and medium-technology industries. Although not significant, cost and organization have a negative sign in model 2 (high-technology) and a positive sign in model 3. In high-technology firms, innovation costs and organizational rigidities reduce the probability of cooperation with U&RI. On the contrary, in less technology-intensive sectors, firms tend to mitigate these difficulties thus increasing their cooperation with public research centres. The fact that none of the factors that reduce the probability of cooperating with U&RI (negative sign) are significant, suggests that factors that hamper innovation or perceived obstacles motivate cooperation with U&RI but they do not discourage it. Hence, we have some evidence to support H1.

Finally, our findings show that the propensity to engage in cooperative arrangements for innovation with universities increases with firm size. The results show that size has a positive and significant effect on cooperation with U&RI ($\beta = 0.960$; $p < 0.01$). The greater the size of the firm, the greater its propensity to cooperate. Moreover, this positive effect is significant in both industries, although it is higher in low- and medium-technology firms ($\beta = 1.120$; $p < 0.01$) than in high-technology industries ($\beta = 0.747$; $p < 0.01$). This finding is similar to previous studies (Tether, 2002) and reflects the greater resources of larger firms, which makes them attractive to these institutions, but also the greater awareness of larger firms as to the services available from U&RI.

CONCLUSION

Corporate entrepreneurship activities have a high degree of risk, and firms try to improve the odds of innovation through cooperation with universities and research institutions. Cooperation with U&RI is particularly important for firms that operate in low- and medium-technology sectors.

These firms seek cooperation in the absence of formal R&D activities on their own part. This chapter aimed to study how a firm's innovation strategy influences the decision to engage in R&D cooperation with U&RI, and the main motivations for these arrangements. Our purpose was to answer the question of whether the balance a firm maintains with internally conducted R&D influences its propensity to cooperate with U&RI and whether there is a different pattern of cooperation regarding the technology intensity of the industry in which the firm operates.

We gathered information on the firms' innovation and cooperation activities from the Spanish CIS3. Our final sample consisted of 9684 firms in low- and medium-technology industries and 2094 firms in high-technology sectors. We carried out a non-parametric test to compare both types of industries in terms of innovation strategy and cooperation activities. Results of this analysis showed that the two sub-samples behave differently, suggesting a further and separate analysis on the factors that affect cooperation with U&RI. We tested three logit models, one for each type of industry, and one for the whole sample.

Our findings show that greater technological intensity of the environment fosters cooperation with U&RI. In sectors with higher complexity of technology, R&D cooperation with U&RI is more frequent than in sectors with lower complexity of technology. This is consistent with previous literature (Santangelo, 2000; Orsenigo et al., 2001; Hagedoorn, 2002). Our results also showed that motivations for cooperating are different in high-technology industries compared to low- and medium-technology sectors. Firms cooperate with U&RI in low-technology sectors basically because they have some difficulties financing their innovation projects. On the contrary, in high-technology industries, apart from a lack of finance for innovation, firms are motivated to cooperate with U&RI as a way of reducing the risks of CE activities and to gain information on the market. However, the innovation strategy of the firm similarly affects its propensity to cooperate with U&RI irrespective of the type of industry in which the company operates.

Internal R&D capability is critical to basic research and research-based innovation. Moreover, high R&D intensity firms seek collaboration with U&RI. Firms that devote a significant amount of resources to research and product development, while focusing on their internal research capability, would utilize U&RI in order to advance their research-based innovation (Hall and Bagchi-Sen, 2007). Cooperation with these institutions would allow these firms access to physical and technological resources. Our findings show that firms that carry out internal R&D have a greater propensity to cooperate with U&RI. This result is in accordance with the idea that internal R&D provides the capacity to absorb the knowledge generated by U&RI. Additionally, all innovation strategy factors have a positive and significant effect on cooperation, and this holds for both sub-samples. This finding supports Cohen and Levinthal's (1990) absorptive capacity. Therefore, we can affirm that companies with internal R&D capabilities have more probabilities of cooperating with U&RI irrespectively of the industry. These internal R&D initiatives provide them with the necessary capacity to recognize and take advantage of external knowledge.

Moreover, we found that firms that invest in external R&D and acquire external knowledge, have a greater propensity for cooperating with U&RI. Thus, the degree of openness of the firms regarding innovation, positively affects their cooperation activities. From our results we can conclude that the options of either carrying out internal R&D activities or acquiring them externally through purchase or cooperation are not mutually exclusive. A future line of research would be an analysis of the joint effect of internal and external innovation expenses from a configurational approach.

The propensity of carrying out R&D cooperation with U&RI depends on the size of the firm, as was previously shown (Cohen et al., 2002b). Larger firms are more likely to cooperate with U&RI. Our empirical analysis showed a significant and positive effect of size on the probability of cooperation with U&RI. This finding could also be indicating that firms have different motivations for cooperating with these institutions according to their size. We also found that size has a greater impact on the propensity to cooperate in low- and medium-technology industries. An interesting further line of research would be to investigate whether the differences in motivations considered in this chapter are maintained depending on the size of the firm. Future research should analyse the motivations and innovation strategy in each type of industry, comparing small and medium sized enterprises with large companies.

One of the limitations of our chapter is that it is cross-sectional, which means that any causality effect should be considered with caution. Future research should approach this issue from a longitudinal perspective. Longitudinal studies would be able to address causality as well as analyse the relationship between cooperation, CE activities and technology intensity of the industry more accurately. Nevertheless, the results of our research should help managers and governments (policy makers) discover or recognize the firm-level innovation strategies that favour cooperation with U&RI, as well as motivations for cooperating with these institutions. Promoting these factors will notably increase cooperation with U&RI. This interaction between firms and publicly funded knowledge institutions is an important determinant of innovation and is strongly related to economic growth and national competitiveness. Cooperation between U&RI and private firms for CE activities is a way of converting publicly funded research into commercialized innovations and productivity growth. Policy makers aiming to increase R&D cooperation between these agents should be aware that motivations on the part of the firms are different depending on the technology intensity of the industry in which they operate. However, in order to recognize and take advantage of the knowledge generated by publicly funded institutions, firms need to have some internal R&D initiatives. Therefore, policies aimed at increasing cooperation between firms and U&RI should be filled with those policies that promote the fact that firms develop R&D on their own part. Policy makers should promote internal R&D on the part of the firms. Firms without absorptive capacity will not be able to either recognize or absorb the knowledge generated by public research institutions. Governments should make an effort to increase the ability of firms to carry out their own internal R&D. These internal R&D initiatives would provide them with the necessary capacity to recognize external knowledge and the ability to take advantage of cooperation with U&RI.

ACKNOWLEDGEMENT

A previous version of this chapter was presented at the XXI RENT Conference in Cardiff. We are grateful to conference participants for their comments. Financial support from Junta de Comunidades de Castilla-La Mancha, Consejería de Educación y Ciencia, España, PAI07-0099-3219, is gratefully acknowledged.

NOTES

1. Fontana et al. (2006) provide information about the number of firm–university R&D projects, which allows them to study the determinants of the extent of firm–university collaboration.
2. In their paper, openness is considered a set of activities carried out by the firm that can be divided into three components: searching, screening and signalling.
3. In the Spanish survey – CIS3 – innovation is defined as a new or significantly improved product (goods or service) introduced into the market (product or service innovation) or the introduction within the firm of a new or significantly improved process (process innovation).
4. Following Tether (2002) we are assuming that firms have entered into cooperation to reduce these difficulties and that cooperation agreements were not themselves the source of difficulty.
5. This openness could also show a lack of internal resources to carry out innovation activities.

REFERENCES

Acosta, J. and A. Modrego (2001), 'Public financing of cooperative R&D projects in Spain: the concerted projects under the national R&D plan', *Research Policy*, **30**, 625–41.

Azagra-Caro, A., F. Archontakis, A. Gutierrez-García and I. Fernandez-de-Lucio (2006), 'Faculty support for the objectives of university–industry relations versus degree of R&D cooperation: the importance of regional absorptive capacity', *Research Policy*, **35**, 37–55.

Bayona, C., T. García-Marco and E. Huerta (2001), 'Firms' motivations for cooperative R&D: an empirical analysis of Spanish firms, *Research Policy*, **30**, 1289–307.

Bayona, C., T. García-Marco and E. Huerta (2002), 'Collaboration in R&D with universities and research centres: an empirical study of Spanish firms', *R&D Management*, **32**, 321–45.

Bercovitz, J.E.L. and M.P. Feldman (2007), 'Fishing upstream: firm innovation strategy and university research alliances', *Research Policy*, **36** (2), 930–48.

Bonaccorsi, A. and A. Piccaluga (1994), 'A theoretical framework for the evaluation of university–industry relationships', *R&D Management*, **24**, 229–47.

Cohen, W., A. Goto, A Nagata, R. Nelson and J. Walsh (2002a), 'R&D spillovers, patents and the incentives to innovate in Japan and the United States', *Research Policy*, **31**, 1349–67.

Cohen, W. and D. Levinthal (1990), 'Absorptive capacity: a new perspective on learning and innovation', *Administrative Science Quarterly*, **35**, 129–52.

Cohen, W., R. Nelson and J. Walsh (2002b), 'Links and impacts: the influence of public research on industrial R&D', *Management Science*, **48**, 1–23.

Combs, K. (1999), 'The role of information sharing in cooperative research and development', *International Journal of Industrial Organization*, **11**, 535–51.

Covin, J. and M. Miles (1999), 'Corporate entrepreneurship and the pursuit of competitive advantage', *Entrepreneurship Theory and Practice*, **23**, 47–63.

Deeds, D.L. and C.W.L Hill (1996), 'Strategic alliances and the rate of new product development: an empirical study of entrepreneurial biotechnology firms', *Journal of Business Venturing*, **11**, 41–55.

Fontana, R., A. Geuna and M. Matt (2006), 'Factors affecting university–industry R&D projects: the importance of searching, screening and signalling', *Research Policy*, **35**, 309–23.

Fritsch, M. and R. Lukas (2001), 'Who cooperates on R&D?', *Research Policy*, **30**, 297–312.

Gonard, T. (1999), 'The process of change in relationships between public research and industry: two case studies from France', *R&D Management*, **29** (2), 143–53.

Greis, N.P., M.D. Dibner and A.S. Bean (1995), 'External partnering as a response to innovation barriers and global competition in biotechnology', *Research Policy*, **24**, 609–30.

Hagedoorn, J. (1993), 'Understanding the rationale of strategic technology partnering: interorganisational modes of cooperation and sectoral differences', *Strategic Management Journal*, **14** (5), 371–85.

Hagedoorn, J. (1995), 'Strategic technology partnering during the 1980s: trends, networks, and corporate patterns in non-core technologies', *Research Policy*, **24**, 207–31.

Hagedoorn, J. (2002), 'Inter-firm R&D partnerships: an overview of major trends and patterns since 1960', *Research Policy*, **31**, 477–92.

Hagedoorn, J., A.N. Link and N.S Vonortas (2000), 'Research partnerships', *Research Policy*, **29**, 567–86.

Hall, L.A. and S. Bagchi-Sen (2007), 'An analysis of firm-level innovation strategies in the US biotechnology industry', *Technovation*, **27**, 4–14.

Hamel, G. (1991), 'Competition for competence and inter-partner learning within international strategic alliances', *Strategic Management Journal*, **12**, 83–103.

Häusler, J., H.-W. Honh and S. Lütz (1994), 'Contingencies of innovative networks: a case study of successful inter-firm R&D cooperation', *Research Policy*, **23**, 47–66.

INE (1998), 'Encuesta sobre innovación tecnológica de las empresas', available at: www.ine.es.

INE (2005), 'Encuesta sobre innovación tecnológica de las empresas', available at: www.ine.es.

Jarillo, J. (1988), 'On strategic network', *Strategic Management Journal*, **19**, 31–41.

Jones-Evans, D. and M. Klofsten (1998), 'The role of the university in the technology transfer process: a European view', *Science and Public Policy*, **25** (6), 373–80.

Jones-Evans, D., M. Klofsten, E. Anderson and D. Pandya (1999), 'Creating a bridge between university and industry in small European countries: the role of the Industrial Liaison Office', *R&D Management*, **29** (1), 47–56.

Khandwalla, P.N. (1987), 'Generators of pioneering innovative management: some Indian evidence', *Organization Studies*, **8** (1), 39–59.

Laursen, K. and A. Salter (2004), 'Searching low and high: what types of firms uses universities as a source of innovation?', *Research Policy*, **33**, 1201–15.

Miller, D., C. Droge and J. Toulouse (1988), 'Strategic process and content as mediators between organizational context and structure', *Academy of Management Journal*, **31**, 544–69.

Miller, D. and P.H. Friesen (1982), 'Innovation in conservative and entrepreneurial firms: two models of strategic momentum', *Strategic Management Journal*, **3**, 1–25.

Naman, J.L. and D.P. Slevin (1993), 'Entrepreneurship and the concept of fit: a model and empirical tests', *Strategic Management Journal*, **14**, 137–53.

Okubo, Y. and C. Sjöberg (2000), 'The changing pattern of industrial scientific research collaboration in Sweden', *Research Policy*, **29** (1), 81–98.

Orsenigo, L., F. Pammolli and M. Riccaboni (2001), 'Technological change and network dynamics. Lessons from the pharmaceutical industry', *Research Policy*, **30**, 485–508.

Robertson, T. and H. Gatignon (1998), 'Technology development mode: a transaction cost conceptualisation', *Strategic Management Journal*, **19**, 515–31.

Rothaermel, F. (2001), 'Complementary assets, strategic alliances, and the incumbent's advantage: an empirical study of industry and firm effects in the biopharmaceutical industry', *Research Policy*, **30** (8), 1235–51.

Santangelo, G.D. (2000), 'Corporate strategic technological partnerships in the European information and communications technology industry', *Research Policy*, **29** (9), 1015–31.

Santoro, M.D. and A.K. Chakrabarti (1999), 'Building industry–university research centres: some strategic considerations', *International Journal of Management Reviews*, **1** (3), 225–44.

Sarkar, M.B., R.A.J. Echambadi and J.S. Harrison (2001), 'Alliance entrepreneurship and firm market performance', *Strategic Management Journal*, **22**, 701–11.

Schartinger, D., C. Rammer, M.M. Fischer and J. Fröhlich (2001), 'Knowledge interactions between universities and industry in Austria: sectoral patterns and determinants', *Research Policy*, **31** (3), 303–28.

Sundbo, J. and F. Gallouj (2000), 'Innovation as a loosely coupled system in services', *International Journal of Services Technology and Management*, **1** (1), 15–36.

Teece, D. (1986), 'Profiting from technological innovation: implications for integration, collaboration, licensing and public policy', *Research Policy*, **15**, 285–305.

Teng, B. (2007), 'Corporate entrepreneurship activities through strategic alliances: a resource-based view approach toward competitive advantage', *Journal of Management Studies*, **33** (1), 119–42.

Terziosvki, M. and J.P. Morgan (2006), 'Management practices and strategies to accelerate the innovation cycle in the biotechnology industry', *Technovation*, **36**, 545–52.

Tether, B.S. (2002), 'Who co-operates for innovation, and why: an empirical analysis', *Research Policy*, **31**, 947–67.

Thornhill, S. (2006), 'Knowledge, innovation and firm performance in high- and low-technology regimes', *Journal of Business Venturing*, **21**, 687–703.

Tsang, E. (1998), 'Motives for strategic alliances: a resource-based perspective', *Scandinavian Journal of Management*, **14** (3), 207–21.

Vonortas, N.S. (1997), *Cooperation in Research and Development*, Boston, MA: Kluwer Academic Publishers.

Williamson, O.E. (1985), *The Economic Institutions of Capitalism*, New York: Free Press.

Zahra, S.A. (1993), 'A conceptual model of entrepreneurship as firm behaviour: a critique and extension', *Entrepreneurship: Theory and Practice*, **17**, 319–40.

Zahra, S.A. (1995), 'Corporate entrepreneurship and company performance: the case of management leveraged buyouts', *Journal of Business Venturing*, **10**, 225–47.

12. ICT-related small firms with different collaborative network structures: different species or variations on a theme?

Vinit Parida and Mats Westerberg

INTRODUCTION

Small firms make up the backbone of the modern economy and are an important source of employment and growth (Storey, 1994). Thus, it is essential to understand more about them and how they become successful. As these firms constitute a large heterogeneous group, we have in this study focused on a single industry, namely ICT (information and communication technology) related small firms. These firms deal with technologically oriented products or services, such as developing software, mobile functions and so on. This industry is interesting for several reasons. First, small firms operating in this high-tech industry have the potential to work globally, since many tools in the ICT-related firms tend to be the same all over the world. Second, as they represent a high growth potential industry, they have the potential to generate a higher level of employment and economic development compared with other industries (Delmar et al., 2003). Third, as these firms operate in a dynamic environment, securing their source of competitiveness holds special and urgent value. Finally, many ICT-related small firms are important partners to other firms, which indicates that securing success for this industry can also benefit other firms. Taken together, ICT-related small firms are the forerunners in developing global markets that benefit both themselves and other firms they work with. Investigating how these firms operate and achieve competitive advantage is therefore interesting for both researchers and practitioners.

Even if heterogeneity is decreased, all ICT-related small firms are certainly not similar. An important aspect that may separate different firms in this industry from each other is how they choose to collaborate with other firms. In Sweden, some 60 per cent of small firms have some kind of organized collaboration with at least one other firm and another 15 per cent have some sort of collaboration with another type of partner (Westerberg and Ylinenpää, 2003). Therefore, a firm's collaborative network structure seems to be a potential construct for reducing heterogeneity. Traditionally, network structure represents 'the pattern of relationships that are engendered from the direct and indirect ties between actors' (Hoang and Antoncic, 2003, p. 166). However, this study focuses only on those ties or relationships that are *strategic* (contributing to the firm's revenue) and *repetitive* (represented by continuous interactions) in nature. By doing so, we only focus on those relationships that have important value for the small firms. In addition, a firm's collaborative network structure can have three dimensions, namely the type of partner (for example, small firms, large firms, universities or government agencies); the type of relationship with the partner (supplier, customer or other) and finally, the number of relations in each category. For different structures of partner setup, other characteristics of the firm, and also how these characteristics are linked to performance, may differ. Therefore, this study uses collaborative network structure as a basis for the analysis and investigates whether firms displaying dissimilar collaborative network structures also display differences in other areas. The characteristics we touch upon in this study are networking capability, ICT capability and entrepreneurial orientation. The motivation for selecting each of these constructs is presented next.

The first differentiating characteristic in our study is 'entrepreneurial orientation' (EO). EO is also our chosen dependent variable because it has been shown to have a stable relation to firm performance in several studies and when environmental dynamism is higher, this link tends to be greater (Wiklund, 1999; Lumpkin and Dess, 1996; Walter et al., 2006). Thus, by being proactive, risk taking and innovative, a small firm can achieve competitive advantage in a more dynamic environment (Covin and Slevin, 1991). Regarding the level of EO and network structure, it would be interesting to explore whether the level of EO differs for different types of collaborative networks and whether there are different links to EO from other firm characteristics, depending on the collaborative network structure.

The 'other characteristics' that we study as independent variables are general characteristics such as firm age, firm size (number of employees and turnover), and firm capabilities. Regarding firm capabilities, we address two specific capabilities, namely networking and ICT (information and communication technology) capability. Networking capability is defined as a firm's 'ability to develop and utilize inter-organizational relationships to gain access to various resources held by other actors' (Walter et al., 2006, p. 542). Thus, having ample networking capability seems to be the key to getting a functional collaborative network. Firms with previous experience of networking can be more capable than firms without any previous experience (Gulati et al., 2000). Since we study small firms operating in a high-technology industry, we expect them to be extensive users of networking and also to have significant networking capability (Hagedoorn et al., 2006). Furthermore, it has been observed that high networking capability leads to being more entrepreneurial and achieving better performance (Walter et al., 2006). Furthermore, as the firms under study are ICT-related small firms, we expect many of them to be high on ICT capability. According to Matlay and Addis (2003), ICT capability can be broadly defined as firm's ability to use a wide array of technology, ranging from database programs to local area networks. In simpler terms, ICT capability is a firm's ability to strategically use information and communication technology in their business activities such as use of emails, websites, e-commerce, web conferencing, intranet, extranet and other similar functions. By limiting our study to strategically used ICT capability, we stress high level ICT usages that can lead to competitive advantage (Johannessen et al., 1999). For small firms, ICT capability can be especially valuable, as ICT can bring many advantages at relatively low cost. By a rather low investment in ICT, a small firm can achieve a high degree of effectiveness and innovativeness (Venkatraman, 1994; Gago and Rubalcaba, 2007). It will therefore be interesting to observe the level of networking and ICT capability for small firms with different collaborative network structures and also how these capabilities are related to EO.

Based on the above background, the purpose of this study is to investigate how different collaborative network structures of ICT-related small firms can be linked to ICT and networking capabilities and entrepreneurial orientation, both in terms of absolute levels and in terms of relations between capabilities and entrepreneurial orientation. This purpose can be further sub-divided into three research questions:

- RQ1: Can ICT-related small firms be differentiated based on their collaborative network structure?
- RQ2: Do ICT-related small firms with dissimilar collaborative network structures also have dissimilarity in terms of their ICT capability, networking capability and entrepreneurial orientation?
- RQ3: Does the influence of ICT capability and network capability on entrepreneurial orientation differ based on an ICT-related small firm's collaborative network structure?

This study has two main contributions. First, it aims to differentiate small firms based on their collaborative network structure and so will contribute towards the literature of 'inter-organization network research' (Kale et al., 2002; Anand and Khanna, 2000; Powell et al., 1996). Second, our study does not only relate inter-firm networking to entrepreneurial orientation, but also relates network structure to entrepreneurial orientation, both directly in terms of differences in absolute levels and indirectly in terms of relations. Therefore, this chapter also contributes towards the entrepreneurship literature (Lumpkin and Dess, 1996; Wiklund, 1999; Covin and Slevin, 1991). This study is divided into five sections. After the introduction, we discuss the theoretical background of this study. In the third section, the methodological aspects are presented followed by the empirical results in the fourth section. Finally, in the last section we discuss the results and offer some conclusions regarding the research.

LITERATURE REVIEW

Why do small firms network? What are the underlying reasons for it? When reviewing the literature, there were several answers offered. When boiling it down, it seems the main benefits of networking for small firms come in the form of access to technical or commercial resources (Hoang and Antoncic, 2003; Baum et al., 2000), enhanced organizational learning (Kale et al., 2002; Oliver, 2001) and innovation (Pittaway et al., 2004; Powell et al., 1996). During the start-up phase, a small firm's network can provide it with external knowledge and guidance. Networking also helps small firms to get noticed and recognized in their respective industry. According to Stuart (2000), this recognition or legitimacy has links to better performance. The inter-firm relationships can also facilitate organizational learning. However, assuming that learning within the organizational structure is complex, it will be even more complex in a network setting. Thus firms also have to be capable of identifying and using external knowledge for learning, which closely relates to the concept of 'absorptive capability', that is, a firm's ability and capacity to identify and utilize external knowledge for commercial success (Cohen and Levinthal, 1990). According to Oliver (2001), learning from networking is not linear throughout the life cycle of small firms. The level of learning differs based on the experience and needs of the firms. Finally, one of the most critical outcomes from networking results in innovations. According to Powell et al. (1996), the locus of innovation is no longer within individual firms but in their network. When firms collaborate, new ideas emerge because each firm brings its unique competence to the network. The chances of a successful innovation increase when it is developed within a network as it tends to be more technologically and economically viable (Pittaway et al., 2004). Now that we have established the main benefits from networking, we focus on the firm's collaborative network structure.

Collaborative Network Structure

Networking is considered to be an important activity by both small and larger firms (Oliver, 2001; Lorenzoni and Lipparini, 1999). However, each firm has its own unique way of collaborating with other firms, but it is still likely that we will find similarities in the collaborative network structure among a population of firms. The view of differentiating small firms based on their collaborative network structure has not been widely researched (Pittaway et al., 2004) and was motivated based on our qualitative pre-study of three small ICT-related Swedish firms (Parida and Westerberg, 2006). One of the main findings from the pre-study was the occurrence of different collaborative network structures used by the small firms. Each firm's collaborative network structure was not just limited to its networking activity, but was also linked to its entire business model and strategy. For example, one of the firms collaborating with many small firms located a long distance away invested heavily in ICT capability because the CEO believed that it was the only way the firm could maintain close functional relations with its partners.

As explained before, we examine a firm's collaborative network structure from three dimensions. First, the type of partner, which can be small firms, large firms, universities or government agencies; second, the type of relation with the partner (supplier, customer or other); and third, the number of relations in each category. In addition, we only focus on those ties or relationships that are *strategic* (contributing to the firm's revenue) and *repetitive* (continuing interactions) in nature. This results in identification of only other actors' relationships that are valuable to the focal firm.

So why is it interesting to group firms based on their collaborative network structure? According to Ostgaard and Birley (1994), looking into different network structures helps us to understand more about firms. Firms develop different network structures, because they want to have a specific strategic focus (Koch, 2004) or an innovation focus (Gemunden et al., 1996). Alternatively, they aim towards a different performance level (Baum et al., 2000). From the literature review, we found only a handful of studies that have investigated the effects of networking structure. A study by Koch (2004) examined one segment that collaborated with few companies and a software house, and another with a more complex and extensive innovation network. The results showed that negotiations, shifting positions and interaction between internal and external collaborating actors are important for network success. In another study, seven different types of technologically oriented network configurations were identified. The results showed that different network configurations have different outcomes in terms of product and process innovation (Gemunden et al., 1996). Furthermore, Ostgaard and Birley (1994) empirically supported the idea that entrepreneurial firms often formed network structures based on their strategic orientation compared to other firms. Thus, we believe that differentiating small firms based on their collaborative network structure should provide us with interesting and diverse results as indicated by previous studies.

Firms tend to have relations with various partners, such as customers, suppliers, competitors, or public organizations (universities or government institutions) (Walter et al., 2006). Let us briefly examine the main reasons for becoming involved with each partner.

Customer collaboration

According to Pittaway et al. (2004), collaborating with customers is the most favoured form of collaboration for achieving innovation. Customer involvement in the production process makes the end product closer to the firms' needs and wants (Jacob, 2006). In high-technology industries, small firms collaborate with large firms at customer level because they lack marketing capabilities. Thus through collaboration small firms are able to sell their products to a large number of customers and, according to Jacob (2006), such customer integration has direct links to market success.

Supplier collaboration

Small firms usually collaborate with suppliers with long-term plans as they commit significant resources to these forms of collaboration. Strong collaboration creates a sense of belonging and trust, which helps in motivating different actors to focus more on network goals rather than their own goal. Furthermore, as repeated transactions occur with suppliers, small firms are able to reduce the costs of production, improve the quality of products and services, increase the rate of product development, and improve the level of productivity (Bradley et al., 2006; Arend, 2006).

Partnership collaboration

This form of collaboration can involve actors or partners that don't necessarily share any direct relationships through their value chain. These actors form partnerships with different motives; for example, a university might collaborate in partnership to spread and publish knowledge of its research work. Similarly, government institutions might collaborate with firms to support regional development in the form of employment and increased taxes (Etzkowitz and Leydesdorff, 2000). Small firms can also form partnerships with larger firms to enter international markets (Audretsch and Feldman, 2003); with universities to get new and high technological knowledge (Pittaway et al., 2004); and with government institutions to gain recognition and legitimacy (Baum and Oliver, 1991).

Entrepreneurial Orientation

Entrepreneurial orientation captures the firm-level practices, decision making style and strategic orientation of an entrepreneurially oriented firm (Lumpkin and Dess, 1996). Entrepreneurial orientation is, as we have already noted, our dependant variable and proxy for competitiveness. It has been proposed that small firms operating in a turbulent business environment can achieve competitive advantage by acting entrepreneurially, which fits the firm under study (Covin and Slevin, 1991; Wiklund, 1999). EO has also shown a stable relation to firm performance and, as Madsen (2007) observed in a longitudinal study of Norwegian small and medium sized firms, there is a link between EO and better firm performance in term of employment growth.

There are five main dimensions of EO, namely innovativeness, risk-taking, proactiveness, autonomy, and competitive aggressiveness (Lumpkin and Dess, 1996), although most studies measure EO by the first three dimensions. *Innovativeness* implies a firm's willingness to support new ideas, creativity and experimentation, which will result in changing the firm's traditional business practices. *Proactiveness* is about a firm's ability to be prepared for any unexpected scenario and act at an early stage, which can help a firm to change threats into opportunities. Finally, *risk-taking* is associated with a firm's readiness to take daring actions that might lead to substantial losses. It also implies that a firm might invest in unknown ventures where outcomes are unknown but promising (Lumpkin and Dess, 1996). Many studies have supported the idea that successful entrepreneurs are highly active in networking and also achieve better growth (Lee et al., 2001). In our study, it would be interesting to investigate how ICT and networking capability link with EO for small firms with different collaborative network structures.

Network and ICT Capabilities

The previous section explains the importance of external links for achieving access to different benefits. However, this process is not simple and before firms are able to utilize external links, they need to possess and structure their own capabilities (Bougrain and Haudeville, 2002). In this study, we have focused on two seemingly important capabilities for networking and competitiveness, namely networking capability and ICT capability. According to Walter et al. (2006, p. 542), network capability is the 'firm's ability to develop and utilize inter-organizational relationships to gain access to various resources held by other actors'. They conceptualized networking capability as a multidimensional construct consisting of four components, namely coordination, relational skills, partner knowledge and internal communication. All these components are distinct but still related. For example, firms with good relationship skills will be able to get access to external knowledge that, in turn, can enhance their partner knowledge. A firm's *coordination* activities help it in synchronizing with different external partners and achieving mutual benefits. *Partner knowledge* can be important for small firms, as it allows them to better understand and utilize their relationships (Anand and Khanna, 2002). Good partner knowledge can lead to stable and long-term relationships between different actors because they clearly understand each other's needs and wants. *Relationship skills* refer to a firm's ability to maintain healthy relationships, and are an important component of networking capability as firms with such social skills are able to manage several relationships. Effective *internal communication* is the life-blood of an organization. According to Walter et al. (2006), it is important from a relationship perspective that appropriate partner information is disseminated through effective *internal communication* channels. This also enhances firms' learning ability as they are able to reduce misunderstandings and create synergies between partners (Cohen and Levinthal, 1990). These four components capture network capability to some extent, but we feel that previous authors have missed an important aspect related to the *building of new relationships*. Thus, we add a new component that is related to the building of new relationships, which refers to firms' ability to be open to new relationships with new partners. This requires firms to be proactive and to initiate the contact with a new partner. Overall, it can be assumed that firms with a high networking capability will be able to more effectively use their network compared to firms lacking such capability.

A firm with high network capability will be able to identify prospective partners, establish relationships, and utilize the relationships to build competitiveness. However, not all inter-firm relationships are beneficial as some can be difficult to manage and complex in nature (Anand and Khanna, 2000). Thus, firms with a high level of networking capability should be able to strategically position themselves in a network and form relationships with selective strategic partners (Hagedoorn et al., 2006). The ability to form and manage a partnership is important in all industries, but the relevance of such a capability is particularly high in technologically related industries. In a technological industry, the business environment is rapidly changing and this influences firms to innovate regularly, especially as many authors believe that networking can enhance a firm's ability to innovative (Pittaway et al., 2004; Powell et al., 1996). It can also provide new knowledge that can be a source of idea generation and can help it gather information to recognize entrepreneurial opportunities (Hoang and Antoncic, 2003). Thus we can visualize a strong link between network capability and EO.

Similar to networking capability, ICT capability is also an essential tool for promoting networking. In this technologically driven era, ICT capability enables firms to develop an effective communication infrastructure (Dholakia and Kshetri, 2004). From the literature review, we are able to identify three key aspects of ICT, namely for internal use (Levy et al., 2001), use for collaboration (Sarshar and Isikdag, 2004; Levy et al., 2001), and use for communication (Martin and Matlay, 2001). The use of ICT within a small firm can be at different levels and it will accordingly influence organizational skills, knowledge and competence (Caldeira and Ward, 2003). The most basic use of ICT comes in the form of lowering the cost of production, better document handling, and making the internal processes efficient (Levy et al., 2001). Small firms can also use ICT as an important tool for keeping a check on competitors and new ideas. This makes it possible for them to take calculated risks and have effective strategic planning (Fillis et al., 2003). Small firms can also use virtual teams or groupware applications through which they can be in constant communication with their collaborative partners (Sarshar and Isikdag, 2004). This leads to a continuous flow of external information, which can enhance learning for the small firm (Venkatraman, 1994). According to Ruiz-Mercader et al. (2006), when small firms use ICT they increase the individual's capacity to learn by creating knowledge through the extension of memory and effective communication. Thus, an increase in individual knowledge has a significant impact on organizational learning, which positively affects firm performance. External knowledge is important for the learning process and firms with ICT capability are able to take advantage of this opportunity. The investment required by small firms to utilize technological tools is relatively low compared to the benefits they can achieve. One important benefit involves the possibility of collaborating with several actors and therefore small firms are no longer limited because of their size but have an increased opportunity for international business and collaboration (Dholakia and Kshetri, 2004). They can achieve quicker and better performance even in the initial stages.

Some studies argue that using ICT does not necessarily lead to competitive advantage. As most of the ICT tools are readily available for all firms, they don't yield any specific advantage (Johannessen, 1994; Venkatraman, 1994). The expression 'productivity paradox' has also been used to explain this statement. However, we believe that ICT capability is important for most small firms, and it should be particularly vital for ICT-related small firms (Lee et al., 2001). According to the quantitative study by Johannessen et al. (1999), ICT is positively related to innovation and performance, which is a result of the fact that learning and change are achieved by the use of ICT in Norwegian IT companies. It can be assumed that when firms are technologically strong and have a large network, they need a good information and communication flow. This should enhance their skills of environmental scanning that would make them well informed about the external environment and better equipped to take calculative risks and act proactively. Thus, we expect that a firm's ICT capability will influence its EO and firms with high ICT capability will have a more extensive collaborative network structure.

We now go on to test whether we can find different collaborative network structures among small ICT-related firms and to see if there are links between ICT capability, networking capability and EO. In doing so, we will next outline the methodological considerations of the study.

RESEARCH METHODOLOGY

Data Collection and Sample

The research sample consisted of small firms working within the ICT sector in Sweden. The current study is mainly exploratory and is a continuation of a pre-study that was done the previous year (Parida and Westerberg, 2006). Taking the pre-study as the baseline, the studied firms' Swedish industry index code (SNI code: 72 220) was obtained. This code indicates *consultancy-related computer systems or computer software* firms. Sample firms were either manufacturing or trading with ICT products or services. When we searched on this code, we found approximately 9000 active firms, and after putting in parameters of fewer than 50 employees (i.e. small firms according to EU definition) and more than one million Swedish kronor in sales (to ensure an active firm), we ended up with 3907 active firms, which was considered as the total population. From 3907 firms, 1471 were selected for the study in the following way. First, the 3907 firms were divided into five groups based on number of employees: 885 firms have one employee, 983 have two employees, 868 have three to five employees, 473 have six to nine employees and 698 have ten to 49 employees. The goal was to achieve a total number of usable responses exceeding 300, which with a response rate of 20 per cent meant that we needed about 1500 to start with. Even though the smallest companies (in terms of employees) are interesting for study, it was not deemed appropriate that they should be sampled in relation to their actual numbers (i.e. as a random sample over the population) otherwise the vast majority of firms studied would be (small) micro firms. Therefore, a random sample of 100 were drawn from the first three categories, while the entire population was chosen for the latter two. This means that our study reflects the six to 49 employee firms to a higher degree than if we had drawn a random sample from the entire population of small firms.

Three waves of questionnaires were sent by mail during May–July 2007. Each questionnaire included three items: (1) a cover letter, (2) a business reply envelope and (3) an eight-page questionnaire. The cover letter was addressed to the chief executive officer (CEO) of the firm, explaining the motivation for this study. As the unit of analysis was at firm level, and to get a holistic view of firms' operations, it was deemed most appropriate to send the questionnaire to the CEO. The cover letter was signed by the researchers and personalized for each firm. Furthermore, within the cover letter three options were available, which made it clear as to who was not part of the sample. First, all firms should be working with ICT-related products or services; second, they should have more then one million Swedish kronor in sales during last year; and finally, the firm should still be actively conducting business.

From the sample of 1471 firms, 93 were taken out since they did not meet at least one of the three mentioned criteria. Furthermore, six questionnaires did not reach the identified firms and it was not possible to contact them. This reduced the sample size to 1372 firms. We received 306 replies. Of these, four were filled out incorrectly, one was a duplicate, and ten came from firms where the CEO addressed another entity than the one targeted (e.g. a group instead of a single firm). Thus, the workable questionnaires were reduced to 291, giving us a response rate of 21 per cent. From these, 257 were used in this analysis, as a result of missing data in the categories used in this chapter, which makes the usable response rate just below 19 per cent. Although this is not very high, it is sufficient for adequate statistical analysis.

Measurements

In the study, we have used four main variables, namely, collaborative network structure, entrepreneurial orientation, network capability and ICT capability. For all the items (except collaborative network structure) seven-point Likert scales were used, ranging from 'strongly disagree' to 'strongly agree' (see Appendix Table 12A.1).

Collaborative network structure
Collaborative network structure was measured by asking respondents to state the number of organizations they have *strategic* and *repetitive* contact with in ten different categories. These categories are small firms as customer, supplier or partner; large firms as customer, supplier or partner; government agency as customer or partner; and university as customer or partner.

ICT capability

The measurement for ICT capability has been partially adopted from the study of Johannessen et al. (1999) and modified based on our own pre-study of three small Swedish firms in the ICT sector (Parida and Westerberg, 2006). We were able to identify 13 different items that measured different strategic use of ICT. After performing factor analysis, we divided the ICT capability into three main groups based on use of technology for collaboration (3 items), communication (3 items) and internal purpose (4 items) by ICT-related small firms. The alpha-values of ICT capability were satisfactory (collaboration; $\alpha = 0.78$; communication; $\alpha = 0.64$; and internal $\alpha = 0.75$).

Network capability

This variable was mainly measured based on the scale developed by Walter et al. (2006). They conceptualize it as a higher order construct comprising four components (coordination activity, relational skills, partner knowledge, and internal communication). We added another component, namely building new relationships, as a fifth aspect of network capability. All components had three items each. All five sub-aspects of network capability showed good measurement properties, but since we only use it as a single construct we only report reliability for network capability as a whole ($\alpha = 0.76$).

Entrepreneurial orientation

This was our dependent variable for the regression analysis and was measured based on the scale developed by Lumpkin and Dess (1996), where we consider three of the five aspects of EO, namely the 'classical' innovativeness (3 items), proactiveness (3 items), and risk-taking (3 items). The α-value for EO was 0.73, indicating a reliable scale.

In this study, we have five control variables. To control for the environment we use dynamism, hostility and heterogeneity. The measurement scale for environment was according to the study by Miller and Friesen (1983). Firm size was measured using the log-number of employees, and age of the firm was calculated using log-number of the years the firm had been in operation.

Data Analysis

We carried out our analysis using software package SPSS (statistical package of social science) version 14.0. Initially, we used factor analysis to observe any irregularity and whether the items formed as expected.

Using the option of automatic categorization, we divided each of the ten aspects of collaborative network relations (such as university as partner) into seven categories. This was done to standardize each aspect before the cluster analysis. Using the ten standardized aspects as input variables, we performed a number of K-mean cluster analyses. The only solution with clear distinction between clusters was the two cluster solution, basically dividing the firms into one group having a relatively weak collaborative network structure and one group having a relatively strong collaborative network structure. These two clusters were then divided into four by splitting the two into a high networking capability group (≥ 2.00 on a scale from -3 to $+3$) and low networking capability group (<2.00). By doing this, we formed two 'matching' clusters, where the level of networking capability is in line with the size of the collaborative structure, and two 'mismatching' clusters, where we have firms with low networking capability and a strong collaborative network structure, and vice versa. This will enable us to see if the clusters need to be matched for results to be positive. The levels for most variables in each cluster are stated as low (>0.25 below mean), medium (mean ± 0.25) and high (>0.25 above mean) based on their relation to the overall mean. To distinguish differences in absolute level, ANOVA and t-tests were performed. Finally, for relational level, hierarchical regression analysis was performed with EO as the dependent variable for all firms and each cluster.

RESULTS

This section is divided into two parts. The first part presents the results of absolute effects, which were obtained by performing cluster analysis, ANOVA and t-tests. The second part presents the relational effects, which were based on the regression analysis.

Absolute Levels

As indicated, we formed four different clusters (groups) within the ICT-related small firm based on level of collaboration and level of networking (see Table 12.1). These are low collaboration with low networking capability (cluster I), low collaboration with high networking capability (cluster II), high collaboration with low networking capability (cluster III) and high collaboration with high networking capability (cluster IV). As can be noted, firms within cluster IV were mostly high on all the forms of relationships with large firms, small firms, government institutions and university, whereas cluster I was low on all such relationships. Cluster II

Table 12.1   Cluster analysis for ICT-related small firms

	Low collaboration		High collaboration	
	Cluster I Low networking capability (N = 96)	Cluster II High networking capability (N = 34)	Cluster III Low networking capability (N = 75)	Cluster IV High networking capability (N = 52)
Small customer	*Low*	*Low*	***High***	High
Small supplier	*Low*	*Low*	High	High
Small partnership	*Low*	*Low*	High	High
Large customer	*Low*	*Low*	High	High
Large supplier	*Low*	*Low*	High	High
Large partnership	*Low*	***Low***	High	High
Government customer	*Low*	*Low*	High	High
Government partnership	*Medium*	Medium	**Medium**	Medium
University customer	*Low*	*Low*	High	**Medium**
University partnership	*Medium*	Medium	Medium	**Medium**
Networking capability	*Medium*	**High**	*Medium*	**High**
Mean firm size (employees)	*11*	*14*	**18**	**21**
Mean firm size (turnover)	*10*	19	**20**	**26**
Mean firm age	11	*9*	**12**	**12**
ICT internal use	*Low*	**High**	**Medium**	**Medium**
ICT collaboration	*Medium*	**High**	*Medium*	**High**
ICT communication	*Low*	**Medium**	**Medium**	**High**
Entrepreneurial orientation	*Low*	**High**	**High**	**High**

Note: When there are differences between different levels of clusters based on the t-test, the highest ones are **bold**. Cluster level is *italic* when they are lower than bold. And ***bold italics*** are used when cluster levels are lower than bold but higher than italic. All levels that have no significance ($p < 0.05$) are neither in bold nor in italic.

was quite similar to cluster I but still a bit different, such as in the case of relations with large firms as partners. Likewise cluster III was quite similar to cluster IV but still different such as in the case of relations with universities as customers.

In terms of firm size (turnover and employees), clusters I and II were lower than cluster III and IV. For firm age, cluster II is younger than clusters III and IV. Networking capability was naturally high for clusters II and IV and low for clusters I and III. ICT use for collaboration was lowest in clusters I and III and highest in clusters II and IV. For ICT communication and internal use, cluster I was lower than all the others. Finally, for entrepreneurial orientation cluster I was significantly lower than all the other clusters.

Relationship Levels (Capabilities and Entrepreneurial Orientation)

Table 12.2 recapitulates the results from the regression analyses that were performed to observe the effects of ICT capability and networking capability on entrepreneurial orientation for each cluster and for the sample as a whole. In Model I, the analysis includes all firms in the sample. In this model, networking capability ($B = 0.26$; $p < 0.05$) has a medium significant effect on EO, and ICT capability for internal use ($B = 0.10$; $p < 0.10$) and communication ($B = 0.10$; $p < 0.10$) have a weak significant effect on EO. In Model II (96 firms) including the firms with low collaboration and low networking capability, networking capability ($B = 0.55$; $p < 0.01$) has a strong significant effect on EO, while ICT capability for communication ($B = 0.17$; $p < 0.05$) has a medium significant effect. In Models III–V, the overall F-value is not significant, which means that there exits no relationship between the capabilities and EO in these three clusters. Regarding control variables, firm size has a strong significant effect on EO, indicating that larger firms tend to be more entrepreneurial. Environmental hostility also tends to breed EO.

DISCUSSION AND CONCLUSION

Discussion

We started this study with three research questions, namely (1) to investigate whether ICT-related small firms could be divided into different clusters based on their network structure and, if so, investigate (2) how the absolute levels of our independent and control variables differ between the clusters, and (3) how ICT and networking capabilities are linked to entrepreneurial orientation within each cluster. This way of studying small firms on the basis of their collaborative networking structure has seldom been reported (Pittaway et al., 2004). We were able to identify four different clusters and to observe differences in terms of their networking capability, ICT capability, entrepreneurial orientation, firm age, and firm size. Looking specifically at collaboration structure, networking capability and ICT capability, there were some interesting outcomes (Figure 12.1).

Cluster I includes the small firms that have few collaboration partners and low networking capability. These firms seems to be at a disadvantage as they have relatively few contacts and also lack the capability to establish new ones or even maintain existing ones. Many authors have acknowledged that external ties are an important source of new knowledge and competitive advantage, especially in a competitive business environment

Table 12.2   *Regression analysis for ICT-related small firms*

	Model I All firms (N = 257)		Low collaboration				High collaboration			
			Model II Low networking capability (N = 96)		Model III High networking capability (N = 34)		Model VI Low networking capability (N = 75)		Model V High networking capability (N = 52)	
Firm size	0.30***	0.19***	0.47***	0.29***	0.16	0.12	0.02	0.08	−0.15	−0.06
Firm age	0.15	0.18*	0.08	0.15	0.27	0.31	0.10	0.14	0.38	0.19
Environmental dynamism	0.05	−0.00	0.09	−0.01	−0.21	−0.26	−0.01	−0.04	0.06	0.02
Environmental hostility	0.13*	0.19***	−0.01	0.07	0.68**	0.67**	0.20	0.23	0.13	0.18
Environmental heterogeneity	0.06	0.00	0.11	0.06	−0.03	−0.05	−0.05	−0.3	0.06	0.09
ICT internal use		0.10*		−0.04		0.35*		0.1		0.13
ICT collaboration		0.01		−0.06		−0.25		0.28**		−0.05
ICT communication		0.10*		0.17**		−0.17		−0.06		0.20
Networking capability		0.26**		0.55***		0.71		0.09		0.72
Model summary										
R²	0.11	0.21	0.26	0.39	0.20	0.33	0.04	0.16	0.07	0.24
R² adjusted	0.09	0.18	0.22	0.32	0.06	0.07	−0.03	0.04	−0.02	0.08
Std. error of the estimate	1.04	0.99	0.96	0.89	1.19	1.18	1.05	1.01	1.06	1.00
R² change	0.11	0.09	0.26	0.12	0.20	0.12	0.04	0.12	0.07	0.17
F	6.64	7.57	6.30	5.94	1.42	1.29	0.51	1.37	0.75	1.50
Sig.	0.00	0.00	0.00	0.00	0.25	0.29	0.76	0.22	0.59	0.18

Notes:
Dependent variable: entrepreneurial orientation.
$* p < 0.10$, $** p < 0.05$, $*** p < 0.01$.

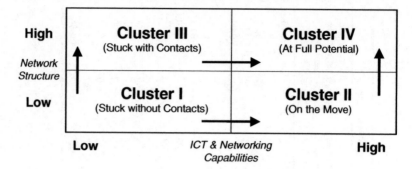

Figure 12.1   Effect of different capabilities and networking structure for ICT-related small firms

(Pittaway et al., 2004; Cohen and Levinthal, 1990). This also holds true here, since firms in cluster I have a significantly lower entrepreneurial orientation than the other firms. The firms in cluster I also have the lowest level of ICT capability, which means that they are not able to strategically utilize ICT and still use it for ad hoc processes. In any case, this would also work against their growth potential (Venkatraman, 1994). We have named this cluster '*stuck without contacts*'. However, since the regression analysis pointed to a rather strong relation between the capabilities (networking and ICT for communication) and entrepreneurial orientation, firms in this cluster may improve their position by building these capabilities and thus move towards cluster II. While it is also possible to move towards cluster III, it seems inappropriate to build a larger network without having a strong networking capability.

In cluster II, we find the firms that have few collaboration partners but high networking capability. These firms were the youngest in the group and although they currently have a rather low collaboration level, they have the ability to change collaboration partners and also to build a stronger collaboration network. Thus, we have named them small firms '*on the move*'. Firms in cluster II were not only high on networking capability but also high on ICT capability. This gives them an advantage as, in terms of networking capability, they had positioned themselves in the right place for future alliances (Hagedoorn et al., 2006). Also, in terms of ICT capability, they can use their technological infrastructure to support internal and external processes for building competitive advantage. These small firms were high on entrepreneurial orientation, which lends supports to authors like Kale et al. (2002) and Gulati et al. (2000) arguing that it's not having a lot of collaboration that is important, but rather to have the right collaboration with selected partners. However, it is also possible that they can use their networking and ICT capability and build more fruitful collaborations and move towards cluster IV as very competitive firms.

Cluster III is where we find firms with many collaborative partners but low networking capability. This seems to be a mismatch since they have a lot of contacts and yet lack the capability to manage these in a way that is beneficial for the firm in the long run. Thus, the name '*stuck with contacts*'. These firms might have invested in many relations but because they have low networking capability, the outcome might be uncertain. Firms within cluster III were also low on ICT capability, which could work against them as without an appropriate level of technological competence, they might find difficult to support several technology-oriented activities, such as using intranet and extranet functions. However, these small firms have the same level of entrepreneurial orientation as clusters II and IV, which means that they are obviously doing fine presently. Over time, if it becomes necessary to renew the network, these firms may face severe problems if they do not develop their capabilities. Therefore, we would like to have a longitudinal dimension where we would be able to detect whether firms in this cluster only manage for a short while or are able to compete successfully for an extended period.

Finally, cluster IV are the firms with many collaboration partners and high networking capability, thus we call them '*at full potential*'. Moreover they are high users of ICT for all three areas (i.e. internal purpose, collaboration and communication). Cluster IV firms are a good example of firms who can combine an extensive collaborative network with ICT and networking capability to achieve entrepreneurial orientation. Thus, we believe that if small firms are able to find the right balance between ICT and networking capability, they will not only perform better but will also increase the possibility of future growth. However, as the entrepreneurial orientation is at the same level in this cluster as in clusters II and III, we can't say that these firms are the most competitive. Again, we would need a longitudinal dimension to untangle the key to success in the longer perspective.

As noted before, we performed regression analysis with entrepreneurial orientation as our dependent variable for all clusters and for the entire sample of firms. Looking at the entire sample, there is a link between entrepreneurial orientation and capability for ICT (internal and communication use) and networking among our firms. Entrepreneurial orientation is linked to proactiveness, risk-taking and innovativeness. By having a high networking capability, firms can create a cushion against environmental threats and can take more daring actions (Lorenzoni and Lipparini, 1999). Also, access to external information is the most important source of innovation (Powell et al., 1996; Pittaway et al., 2004). Small firms can also use ICT for environmental scanning and to scan for changes that can enhance their ability to be proactive (Fillis et al., 2003). Also, communicating new information within and outside the firm by the use of an intranet or extranet enhances learning (Ruiz-Mercader et al., 2006) from different sources such as suppliers, customers and competitors, and can lead to the development of commercially viable innovations (Johannessen et al., 1999). The only cluster where we found a link with entrepreneurial orientation was cluster I. Thus, for the other clusters, more capability in ICT and networking do not lead to higher EO. This might be because these firms already have high EO compared to cluster I firms. In terms of ICT and networking capability, firms may not be required to be more entrepreneurial at the current stage. Another related explanation is that there are diminishing returns on investing in networking and ICT capability; that is, when you have reached a certain level of capability, raising it even higher will not pay off.

This study is of course not without limitations. As mentioned before, it is not possible to make clear-cut generalizations from this study because of the absence of longitudinal data. Also, the number of firms in some clusters is rather small (especially for cluster II), which could be the reason for not having significant relations in the regression analysis.

CONCLUSION

We started this study with the purpose of finding different clusters within ICT-related small firms and of observing how different clusters can have different effects. Within our study, we identified four clusters and each of them had its own unique characteristics. We found that firms with few collaborative partners and lacking networking capability are significantly lower in entrepreneurial orientation compared to the other three groups. Among the other three groups, it seems those with networking capability are better off, but our results do not support this. Cluster III, containing firms with a strong collaboration structure but lacking the tools to handle this (i.e. networking capability) seems to cope anyway. This is a genuinely intriguing finding and future studies need to examine this further to come up with more detailed explanations.

From the regression results, we have clear indications that it pays off in terms of higher entrepreneurial orientation to invest in improving capabilities in ICT and networking. This is especially true if the firm is rather low in these capabilities and lacks a strong collaborative network structure.

Finally, as an answer to the question in the title, it seems that small firms in the ICT industry can work in different ways to produce the same results in terms of entrepreneurial orientation. Some build networks without the capabilities that seem to be needed, while others possess the capabilities but do not build a large network. A third group has the capabilities *and* the large network. It seems it takes different types of logic to work successfully in the three situations and our study is unable to provide any clear answers about this logic at this point. We hope this study has provided some interesting answers and has opened up a number of questions in the area of small firm inter-organization network research.

REFERENCES

Anand, B.N. and T. Khanna (2000), 'Do firms learn to create value? The case of alliances', *Strategic Management Journal*, **21** (3), 295–315.

Arend, R.J (2006), 'SME–supplier alliance activity in manufacturing: contingent benefits and perceptions', *Strategic Management Journal*, **27** (8), 741–63.

Audretsch, D.B. and M.P. Feldman (2003), 'Small-firms' strategic research partnerships: the case of biotechnology', *Technology Analysis and Strategic Management*, **15** (2), 273–88.

Baum J.A.C., T. Caladrese and B.S. Silverman (2000), 'Don't go it alone: alliances, network composition and start-ups' performance in Canadian biotechnology', *Strategic Management Journal*, **21** (3), 267–94.

Baum, J.A.C. and C. Oliver (1991), 'Institutional linkages and organizational mortality', *Administrative Science Quarterly*, **36** (2), 187–218.

Bougrain, F. and B. Haudeville (2002), 'Innovation, collaboration and SMEs' internal research capacities', *Research Policy*, **31** (5), 735–47.

Bradley, F., R. Meyer and Y. Gao (2006), 'Use of supplier–customer relationships by SMEs to enter foreign markets', *Industrial Marketing Management*, **35** (6), 652–65.

Caldeira, M.M. and J.M. Ward (2003), 'Using resource-based theory to interpret the successful adoption and use of information systems and technology in manufacturing small and medium-sized enterprises', *European Journal of Information Systems*, **12** (2), 127–41.

Cohen, W.M. and D.A. Levinthal (1990), 'Absorptive capacity: a new perspective on learning and innovation', *Administrative Science Quarterly*, **35** (1), 128–52.

Covin, J.G. and D.P. Slevin (1991), 'A conceptual model of entrepreneurship as firm behavior', *Entrepreneurship Theory and Practice*, **16** (1), 7–25.

Delmar, F., P. Davidsson and W.B. Gartner (2003), 'Arriving at the high-growth firm', *Journal of Business Venturing*, **18** (2), 189–216.

Dholakia, R.R. and N. Kshetri (2004), 'Factors impacting the adoption of the Internet among SMEs', *Small Business Economics*, **23** (4), 311–22.

Etzkowitz, H. and L. Leydesdorff (2000), 'The dynamics of innovation: from national systems and "mode a" to a triple helix of university–industry–government relations', *Research Policy*, **29** (2), 109–23.

Fillis, I., U. Johansson and B. Wagner (2003), 'A conceptualisation of the opportunities and barriers to e-business development in the smaller firm', *Journal of Small Business and Enterprise Development*, **10** (3), 336–44.

Gago, D. and L. Rubalcaba (2007), 'Innovation and ICT in service firms: towards a multidimensional approach for impact assessment', *Journal of Evolutionary Economics*, **17** (1), 25–44.

Gemunden, H.G., T. Ritter and P. Heydebreck (1996), 'Network configuration and innovation success: an empirical analysis in German high-tech industries', *International Journal of Research in Marketing*, **13** (5), 449–62.

Gulati, R., N. Nohria and A. Zaheer (2000), 'Strategic networks', *Strategic Management Journal*, **21** (3), 203–16.

Hagedoorn, J., N. Roijakkers and H.V. Karneburg (2006), 'Inter-firm R&D networks: the importance of strategic network capabilities for high-tech partnership formation', *British Journal of Management*, **17** (1), 39–53.

Hoang, H. and B. Antoncic (2003), 'Network-based research in entrepreneurship: a critical review', *Journal of Business Venturing*, **18** (2), 165–87.

Jacob, F (2006), 'Preparing industrial suppliers for customer integration', *Industrial Marketing Management*, **35** (1), 45–56.

Johannessen, J.A. (1994), 'Information technology and innovation: identifying critical innovation factors', *Information Management and Computer Security*, **2** (2), 4–9.

Johannessen, J.A., J. Olaisen and B. Olsen (1999), 'Strategic use of information technology for increased innovation and performance', *Information Management and Computer Security*, **7** (1), 5–22.

Kale, P., J.H. Dyer and H. Singh (2002), 'Alliance capability, stock market response, and long-term alliance success: the role of the alliance function', *Strategic Management Journal*, **23** (8), 747–67.

Koch, C. (2004), 'Innovation networking between stability and political dynamics', *Technovation*, **24** (9), 729–39.

Lee, C., K. Lee and J.M. Pennings (2001), 'Internal capabilities, external networks and performance: a study of technology-based ventures', *Strategic Management Journal*, **22** (6/7), 615–40.

Levy, M., P. Powell and P. Yetton (2001), 'SMEs: aligning IS and the strategic context', *Journal of Information Technology*, **16** (3), 133–44.

Lorenzoni, G. and A. Lipparini (1999), 'The leveraging of interfirm relationships as a distinctive organizational capability: a longitudinal study', *Strategic Management Journal*, **20** (4), 317–38.

Lumpkin, G.T. and G.G. Dess (1996), 'Clarifying the entrepreneurial orientation construct and linking it to performance', *The Academy of Management Review*, **21** (1), 135–72.

Madsen, E.L (2007), 'The significance of sustained entrepreneurial orientation of performance of firms: a longitudinal analysis', *Entrepreneurship and Regional Development*, **19** (2), 185–204.

Martin, L. and H. Matlay (2001), 'Blanket approaches to promoting ICT in small firms: some lessons from the DTI ladder adoption model in the UK', *Internet Research*, **11** (5), 399–410.

Matlay, H. and M. Addis (2003), 'Adoption of ICT and e-commerce in small businesses: an HEI-based consultancy perspective', *Journal of Small Business and Enterprise Development*, **10** (3), 321–35.

Miller, D. and P.H. Friesen (1983), 'Strategy-making and environment: the third link', *Strategic Management Journal*, **4** (3), 221–35.

Oliver, A.L (2001), 'Strategic alliances and the learning life-cycle of biotechnology firms', *Organization Studies*, **22** (3), 467–89.

Ostgaard, T.A. and S. Birley (1994), 'Personal networks and firm competitive strategy: a strategic or coincidental match?', *Journal of Businesses Venturing*, **9** (4), 281–305.

Parida, V. and M. Westerberg (2006), 'ICT use for innovation and competitiveness in Swedish industrial service SMEs', paper presented at The 1st Nordic Innovation Research Conference, Oulu, Finland.

Pittaway, L., M. Robertos, K. Munir, D. Denyer and A. Neely (2004), 'Networking and innovation: a systematic review of the evidence', *International Journal of Management Reviews*, **5** (6), 137–68.

Powell W.W., K.W. Koput and L. Smith-Doerr (1996), 'Interorganizational collaboration and the locus of innovation: networks of learning in biotechnology', *Administrative Science Quarterly*, **41** (1), 116–45.

Ruiz-Mercader, J., A.L. Merono-Cerdan and R. Sabater-Sanchez (2006), 'Information technology and learning: their relationship and impact on organisational performance in small businesses', *International Journal of Information Management*, **26** (1), 16–29.

Sarshar, M. and U. Isikdag (2004), 'A survey of ICT use in the Turkish construction industry', *Engineering, Construction and Architectural Management*, **11** (4), 238–47.

Storey, David J. (1994), *Understanding the Small Business Sector*, London: Routledge.

Stuart, T.E. (2000), 'Interorganizational alliances and the performance of firms: a study of growth and innovation rates in a high-technology industry', *Strategic Management Journal*, **21** (8), 791–811.

Venkatraman, N. (1994), 'IT-enabled business transformation: from automation to business scope redefinition', *Sloan Management Review*, **35** (2), 73–88.

Walter, A., M. Auer and T. Ritter (2006), 'The impact of networking capabilities and entrepreneurial orientation on university spin-off performance', *Journal of Business Venturing*, **21** (4), 541–67.

Westerberg, M. and H. Ylinenpää (2003), 'Cooperation among smaller firms and its relation to competence, entrepreneurship and performance', paper presented at the 17th Nordic Conference on Business Studies, Reykjavik, Iceland.

Wiklund, J (1999), 'The sustainability of the entrepreneurial orientation–performance relationship', *Entrepreneurship Theory and Practice*, **24** (1), 37–49.

APPENDIX

Table 12A.1 Descriptives, factor loading and construct reliability

Construct	Items	Loading	Alpha	Mean	S.D
Risk-taking	*In our firms* ... we see bold, wide-ranging acts are necessary to achieve the firm's objectives	0.76			
	... we have a strong aptitude for high risk projects (with chances of high returns)	0.88	0.82	0.43	1.34
	... my firm typically adopts a bold posture when confronted with decisions involving uncertainty, to maximize the exploitation of opportunities	0.85			
Proactiveness	... we tend to be ahead of competitors regarding the introduction of products and ideas	0.78			
	... we typically initiate actions which competitors then respond to	0.86	0.85	0.77	1.26
	... we are often the first to introduce new products and services, new ways to produce these or new administrative methods	0.82			
Innovativeness	... we have a strong emphasis on R&D, technological leadership, and innovations	0.76			
	... changes in product or service lines have usually been quite dramatic to achieve competitive advantage	0.75	0.76	0.97	1.43
	... one of the main goals is to launch many new lines of products/services in next 3 years	0.79			
EO – Entrepreneurial orientation	Risk-taking	0.72	0.76	0.72	1.08
	Proactiveness	0.84			
	Innovativeness	0.84			
Coordination	... we analyse what we would like and desire to achieve with which partner	0.78			
	... we develop relations with each partner based on what they can contribute	0.68	0.74	1.39	1.01

Table 12A.1 (continued)

Construct	Items	Loading	Alpha	Mean	S.D
	. . . we discuss regularly with our partners how we can support each other	0.73			
Relational skills	. . . we have the ability to build good personal relationships with our business partners	0.69			
	. . . we can deal flexibly with our partners	0.78	0.83	1.99	0.87
	. . . we almost always solve problems constructively with our partners	0.83			
Building new relations	. . . we are constantly open to new relations with new partners	0.81			
	. . . we have the ability to initiate a mutual relationship with new partners	0.76	0.82	1.86	1.03
	. . . we have our eyes open to find new partners	0.86			
Partner knowledge	. . . we know our partners' markets	0.83			
	. . . we know our partners' products/procedures/services	0.82	0.87	1.41	1.04
	. . . we know our partners' strengths and weaknesses	0.86			
Internal communication	. . . we have regular meetings for every project	0.75			
	. . . employees develop informal contacts among themselves	0.87	0.76	1.77	1.01
	. . . managers and employees often give feedback to each other	0.79			
Networking capability	Coordination	0.79	0.76	1.69	0.71
	Relational skills	0.79			
	Building new relations	0.68			
	Partner knowledge	0.75			
	Internal communication	0.56			
ICT capability	*The extent to which your company uses ICT in this area:*				
ICT internal use	. . . access information (e.g. market, customer)	0.69*			
	. . . enable strategic planning	0.79*			
	. . . enable cost savings	0.69*	0.75	3.82	1.36
	. . . enable competence/skills development for employees	0.61*			

Table 12A.1   (continued)

Construct	Items	Loading	Alpha	Mean	S.D
ICT collaboration	. . . maintain collaboration with existing business partners	0.84*			
	. . . establish business collaborations with new partners	0.78*	0.78	4.34	1.36
	. . . enable work flexibility (e.g. work outside the office)	0.63*			
ICT communication	. . . handle communication within the firm (e.g. intranet)	0.66*			
	. . . handle external communication with the firm's stakeholders (e.g. extranet)	0.82*	0.75	3.85	1.31
	. . . promote marketing activities	0.57*			

Note: Likert scale: –3 to +3; * Likert scale: 1 to 6.

PART VI

Entrepreneurship and Social Inclusion

13. Does enterprise discourse have the power to enable or disable deprived communities?

Carole Howorth, Caroline Parkinson and Alan Southern

INTRODUCTION

Many local economic development and regeneration initiatives have connected enterprise and deprived areas. They posit enterprise as a tool for releasing human, social and economic potential. Policy makers are keen to promote enterprise as *the* solution to deprivation, recognizing employment opportunities through new business start-up and local growth. In this sense, not only are communities being asked to take responsibility for their own futures by being enterprising (see Blackburn and Ram, 2006), the implication is that they will be held accountable for the lack of enterprise that is leading to their deprivation. This is seen in many UK approaches to local economic development but is particularly evident in the drive for social enterprise over the last ten years and as a broader part of both social and economic regeneration.

Social enterprise is thus attracting significant interest from a policy perspective and also as a new context for the study of entrepreneurship. The rhetoric of social enterprise adopts the language of business and entrepreneurship as a way forward for particular sections of society. Pomerantz (2003, p. 26) expresses a widely held view in writing, 'The key to social enterprise involves taking a business-like, innovative approach to the mission of delivering community services.' The people who run social enterprises are often called 'social entrepreneurs' because they are expected to combine 'entrepreneurial flair with a commitment to giving something back to the community' (Michael, 2006).[1] However, Parkinson and Howorth (2008) found that managers of social enterprises, whom others labelled as social entrepreneurs, did not themselves identify with the entrepreneur label. The application of the entrepreneurship paradigm to this social sphere has been questioned conceptually, practically and ideologically (Krashinsky, 1998; Paton, 2003; Pearce, 2003; Dees, 2004; Cho, 2006) and there are concerns that the repackaging of longstanding community processes as a new form of entrepreneurship is neglecting some of the ideological and political principles at their roots (Pearce, 2003). Berglund and Johansson (2007) argue that the dominant enterprise discourse actually suppresses entrepreneurial initiatives in their study of a region in decline in Sweden.

A vast body of literature points to a range of problematics in understanding the interplay between community, entrepreneurship and deprivation. There is a danger that policy could overlook the conceptual and ideological complexities inherent in every aspect of enterprise and deprived communities. Previous research has highlighted issues around the changing dynamics of poverty (Fitzpatrick, 2004) and social exclusion (Power, 2001; Blackburn and Ram, 2006); the effectiveness of area based policies (Chatterton and Bradley, 2000); the impact of entrepreneurship on deprivation in regeneration and economic development policy terms (Lloyd and Mason, 1984; Haywood and Nicholls, 2004; Nolan, 2003; Southern, 2006); the impact of regional structural effects (Johnson, 2004); the influence of peripherality on munificence (Benneworth, 2004); links between small business and the local community (Curran et al., 2000), and the influence of civic engagement on social-economic well-being (Tolbert et al., 1998).

Previous research alludes to the importance of the relationship between dominant world views encapsulated in enterprise policy and those competing on the ground. Theories on inequitable social relations and social reproduction, particularly those with a Marxist starting point (see for example, Althusser, 1984; Bordieu, 1985, 1989; Foucault, 1972, 1982; Gramsci, 1971), would suggest that hegemonic discourses, in this case the 'grand' discourse of enterprise that has pervaded western society since the 1980s, perpetuate the normative views of those in power and impose 'calls to order' that those subordinated to the discourses are bound to follow. There seems to be a tension in recent literature, however, with critics of this deterministic view finding that counter hegemony is thriving and that groups and individuals are able to contest or appropriate discourses for themselves (Cohen and Musson, 2000; Jones and Spicer, 2005; Moulaert et al., 2007; Parkinson and Howorth, 2008).

Enterprise and entrepreneurship are nevertheless firmly established in the lexicon of regeneration and renaissance. This chapter critically examines the discourse around such policies. It provides a critical perspective on the top down promotion of enterprise targeted at places identified in policy terms as deprived, with particular reference to social enterprise. By reviewing both the discursive features of recent enterprise policy and the discourse analysis of interviews with three levels of social enterprise agents, competing world views are revealed, which raises cautionary points relevant to academic and practitioner worlds. Through an analysis of language, the influence of the enterprise narrative or myth is explored. We attempt to demonstrate how deprived communities have become an arena for a sometimes negotiated, and often contested, space as enterprise policy is formed and particular conceptualizations of enterprise and entrepreneurship are favoured.

In this chapter we analyse the structured discourse that prevails in national and regional policy circles and contrast it with the discourse of three groups: social enterprise support workers, social and local entrepreneurs and community workers. We highlight ideological tensions and confusion that improve our understanding of the mixed results reported for enterprise policy in deprived communities (Blackburn and Ram, 2006). This is extremely important in determining the appropriateness and efficacy of enterprise policy and in developing an understanding of how it works (or not) 'on the ground'.

We first provide a critical overview of UK enterprise policy in deprived areas. We then set out the value of Bordieu's theories of symbolic violence for understanding the subordination of communities that are deemed deprived. We then present some counter arguments that could allow us to perceive communities as more active agents – not constrained by a habitus acquired over time and from experience. Following this we explain the method adopted, which was based on discourse analysis. Our analysis examines the emergence of a structured discourse around recent policy on enterprise, before comparing the language used by three different groups involved in social enterprise activities. Our conclusions highlight the important implications of the study for policy and practice.

ENTERPRISE IN UK LOCAL POLICY: THE SALVATION OF DEPRIVED AREAS

Enterprise has been a central thread in local economic development (LED) from the second half of the twentieth-century, as a strategy for addressing decline, recession and more lately the effects of internationalization, globalization and social exclusion (Blackburn and Ram, 2006; Eisenschitz and Gough, 1993; Wong, 1999). A political response to macro effects impacting on the prosperity of local areas, it has been through various phases throughout 40 years in the UK but always supported by political consensus (Eisenschitz and Gough, 1993). At the same time as a policy push for enterprise, a *lack* of enterprise has characterized political responses to localism, such as anti-enterprise views of British culture of the Thatcher years (Eisenschitz and Gough, 1993) and public policy diagnoses of neighbourhood decline (Kintrea, 2007).

LED has always linked social and economic issues. However, since the election of a Labour government in 1997, enterprise, or at least enterprise policy, has gained an extra dimension: redressing social exclusion in depleted communities, neighbourhoods that conventional wisdom suggest have a deficit in levels of entrepreneurial behaviour. It appears that policy makers and advisers promote enterprise as 'the solution' to deprivation. Moreover, in the most intractably problematic areas, social and community enterprise are positioned as the panacea for entrenched economic and social ills.

This is perhaps most evident in the policy investment in social entrepreneurship and social enterprise over the last decade in the UK. Many clearly locate social enterprise within community or economic development, where it has a political agenda of alternative democratic structures and processes. Pearce (2003) traces the history of the movement in the UK back to the 1970s Job Creation Programme, when the focus was on community development, and the cooperative movement. Haughton (1998) situates the UK movement within sustainable regeneration, itself a response to the failure of top down urban policy approaches throughout the 1980s. Social and community entrepreneurship in the UK emerged out of structures aimed at anchoring the benefits of the local economy within communities. It was not until the end of the 1990s in the UK that the discourse around social enterprises as businesses emerged. Since then, the topic has seen a radical and rapid discursive shift through various agendas, now critiqued (Krashinsky, 1998; Paton, 2003; Pearce, 2003; Dees, 2004; Cho, 2006), including those above, to the social economy and social entrepreneurship.

An ideological vision of enterprise, embodied in LED in the 1960s and 1970s, was captured by Eisenschitz and Gough (1993, p. 4) when talking about LED's vision for local communities to become 'active shapers of their destiny':

> The central way in which [. . .] local resources are conceptualised is as 'enterprise'. Enterprise denotes the initiative not only of business but also of workers, as workers or as would-be entrepreneurs, and of volunteers, organisations and communities groups. In an even wider sense, enterprise suggests the need to shake off past routine, to question past assumptions, to think and act radically; every local organisation, public as well as private, economic as well as social, is to be enterprising in this sense. All local social groups are to be involved, and their collaboration is to constitute the locality as a unified entity, a community, able to fight for its place within the hostile world outside. The movement, then, marches under the banners of local autonomy, enterprise and community.

Some have suggested that this promotion of enterprise as 'the solution' to deprivation is akin to communities being asked to take responsibility for their own futures through their adaptation to enterprising behaviour, while at the same time noting that there is little evidence to support any views that such policy actually works (see for example Blackburn and Ram, 2006). Overall, the presumption of public policy reliant on enterprise as a solution to social and economic ills of target groups or areas has come under attack (Macdonald and Coffield, 1991; Gavron et al., 1998; Servon, 1997; Blackburn and Ram, 2006). Blackburn and Ram (2006, p. 77), for example, explicate the fundamental tension in expecting business and enterprise to tackle social exclusion which is a product of the very capitalist system in which they operate.

The following section considers how one world view (e.g. enterprise is 'the solution') can prevail and become hegemonic.

BORDIEU, SYMBOLIC VIOLENCE AND THE ARTICULATION OF DEPRIVED COMMUNITIES

Bordieu (1989) conceptualizes the process of world views gaining dominance in terms of symbolic violence. Symbolic violence refers to the gradual and complicit subordination of people to ideas and structures, promulgated by those in possession of symbolic capital (Bordieu, 1989; Bordieu et al., 1994). Symbolic violence is the antithesis of physical violence in that it is indirect and socially reproduced, bringing about one's own subordination through a complicity that is neither enforced nor passively deferential (Connolly and Healy, 2004). Instead, symbolic violence is seen as occurring iteratively and stems from individuals' predispositions to the world around them that are developed over time (Connolly and Healy, 2004) – the much cited '*habitus*' Bordieu's work is often reduced to. Through the symbolic violence exerted by dominant groups in society, their values/norms/world view are quietly accepted until they become taken for granted, part of the pre-reflexive agreement of the commonsense world (Bordieu et al., 1994, p. 15).

Interestingly, Bordieu (1989) argues that 'elusive' social collectives such as 'the community' come into being through the very act of being classified or codified. Through words, collectives are nominalized and social divisions become distinguishable. The naming process is a fundamental part of world making and, more specifically, class struggle. In relation to this study, nominalization of areas in terms of deprivation, community and area based regeneration, and local economic development would reproduce social privilege, by different tiers and agents within society. This is not a benign act but a political process: 'The power to make visible and explicit social divisions that are implicit is political power par excellence' (Bordieu, 1989, pp. 23–4).

Bordieu et al. (1994) argue that holders of capital (e.g. physical force, economic capital, informational or cultural capital and symbolic capital) use it to fight for power. Within this fight over social space, the role of the state is paramount, and it is portrayed as the holder of the monopoly of legitimate symbolic violence and the 'repository of common sense' (Bordieu, 1989, p. 22). Official discourse is held up as quasi 'divine'; providing identities, prescribing what people should be doing, recording what people have done. It is of relevance therefore to recognize how the concept of symbolic violence helps us to reflect on the contested space associated with policies aimed at deprived communities. Bordieu's work has been used to look at how broader societal issues affect inequality, particularly in the field of education.[2] Bordieu's theories of symbolic violence are however predicated on subordination and compliance, notions that are challenged in some recent entrepreneurship literature.

ENTREPRENEURSHIP – CHALLENGING HEGEMONY?

Entrepreneurship is no longer accepted solely as an economic entity. The cultural turn in entrepreneurship research has led to a wide body of work focusing on the links between entrepreneurship and different aspects of society or contexts. These range from the reciprocal benefits from the interaction between firms and their local environments (Tolbert et al., 1998; Kilkenny et al., 1999; Laukkanen, 2000; Johannisson et al., 2002) and the informal economy (Portes, 1994; Evans et al., 2004; Williams, 2005) to ethnic minority enterprise (Ram and Smallbone, 2003; Deakins et al., 2007) and the linguistic turn in entrepreneurship studies (Hjorth and Steyaert, 2004; Berglund and Johansson, 2007). Entrepreneurship is conceived as a process taking place in various spaces and dimensions, socially embedded and constructed (Johannisson et al., 2002), communally and relationally constituted (Zafirovski, 1999; Hodson and Kaufman, 1982; Fletcher, 2006; Anderson and Jack, 2002). Entrepreneurial processes have meaning that is specific to a particular time and place (Hjorth and Johanisson, 2003; Fletcher, 2006), perhaps also 'liminal' in that it takes place at the edges or in between structures (Anderson, 2005; Jones and Spicer, 2005). At the level of research at least, entrepreneurship is recognized as a complex social phenomenon.

Despite this acknowledged complexity, the literature points to the hegemonic power of the enterprise discourse in policy and popular media. Ogbor (2000) argues that dominant entrepreneurial discourses portray the entrepreneur as an aggressive hero. It is argued that a 'reproduction of familiar ethnocentric, discriminatory and gender biased assumptions of entrepreneurship' is encouraged (Fletcher, 2003, p. 129). This provides us with the 'grand narrative of entrepreneurs and small businesses' (Perren and Jennings, 2005, p. 176), which presents a narrow understanding of what it means to be entrepreneurial and is reflected by locking into a specific 'enterprise solution'. It provides an understanding of a particular policy drive (i.e. more enterprise as it is uncritically good for society), a particular objective (i.e. more entrepreneurs as their behaviour will give us, uncritically, more enterprise) at a particular scale (i.e. the local, for it is here where the answers to global forces can be found.)

In terms of popular readings of this discourse, Anderson (2005) points to the persistent power of the heroic entrepreneurial metaphor. Nicholson and Anderson (2005) propose that the myth embodied in cultural beliefs, popular literature and journalism becomes self-perpetuating; mystery is created around the myth of the entrepreneur and is perpetually reinforced. The mystery shrouding the myth grows; the myth becomes shorthand and eventually 'the uncorrected "collective memory"'. (Nicholson and Anderson, 2005, p. 166). The discourse of the enterprise culture can be seen as reasserting individualism (Nicholson and Anderson, 2005).

In a macro sense, therefore, the dominant discourse of entrepreneurship fits into a neo-liberal world view of how social and economic problems should be addressed. In line with Bordieu, above, much of this work assumes that language is a reflection of power relations, struggles and dynamics (Foucault, 1972, 1982). A Foucauldian stance is adopted in that discourses themselves are creative and determine how power and knowledge are produced (see Parker, 1999; Ahl, 2007).

However, at a micro level there are challenges to the hegemony of enterprise or entrepreneurship discourses. The Foucauldian perspective and its antecedents are criticized for assuming that the individual is slave to ideologies or discourses and is powerless to resist (Cohen and Musson, 2000; Jones and Spicer, 2005). That view of the individual is seen as deterministic, leaving no room for individuals to resist and find their own alternative discourses. An alternative view is that individuals appropriate or re-write the discourse to make sense of their specific realities. Various studies show how individuals and groups reproduce idealized views of entrepreneurs and what it means to be entrepreneurial, while simultaneously challenging and re-writing the enterprise discourse (Fletcher, 2006; Cohen and Musson, 2000). Contrary to the hegemonic view, Cohen and Musson (2000) present individuals as able to discriminate between discourses and appropriate them to their circumstances, with some elements of the business or enterprise discourse being appropriated and others rejected. Cohen and Musson (2000) argue that meaning cannot be solely constructed by those in positions of power to exclude or include certain groups, since this is also alterable by the subjects of the discourse.

In their study of urban development, Moulaert et al. (2007) found that the hegemonic discourse was neither omnipotent nor self-fulfilling in practice and that policy and practice remain pragmatic in the face of the rapid advance of neo-liberal logic. Instead, 'counter-hegemonic forces' make up part of the patchwork of local agents, and through social innovation can actually permeate macro structures (Moulaert et al., 2007, p. 202). They also found that the gap between practice and the 'grand discourse' is wider as people are closer to real communities, where the connection to path dependency is stronger. As Begg (2002) argues, it is at the local level that discourse is challenged and reproduced.

In terms of enterprise policy, this indicates the potential for communities or groups to author their own futures to a degree, in spite of social reproduction of asset-poor communities by the state through the hegemonic discourse of enterprise. This empowerment is a powerful tenet of social regeneration and social inclusion initiatives, as well as social enterprise.

The above discussions present two connected but different perspectives on the power of discourse in terms of how it is authored and, critically, how it is reproduced. This study seeks to understand which perspective helps to explain the effects of the enterprise discourse within deprived areas. It looks first at the discourse in UK enterprise policy, which provides the discursive context within which communities and agencies may be working, and then at interview data to provide a snapshot of how different actors embrace or contest these discourses in articulating their own situations.

METHOD

The research method is discourse analysis.[3] We draw broadly on Fairclough (1989, 1992, 1995) and Weiss and Wodak (2003), whose works on critical discourse analysis (CDA) suggest that discourse is more than reflective of social power situations, in that language influences, as much as it is influenced by, social practice. Discourse must therefore be studied in reference to the social and political context (Fairclough and Wodak, 1997). Critical discourse analysis includes situations, objects of knowledge and the social identities of and relationships between people and groups of people (Weiss and Wodak, 2003). Language is constitutive of meaning, the 'prism through which we conceptualise the world' (Jacobs, 2004, p. 819) and is seen as a social practice shaping, and shaped by, social relations and structures. Analysis is critical in that it is explicitly linked to the researchers' interest in a social issue – in this case enterprise policy and its effects on people in its targeted deprived areas.

In particular we refer to the Frankfurter school of discourse analysis. We conducted a loose CDA on our interview data, which followed a three-stage framework of text production (the macro context within which statements are made, how they connect to other debates and how the interviewees generally framed their spoken texts), text analysis (the micro processes of discourse that shape the text (Fairclough, 1992), including modality and word meaning) and finally social practice (effect of the texts on wider power relations and ideologies). To analyse the prevailing discourses in UK policy, we used a broader approach, analysing statements from key documents out of which current UK enterprise policy in deprived areas emerged.

The study was based in a defined UK area of deprivation, which has persistently ranked in the worst 10 per cent of areas in the UK according to the Index of Multiple Deprivation (IMD).[4] These indices are the basis for governments to develop area-based responses to the persistence of poverty and social exclusion, including initiatives aimed at increasing levels of enterprise such as the Neighbourhood Renewal Fund. The study thus focuses on one specific deprived area, which qualifies for a range of particular funding streams and enterprise development assistance, in order to provide a similar geographical basis for participants' experiences.

Semi-structured and unstructured interviews were held in 2006 with ten individuals taking part in a learning and development programme for social enterprise managers or social entrepreneurs. These included three enterprise support workers; three managers of social enterprises with varying experience, plus one local entrepreneur involved in starting up a social venture; and two community leaders, one of whom managed a community centre and the other managed a community gym, but both were involved in activities labelled as social enterprise. Table 13.1 provides a summary of the basic characteristics of the interviewees. All interviews were recorded, lasted between one and one and a half hours and took place mainly at the interviewees' own workplaces. In addition, the researchers observed and recorded a steering group meeting of a three-year social enterprise support initiative, involving 11 participants, including representatives of local and regional funding bodies, officers from two local authorities, (social) enterprise support agencies, one social enterprise representative and an academic. The recordings were transcribed verbatim.

Table 13.1   Characteristics of interviewees

Support workers:*		
SW1	M	Director of a cooperative consultancy
SW2	F	Project manager of an SE support project
SW3	M	Local authority officer with remit for supporting social and community enterprise
Social entrepreneurs:*		
E1	M	Manager of a white goods recycling enterprise
E2	F	Manager of a disability project
E3	M	Manager of a community gym
E4	M	Director of a sea training school
Community leaders:*		
CL1	F	Community centre manager
CL2	M	Setting up a community gym

Note: * These labels were allocated by the researchers to distinguish between categories of local actors, and may not necessarily be used or accepted by the participants.

After an initial reading of the entire interviews, sections of the interviews of one page or less were selected for analysis. The excerpts were chosen to be most revealing in terms of how the enterprise discourse, texts or content were reproduced or contested. More precisely, the sections were chosen that give insights into at least one of three factors: how the enterprise discourse was manifest or contested; how the discourse might have the effect of including or excluding different agents; or self-representation in relation to the enterprise discourse. Within-group analysis was undertaken on the ten interviews in three groups: support workers, entrepreneurs and community leaders. Cross-group comparisons were then made.

ANALYSIS AND FINDINGS

As stated above, the analysis examined two levels of discourse: the prevailing discourses in UK enterprise policy, with specific reference to social enterprise; and the enterprise discourse as embraced by local actors when asked to talk about their own perceived realities. The former aims to set the discursive context within which local actors operate. The latter aims to understand how the enterprise discourse, including the texts or content from these prevailing discourses, is reproduced or contested in our own interview data.

Prevailing Discourses in UK Enterprise Policy: Structuring a Discourse of (In)Equality

The following section looks at the language used in constructing policy. It is based on selective quotes, all from the point at which the current strand of UK enterprise policy emerged.

The first comes from the Policy Action Team 3 (PAT 3), a group of policy makers and practitioners who brought together the new view on enterprise. These could be referred to as the visionaries who sought to introduce the 'Third Way' into ideas about enterprise from the 1997 watershed. From their initial document we see clearly stated the intention of the new Labour administration in 1999 to draw on enterprise to address matters of social and economic exclusion. This document, titled simply but with some degree of force 'Enterprise and Social Exclusion', set the tone for what was to follow:

> A shortage of jobs, local services and enterprise is one aspect of exclusion facing people in disadvantaged neighbourhoods. The challenge in economic terms is to *rebuild* livelihoods and *restore* robust local markets. Sustainable neighbourhood *renewal* will not happen without enterprise *development*. Conversely, enterprise development will be of only marginal relevance unless it is part of a wider strategy to develop people's skills and self-esteem and help them use mainstream services from which they feel excluded. (Policy Action Team 3, 1999, p. 6, emphasis added)

This extract presents a structural perspective related to societal rebuilding, restoration, renewal and development. In this sense we see language associated with construction and physical action used as a metaphor, with the key 'tool' (to continue the metaphor) being enterprise. Furthermore:

> [p]romoting enterprise to expand employment *opportunities* can build *confidence* and capacity and offer a route out of exclusion through *economic opportunity*. Enterprise development should therefore be an important indicator of the success or failure of neighbourhood renewal. (Ibid.)

Not only is the metaphor embellished as demonstrated in this extract, but brought into play is the idea of new *economic* opportunities emerging. This emergence is an important feature in the language of enterprise and how it is associated with depleted communities. It is entirely consistent with the views of Blackburn and Ram (2006, p. 74) when they state 'the notion of "enterprise" has been positioned as a key means of helping to overcome social exclusion'.

Following the view from the group of experts who made up PAT 3 comes a second example to demonstrate how politicians support the policy initiative that brought in the Phoenix Fund. The Phoenix Fund was an initiative that came from the PAT 3 report and was established in 2000 aimed at encouraging entrepreneurship in disadvantaged areas. Patricia Hewitt, the then Trade and Industry Secretary commented on this initiative: 'The Government is committed to *enterprise for all*, no matter where people live or whatever their circumstances. The new money will help more people start up in business' (Business Hotline Publications, 2003, p. 1, emphasis added). This line of 'enterprise for all' was pushed further by the Small Business Minister, Nigel Griffiths. Griffiths outlined the role of Community Development Finance Institutions (CDFIs), a means by which finance for enterprise could be accessed in depleted communities. He stated:

> The Government recognises that CDFIs have a vital role to play in providing finance to some of our most *imaginative and tenacious* entrepreneurs. CDFIs are filling a vital gap in *access to finance in more disadvantaged communities*, forming a bridge between the public and private sectors. CDFIs are helping us to provide enterprise opportunities for all, and ensure that the best possible support is in place for those who want to start or grow their own business – *no matter what their background*. (Small Business Service Press Release, 14 April 2004, emphasis added)

Enterprise, still in its heroic sense, has become an egalitarian mantra and is inclusive and for all. Such is the reiterated message. This is reflected in the name of this initiative, 'Phoenix', that refers to a mythical bird that is reborn from the ashes in much the way that politicians seek enterprise to be the magical remedy from which depleted communities can be reborn.

A third example, as part of the structured discourse, comes from the cautious but realistic practitioner, the Bank of England who (prior to the Phoenix initiative but in response to PAT 3) looked at finance for small businesses in deprived areas. The Bank noted how the promotion of enterprise in depleted communities can assist the circulation of money within a neighbourhood and provide much-needed jobs. They state:

> The causes of social and financial exclusion are complex and there are a *variety of symptoms*. The nature of deprivation in a particular area depends on *many factors*, including its history, the origin and duration of its economic problems and the particular industry or industries which have declined. (Bank of England, 2000, p. 3 emphasis added)

This is a cautionary tale to indicate that the private sector is not wholly responsible for the vagaries suffered by those living in depleted communities. It is a change in emphasis from the language used by policy makers and politicians, a contrast to the metaphor of building, seizing opportunity and inclusion. It is further embellished through the Bank's report, for example: 'While the promotion of businesses in deprived areas can have a number of positive impacts on local people, several studies have stressed that business establishment on its own should not be viewed as a primary tool for tackling deprivation' (ibid, p. 14). The almost defensive position of the Bank noted here not only seeks to exonerate the private sector from the responsibility for social and economic exclusion but is also apologetic for enterprise not being the answer for such problems. In this respect they may well be correct. However this is not the point but that they, the Bank of England, are an important part of the structured discourse on enterprise in deprived communities.

In a review of core policy and strategy texts on social enterprise from national, regional and local agencies, Parkinson and Howorth (2008) highlight many similar concepts: for example, 'doing lots with very little, financial independence through sustainability, contributing to the mainstream economy, bringing business discipline to social ventures, innovating for change, helping people take charge of their lives and futures'. It is assumed that social enterprises will take on the existing business model, which excludes the potential to develop new models. For example, 'Social enterprises must see themselves as businesses, seek to become more professional and continuously raise their standards of performance and their ambitions' (DTI, 2002). And social enterprises are encouraged to be part of the mainstream economy: 'social enterprise should "become part of the solution to reviving and strengthening local economies" but should not be seen as a side show to the real economy' (NWDA, 2003). Pearce argues that there has been a shift in language from political engagement to problem fixing, collective action to individual entrepreneurs, and from democratic structures to a focus on social purpose (Pearce, 2003). The charge is that in the rise of the social enterprise agenda, *community* has been sidelined discursively, and complex values and meanings behind the *social* ignored.

It is important to note that we are not suggesting that these initiatives are wrong or that they are intrinsically flawed. What we are suggesting is that the policy drive may bring with it a particular discourse that is limited. It is possibly restrictive in that it could reduce the entrepreneur who operates in a depleted community (and his or her voice) to being a passive recipient of the dominant policy discourse. It takes little if any account of the contested space that is policy formation, or the contested space that is entrepreneurship and business in deprived communities.

By locking into this narrow, particular view of enterprise, the social regenerative potential from initiatives that manifest in new forms of social or local enterprise may be lost. No account is taken of effects on family and kinship, the raising of aspirations and self-esteem and the impact on the community psychology that prevail in localized neighbourhoods. In fact, the structured discourse not only acts as an exclusive narrative but it brings into play individual actors as part of an economic response, at the expense of local politics and alternative ideals about the meaning of enterprise (Gibson-Graham, 2006).

Our aim in the second analysis is to look at the language of those individuals and consider the extent to which they challenge or appropriate the structured policy discourse. As we attempt to do this we seek to identify those ideological tensions and contradictions that become apparent within individuals as well as between groups in depleted communities. This can help draw out some of the complexities that are implicit in policy objectives; not least the potential of enterprise policies aimed at deprived communities in reinforcing inequitable social relations and economic inequity.

ANALYSIS OF INTERVIEW DATA

The findings discuss use of, and associations with, the enterprise discourse promoted in the policies, among each of the three groups. We summarize briefly the main issues at the end of each section before discussing the findings in relation to each other, particularly the intended and unintended effects of the enterprise discourse as it is reproduced by the different groups.

Support Workers

The support workers display a polarized conceptualization of (social) enterprise, in which enterprising activities are defined in contrast to funding dependency. Funding and grant schemes are seen as both the driver behind the existence of many social enterprises and their weakness. Enterprise on the other hand, and trading in particular, is positioned as the antidote to dependency and complacency.

In the following extract, Support Worker 1 (SW1) contrasts positively framed enterprising activities (income generation, trading) with more negatively framed 'looking for funding':

> I think we need to make things reasonably clear that people who are interested in enterprising activities, income generation, becoming a trading organisation and we will assist them. I think if they're interested . . . if they're only going to be looking for funding then I don't think . . . you know, I think there's other . . . there's other people that are in that market. (SW1)

It becomes clear that he considers the priority is to help existing social enterprises, operating within a constituted framework (by omission, therefore, individuals and communities engaging in social entrepreneurship more widely), to achieve income through trading. This is also seen in the views of SW 2, who equates 'true' social enterprise with sustainability, defined as generating money to cover costs:

> SW2:   Oh gosh . . . I would say it's a business that's run with social aims [. . .] But on the whole, if it's true social enterprise it should be able to sustain itself.
> I: What do you mean by sustainable?
> SW2:   Pay its own bills, pay its core costs, yeah, not be a funding junkie, as we say . . .

Trading is presented here in opposition to dependence and the 'false' state of relying on funding. The negative association with funding is further compounded by use of the drugs-related term 'junkie'. In the steering group meeting, various references are made to the other side or the other way, which reinforce this polarization:

> M: . . . it's gone more to the other side now . . . the other way, you know, looking for grants.
> F: Yeah
> M: Looking for grant schemes and writing business plan and people obviously know stuff. Now it's turned the other way round, which I think a lot of social enterprises are going that way now.

The effect of this dichotomy is to marginalize the social and exclude other forms of organization and activity. Interestingly, in the steering group meeting, there is overt discussion of this shift to a business language, which it is claimed offers relief from the jargon presumably prevailing in the social sector:

> M: And kind of the business plan was the way of getting some money, so it was a sort of means to an end. Whereas now, there seems to be much more talk about having a sustainable business plan and all those types of issues have come to the forefront. And then the funding's kind of an add-on that they may be able to get. But first and foremost, it's a plan for a business and not just . . .

In fact, achieving this discursive shift to a language, in which the business plan is more meaningful, is held as a triumph in its own right. The statement 'and not just . . . ', above, has the effect of marginalizing other forms of social enterprise organization. This is perpetuated by SW2 who is dismissive of not just the term social enterprise but of the people involved, whose activities she compares against enterprise:

I: Why do you think they don't think of themselves as being a social enter-
        prise then?
SW2:   I think they just sort of think of themselves as doing a service. I just
        don't think that they even think that's what they are, community sort of
        businesses or whatever they want to call themselves. . . . They just don't,
        they just think 'oh we're a bunch of ladies who get together and . . . ',
        yeah.

In the process, the social element of the social enterprise's endeavours is
tacitly (and, at points, overtly) discredited. In the following excerpt from
Support Worker 3's interview, a valuable social service is praised in its
own right but critiqued for attempting to be a social enterprise:

SW3:   . . . there was a review of the service about two years ago now I think,
        that gave it a glowing report . . . It showed categorically that there was
        an improvement in the reading of the people that they'd worked with.
        But where's the income? [. . .] It's a great project, brilliant outcomes, all
        that stuff, but who's going to pay for it?

Paradoxically, we find out later that the reason for the project's transition
was externally driven; to take on a separate status from the county council
(the local authority that employs SW3), in order to continue accessing
funding.

Within the support workers' narrative of becoming business-like, the
two main tenets are sustainability and money/income, all interconnected
and used interchangeably. Paying bills appears central to the support
workers' construction of enterprise. The same point is made in the steering
group meeting, where consensus on this resonates:

F: . . . But you've still got to be business-like and you've still got to pay
        your bills. And that's the point.
F: That's the point, yes.

In both excerpts, sustainability appears to be the end goal of enterprise,
and the imperative for social enterprises is the process of becoming sustainable. Social need, usually closely associated with social entrepreneurship, is backgrounded by this emphasis on sustainability.

The enterprises' ability to generate money and thereby become sustainable becomes a condition of support from the social enterprise support
project. While rhetorical emphasis is placed on good relationships built
on trust between social enterprises and the project, this relationship is
both conditional and transformational in its agenda. In the following
extract from the steering group meeting, support is seen to depend more
on viability than need:

F: . . . I want to see this happen anyway if we possibly can. But to take the previous point, you know, is it a viable business. If it is, then we'll pull out stops and make it happen.

M: yeah

F: yeah, if it's got the right . . .

M: if it's got legs?

F: yeah.

In this organizational perspective on social enterprise, there is less value given to entrepreneurship or being entrepreneurial. In line with accepted understandings of entrepreneurship, being entrepreneurial is defined primarily in terms of packaging resources and the notion of spotting or generating ideas. The familiar neo-conservative perspective of the heroic individual entrepreneur is reinforced, by SW1 and SW3 particularly. SW3 places emphasis on the individual, in spite of earlier value placed on idea generation being a community or collective process:

SW3:   Usually you need someone who is very committed to delivering that project and it usually is one person. [. . .] but it tends to be one person that that has the sort of . . . not necessarily the idea but the wherewithal to take the idea forward.

I: yeah, what do you mean by [wherewithal] . . . ?

SW3:   I suppose I mean the . . . whatever the social enterprise version . . . of Alan Sugar is.

There appears to be some tension between this perspective and other ideological positions on power. SW3, despite the above statements, promotes a grassroots community action ideology, in which local people are the holders of power in terms of both creating ideas and bringing about change. There is also an interesting ideological contrast between SW1 and SW2. One displays firm commitment to social ownership and suggests that involvement in social enterprise should be democratic; the other expresses clear views that local people should earn the right to involvement through entrepreneurial skills (for which read business knowledge):

SW1:   . . . because ownership of course is not included in the government social enterprise definition, then the argument about something being social enterprise because it is socially owned doesn't wash. I mean I think my position is that if it's socially owned, it's a social enterprise.

I: Right, what if it's not socially owned?

SW1:   Well, if it's not socially owned, it's probably not a social enterprise.

Contrast this with:

SW2:   And these people don't even really know . . . some of them off the estate don't even know how to read a business . . . a spreadsheet, never mind

> [. . .] and I think the trouble is that some of these need entrepreneurial
> skills and they just . . . you know, how do you say, 'well I'm sorry,
> you've got to live in the estate but you have to be an entrepreneur
> type person or have some business knowledge before we'll let you on'?
> (laughs).

Finally, there is an interesting struggle in the steering group meeting over
a social enterprise's identity or status, between the manager of that social
enterprise and a representative of a support organization. Not only does
this show clearly the perceived demarcation between social and business,
discussed above, but it also betrays dynamics of power, with the steering
group member (F here) contradicting the social enterprise manager and
informing him of his organization's actual status:

> M: I think we're more of a business now than what we were when we set
>   out because we weren't . . . it wasn't a business was it really, but now it's
>   more of a business than it is a social enterprise.
> F: well no, you're a social enterprise but you . . .
> M: yeah, but it's gone more to the other side . . .

Importantly, it also shows an eagerness on the part of the social enterprise
manager to conform to the 'business-like' agenda being discussed within
the steering group, by aligning his organization more closely with a business than a social organization. The tussle around definitions between the
two speakers exposes his desire to play along with the funders and local
authority representatives.

In summary, analysis of the excerpts from the support workers'
interviews reveals overt statements about inclusion and exclusion in
social enterprise, reinforced by discursive practices. The enterprise and
sustainability discourses are used semi-interchangeably and as shorthand
for business (also business-like behaviour) and money. They are used
particularly in reference to helping existing organizations to make the
transition out of the apparently dead-end social sector into the more
positive arena of enterprise. There is less focus on being enterprising or
entrepreneurial, and where entrepreneurial references are made, some
familiar conventional/popular assumptions reinforced. While mainly
reproducing government rhetoric, the support workers nonetheless show
some resistance to policy level assumptions about social enterprise in their
communities. This is important to highlight as it suggests the prevailing
discourses at policy level are not necessarily reproduced wholesale at the
local/regional agency level, as might be assumed. Ideological tensions are
also apparent between members of this group regarding inclusion and
ownership.

Social Entrepreneurs

Enterprise is often equated with freedom and independence by this group. This freedom can be either political or, more usually, pragmatic in terms of bureaucratic funding and grants:

> E1:   . . . As you know with previous organisations [in the voluntary sector], that was the problem. You would always have to sit there and say 'yes, sir', 'no, sir' to people. But now we don't, I can say what I like to whom I like and not worry about it. I'm quite free in that way, you know.

Like the support workers, the entrepreneurs often re-write enterprise as *business*, though *project* is more common. Where business is referred to, however, it emerges as conceptually tricky for the speakers. How to bridge delivery of a service with talk of a market is one example of this tension from Entrepreneur 1 (E1):

> E1:   . . . but I feel it's slightly more difficult for something like this project because you're not selling a commodity, you're not selling a widget or manufacturing a widget to sell to somebody.
> I: that the public understands?
> E1:   Exactly. What we do is sell something totally unseen. And some will be totally unquantifiable, you know, and we'll be creating youth workers. How do you measure a smile? How do you put that down on a piece of paper?

Money and sustainability are again dominant themes, as with the support workers. Pricing and charging are highlighted by E2 as another example of the tension between her construction of enterprise and her organization's commitment to its social service or product. Here sustainability is seen as a barrier:

> E2:   . . . you know, it's a problem here because how am I going to make it self-sustainable, that learning centre self-sustainable? Because I can't hire out the facilities because they're too small. [. . .] So you're depending on funders saying, 'yeah, you've got a really brilliant idea, we'll keep chucking money at you' even though you're not going to exist after three years because you'll be going to the same funders again.
> I: So where does it [end up]?
> E2:   Well, it won't will it, it will eventually . . . it will die because there'll be no way of sustaining it. Unless people pay and people haven't got the money to pay.

With this emphasis on charging, there appears to be slightly less emphasis on income generation per se than among the support workers group. Referring to the national and regional bodies of the NHS (National

Health Service) and PCT (Primary Care Trust), one social entrepreneur expresses fatigue at the push for income generation and states his ideological disregard for the capitalism he associates with profiteering enterprise:

> E3:　　But I can see . . . like the NHS or PCT can't keep forking money out. But . . . and the sad thing is the exercise on referrals going . . . in an ideal world, somebody with diabetes could get referred in and just pay the same price as prescriptions, for example, £6.20 or whatever it is, would last them for 12 weeks of exercise. But money talks really, so that . . . Yeah, I mean I wouldn't want to do it as a business as such because I wouldn't want to kind of make a profit out of other people's ill health and stuff. But yeah.

Sustainability is central in their construction of social enterprise. Often, views about sustainability and the business drive appear confused. Interestingly, profit is only mentioned by the SME manager (E4); other concepts associated with trading by the support workers, such as sales and markets, are absent – or are used to emphasize the social value of their work. This might indicate that the commercial imperative of trading, sought by the support workers as the route to sustainability, is marked on the surface of the social entrepreneurs' texts at best. In other words, the social entrepreneurs seem to be echoing some of the texts of the enterprise/business discourse but in the process contesting their validity or meaning for this group.

Indeed, sustainability is frequently talked about with despondency, as if it were the unattainable holy grail, as seen in E2's excerpt above. There appears to be discomfort also around the drive for enterprise generally. The pressure to be business-like, in particular balancing this top-down agenda with their day-to-day pressures to deliver a needed service, is expressed by E3:

> E3:　　Well I'll not deny it . . . I don't know, I maybe wish it was a bit easier to get money on merit if you like. Instead of having to have a precise costing for everything, I would like it if somebody could just say, 'here's like . . . you know, it looks like a good business plan, here's £300,000, see how it gets on [. . .] And if I hadn't had to do all that I could have put so much more time into promotion and marketing and actually getting people in and making the service better.

However, this is counterbalanced by a tired unease with funding and grants. Both funding and enterprise therefore, the two concepts seen with the support workers to form a polemic binary in which enterprise (sustainable business) is positive and grant dependency negative, are equally negative for the social entrepreneurs.

The four interviewees tend to detach themselves from the entrepreneurial identity they associate again with the popular heroic myth. Here

E2 lists vision, audacity and independence among qualities of the entrepreneur, even though she was asked to talk about social entrepreneurs:

> I: So how would you define him as a social entrepreneur?
> E2:   He just went out for it, he just went out for it. He's got the confidence. I mean he started off as a salesperson and then he worked for a company in London as a salesperson. And then he went into partnership with someone. And then he had the gall to get out of the partnership and his wife was behind him and everything. And to put his house up and everything and to have a dream and go for it. That's a social entrepreneur; someone who has got this vision and this goal and they go for it and just take the risk . . .

The speaker is assigning popular characteristics of an entrepreneur to social entrepreneurs but, interestingly, does not at any point, either in this excerpt or later, question her total omission of the social – meaning social action or purpose. The result is that the social is subsumed under the popular discourse of the entrepreneur, betraying the fact that this interviewee, like others in this study, refers to the dominant 'mainstream' understanding of entrepreneurship, even if echoing the social entrepreneurship discourse. As seen, this is often a way of detaching themselves from an identity they see as foreign to their roles in society.

In summary, the enterprise discourse in the social entrepreneurs' texts does reproduce many of the same tenets as the support workers – sustainability, business, money. However, as much as these are echoed, they are also challenged in the context of the speakers' social activities and purposes. Noteworthy is that enterprise is also defined in their narratives as freedom and independence from funding regimes. Funding is negatively framed, as it was by the support workers. However, enterprise is equally negatively reproduced, for creating friction with social objectives and pressure to become business-like. The speakers detach themselves from the individual entrepreneurial identity put forward by the support workers, preferring to portray their roles in the social entrepreneurship process as building and expanding. They place emphasis on their teams in generating new ideas and little value on public sector support. In the process, they seem to resist the notion that formal enterprise creation, so central to the prevailing discourses at policy level and the support workers, is the key to improving the enterprise capacity of their areas.

Community Leaders

Community leaders are expected to have had less exposure to the social enterprise discourse. As with the social entrepreneurs, enterprise is associated with independence and, in CL1's case, with grassroots development.

> CL1:   Well yeah, it is a social enterprise. We started at the bottom and we're sort of branching out, so it is a social enterprise [. . .] We've got to start out in our own right now, we're not having housing anymore and we're starting out in our own right.

However, these two interviewees tend to talk far less about business than the previous two groups, referring more usually to project or venture, perhaps reflecting their start-up status or, as is our presumption, their interest in community development and social inclusion over (social) enterprise. They prefer to talk about local issues, particularly people:

> CL2:   I live right in the middle of heroin alley and I've kept my lads off the drugs but they're still into having a tipple you know, having a drink or two.
>
> CL2:   I said, it's time to move on. That's why I've created something like this, not only for my own but for other families' kids [. . .] Like sometimes I'm battling here, like I say, for nearly three or four year and they always put somebody in front of you like, where many a fella would have just got. . . . I believe in what I do.

Enterprise for them is clearly secondary to the social issues faced by their communities. The enterprise entity is the means to the social end, much more so than in the previous interviews. The legal aspect of incorporation is held as merely allowing them to achieve their goals. The social focus of the community gym is also forefront in CL2's mind when asked about enterprise:

> I: Okay, how do you see this enterprise generally, how do you see it going?
>
> CL2:   I do, aye. I really believe it'll take right off. And I do believe that we will be employing a few people in here like, that's a bonus.
>
> I: How many are you intending to employ or hoping to?
>
> CL2:   Well I'd like to employ everybody and their fathers but you can't can you.
>
> I: No.
>
> CL2:   But I've got lads that's came in here and gone to college and got their certificates for being gym instructors and nutrition. Three lads in particular that's got their certificates six weeks ago, the same three wouldn't go to school, couldn't get them to school.

The same themes of sustainability and money are again prominent, although less so than with the social entrepreneurs, and again contested by their ideological difficulties with pricing/charging in respect of their audiences. Sustainability appears more closely connected to them as individuals in their eyes and articulated in terms of tenacity, as is evident with CL2:

> CL2: I had to convince him. So I went and I bought half a gym that was closing down and get the men organised. And he come and he goes, 'I'm going to get behind this club'. I said, 'we're not here for show, we're here to do business, like.'
>
> CL2: This is a big venture, you know what I mean, so you've got to be staying with it all the time.
>
> I: Yeah. Do you feel daunted by it?
>
> CL2: No, never been put off it once. If I had, there wouldn't have been anybody because everything is on me. If I walk away, this club closes. I won't be walking away.

Indeed, both these speakers seem more attached to an entrepreneurial identity that they associate with fighting the local corner and the status that comes with that:

> CL1: My strength is because I have no fear, nothing fazes me. If somebody knocked on the door and said 'my child's just been molested' then I'd bring them in, I'd sit them down, I'd point them in the right direction and I'd get them every help they need. [. . .] I have no fear as I'm not afraid to tackle anything. You know, if it benefits the people of [place] . . . then I will go for it, within reason.

Ideas, as with the social entrepreneurs, are generally portrayed as coming from the community around them. This is the source of some pride for CL2, talking again about one of his protégés from the local neighbourhood:

> CL2: Out of them three lads, one of them's starting off his own business. [. . .] Because like I had to mentor him and all that [. . .] But he's gone on his . . . with doing that, he can take himself further. Well that's great isn't it?

The enterprise discourse in the community leaders' texts again reproduces the same tenets as the support workers – sustainability and money. Business, however, is far less prevalent, with the interviewees preferring to talk about their projects or social ventures and, more prominently, the people affected. Sustainability is re-written as tenacity and longevity and linked to their influence and/or the physical assets pertaining to their projects. This is reflective of a more political narrative overall, in which enterprise is subjugated under discourses of community or social action.

In keeping with this, the speakers attach themselves to a more radical entrepreneurial identity, in which their roles are perceived as fighting and battling on behalf of people in their specific communities.

Our analysis suggests that the three groups interviewed reproduce aspects of the policy discourse with differing degrees of loyalty to the texts and content. This seems to be on a spectrum that corresponds to the hierarchy, represented by our three categories, albeit somewhat artificial (support workers at the top being closer to policy speak; community leaders at the bottom being furthest removed). Almost on the same sliding scale, however, all groups also contest or re-write aspects of the enterprise discourse to suit their ideological concerns and social morality. This is certainly too small a sample to reach general conclusions but it does appear that the community leaders, who are likely to have had less exposure to the social enterprise discourse, remain more focused on social aims even when prompted by the enterprise discourse. Equally, the enterprise discourse finds fewer reverberations among the social entrepreneurs' excerpts than among the support workers', drawing less on business and management speak. Where they do use it, it is discursively demarcated as separate from the discourse of social need that is otherwise dominant. Business discourses were more prevalent among interviewees who were closer to policy makers, particularly support workers, and vice versa.

CONCLUSION

This analysis suggests that the application of the enterprise discourse to the social sphere, in the guise of the social enterprise agenda (and the micro-rhetoric of sustainability in particular) does have the potential to lock out certain players and activities. At the level of the support workers, the focus on enterprise is seen to negate the social values and ideologies seen elsewhere as important to the speakers (social ownership in the case of SW1; community action and development in the case of SW3). The discourse of enterprise presented by social enterprise policy is allowed to work dominantly and to delimit discussion of social value. With this, exclusionary effects are seen to potentially lock out less business-minded people or activities that do not comply with the legally constituted forms of social enterprise organization – both of which are particularly significant given the context of deprived communities.

Importantly, however, the residual lock-out effect on the two groups working 'on the ground' seems to be resisted by the speakers, who echo the rhetoric of becoming business-like or sustainable, but do not allow it to violate social values.

Therefore, while the enterprise discourse may reinforce conventional understandings common to the popular myth of entrepreneurship and those promoted by social enterprise policy, in other ways it is contested and appropriated by all three groups. The support workers focus on existing organizations becoming more business-like, with emphasis on money and viability, yet challenge ideologies at the heart of these perspectives. The social entrepreneurs and leaders echo the imperative of becoming business-like, possibly playing along with the game for politically expedient purposes and resources, but establish clear discursive boundaries between being business-like and serving important social needs.

In respect of Bordieu's symbolic violence concept, this study has certainly highlighted explicit use of a business dominated discourse of social entrepreneurship. This could risk subordinating the very people and activities in deprived communities that the policy is overtly attempting to support. The rhetoric as it is interpreted and enacted by the support workers can be seen to reinforce inequitable social relations among poor areas and 'people on the estate', who are positioned as not business-like and therefore not enterprising, in need of fixing by external intervention. In the process, welfare and social regeneration objectives that are clearly forefront for the social entrepreneurs and community leaders are underpinned by a neo-liberal view of enterprise as a tool of economic regeneration. In line with Bordieu, the discourse at all levels, from the policy statements down to the community leaders, appears to lead to the social reproduction of privilege and social inequalities.

However, this process – seen largely by Bordieu as a political process controlled predominantly by those in power – is not necessarily played out in the case of the enterprise discourse. Instead, the discussions in the second section of this chapter highlight the popular and collective processes by which the enterprise discourse and myths work – and are allowed to work – hegemonically. We would suggest, from this study, that the prevailing discourses of UK enterprise policy work are controlled as much by cultural as by political factors and work hegemonically on all tiers of agency. While the state, as holder of the monopoly of symbolic violence, is certainly important in the interview texts, it is important to recognize the role of individuals and social collectives in co-constructing and perpetually reinforcing/redefining the enterprise discourse.

Indeed, the analysis revealed competing world views that undermine the subordination effect of the enterprise discourse. As in Moulaert et al. (2007) and Begg (2002), our analysis suggests that it is at the micro level (i.e. furthest removed from the state) that the discourse is most clearly contested. Ideologies appear to be strikingly different on the ground in comparison to macro or meso levels. In some ways, the enterprise discourse appears to have developed iteratively over time until it has become an entrenched part of modern western society, a taken for granted and shared way of understanding the world. At an individual level, though, people effectively resist (either through appropriation or negation) the discourse by defaulting to the dominant popular myth of the entrepreneur or enterprise and then demarcating boundaries between that world and their own.

This has implications for entrepreneurship research and discourse studies. It seems clear that caution is required at multiple levels but not least by researchers, who may be tempted as Eisenschitz and Gough suggest (1993) to overplay the power of policy discourse at the local level, or indeed generate their own symbolic violence through uncritical pursuance of taken for granted assumptions. It is tempting to look at policy statements as indeed quasi divine, to use Bordieu's terms, and to assume hegemonic discourses are politically sustained for political gains. Ultimately, we would question whether the prevailing discourse in this case stems from the producers of policy, from the hegemony of the enterprise discourse itself given its pervasiveness in western societies (in that the state as creator of policy is as much an unwitting reproducer of the enterprise discourse's symbolic capital as its subjects), from the meso level intermediaries through their interpretation and enactment of the rhetoric or, significantly, from the masses perpetuating the popular myths of enterprise and entrepreneurship.

The study has highlighted certain questions for further research. What is not clear, yet, is how far the symbolic violence inherent in the rhetoric and intermediaries' texts filters from the meso to the micro level, where social enterprise is enacted. Also worth further research might be the residual impact of official enterprise discourses on the propensity of communities more widely to engage in enterprising activities, or consider themselves to be enterprising. Further research could examine to what extent local actors may be echoing the texts and content of the enterprise discourse for the sake of playing along with policy and funding discourses and how this affects the behaviours, actions or outcomes of people engaged in enterprise activities (in deprived communities and elsewhere).

The study also reveals implications for UK policy on enterprise in deprived areas and social enterprise. Policy makers need to reflect on the implicit demands on the subjects of the policies, in this case people engaged with social enterprise, and how any symbolic capital may be handled down the hierarchy of local regimes. In particular, they need to be wary about the possible symbolic violence on already vulnerable communities in reinforcing social inequalities and privilege. At the same time, however, given the entrenched cultural attachments to enterprise and entrepreneurship seen in our interview texts – and the competing influence of ideologies and social morality for those on the ground – expectations about the potential for enterprise interventions that derive from mainstream enterprise discourses need to be realistic. Practitioners, in turn, should avoid further distilling inequality for people in the most deprived areas by reproducing permissions to be part of the enterprise culture, based on a business-led conceptualization of enterprising potential.

NOTES

1. Often, the terms 'enterprise' and 'entrepreneurship' are used interchangeably with little attempt to distinguish between the two. The definition of 'entrepreneurship' is probably more contested than that of 'enterprise' (see Howorth et al., 2005). Parkinson and Howorth (2008) identify that in the field there is much overlap between the two. For the purposes of this chapter, enterprise is used when referring to specific organizations and in relation to government policy. Entrepreneurship is used to refer to the art of acting in an enterprising manner and the academic field of study. However, in the analysis participants' own use of the terms are reflected.
2. Connolly and Healy (2004) in their study of working- and middle-class boys in Belfast, examined the way social structures and processes of inequality are incorporated differently by the two different groups. The working-class boys' world view, their habitus, was linked with territoriality and localism and reinforced, through schooling, their subordination. In a similar study in the US, Herr and Anderson (2003) found that symbolic forms of violence in school helped reinforce social inequality and inequitable social relations. Their work highlights how, even where pupils (the victims of symbolic violence) are assisted to challenge the macro discourse (in this case, of meritocracy), their challenge may still leave them and their teacher vulnerable to the symbolic violence inherent in the system of educational leadership. Indeed, and perhaps ironically, it also requires us as researchers to reflect on not only the role of policy making, but of research and education, in perpetuating symbolic violence if we fail to challenge assumptions embodied in the social problems that, Bordieu would argue, are created partly by the state.
3. See Achtenberg and Welter (2007) for an overview of discourse methods in entrepreneurship research.
4. The UK government provides a measure of deprivation in England, Wales, Scotland and Northern Ireland. Each administrative authority formulates their respective count, with for example the Department for Communities and Local Government deriving the Index of Multiple Deprivation for England. In the case of England, the indices consist of income, employment, health and disability, education, skills and training, housing and services, crime and living environment. These are weighted unequally to derive an aggregated measure. Deprivation measures are built up from the smallest geography, which is currently the 'Lower layer Super Output Area (LSOA)' that for lay person usage is smaller than a ward or neighbourhood. This provides the basis for aggregation to compare district level indices of deprivation for instance. See Department for Communities and Local Government (2007) for more technical detail.

   While the measures provide us with detail on deprivation, the data are not all comparable across time. Although figures for 2007 can be compared with 2004 figures, they cannot be compared with figures for 2000 and for 1998. Crucial therefore, is the interpretation of measures and the need for a qualitative understanding of what deprivation means for a community, and within a community. Of even greater value is the longstanding debate on poverty initiated by those such as Booth and Rowntree but relevant in its current context by reference to the work of Townsend (Townsend, 1970, 1979) and more recently Alcock (1993) and Lister (2004).

REFERENCES

Achtenberg, L. and F. Welter (2007), 'Media discourse in entrepreneurship research', in H. Neergaard and J.P. Ulhoi, *Handbook of Qualitative Research Methods in Entrepreneurship*, Cheltenham, UK and Northampton, MA, USA: Edward Elgar, pp. 193–215.

Ahl, H. (2007), 'A Foucauldian framework for discourse analysis', in H. Neergaard and J.P. Ulhoi, *Handbook of Qualitative Research Methods in Entrepreneurship*, Cheltenham, UK and Northampton, MA, USA: Edward Elgar, pp. 216–50.

Alcock, P. (1993), *Understanding Poverty*, Basingstoke: Macmillan.

Althusser, L. (1984), *Essays on Ideology*, London: Verso.

Anderson, A.R. (2005), 'Enacted metaphor: the theatricality of the entrepreneurial process', *International Small Business Journal*, **23** (6), 585–603.

Anderson, A.R. and S.L. Jack (2002), 'The articulation of social capital in entrepreneurial networks: a glue or a lubricant?', *Entrepreneurship and Regional Development*, **14** (3), 193–210.

Bank of England (2000), *Finance for Small Businesses in Deprived Communities*, November 2000, London: Bank of England, Domestic Finance Division.

Begg, I. (2002), *Urban Competitiveness: Policies for Dynamic Cities*, Bristol: Policy Press.

Benneworth, P. (2004), 'In what sense "regional development"? Entrepreneurship, underdevelopment and strong tradition in the periphery', *Entrepreneurship and Regional Development*, **16**, 439–58.

Berglund, K. and A.W. Johansson (2007), 'Entrepreneurship, discourses and conscientisation in process of regional development', *Entrepreneurship and Regional Development*, **19** (6), 499–525.

Blackburn, R. and M. Ram (2006), 'Fix or fixation? The contributions and limitations of entrepreneurship and small firms to combating social exclusion', *Entrepreneurship and Regional Development*, **18** (1), 73–89.

Bordieu, P. (1985), 'The social space and the genesis of groups', *Theory and Society*, **14** (6), 723–44.

Bordieu, P. (1989), 'Social space and symbolic power', *Sociological Theory*, **7** (1), 14–25.

Bordieu, P., L. Wacquant and S. Farage (1994), 'Rethinking the state: genesis and structure of the bureaucratic field', *Sociological Theory*, **12** (1), 1–18.

Business Hotline Publications (2003), 'The no-nonsense guide to government rules and regulations for setting up your business', available at: http://www.business-hotlinepublications.co.uk/case_study.asp?id=16, accessed July 2008.

Chatterton, P. and D. Bradley (2000), 'Bringing Britain together?', *Local Economy*, **15** (2), 98–111.

Cho, A.H. (2006), 'Politics, values and social entrepreneurship: a critical appraisal', in J. Mair, J. Robinson and K. Hockerts (eds), *Social Entrepreneurship*, Basingstoke: Palgrave Macmillan.

Cohen, L. and G. Musson (2000), 'Entrepreneurial identities: reflections from two case studies', *Organization*, **7** (1), 31–48.

Connolly, P. and J. Healy (2004), 'Symbolic violence, locality and social class: the educational and career aspirations of 10–11-year-old boys in Belfast', *Pedagogy, Culture and Society*, **12** (1), 15–33.

Curran, J., R. Rutherford and S. Lloyd-Smith (2000), 'Is there a local business community?', *Local Economy*, **15** (2), 128–43.

Deakins, D., I. Mohammed, D. Smallbone, G. Whitham and J. Wyper (2007), 'Ethnic minority businesses in Scotland and the role of social capital', *International Small Business Journal*, **25** (3), 307–26.

Dees, G. (2004), 'Rhetoric, reality and research: building strong intellectual foundations for the emerging field of social entrepreneurship', paper presented at the 2004 Skoll World Forum on Social Entrepreneurship, March 2004, Oxford.

Department for Communities and Local Government (2007), *The English Indices of Deprivation 2007*, Wetherby: Communities and Local Government Publications.

DTI (2002), *Social Enterprise: A Strategy for Success*, London: Department of Trade and Industry.

Eisenschitz, A. and J. Gough (1993), *The Politics of Local Economic Policy*, Basingstoke: Macmillan.

Evans, M., S. Syrett and C. Williams (2004), *The Informal Economy and Deprived Neighbourhoods: A Systematic Review*, London: Office of the Deputy Prime Minister.

Fairclough, N. (1989), *Language and Power*, London: Longman.

Fairclough, N. (1992), *Discourse and Social Change*, Cambridge: Polity Press.

Fairclough, N. (1995), *Critical Discourse Analysis: The Critical Study of Language*, London: Longman.

Fairclough, N. and R. Wodak (1997), 'Critical discourse analysis', in T. van Dijk (ed.), *Discourse as Social Interaction*, London: Sage.

Fitzpatrick, S. (2004), 'Poverty of place', keynote address at the University of York, 14 December 2004, Joseph Rowntree Foundation.

Fletcher, D.E. (2003), 'Framing organisational emergence: discourse, identity and relationship', in C. Steyaert and D. Hjorth (eds), *New Movements in Entrepreneurship*, Cheltenham, UK and Northampton, MA, USA: Edward Elgar, pp. 125–42.

Fletcher, D.E. (2006), 'Entrepreneurial processes and the social construction of opportunity', *Entrepreneurship and Regional Development*, **18** (5), 421–40.

Foucault, M. (1972), *The Archaeology of Knowledge*, New York: Pantheon Books.

Foucault, M. (1982), 'The subject and power', in H. Dreyfus and P. Rabinow, *Michel Foucault: Beyond Structuralism and Hermeneutics*, Chicago: University of Chicago Press.

Gavron, R., M. Cowling, G. Holtham and A. Westall (1998), *The Entrepreneurial Society*, London: IPPR.

Gibson-Graham, J.K. (2006), *The End of Capitalism (As We Knew It): A Feminist Critique of Political Economy*, Minneapolis: University of Minnesota Press.

Gramsci, A. (1971), *Selections from the Prison Notebooks*, trans. Q. Hoare and G. Nowell-Smith, London: Lawrence & Wishart.

Haughton, G. (1998), 'Principles and practice of community economic development', *Regional Studies*, **32** (9), 872–77.

Haywood, G. and J. Nicholls (2004), 'Enterprise dynamics in the 20% most deprived wards in England', Betamodal Ltd.

Herr, K. and G. Anderson (2003), 'Violent youth or violent schools? A critical incident analysis of symbolic violence', *International Journal of Leadership in Education*, **6** (4), 415–33.

Hjorth, D. and B. Johannisson (2003), 'Conceptualising the opening phase of regional development as the enactment of a regional identity', *Concepts and Transformations*, **8** (1), 69.

Hjorth, D. and C. Steyaert (2004), *Narrative and Discursive Approaches in Entrepreneurship*, Cheltenham, UK and Northampton, MA, USA: Edward Elgar.

Hodson, R. and R.L. Kaufman (1982), 'Economic dualism: a critical review', *American Sociological Review*, **47** (6), 727–39.

Howorth, C., S. Tempest and C. Coupland (2005), 'Rethinking entrepreneurship methodology and definitions of the entrepreneur', *Journal of Small Business and Enterprise Development*, **12** (1), 24–40.

Jacobs, K. (2004), 'Waterfront redevelopment: a critical discourse analysis of the policy-making process within the Chatham Maritime Project', *Urban Studies*, **41** (4), 817–32.

Johannisson, B., M. Ramirez-Pasillas and G. Karlsson (2002), 'The institutional embeddedness of local inter-firm networks: a leverage for business creation', *Entrepreneurship and Regional Development*, **14** (4), 297–315.

Johnson, P. (2004), 'Differences in regional firm formation rates: a decomposition analysis', *Entrepreneurship Theory and Practice*, **28** (5), 431–45.

Jones, C. and A. Spicer (2005), 'The sublime object of entrepreneurship', *Organization*, **12** (2), 223–46.

Kilkenny, M., L. Nalbarte and T. Besser (1999), 'Reciprocated community support and small town–small business success', *Entrepreneurship and Regional Development*, **11** (3), 231–46.

Kintrea, K. (2007), 'Policies and programmes for disadvantaged neighbourhoods: recent English experience', *Housing Studies*, **22** (2), 261–82.

Krashinsky, M. (1998), *Does Auspice Matter? The Case of Day Care for Children in Canada*, New Haven and London: Yale University Press.

Laukkanen, M. (2000), 'Exploring alternative approaches in high-level entrepreneurship education: creating micro-mechanisms for endogenous regional growth', *Entrepreneurship and Regional Development*, **12** (1), 25–47.

Lister, R. (2004), *Poverty*, Cambridge: Polity Press.

Lloyd, P. and C. Mason (1984), 'Spatial variations in new firm formation in the United Kingdom: comparative evidence from Merseyside, Greater Manchester and South Hampshire', *Regional Studies*, **18** (3), 207–20.

Macdonald, R. and F. Coffield (1991), Risky *Business? Youth and the Enterprise Culture*, London: Falmer Press.

Michael, A. (2006), 'Securing social enterprise's place in the economy', Social Enterprise Coalition Conference, Manchester, 25 January 2006, SBS press release, available at: www.sbs.gov.uk/sbsgov/action/news.

Moulaert, F., F. Martinelli, S. Gonzalez and E. Swyngedouw (2007), 'Introduction: social innovation and governance in European cities: urban development between path dependency and radical innovation', *European Urban and Regional Studies*, **14** (3), 195–209.

Nicholson, L. and A.R. Anderson (2005), 'News and nuances of the entrepreneurial myth and metaphor: linguistic games in entrepreneurial sense-making and sense-giving', *Entrepreneurship Theory and Practice*, **29** (2), 153–72.

Nolan, A. (2003), *Entrepreneurship and Local Economic Development: Policy Innovations in Industrialised Countries*, Paris: OECD.

NWDA (2003), *Social Enterprise Survey*, Warrington: North West Development Agency.

Ogbor, J.O. (2000), 'Mythicizing and reification in entrepreneurial discourse: ideology-critique of entrepreneurial studies', *Journal of Management Studies*, **37** (5), 605–35.

Parker, I. (1999), *Critical Textwork: An Introduction to Varieties of Discourse and Analysis*, Buckinghamshire: Open University Press.

Parkinson, C. and C. Howorth (2008), 'The language of social entrepreneurs', *Entrepreneurship and Regional Development*, **20** (3), 285–309.

Paton, R. (2003), *Managing and Measuring Social Enterprises*, London: Sage.

Pearce, J. (2003), *Social Enterprise in Anytown*, London: Calouste Gulbenkian Foundation.

Perren, L. and P.L. Jennings (2005), 'Government discourses on entrepreneurship: issues of legitimization, subjugation, and power', *Entrepreneurship Theory and Practice*, **29** (2), 173–84.

Policy Action Team 3 (1999), *Enterprise and Social Exclusion, National Strategy for Neighbourhood Renewal, Social Exclusion Unit PAT 3*, London: HM Treasury.

Pomerantz, M. (2003), 'The business of social entrepreneurship in a "down economy"', *Business*, **25** (3), 25–30.

Portes, A. (1994), 'The informal economy', in N.J. Smelser and R. Swedberg (eds), *The Handbook of Economic Sociology*, Princeton, NJ: Sage Foundation, pp. 426–49.

Power, A. (2001), 'Social exclusion and urban sprawl: is the rescue of cities possible?', *Regional Studies*, **35** (8), 731–42.

Ram, M. and D. Smallbone (2003), 'Policies to support ethnic minority enterprise: the English experience', *Entrepreneurship and Regional Development*, **15** (2), 151–66.

Servon, L.J. (1997), 'Microenterprise programs in US inner cities: economic development or social welfare?', *Economic Development Quarterly*, **11** (2), 166–80.

Small Business Service (2004), 'Griffiths unveils new Phoenix Fund for disadvantaged communities', Press Release, 14 April 2004, London, DTI.

Southern, A. (2006), 'Enterprise and regeneration', paper presented at First Lancaster Social Entrepreneurship Research Seminar, Lancaster University, September 2006.

Tolbert, C. M., T.A. Lyson and M.D. Irwin (1998), 'Local capitalism, civic engagement and socio-economic well-being', *Social Forces*, **77** (2), 401–27.

Townsend, P. (ed.) (1970), *The Concept of Poverty*, London: Heinemann.

Townsend, P. (1979), *Poverty in the United Kingdom*, London: Heinemann.

Weiss, G. and R. Wodak (2003), *Critical Discourse Analysis: Theory and Interdisciplinarity*, Basingstoke: Palgrave Macmillan.

Williams, C.C. (2005), 'Tackling undeclared work in advanced economies: towards an evidence based public policy approach', *Policy Studies*, **25** (4), 243–58.

Wong, C. (1999), 'Determining factors for local economic development: the perception of practitioners in the North West and Eastern regions of the UK', *Regional Studies*, **32** (8), 707–20.

Zafirovski, M. (1999), 'Probing into the social layers of entrepreneurship: outlines of the sociology of enterprise', *Entrepreneurship and Regional Development*, **11** (4), 351–71.

14. Transnationalism, mixed embeddedness and Somali entrepreneurs in Leicester

Trevor Jones, Monder Ram and Nicholas Theodorakopoulos

INTRODUCTION

In a recent critique of current ethnic minority business (EMB) literature, the present authors draw special attention to what they see as an unfortunate tendency towards *ahistoricism*, in which ethnic entrepreneurs are presented as essentially an unprecedented novelty, subject to few if any of the historical forces and economic laws governing the generality of small business operators (Jones and Ram, 2007). To judge from one tenaciously persistent strand of UK literature running from Werbner (1980) through to Basu and Altinay (2002), we might be forgiven for concluding that EMB use of informal social capital networks in business is a new innovative practice, the product of unique cultural attributes. Naturally such context-free interpretations cannot go unchallenged, with Light (2007) reminding us of Granovetter's (1985) definition of social embeddedness as the universal basis of all entrepreneurial activity for all groups at all times. Far from exceptional – or, come to that, exceptionally successful – postwar immigrant businesses in Europe are better seen as the latest recruits to a time-honoured occupation, whose rules of engagement are harsh and ruthlessly enforced by the capitalist market (Bechofer and Elliott, 1978; Rainnie 1989). In this precarious struggle for survival, social capital has always been an indispensable prop. For EMBs faced with additional costs imposed by racist barriers (Ram and Jones, 2008), the availability of cheap capital and labour from family and community takes on extra urgency. More recently these principles have been further elucidated by Kloosterman et al.'s (1999) theory of *mixed embeddedness*. As well as recognizing that EMBs are indeed firmly grounded in their own special heritage cultures, these authors also insist that ethnic business outcomes are even more decisively shaped by the 'wider economic and institutional context into which immigrants are inevitably also inserted' (Kloosterman et al., 1999, p. 252). There is an ever-present danger that structural limitations may be ignored in the promotion of ethnic agency.

Yet, indestructible as a mutant virus, ethnic exceptionalism has once more re-emerged in the currently fashionable guise of transnationalism. Here the focus is upon the permanent cross-border social networks that many immigrant groups maintain both with the country of origin and throughout their diasporas (Portes, 1996). Notably, there has been relatively little British research on the role of diasporic networks in promoting EMB competitiveness, though recent years have seen an emergent awareness of the possibilities here (Henry et al., 2002; Hepburn, 2004; Kitching et al., 2009; McEwan et al., 2005; Sepulveda et al., 2006).

As convincingly demonstrated by McEwan et al. (2005), transnational trading and investment linkages may offer a hugely expanded sphere of social capital, in which EMB retains all the advantages of preferential insider access but this time with no geographical limits. In the same vein, Bagwell (2006) in her study of Vietnamese businesses in London stressed the role of global family networks in providing business ideas, advice and finance, and market opportunities. For these authors, transnational social capital offers a genuine comparative advantage in place of the sweated labour and other desperate cost-cutting practices traditionally used to survive in marginal activities shunned by mainstream businesses (Jones et al., 2000). This has led to impressive growth and earnings far beyond those enjoyed by the standard EMB. Yet, as the authors themselves concede, their case studies may be unrepresentative of the rank and file of EMB, a qualification in line with a more cautious school of thought, which warns that any pay-off from transnationalism is contingent on a complex range of other variables (Morawska, 2004; Portes et al., 2002). Particularly vulnerable to this external context are the more recent smaller but more socially differentiated groups who embody what Vertovec (2006) calls the new 'superdiversity'. Typical of these are overseas Somalis, the subject of the present chapter, a community for whom transnationalism is virtually a defining hallmark. Apparently released from the traditional prison of space by cheap air travel, the internet and other communications technology, the lives of many Somali business operators revolve around a constant flow of information, remittances and other exchanges with Somalis world-wide (Lindley, 2005). Such a high degree of spatial liberation might be thought to provide the ultimate litmus test of the entrepreneurial effectiveness of transnationalism. Accordingly we examine the case histories of 25 Somali enterprises in Leicester to discover how far the cross-border marshalling of business resources can overcome the usual constraints on EMB. Crucially, however, this exercise is performed within the rubric of mixed embeddedness, moving beyond itemizing their social capital, global and otherwise, to fixing them within their political-economic environment. As we shall see, although the deregulated UK regime is much more favourable than elsewhere in Europe to the formation of overseas Somali business firms, their performance tends to founder against the rock of hostile local market conditions.

TRANSNATIONAL ECONOMIC NETWORKS

Although, as Portes et al. (1999) note, migrants' overseas networks have profound political and cultural repercussions, for present purposes the focus is on the economic and specifically the entrepreneurial, the way in which immigrant self-employment is nurtured by diasporic connections. In Britain, recent years have witnessed the emergence of interest in the role of overseas connections as a competitive resource for EMB (Sepulveda et al., 2006; Henry et al., 2002; Hepburn, 2004; McEwan et al., 2005; Kitching et al., 2009), with McEwan et al. (2005) providing an especially useful analysis of outstandingly successful ethnic firms in Birmingham, who appear to be differentiated from the general mass of plodders and strugglers by their strong commercial links to the home country and to other overseas co-ethnic business clusters. Outstanding here is the Chinese business community, among whose members are several prototypically transnational operators, whose operations have clearly achieved extra competitive vigour through cultivating their trading, investment and information exchange with Hong Kong, the place of origin for most Birmingham Chinese, as well as other parts of their diaspora. Among many eye-catching instances of the transnational dividend is a major supermarket employing more than 70 workers locally and sourcing a huge range of foods and other imports preferentially via ethnic trading channels from South East and East Asia. Also cited is the role of overseas Chinese investment in the lavish redevelopment of the city's Chinese quarter. Alongside this, the city is now the location for numerous ethnic food manufacturers, South Asian as well as Chinese, catering to a nationwide clientele of supermarkets. The authors also celebrate creative industries like the local Bhangra music industry, the vibrant offspring of 'innovation, fusion and transnationalism' (McEwan et al., 2005, p. 927); and broadcasting ventures in partnership with India-based companies. When all this is added to similar work by other authors such as Dwyer and Jackson (2003) on the fashion industry, a plausible case can be made for transnationalism as a decisive shaper both of the urban economy and of the ethnic entrepreneur.

From McEwan et al.'s economic geography perspective, such

transnationally boosted EMB has to be seen as a highly proactive key element in a local economy now increasingly enmeshed in a multitude of evolving global linkages (Dwyer and Jackson, 2003), a refreshing change of direction that attempts to recast losers as winners, indeed as emergent leaders in the development of the local economy. Through their membership of diasporic communities, ethnic entrepreneurs may enjoy a decisive competitive advantage over non-members, with privileged insider access to all manner of global commercial resources. Moreover, as post-industrial cities like Birmingham continue to reposition themselves in relation to economic globalization, what could be more natural than that this move be led by those of its local business community whose identity is itself 'globalized'?

Essentially this is part of a recent 'globalization-from-below' discourse (Light, 2007; Portes, 1996, 1999; Portes et al., 2002; Vertovec, 2006), which seeks to depart from the notion of migrants as victims of structural forces and to highlight instead the opportunities opened up by globalization for profitable entrepreneurial strategies. Applying this to the EMB literature, we would argue that the central significance of transnationalism for the entrepreneurs themselves is its opening up of access to vastly enlarged *social capital*. Ever since Granovetter's (1985) path-breaking account of economic transactions as embedded in social relations, social capital has become central to enterprise studies, with its emphasis on personal net-works of trust as the principal source of business resources. Since shared ethnicity is one of the most potent of all forms of trust, it is unsurprising that EMB studies have continually singled out ethnic minority entre-preneurs as benefiting from more than usually dense and solidary social networks of trust (Janjuha-Jivraj, 2003). These comprise a fertile source of labour, capital and myriad other kinds of informal business support, often available at below market rates (Flap et al., 2000; Nee and Sanders, 2001; but see Jones and Ram, 2007, and Ram et al., 2007) on the perils of over-arguing ethnic specificity). Since access to these networks is effec-tively closed to group outsiders, there is a strong element of protectionism in which group members enjoy key business resources on advantageous terms denied to non-members. McEwan et al.'s (2005) contribution is to draw attention to the way these insider networks can now operate on a hugely expanded geographical scale, thanks to the 'time–space compres-sion' (Kivisto, 2001) created by advanced communication technologies. No longer must EMB social capital be restricted by local family and community networks, since entrepreneurs can now enjoy a global range without losing any of their preferential insider dealings.

Such is the rationale of McEwan et al.'s (2005) cases, much of whose competitive life force derives from exclusive access to ethnic financial and trading connections virtually world wide. Important though this may be, however, there are widespread doubts about how far transnational entrepreneurs are representative of EMB as a whole (Portes et al., 2002). Significantly, McEwan et al. (2005, p. 927) themselves recognize the possibility that these ventures may be unrepresentative of an EMB economy more generally 'characterized by low wages, poor working conditions and racism'. For seasoned researchers in the field, this need to guard against a (perhaps understandably) over-enthusiastic celebration of the entrepreneurial achievements of disadvantaged groups (see for example, Gidoomal, 1997) is a matter of eternal vigilance. As noted in the introductory section, EMB is more typically beset by a widespread poverty of resources and a struggle for survival against heavy external barriers (Jones et al., 1994; Light and Gold, 2000). Historically, dynamic high performance EMB firms are always a tiny minority (Jones et al., 1994), a reflection not only of conditions peculiar to racialized minorities but pertaining also to the general population of independent firms, with survey after survey showing the 'fast trackers' to be heavily outnumbered by the 'trundlers' and the failures (see Storey, 1994 for summary). At the highest level of generalization, this expresses the continuing concentration of capital (Harvey, 1993), a seemingly inevitable tendency irrespective of globalization, transnationalism or any other form of restructuring (Kieley, 2007; Virdee, 2006). In a competitive capitalist system, structural shifts cannot be expected to do away with winners and losers but simply to shuffle the pecking order, creating new opportunities for a few while annihilating the many. Globalization, as Hay and Watson (1999, p. 420) remind us, 'may well be empowering for those already empowered by their access to capital'. This, we suspect, is the underlying rationale for McEwan et al.'s (2005) high performing entrepreneurs. Certainly they are to be congratulated on their vision and their strategic deployment of their cross-border cross-cultural networks to take advantage of a changing world. In the final analysis, however, they must be seen as a minority of a minority, thriving by virtue of exceptional advantages by definition denied to the great struggling mass of EMB owners.

These warnings must act as a constant guide when assessing the business histories of Somalis in Leicester. Of the many research-worthy qualities of this new immigrant community, it was their genuinely transnational orientation that principally attracted our attention, a cross-border solidarity given additional strength by (in many cases) refugee status and 'political convulsions at home' (Portes, 1999, p. 464). As entrepreneurs, these global linkages offer potentially their greatest advantage. Given that this is in many other senses an acutely disadvantaged group, we might see this as the ultimate test of transnationalism, a question of whether diasporic networks alone can overcome both the poverty of other resources and an unfavourable local commercial environment.

METHODS

Somalis and Leicester are a particularly apposite conjunction to test the connection between 'superdiversity', transnationalism and entrepreneurship. The Somali community can be seen as a 'critical case' in that it is new, comparatively small in the UK (although growing), quite highly dispersed, transnationally linked and socio-economically differentiated (Vertovec, 2006, p. 1). With over one million Somalis living abroad and labour constituting its principal export, Somalis are truly a 'globalized' society (Lindley, 2005). Diasporic connections extend to Canada, the USA, Scandinavia, as well as the UK (Bang Nielsen, 2004). Transnational links are supported by an elaborate informal remittance system and 'multi-local' (Vertovec, 2006) attachment that characterize social networks among many Somalis (Bang Nielsen, 2004).

Leicester has hosted a major concentration of British Indians since the 1960s; but over the last decade or so it has followed the national trend of increasing ethnic diversity, with a growing influx from the Middle East and Africa, including Somalia itself. Now estimated (typically imprecisely) at between 6000 and 17000 (Daahir et al., 2004; LCC, 2006), Somalis have been attracted to the city by the presence of a pre-existing Somali community and by perceptions of the UK's multi-cultural tolerance, allowing them to practise their Muslim religion more freely than in many other European countries (Daahir et al., 2004). Almost 40 per cent of the population is made up of ethnic minorities (LCC, 2006).

A qualitative research design was adopted to examine the nature of transnational links and the actual experiences of Somali business owners in Leicester. This comprised face-to-face, in-depth interviews with 25 Somalis in business, and 25 employees/volunteers (one from each enterprise). Basic profile data of the firm, such as activities, employment size, age, location and sectors, along with information on the entrepreneur, including age, gender, ethnicity, migrant status, management qualifications/training and experience, as well as motives for starting and running the business were considered. Furthermore, a semi-structured interview protocol was used to assess the drivers and inhibitors impacting Somali entrepreneurship. The research design was enhanced by considering three focus groups (one of which was all-female). These helped clarify some of the issues revealed during the interviews and delved deeper into respondents' experiences of enterprising in Leicester.

Conducting research in communities that have often been subjected to hostile political coverage like the Somalis presents challenges with regard to accessing the right informants (Faugier and Sargeant, 1997; Harris, 2004; Jones et al., 2006). A snowball sampling method was used since this is particularly effective for accessing 'hidden' populations (Hendricks and Blanken, 1992) and more suitable for small sample sizes (Black and Champion, 1976). It is cost-efficient, while refusal rates are minimized with the process of referrals from gatekeepers/participants (Penrod et al., 2003). To circumvent potential challenges related to sample bias, the researchers adopted an enhanced snowballing approach, known as chain referral sampling or multiple-snowballing. 'This technique maximizes variation in the determinants identified by the researcher as critical to the phenomenon or concept of interest' (Penrod et al., 2003, p. 105). In this study, care was been taken to direct referral strategically, in order to increase variation in the sampled population; the object was to minimize sample bias by enhancing the scope and hence the generalizability of the findings. Different gatekeepers were recruited to locate and gain access to suitable participants of different business sectors and backgrounds in Leicester.

Notably, to overcome the trust barrier, data collection was undertaken with the assistance of a trusted intermediary, who had extensive links with the Somali community and a track record of effective collaboration with the university sector. However, devising the interview protocols and undertaking all data analysis, interpretation and presentation activities was incumbent on the researchers. In order to analyse data systematically and create an audit trail (i.e. documenting data analysis and interpretation procedures) the QSR NVivo software package was used.

SOMALI ENTERPRISE AND TRANSNATIONALISM

Typical of many newly arrived Third World origin immigrant groups, Somalis in Leicester are highly dependent on the social capital embedded in tight-knit ethnic and especially kinship networks. This is operative across a whole range from the settling-in process to the launching and support of business ventures. In the former case, the already settled community plays an invaluable role in sheltering and mentoring new arrivals to the UK. A typical account is provided below:

> family friends guided us to the main service offices in the city, assisted us in locating good housing . . . this helped us to settle into Leicester life very quickly. (Owner-manager Beta)

When it comes to business itself, family and community social capital comes into play to major effect, notably in the form of cheap and reliable labour.

Moreover, as suggested, one very distinctive aspect of Somali networks is their extensive transnational scope, with many families maintaining ties of mutual aid with members in Somalia itself and throughout the diaspora. Indeed, this constant long distance inter-communication is strikingly evocative of Portes's (1996, p. 3) definition of transnational migrants as 'communities that sit astride political borders . . . "neither here nor there" but in both places simultaneously'. Significantly, these networks, 'simultaneously dense and extensive over long physical distances' (Portes, 1996, p. 8), constitute a substantial addition to the stock of social capital, in both material and intangible ways. As Box 14.1 indicates, family members contribute moral support and motivation, as well as much needed financial assistance in some cases.

From these comments we can appreciate how deeply Somali enterprise in Leicester is enmeshed in a sprawling 'transnational field' (Vertovec, 1999) of insider social relationships, a potentially rich repository of business resources extending far beyond what would be available to an isolated entrepreneurial minority solely dependent on its own locally resident community. Here we note that in almost every place Somalis have settled, they have achieved high rates of self-employed business ownership, creating what amounts to an entrepreneurial diaspora (Horst, 2002). Somali business owners in Leicester are typically in perpetual touch with similarly entrepreneurial relatives and friends in mainland Europe, North America and the Arab world as well as elsewhere in Britain. They perfectly exemplify Portes's (1996, p. 9) notion of a 'class of entrepreneurs who shuttle regularly across countries and maintain daily contact with events and activities abroad'. As R2 tells it, 'We are in constant contact via the net and through visits at least once a year' (Owner manager Xi). This is a reminder of the way in which twenty-first-century transnationalism is enabled by cheap air travel and new communication technologies. Though e-mail is not a face-to-face exchange in the narrow literal sense, it can nevertheless operate as an effective means of cementing social bonds over global space. Indeed, the internet might almost have been invented with communities like the Somalis in mind. Liberated from old-fashioned spatial bonds, Somali business is in effect now able to operate as a virtual entity across four continents, undeterred by sheer distance or even the Atlantic Ocean itself.

In practical terms, one benefit of this is that entrepreneurs R2 to R6 have been able to tap into much needed financial assistance from vastly distant sources. Given the crippling obstacles to raising capital typically

BOX 14.1 RESPONDENTS' COMMENTS ON WORLDWIDE KINSHIP AND SOCIAL LINKAGES

R1: I have family members in Dubai, Canada and USA. They are all in business and help with business ideas and encouragement. (Owner-manager Pi)

R2: I needed about £20,000 to start this business. I got initial supplies from my uncle who has a business in Dubai. This made it easier to get cheaper products. Hopefully we can expand in future and my Dubai relative is willing to provide the funds. (Owner-manager Xi)

R3: I borrowed £5,500 from my brother in Montreal for a start-up, an interest-free loan to be paid back over the next two years. (Owner-manager Upsilon)

R4: Two of my friends in Dubai lent me £6,000. This was much needed assistance for starting my business. I am thankful for such true friends. (Owner-manager Alpha)

R5: I have family members in the USA, Europe, Dubai, Saudi Arabia and Canada and close friends who come from my clan back home. We are all very close. My cousin in the USA lent me the money to start the business. (Owner-manager Eta)

R6: My family abroad play a good role, both financial and in terms of business ideas. If I need to buy more goods, I request to borrow some money and I repay them after I have sold the goods. I do the same for them whenever they need help from me. (Owner-manager Lambda)

R7: I have relatives in Toronto and Houston, I keep in constant contact with them. My uncle gave me most of the money towards the start-up of my business. I value my relatives, not just for the material things but for the support and the fellowship. This is the great value of the extended family in Somalia. (Owner-manager Omicron)

R8: I have a lot of friends in other countries and I contact them regularly. They order tickets from my agency. (Owner-manager Iota)

R9: I have family who live mostly in Africa, America and Europe as well as the UK, especially in London, Nottingham and Birmingham. They are mostly running businesses and we call each other to exchange business tactics and experience. We work together to find suitable business places around the world. (Owner-manager Nu)

R10: Members of my family have businesses in Dubai, Canada and the USA. I have been in a business environment since childhood and I had to start a business of my own once I got here, as it was something I had always desired. I like the independence and dignity it gives. I am my own boss and it is also a source of great personal pride. (Owner-manager Rho)

faced by EMB (Jones et al., 1994; Ram et al., 2002b), this advantage can hardly be exaggerated and it is apparent that overseas funding has played an important part in the start-up of several businesses in the present sample. It might also contribute to the expansion plans of firms like R3 and R4, who otherwise might be obliged to delay any growth through lack of space and stock.

At this stage, however, we need to consider the entrepreneurial advantages of these cross-border linkages with caution. Though it would indeed be pleasant to report on transnationalism as a true force for entrepreneurial empowerment, in the present case the inescapable impression is of an entrepreneurial minority essentially stuck in much the same rut as any other chronically under-resourced group of racialized entrepreneurs. One immediate explanation for this disappointing outcome is that by no means all Somalis in Leicester do enjoy access to these fertile international channels of market intelligence, low cost supplies and financial capital. On the contrary, there are sharp class divisions within the community, which in this case means that transnationalism tends to be the preserve of better off individuals. Our findings suggest that those excluded from transnational linkages perform less well than those who do enjoy them. Whether this is because these are generally the least well resourced is not clear at this stage.

More to the point, however, it has to be recognized that even those Somalis who do benefit from such linkages do not generally present a picture of rude entrepreneurial health. On the contrary, all the signs point to a set of marginal and often precariously surviving firms, typified by one respondent who laments: 'Any small situation in my life can cause my business to fail' (Owner-manager Gamma). For perhaps a majority of these firms, transnational social capital manifests itself mostly in the form of information exchange and moral support rather than the lavish financial backing required to break the constraints in which EMB is customarily confined. While these intangibles certainly do contribute hugely to entrepreneurial motivation, confidence and morale, all the evidence from the present survey points to the transnational dimension as offering little more than a buffer for a set of firms that, in almost every respect, are simply reproducing the age-old EMB symptoms of marginality and precarious survival. Business life for many Somalis in Leicester is, as one shopkeeper complains, 'hard work without much return', echoing one of the long-running refrains of ethnic business studies.

Entrepreneurs themselves clearly recognize these drawbacks and one aspiring Somali business entrant went so far as to tell us: 'I have a very poor opinion of Somali business. Products are rubbish' (Focus group participant FG1). While this might seem a little over-judgemental, it accurately captures a sense of social exclusion and frustration at unrealized potential. In classic mode, Somali firms in Leicester are locked into that *demi-monde*, described by Kloosterman as 'the lower end of the distribution of firms: very small scale, low value-added and labour intensive, with a small capital to labour ratio' (Kloosterman, 2000, p. 95). Unhappily, many of the negative symptoms of this are present in particularly acute form in the present sample. Tellingly, the overwhelming majority of these firms are located in the least rewarded and indeed least desired sectors of the economy (Table 14.1), perhaps the most graphic indicator of entrepreneurial disadvantage (Ram and Jones, 2008). Corner shop retailing and consumer services like catering are the historic preserve of immigrant entrepreneurs in western cities and this over-reliance on these over-crowded low yielding onerous activities looms large once again in the present sample. Apart from a few exceptions dealing in lines like travel agencies and computer repair, there is a lack of diversity, with firms largely confined to low order retailing and restaurants. Of the 25 firms listed in Table 14.1, 12 are wholly or partially reliant on retailing activities and a further six run restaurants or cafes. Though such a limited sample is not claimed as statistically representative, it is more than indicative of a quite inordinate degree of sectoral concentration.

In substance, then, there is very little here to distinguish Somali enterprise from the general run of EMB. Moreover, there is a palpable sense of history repeating itself. The resemblance to the first wave of struggling South Asian businesses in Britain as charted by early researchers like Aldrich et al. (1981) and Rafiq (1985) is almost uncanny. The only

Table 14.1 Sample of Somali firms in the study

Business name pseudonym	Sector	Ownership	Tenure (months)	No. of employees	No. of helpers	Owner's gender	Age	Education	Growth orientation	Net income
Alpha	Retail	Sole Trader	84	0	1	Male	25–34	Secondary	No	Static
Beta	Retail	Partnership	24	0	3	Male	45–54	Graduate	Yes	Static
Gamma	Retail	Sole Trader	36	0	1	Female	45–54	Secondary	Yes	Falling
Delta	Retail	Sole Trader	6	0	1	Male	35–44	Secondary	Yes	Static
Epsilon	Retail	Sole Trader	6	0	1	Male	45–54	Secondary	Yes	N/A
Zeta	Retail	Sole Trader	24	0	2	Male	45–54	GCSE	Yes	Static
Eta	Services/café/retail	Sole Trader	24	0	1	Male	45–54	Primary	Yes	Rising
Theta	Electronics/comp. repair	Sole Trader	36	1	0	Male	25–34	NVQ	Yes	Static
Iota	Travel agent/media	Ltd	24	0	1	Male	45–54	Graduate	Yes	Static
Kappa	Travel agent	Ltd	36	1	0	Male	35–44	NVQ 2	Yes	Rising
Lambda	Retail/comp. repair	Sole Trader	10	0	1	Male	45–54	Secondary	No	Static
Mu	Hairdressers/retail	Sole Trader	11	0	1	Male	35–44	Primary C	No	New
Nu	Imports/exports/distrib./retail	Ltd	24	0	1	Male	35–44	GCSE	Yes	Static
Xi	Intern. café & tel./retail	Ltd	24	0	1	Male	35–44	GCSE	Yes	Static
Omicron	Intern. café/comp. sales & repair	Sole Trader	24	0	2	Male	45–54	Secondary	No	Static
Pi	Restaurant & indoor games	Sole Trader	48	2	1	Male	45–54	NVQ 3	Yes	Rising
Rho	Retail	Sole Trader	8	0	1	Female	35–44	NVQ 2	Yes	Static
Sigma	Tel./money transfer/food intern. café/money	Sole Trader	10	0	2	Male	45–54	NVQ 2	No	Static
Tau	Transfer/food	Partnership	17	1	0	Male	35–44	Secondary	No	Rising

Table 14.1 (continued)

Business name pseudonym	Sector	Ownership	Tenure (months)	No. of employees	No. of helpers	Owner's gender	Age	Education	Growth orientation	Net income
Upsilon	Auto repairs	Sole Trader	60	4	0	Male	25–34	Secondary	Yes	Rising
Phi	Restaurant	Sole Trader	36	3	0	Male	45–54	Secondary	Yes	Rising
Chi	Retail/grocers	Sole Trader	18	1	0	Male	55+	Secondary	Yes	Rising
Psi	Internet café/tel.	Ltd	36	1	0	Male	45–54	Secondary	Yes	Rising
Omega	Butcher/grocer	Sole Trader	12	1	0	Male	45–54	Secondary	Yes	Rising
AlphaEn	Retail/grocer	Sole Trader	18	0	1	Male	35–44	NVQ3	Yes	Rising

hint that almost three decades have passed is the presence of a handful of internet cafes, though this may be more a reflection of changing style than anything of practical substance. Furthermore, given that the majority of early Asian entrepreneurs were manual workers displaced by industriali-zation, whereas the Somalis appear to be a largely self-selected group of entrepreneurially motivated individuals (Daahir et al., 2004; Ram and Patton, 2003), the lack of contrast is even more striking. To some degree, their disadvantage may be a partial product of their newness, and evidence from a focus group of aspiring business owners suggests the possibility of some diversification in the near future. Optimistically, one of these aspir-ants is qualifying to become a self-employed accountant, while another intends to start a building firm. Each of these proposals would, if realized, represent a significant breakout from the present sectoral trap. As yet, however, these are but miniscule straws in the wind and history suggests that a tiny minority of Somali firms might be hugely successful, a great many will die and the in-between majority will exist on the basis of much sweat and tears.

Even more directly indicative of a struggle for survival is the finding that many if not most of the firms interviewed depend for their viability on that other typical EMB last resort of low paid or even unwaged labour. In itself, this is a further expression of *under-capitalization*, yet another of the congenital disadvantages facing immigrant business owners (Ram et al., 2002a). Very much in the manner of every other entrepreneurial minor-ity, the Somali business economy is based on the substitution of labour for capital; labour that comes cheaply because it is provided by family members and co-ethnics on a personal rather than a contractual basis (Ram et al., 2007). This cost-cutting strategy is absolutely central to the Somali business economy. According to the candid testimony of one of the retailers: 'employing Somali co-ethnics is a means of getting assistance without paying a high salary' (Owner-manager Zeta).

Several of the workers interviewed told us they were not taking any pay at all. Strictly speaking, the labour process in many of these operations is not based on 'employees' in the true sense but on 'helpers'. This apparently flagrant injustice is in a great many cases rationalized in terms of mutual benefits and deferred gratification, with workers/helpers viewing their situation as a kind of business apprenticeship. A couple of representative quotes give the flavour of this: 'I am keen to get into business. I am not getting full pay but I am gaining experience' (Worker Lambda). 'I don't get paid but the important thing is to learn a skill' (Worker Gamma). Apart from the consideration that entrepreneurial apprenticeship is a complex and intensely contested notion in itself (Ram et al., 2001), this widespread reliance on uncosted labour is hardly suggestive of an entrepreneurial economy dynamized by transnationalism or any other extraordinary innovation. This impression is reinforced by the further widespread use of unwaged family members, typified by one retailer, assisted in running his shop by his wife, who explains: 'She is not paid a salary at all. What we make in the shop is sufficient for the family and we can't afford a second salary' (Owner-manager AlphaEn). As ever, there is no straightforward black and white verdict on a highly traditional informal labour process, where the distinction between the domestic and the productive spheres is blurred to the point of invisibility; and where there is constant trade-off between material and non-material rewards, monetary versus personal considerations (Ram et al., 2007).

Indeed, from a purely humanistic viewpoint, we might rejoice with Werbner (1999) that, in a consumerist age of unprecedented materialism, sentiment and cultural values are still capable of trumping cold-blooded calculation. Reassuringly, a further acquaintance with the burgeoning literature on the informal economy (Leonard, 1998; Williams, 2006) offers a mass of evidence on the pervasive influence of altruistic work motivations. Yet, while freely acknowledging all this, our point is simply that reliance on informal practices to the extreme degree evident in the present case betrays a serious lack of economic resources as understood in the conventional sense. Since market imperatives are ultimately a matter of commercial life or death, they cannot be wished away by other-worldly idealism.

More specifically for present purposes, it is clear that cross-border linkages do not pay off for Somalis in the way they do for the cases outlined by McEwan et al. (2005). Highly dynamic transnational networks do not seem to translate into highly dynamic business performance. In effect, the business resources generated by Somali diasporic social networks are insufficient to compensate for deficiencies in forms of capital (Nee and Sanders, 2001) other than social capital. Not only are Somali entrepreneurs seriously starved of financial capital but they also lack human capital, in the shape of educational and professional qualifications recognized in the UK. This is compounded by problems with what Nee and Sanders (2001) would call 'cultural capital', with language barriers one of the many symptoms of social dislocation suffered by any recently arrived migrant community. Arguably this goes far to explain both a high degree of reliance on self-employment as a refuge for individuals ill equipped to compete in the open labour market; and for their struggle to thrive in that most demanding of occupations. Even so, we would argue that personal resource inadequacies tell only part of the story and need to be located in their proper context in order to arrive at anything approaching a full explanation.

THE STRUCTURAL CONTEXT

Following Rainnie's (1989) argument that, irrespective of ethnic identity, small firms can only be properly understood in relation to their external context, we would move the analysis beyond internal group resources to a consideration of the way these interact with the external environment. Here we are especially interested in what Waldinger et al. (1990) call the 'opportunity structure'; that is, the mix of entrepreneurial possibilities and hazards presented by the receiving society that Somali entrepreneurs must negotiate. In the EMB field, the most advanced theorization of this political-economic context is offered by Kloosterman et al.'s (1999, see also Kloosterman, 2000; Kloosterman and Rath, 2001, 2003) *mixed embeddedness* model. Here they seek to reinterpret the position of ethnic entrepreneurs by examining 'not only their rather concrete embeddedness in social networks of immigrants but also their rather more abstract embeddedness in the socio-economic and politico-institutional environment of the country of settlement' (Kloosterman and Rath, 2001, p. 190). They worry about an over-emphasis in the EMB literature on ethnic social capital and internal group characteristics at the expense of a full analysis of the opportunity structure.

Such theorizing does of course require intensely delicate tightrope walking, since we should never lose sight of the actors themselves, of what Virdee (2006, p. 614) calls 'the self-activity of racialized minorities in reshaping . . . adverse circumstances'. Even so, Kloosterman and Rath (2003, p. 5) are adamant that 'many researchers confine themselves to exploring and refining agency . . . instead of elaborating on the interplay of agency and structure'. Ever mindful that ethnic entrepreneurs should never be depicted as pawns or victims, they nevertheless insist that even active agents 'have to accept the specific socio-economic make-up of their new place of living' (Kloosterman and Rath, 2001, p. 196). Yet, while ethnic entrepreneurs are certainly never without some degree of strategic choice, they must ultimately conform to stringent rules and tight parameters laid down by the market. Here we note that this interaction between a narrow range of strategic options and a narrow range of market opportunities is a universal non-ethnic-specific principle applying to all but the very largest corporations with monopolistic leverage (Scase, 2002). For various reasons, however, the straitjacket is laced even tighter on EMB than it is for the general run of enterprises (Ram and Jones, 2008).

Bearing all this in mind, we now attempt to understand the Somali entrepreneurial position through their struggle to come to terms with the harsh laws laid down by the market. For Kloosterman and Rath (2001), the market forces impinging on EMB are heavily conditioned by the political and institutional as well as the purely economic. High importance is attached to differences in national government regulatory regimes, where the relatively deregulated economies of North America and Britain have been shown to offer a very favourable environment for immigrant entrepreneurs. By contrast, the much more tightly regulated regimes of continental Europe place all manner of legal and institutional barriers to their business entry (Haberfellner, 2003), with the result that EMB development in those countries lags significantly behind that in Britain.

In itself, this has an immediate bearing on British-based Somali entrepreneurs, many of whom were previously resident in the Netherlands and Denmark, where their business ambitions had been thwarted (Bang Nielsen, 2004). Our sample contains many of these secondary migrants. Characteristic is the account provided by one of our respondents: 'When I went to business school in Holland my objective was to go into business there. However, that proved harder than I thought. When I visited Leicester and saw what Somali people had achieved there, I decided to move' (Owner-manager Omicron). On the face of it, this is a textbook example of positive agency, a migrant not only positively motivated towards entrepreneurship but also able to use transnational links to transcend structural barriers. Unhappily, this would be a simplistic interpretation, since any idea of deregulated Britain as a land of opportunity for migrant business founders on the fundamental distinction between quality and quantity. As demonstrated by Barrett et al. (2003), the absence of any formal entry barriers certainly does permit the proliferation of vast numbers of EMB in the UK, but in the long run this merely ensures a surfeit of firms and cut-throat competition. In the general absence of effective business resources, above all financial capital, the majority of these great swarms of little firms are destined to eke out an existence on the economic margins.

This could hardly be more graphically illustrated than by the position of Leicester Somalis. At the very outset, their freedom of movement has been drastically circumscribed by their extremely modest stocks of financial and other resources. Very much in the mode of every other newly arrived set of raw entrepreneurs, they have had little choice but to gravitate towards low threshold sectors, markets that are the easiest to enter because they 'require only small outlays of capital and relatively low levels of education' (Kloosterman and Rath, 2001, p. 191). Self-evidently, this accounts for their enormous over-representation in micro-scale retailing and catering, where the need for minimal outlay on premises, equipment and stock has offered a business opening to several of our most cash-strapped respondents. In one case, 'I was an indigent refugee with no resources of any kind. I only had a small amount of pocket money given by government officials'

(Owner-manager Chi). That he is now running a shop is a great source of personal pride – though not, regrettably, of great personal wealth.

As repeatedly noted by EMB researchers, the down side of easy entry is that it almost by definition guarantees only poor earnings (Aldrich et al., 1981; Jones et al., 2000), given the elementary rule that returns on capital are proportionate to the investment. What comes out is determined by what goes in. Coupled with this, 'low entry barriers are synonymous with high levels of competition . . . as a result, profits tend to be low, failure rates high and the . . . mere existence of the firm increasingly depends on informal or illegal practices' (Engelen, 2001, p. 217). On this last point, another recurrent theme in the recent British literature concerns the use of illegal immigrant workers and the undercutting of the National Minimum Wage as desperate cost-cutting survival strategies for marginal EMB (Jones et al., 2004, 2006; Ram et al., 2007). In the present case, some Somali entrepreneurs are found to be using precisely this survival stratagem, though theirs is a perfectly legal version in that their unpaid 'helpers' do not come within any sort of official definition of 'employee'. Even so, their function – low cost survival lifeline – is essentially the same as any other invisible labour force, as is that of the many unpaid family members. In terms of the ever-present agency/structure dialectic, this deployment of invisible labour certainly comes within the literal definition of autonomous decision-making, while at the same time underlining the rather desperate nature of the options open to bottom end business owners. 'Hobson's Choice' would be the most realistic description of their room for manoeuvre.

At root, all this is a reflection of Engelen's (2001) point about high levels of competition. By definition, the very ease of entry to these low value sectors is a virtual guarantee that they will attract vast numbers of small scale entrepreneurs too poorly resourced to seek their salvation in more demanding sectors of the market. Jones et al. (2000) use the term 'entrepreneurial overpopulation' to describe the way that the consumer potential in these markets is insufficient to support the number of firms at an economic level of return. This apparent violation of the neo-classical principle of equilibrium stems from the fact that Somalis, like any other micro business proprietors, are not rationally calculative and are prepared to operate for returns well below anything likely to be deemed 'economic' by the yardsticks of capitalist accountancy.

This interpretation is forcefully borne out by our sample responses. When asked about their most pressing problems, Somali entrepreneurs repeatedly cite intense competition as one of the highest hurdles in their path. For many, the impossibility of drumming up sufficient custom to earn a decent living is a consequence of direct competition with a multitude of other ethnic minority firms, owned by Indians and other much longer settled groups. Now deep-rooted, with accumulated capital and an established local customer base, supply chains and other commercial links built up through time and familiarity, these incumbent competitors are difficult to live with and still more so to displace. This is especially so in Leicester, where the entrepreneurial position of Indians and East African Asians is extraordinarily far reaching (Ram and Patton, 2003). The practical effects of this built-in competitive disadvantage are highlighted by the complaint of a barely profitable shopkeeper: 'Along this street there are many Asian businesses that are well financed and can attract more customers than I can because they have more products' (Owner manager Beta). Expressing a widespread perception of a kind of ethnic monopoly and superiority of the Asian customer base, respondents claim: 'Currently the Asians are supplying everyone's needs' (Owner-manager Zeta). 'In this location, most businesses are owned by Asian people. Hence it is difficult to compete, as they have a larger population to service' (Owner-manager Rho).

Likewise, one of the food retailers defines his own greatest problem as 'Competition from other cash and carry shops in the neighbourhood with much greater variety of products' (Owner-manager AlphaEn). Once again we are reminded of the inter-relationship between market position and capital, the lack of which is the prime cause of poor market choice and inability to compete on level terms.

There are countless historical precedents and the EMB literature on 'vacancy chains' is illuminating here (Ram and Jones, 2008). According to this perspective, newly arrived immigrant groups tend to establish themselves in business by taking over business opportunities vacated by their previous incumbents, a process of entrepreneurial succession that often proceeds hand-in-hand with residential succession (Aldrich and Reiss, 1976). In cities like Leicester during the 1970s, this took the form of South Asian shops and services inserting themselves into the space abandoned by white owners (Aldrich et al., 1981). Now, in the latest round, another wave of newcomers like Somalis are inserting themselves in much the same way. As suggested by Ram and Patton (2003), there is in Leicester an emerging trend for the established South Asian entrepreneurs to move to higher level business or out of self-employment altogether. Already this is opening up space for them to move into, but as yet Asian business is still omnipresent and competitively formidable. Even where Somalis can find space, they are still confined to low level market opportunities, which is of course the very reason why Asians are willing to abandon them. In addition, there is no necessary guarantee that the tendency will continue far enough and fast enough to completely accommodate Somali demands for business opportunities.

Before closing this discussion of sectoral constraints, we must strongly emphasize that, powerful though the structural forces may be, Somali enterprise should not be simply dismissed as passively allocated to a position in some sort of racialized division of labour. On the contrary, their position is neither immutable nor non-negotiable. This is best seen in the attitudes of the focus group of young would-be entrepreneurs, many of whom show not a little strategic vision. Among other issues like the need for training and access to business support, there is widespread awareness of the need for sectoral diversification and widening of the customer base. 'We need to penetrate into communities other than Somali. That is the only way Somali business can gain more customers' (Owner-manager Epsilon). 'The more people our businesses can appeal to, the better the amount of trade we can do' (Owner manager Nu). 'Opening to other markets should be assisted' (Owner manager Tau). Even with this awareness and will to conquer barriers, however, these barriers must still be recognized as formidable. If past precedents are any guide, it is likely to be only the very best equipped who will scale them. Once again, options are available but within a very narrow range.

THE URBAN SPATIAL DIMENSION

Closely articulated with the sectoral dimension is the spatial dimension, whose influence on the mix of opportunities and constraints often tends to reinforce that of sector. In the preceding discussion we frequently used the term 'space' in an essentially non-geographic sense to denote the scale of market opportunities available to competing entrepreneurial minorities. Yet there is a more literally spatial dimension to the opportunity structure, as Kloosterman and Rath (2001, p. 197) remind us, 'Access to markets and their growth potential differ not only from city to city but from neighbourhood to neighbourhood within cities'. Just as EMB tends to be excluded from the plum sectors of the economy, so too is it from the prime urban locations and sites (Rekers and Van Kempen, 2000). A further reminder of this is given by our respondents, whose repeated complaints about the drawbacks of their physical location are closely related to their competitive disadvantages: 'The place of my business premises is not that good. My business could grow well if I got good premises' (Owner-manager Nu). 'The thing is, we need a bigger space in a better location' (Owner-manager Delta). 'My shop premises are not in the right place' (Owner-manager Iota). 'My shop is not in an attractive location, therefore my competitors can defeat me' (Owner-manager Gamma).

As argued by Rekers and Van Kempen (2000), access to prime locations and quality premises is strictly rationed by capital and thus denied to most small immigrant entrepreneurs. In the case of the small retail and consumer service outlets that predominate in the Somali enterprise economy, customer potential depends in the first instance on the size and affluence of the local resident population. This is picked up by one of the focus group discussants, whose business entry strategy includes 'looking for rich areas'. Theoretically, the optimum formula is to be the only specialist business in a highly affluent suburb (Jones et al., 2006). Needless to say, in practice most Leicester Somalis ply their trade cheek by jowl with a host of competitors in the least rich areas of the city. Given the reliance on family and co-ethnic labour and other community links, firms are overwhelmingly located within or near the main Somali residential clusters. Largely because of the asylum dispersal process, these are concentrated in relatively deprived areas like Highfields and South Braunstone (LCC, 2006), ensuring a rather depressed customer base of low income local residents, Somali and non-Somali alike. On top of this, such urban stress locations usually impose all manner of additional security costs (Jones et al., 2000). Several respondents echo the aggrieved shopkeeper's account: 'There is a big problem of stock and vandalism, especially by local kids' (Owner-manager Rho).

A further aspect of market location explored by Ram et al.'s (2002a) study of curry houses is the agglomeration effect, the strategic cluster of shops and services, where each individual firm benefits from the presence of others in what is a recognized port of call for shoppers and diners. It seems that few of our respondents benefit from this and there are several complaints about the 'lack of passing trade'. Continuing the rather pessimistic theme, we must nevertheless remind ourselves that entry to such retail and service centres is rationed by higher rents and other costs.

One particularly unpleasant barrier that finally rears its head at this spatial level is racism. While racism may well be implicated in an impersonal sense in other aspects of business resource allocation, it is rarely directly identified as such by our respondents. On the contrary, more than one of them go out of their way to praise what they see as Leicester's multicultural inclusiveness. However, when it comes to business premises there is widespread perception of discrimination, voiced by the focus group member who claims, 'There are some areas who say "no place" when Somali people apply to rent. They are simply hostile' (Owner-manager Kappa). In the Somali case, exclusionary practices in the local property market are undoubtedly reinforced by negative stereotyping of asylum-seekers and refugees. Whatever the reason, its practical effect is to unfairly restrict access to business property as well as housing. Hence our respondents' long string of complaints about inadequate premises in sub-prime locations.

CONCLUSION

In a field where historical and structural context are often ignored and insufficiently theorized, the link between 'transnationalism' and entrepreneurship is potentially a seductive one, chiming as it does with complementary discourses on 'globalization from below' and the contribution of 'ethnic diversity' to competitiveness. The extant (and largely non-UK) literature on the phenomenon of transnational entrepreneurship has documented how EMBs use their diasporic networks to access an array of valuable resources additional to those available locally (Zhou, 2004).

Yet, amid the feverish enthusiasm for this novel addition to ethnic agency, vital structural elements are unaccounted for and the present chapter has attempted to apply a corrective through the introduction of Kloosterman et al.'s (1999) theory of mixed embeddedness to examine the (often negative) impact of the structural environment. As well as bridging a conceptual gap here, we might also claim to have bridged a transatlantic gap, a tendency among the highly influential American pace-setters in this field to ignore mixed embeddedness and other European theoretical contributions. Empirically, the chapter has examined the extent to which UK-based Somalis – a community emblematic of the new era of 'super-diversity' – are drawing on their transnational links to establish small enterprises. Here it became immediately evident that the transnational co-ethnic links of Somalis served as a crucial resource for the nurturing of small business activity. For the many 'secondary' movers in the sample, pre-existing ties in the UK were crucial to the identification of places to settle, labour market information, and an array of other resources. Somalis routinely drew on transnational links to access finance, labour and commercially useful information. Though the utilization of co-ethnic social capital is a much remarked upon feature of ethnic minority enterprise (Jones and Ram, 2007), its centrality to the operation of most of the firms in the sample is nonetheless surprising. But as the day-to-day experiences of our business owners and workers illustrate, this falls considerably short of neo-liberal depictions of the propitious consequences of globalization. The political-economic context imposes harsh constraints on Somali business activity that cannot be circumvented by the mobilization of social capital, be it local or transnational. In the light of these constraints, transnational entrepreneurship is likely to be the preserve of a minority of minorities.

By illuminating the dynamics of 'transnational' Somali business activity, we have begun to address a gap in the literature on ethic minority enterprise, which has struggled to address the 'diversification of diversity' (Vertovec, 2006) that attends the arrival of new communities in the UK.

Moreover, in the field of migration, there has been much discussion on the importance of 'conditioning factors' in explaining the 'integration' of new arrivals (Castles et al., 2002). One set of factors are undoubtedly the different 'forms of capital' (Nee and Sanders, 2001) that new arrivals draw on; that is, immigrant incorporation or integration is largely a function of the social, financial and human capital of families, as well as how these resources are used by individuals within and apart from the structure of ethnic networks and institutions. However, these resources have to be set against the conditions of the receiving context, which include the nature of the product and labour markets in which new arrivals operate, distribution, segregation/concentration in specific areas, and the support available to pursue business opportunities. We have shown how both sets of factors interact.

The findings also present challenges to policy makers. Though diasporic sources of capital and capital were routinely used by this truly 'globalized' community, policy makers could fruitfully explore ways in which they could be developed (Lyon et al., 2006). In conjunction with this, interventions to improve the local context for migrant entrepreneurship could boost both local regeneration and Somali business activity itself, a thrust congruent with the government's agenda to promote 'enterprise for all'. However, the *quality* of the businesses reported here is highly questionable, as indicated by the widespread nature of 'informal' activity in the sample (see also Sepulveda et al., 2006). Policy makers face the difficult choice of ignoring such practices, condoning informality, or attempting to transition such enterprises into the 'formal' economy. Future research in this area, examining and/or enacting successful transitions, would be beneficial.

REFERENCES

Aldrich, H. and A. Reiss Jr. (1976), 'Continuities in the study of ecological succession: changes in the racial composition of neighborhoods and their businesses', *American Journal of Sociology*, **81** (4), 846–66.
Aldrich, H., J. Cater, T. Jones and D. McEvoy (1981), 'Business development and self-segregation: Asian enterprise in three British cities', in C. Peach, V. Robinson and S. Smith (eds), *Ethnic Segregation in Cities*, London: Croom Helm.
Bagwell, S. (2006), 'UK Vietnamese businesses: cultural influences and intercultural differences', *Environment and Planning C: Government and Policy*, **24**, 51–69.
Bang Nielsen, K. (2004), 'Next stop Britain: the influence of transnational networks on the secondary movement of Danish Somalis', Working Paper no. 22, Centre for Migration Research, Sussex.

Barrett, G., T. Jones and D. McEvoy (2003), 'United Kingdom: severely constrained entrepreneurialism', in R. Kloosterman and J. Rath (eds), *Immigrant
Entrepreneurs: Venturing Abroad in the Age of Globalisation*, Oxford: Berg.

Basu, A. and E. Altinay (2002), 'The interaction between culture and entrepreneurship in London's immigrant businesses', *International Small Business Journal*, **20**
(4), 371–94.

Bechofer, F. and B. Elliott (1978), 'The voice of small business and the politics of
survival', *Sociological Review*, **26**, 57–88.

Black J.A. and D.J. Champion (1976), *Methods and Issues in Social Research*,
Chichester: John Wiley and Sons.

Castles, S., M. Korac, E. Vasta and S. Vertovec (2002), 'Integration: mapping the
field', Home Office Online Report 28/03.

Daahir, J., M. Bargchi and T. Abdishakur (2004), 'Mapping Somali children's
educational needs in Leicester', report submitted to LCC, Leicester Partnership
through Neighbourhood Renewal Funding, Regent College, Leicester.

Dwyer, C. and P. Jackson (2003), 'Commodifying difference: selling EASTern
fashion, *Environment and Planning D*, **21** (3), 269–91.

Engelen, E. (2001), '"Breaking in" and "breaking out": a Weberian approach to
entrepreneurial opportunities', *Journal of Ethnic and Migration Studies*, **27** (2),
203–23.

Faugier, J. and M. Sargeant (1997), 'Sampling hard to reach populations', *Journal
of Advanced Nursing*, **26**, 790–797.

Flap, H., B. Bulderand and A. Kumcu (2000), 'The social capital of ethnic entrepreneurs and their business success', in J. Rath (ed.), *Immigrant Businesses: The
Economic, Political and Social Environment*, London: Macmillan.

Gidoomal, R. (1997), *The UK Maharajahs: Inside the Asian Success Story*,
London: Nicholas Brealey.

Granovetter, M. (1985), 'Economic action and social structures: the problem of
embeddedness', *American Journal of Sociology*, **91** (3), 481–510.

Haberfellner, R. (2003), 'Austria: still a highly regulated economy, in R.
Kloosterman and J. Rath (eds), *Immigrant Entrepreneurship: Venturing Abroad
in the Age of Globalisation*, Oxford: Berg.

Harris, H. (2004), *The Somali Community in the UK: What We Know and How
We Know It*, London: King's College, Information Centre about Asylum and
Refugees in the UK (ICAR).

Harvey, D. (1993), *The Condition of Post-Modernity*, Oxford: Blackwell.

Hay, C. and M. Watson (1999), 'Globalisation: sceptical notes on the 1999 Reith
Lectures', *Political Quarterly*, **70** (4), 418–25.

Hendricks, V.M. and P. Blanken (1992), 'Snowball sampling: theoretical and
practical considerations', in V.M Hendirck, P. Blanken and N. Adrians (eds),
Snowball Sampling: A Pilot Study on Cocaine Use, Rotterdam: IVO.

Henry, N., C. McEwan and J. Pollard (2002), 'Globalisation from below:
Birmingham postcolonial workshop', *Area*, **34** (2), 117–27.

Hepburn, J. (2004), *Ethnic Minority Entrepreneurship in the UK*, London: Business
in the Community and Lloyds TSB.

Horst, C. (2002), 'Transnational dialogues: developing ways to do research in a
diasporic community', unpublished paper, Transnationalism Seminar, Utrecht
University, CERES Summer School, 26–28 June.

Janjuha-Jivraj, S. (2003), 'The sustainability of social capital within ethnic
networks', *Journal of Business Ethics*, **47** (1), 31–43.

Jones, T. and M. Ram (2007), 'Re-embedding the ethnic business agenda', *Work, Employment and Society*, **21** (3), 439–57.

Jones, T., G. Barrett and D. McEvoy (1994), 'Raising capital for the ethnic minority firm', in A. Hughes and D. Storey (eds), *Finance and the Small Firm*, London: Routledge.

Jones, T., G. Barrett and D. McEvoy (2000), 'Market potential as a decisive influence on the performance of ethnic minority business', in J. Rath (ed.), *Immigrant Businesses: The Economic, Political and Social Context*, London: Macmillan.

Jones, T., M. Ram and P. Edwards (2004), 'Illegal immigrants and the Asian underground economy in the West Midlands, *International Journal of Economic Development*, **6** (1), 92–113.

Jones, T., M. Ram and P. Edwards (2006), 'Shades of grey in the black economy', *International Journal of Sociology and Social Policy*, **23** (2), 9–10,

Kieley, R. (2007), 'Globalisation and poverty and the poverty of globalisation theory', *Current Sociology*, **53** (6), 895–914.

Kitching, J., D. Smallbone and R. Athayde (2009), 'Ethnic diasporas and business competitiveness: a study of minority-owned enterprises in London', *Journal of Ethnic and Migration Studies*, **35** (4), 689–705.

Kivisto, P. (2001), 'Theorizing transnational immigrants: a critical review of current efforts', *Ethnic and Racial Studies*, **24** (4), 549–77.

Kloosterman, R. (2000), 'Immigrant entrepreneurship and the institutional context: a theoretical exploration', in J. Rath (ed.), *Immigrant Businesses: The Economic, Political and Social Environment*, London: Macmillan.

Kloosterman, R. and J. Rath (2001), 'Immigrant entrepreneurs in advanced societies: mixed embeddedness further explored', *Journal of Ethnic and Migration Studies*, **27** (2), 189–201.

Kloosterman, R. and J. Rath (2003), 'Introduction', in R. Kloosterman and J. Rath (eds), *Immigrant Entrepreneurs: Venturing Abroad in the Age of Globalisation*, Oxford: Berg.

Kloosterman, R., J. Van Leun and J. Rath (1999), 'Mixed embeddedness: (in) formal economic activities and immigrant businesses in the Netherlands', *International Journal of Urban and Regional Research*, **23** (2), 252–66.

LCC (2006), *The Diversity of Leicester: A Demographic Profile*, Leicester: LCC Community Cohesion Project Team and LPIG, October.

Leonard, M. (1998), *Invisible Work, Invisible Workers*, Basingstoke: Macmillan.

Light, I. (2007), 'Global entrepreneurship and transnationalism', in L. Dana (ed.), *Handbook of Research on Ethnic Minority Entrepreneurship*, Cheltenham, UK and Northampton, MA, USA: Edward Elgar.

Light, I. and S. Gold (2000), *Ethnic Economies*, San Diego, CA: Academic Press.

Lindley, A. (2005), 'Somalia country study', Working paper, Oxford Centre on Migration, Policy and Society, Oxford.

Lyon, F., L. Sepulveda and A. Botero-Jethwa (2006), 'Enterprising refugees: their impact, constraints and lessons for support providers', proceedings of the 29th ISBE National Small Firms Conference, Cardiff, 30 October – 1 November.

McEwan, C., J. Pollard and N. Henry (2005), 'The "global" in the city economy: multicultural economic development in Birmingham', *International Journal of Urban and Regional Research*, **29** (4), 916–33.

Morawska, E. (2004), 'Immigrant transnational entrepreneurs in New York: three varieties and their correlates', *International Journal of Entrepreneurial Behaviour and Research*, **10**, 325–48.

Nee, V. and J. Sanders (2001), 'Understanding the diversity of immigrant incorporation: a forms-of-capital model, *Ethnic and Racial Studies*, **24** (3), 386–411.

Penrod, J., D. Preston, R.E. Cain and M.T. Starks (2003), 'A discussion of chain referral as a method of dampling hard-to-reach populations', *Journal of Transcultural Nursing*, **14** (2), 100–107.

Portes, A. (1996), 'Transnational communities: their emergence and significance in the contemporary world system', in R. Korzeniewicz and W. Smith (eds), *Latin America and the World Economy*, Westport, CT: Greenwood Press.

Portes, A. (1999), 'Conclusion', *Ethnic and Racial Studies*, **20** (2), 463–77.

Portes, A., L. Guarnizo and P. Landolt (1999), 'The study of transnationalism: pitfalls and promise of an emergent research field', *Ethnic and Racial Studies*, **22** (2), 217–37.

Portes, A., W. Haller and L. Guarnizo (2002), 'Transnational entrepreneurship: the emergence of an alternative form of immigrant economic adaptation', *American Sociological Review*, **67**, 278–98.

Rafiq, M. (1985), *Asian Businesses in Bradford: Profile and Prospect*, Bradford: Bradford Metropolitan Council.

Rainnie, A. (1989), *Industrial Relations in Small Firms*, London: Routledge.

Ram, M. and T. Jones (2008), *Ethnic Minorities in Business*, 2nd edn, Milton Keynes: Small Business Research Trust.

Ram, M. and D. Patton (2003), *A Strategy for the Support of Black and Minority Ethnic Businesses in Leicestershire*, Leicester: Business Link Leicestershire.

Ram, M., T. Abbas, B. Sanghera, G. Barlow and T. Jones (2001), 'Apprentice entrepreneurs? Ethnic minority workers in the independent restaurant sector', *Work, Employment and Society*, **15** (2), 353–72.

Ram, M., T. Jones, T. Abbas and B. Sanghera (2002a), 'Ethnic minority enterprise in its urban context: South Asian restaurants in Birmingham', *International Journal of Urban and Regional Research*, **26** (3), 24–40.

Ram, M., D. Smallbone and D. Deakins (2002b), 'Ethnic minority businesses in the UK: access to finance and business support', British Bankers Association, London, September, 133 pp.

Ram, M., P. Edwards, and T. Jones (2007), 'Staying underground: informal work, small firms and employment regulation in the UK', *Work and Occupations*, **34** (3), 290–317.

Rekers, A. and R. Van Kempen (2000), 'Location matters: ethnic entrepreneurs and the spatial context', in J. Rath (ed.), *Immigrant Businesses: The Economic, Political and Social Environment*, London: Macmillan.

Scase, R. (2002), 'Employment relations in small firms', in P. Edwards (ed.), *Industrial Relations: Theory and Practice*, Oxford: Blackwell.

Sepulveda, L., F. Lyon and S. Syrett (2006), *Refugee, New Arrivals and Enterprise: Their Contributions and Constraints*, London: Small Business Service and Business Link.

Storey, D. (1994), *Understanding the Small Business Sector*, London: Routledge.

Vertovec, S. (ed.) (1999), *Migration and Social Cohesion*, Cheltenham, UK and Northampton, MA, USA: Edward Elgar.

Vertovec, S. (2006), 'The emergence of super-diversity in Britain', Working paper no. 25, University of Oxford.

Virdee, S. (2006), '"Race", employment and social change: a critique of current orthodoxies', *Ethnic and Racial Studies*, **29** (4), 605–28.

Waldinger, R., H. Aldrich and R. Ward (1990), 'Opportunities, group characteristics and strategies', in R. Waldinger, H. Aldrich, R. Ward and associates (eds), *Ethnic Entrepreneurs: Immigrant Business in Industrial Society*, Newbury Park, CA: Sage.

Werbner, P. (1980) 'From rugs to riches: Manchester Pakistanis in the textile trade', *New Community*, **9**, 84–95.

Werbner, P. (1999), 'What colour success? Distorting values in studies of ethnic entrepreneurship', *Sociological Review*, **47**, 548–79.

Williams, C. (2006), *The Hidden Enterprise Culture*, Cheltenham, UK and Northampton, MA, USA: Edward Elgar.

Zhou, M. (2004), 'Revisiting ethnic entrepreneurship: convergences, controversies, and conceptual advancements', *International Migration Review*, **38** (3), 1040–74.

15. The emergence of entrepreneurial potential in transition environments: a challenge for entrepreneurship theory or a developmental perspective?

Friederike Welter and David Smallbone

INTRODUCTION

The importance of analysing entrepreneurship in its social context has recently been emphasized in the mainstream entrepreneurship literature (Davidsson, 2003). Under transition conditions, entrepreneurship has distinctive characteristics and behaviours, reflecting the specific external conditions pertaining and the wider social context. This includes forms of self-employment and part-time businesses (Arzeni, 1996); where self-employment can provide a means of 'self-help' support for those who have lost their jobs through restructuring, or who have been unable to find employment. Other forms of entrepreneurship range from nomenclature businesses where well-connected party officials and directors of former state enterprises used their privileges to gain from privatizing businesses or setting up new ventures, to a variety of types of formal and informal microenterprise and small enterprise activity, often involving different members of a household on a paid and unpaid basis (Smallbone and Welter, 2001).

In such a context, researchers often discuss the contribution of 'simple' entrepreneurial activities, sometimes categorizing such activities as necessity-driven entrepreneurship, or proprietorship rather than entrepreneurship, or in the case of petty trading as arbitrage, rather than entrepreneurship, with little development potential. However, it can be argued that reality is more complex, making such a dichotomy overly simplistic in practice, particularly in a rapidly changing and hostile environment, and one where there is evidence of entrepreneurs having considerable human capital (e.g. Smallbone and Welter, 2001; Wasilczuk, 2000), which is likely to increase their adaptive capacity. Research has shown that in the context of hostile environments, such as in a transition context, where property rights are not fully ensured and governments do not foster entrepreneurship and small business in practice, entrepreneurship can emerge from humble origins, frequently involving bootstrapping solutions undertaken by entrepreneurs in the face of serious institutional deficiencies.

As a consequence, an analysis of entrepreneurship development and entrepreneurial potential in such conditions needs to be grounded in the context that pertains in such environments, if it is to accurately reflect the empirical reality, with implications for existing entrepreneurship theory. This chapter focuses on the relationship between petty trading and entrepreneurship. This is because, on the one hand, such activity may be dismissed as 'arbitrage', operating outside the confines of the formal economy and highly dependent on relative price differentials on either side of the border, while on the other hand, it may be seen as a potential mechanism for entrepreneurial individuals to accumulate resources that can subsequently be invested in the development of more substantial ventures, in conditions where resource mobilization for entrepreneurship is extremely difficult. It is an assessment of this aspect that forms the focus of the chapter.

In this context, the specific aim of the chapter is to investigate an under-researched source of entrepreneurship in transition economies, namely 'petty trading' or arbitrage activity. The proposition is that in resource- and institutionally deficient environments, the entrepreneurial process may include an evolution from simple trading activity, much of which may take place outside the formal economy, to productive and more formal entrepreneurial activities. Although the chapter is an exploratory one, the underlying aim is to demonstrate a need to adapt conventional views of the entrepreneurial process, based largely on experience in mature market environments, to incorporate distinctive characteristics of the context found in transition environments. This is important if entrepreneurship is to be viewed in its social context and theories of entrepreneurship are to be applicable in a wide variety of external conditions. The methodology employed is qualitative, involving the use of case studies of individual entrepreneurs and enterprises, drawn from a recent project on cross-border entrepreneurship in three of the newly independent states (NIS).

The rest of the chapter is divided into four main sections: firstly, a review of relevant literature; secondly, a description of the methodology employed; thirdly, a presentation and discussion of case study evidence to explore the emergence of entrepreneurial potential; and lastly, conclusions and implications for both theory and policy.

LITERATURE REVIEW: INFORMAL AND FORMAL ENTREPRENEURSHIP

In reviewing some of the key literature relevant to a discussion of the entrepreneurial potential of those involved in petty trading activities, this section is divided into three main parts. The first discusses Scase's distinction between entrepreneurship and proprietorship, which he argues best describes the majority of business owners in transition conditions. The second reviews literature that specifically refers to a development path from informal to formal types of entrepreneurial activity. The final part emphasizes the heterogeneity of types of informal activity.

Entrepreneurship or Proprietorship?

Some authors have questioned the extent to which 'entrepreneurship' really exists in transition economies and thus the nature of its contribution to economic transformation. For example, according to Scase (1997, 2003), most business ownership in transition conditions may be more appropriately characterized as proprietorship rather than entrepreneurship, based on the motivation of those involved, but with implications also for their business behaviour and contribution to economic development. He distinguishes between entrepreneurship and proprietorship, based on 'contrasting psychologies of business founders; their attitudes towards trading; and their orientation towards capital accumulation' (Scase, 2003, p. 67). According to Scase, entrepreneurship refers to a person's commitment to capital accumulation and business growth, whereas proprietorship describes the ownership of property and other assets, which may be used for trading purposes to realize profits, but are not utilized for longer term purposes of capital accumulation. Any surpluses generated by proprietors are likely to be consumed rather than reinvested for business purposes, and much of Scase's proprietorship is likely to be undertaken outside the formal economy.

In the pursuit of capital accumulation and long-term growth, an entrepreneur may forgo personal consumption and may actively search out market opportunities, which involves taking risks and coping with uncertainty. In the case of proprietorship, according to Scase, the motives of individuals are quite different, since surpluses are not reinvested in the business for future long-term capital accumulation but rather are consumed and used to sustain living standards. According to Scase, in the transitional economies of Russia and Central Europe, proprietorship rather than entrepreneurship best describes the majority of small business activity. His assessment is that while small businesses may be numerically significant, particularly in sectors such as services and retailing, offering employment and providing income for those involved, the proprietors who own and run most of these firms are incapable of constituting an indigenous force for economic development.

The central proposition being examined in this chapter challenges the simple dichotomy adopted by Scase, in emphasizing the development potential of some of the individuals who Scase classifies as 'proprietors'. The rapidly changing nature of external conditions in transition environments, together with the learning capability of some individuals, may result in their motives and aspirations changing over time, interacting with external environmental changes.

Informal Activities as Seedbed for Enterprise Development?

An important part of the context for a discussion of entrepreneurial and trading activities in post-Soviet societies is the legacy inherited from the Soviet period. During Soviet times, different forms of private entrepreneurial activities co-existed alongside state ownership and entrepreneurship within state enterprises. Conceptually, researchers have distinguished between, on the one hand, a formal economy, which included state enterprises and legalized private enterprises and, on the other, the grey economy, which itself consisted of the second and the illegal economy. The 'second economy' included any form of unlicensed but tolerated private entrepreneurial activities. This included unlicensed activities in the private sector that were not officially recorded, as well as the clandestine use of state property (e.g. raw materials, machines, labour, services) for private business activities (Dallago, 1990). In other words, informal entrepreneurial behaviour existed within state owned enterprises during the communist period as a necessary response to the constant shortage of materials. Finally, during the socialist period an illegal economy existed, made up of quasi-criminal activities within state enterprises (i.e. bribes, theft of resources) and also criminal private activities. However, in some countries (such as the former Soviet republics) any type of private business activity could technically be considered to be part of the illegal economy, as prior to the start of the reform process in the late 1980s, no private business activity was legally acceptable. As a consequence, the legacy of entrepreneurship inherited from the communist period is complex (Rehn and Taalas, 2004, p. 243), not least because the same authors argue that entrepreneurship flourished in the daily lives of individuals during the Soviet period, as people struggled to cope with material shortages that were a common occurrence in the Soviet system.

Against this background, it is hardly surprising that informal economic activity has flourished during the transition period. While the informal sector in developing countries has been reviewed extensively, so far few studies exist on its 'analogue' in a post-Soviet context. Informal activities include a wide variety of activities on a 'cash-in-hand-basis', some of which may be viewed as specific features of the post-Soviet period. These include petty trading or shuttle trading, where traders trade across borders, and the widespread use of informal employment. Such activities may be used to supplement an individual's income from the formal economy, but in some circumstances may constitute the sole income for a household or family. With reference to the former, Williams et al. (2007) found that 51 per cent of all Ukrainian households reliant on informal strategies to earn income are multiple-earner households; only 6 per cent are no-earner households (i.e. with no employment possibilities outside the informal sector), while nearly two thirds of self-employed entrepreneurs have no licence and are thus operating informally and illegally. Williams (2005a) also finds informal activities to be a widespread phenomenon, with just two thirds of households in post-Soviet economies relying on incomes earned in the formal sector.

Some judge such informal activities as a transient phenomenon (e.g. see Welter, 1989 for a review of the respective literature), while others refer to 'a regression to an earlier form of subsistence; for example, peasant-style self-sufficiency as a survival mechanism' (Wallace and Latcheva, 2006, p. 84). These authors suggest a typology of different types of informal activities, distinguishing between, on the one hand, activity at the household level that is non-monetized and alegal, such as 'growing own food' or 'repairing the house' (ibid., p. 85), and on the other, 'earnings of a second job' or 'incidental earnings', which are classified as part of the black economy; that is monetized and outside the law. An empirical study of Moscow households emphasizes the 'multiple economies' that existed during the transition period, including formal and informal, private and state as well as those operating in monetized and non-monetized spheres (Pavlovskaya, 2004). The author points out that these 'sub-economies' are not to be seen as dichotomies, but rather as being complementary to one another; with boundaries that are permeable and fuzzy, which is a key argument in this chapter. Several empirical studies show that legal and illegal (or grey) activities co-exist in a transition context, with most new and small firms involved in both productive and rent seeking activities at the same time (e.g. Rehn and Taalas, 2004; Scase, 2003; Smallbone and Welter, 2001).

The fuzzy boundaries between formal and informal activities have consequences for our understanding of entrepreneurial activities in transition environments. They suggest that informal activities may be a seedbed for more substantial entrepreneurial ventures, as several authors have previously argued for developing and transition economies (e.g. Bennett and Estrin, 2007; Guariglia and Kim, 2006; Maloney, 2004; Smallbone and Welter, 2006; Williams et al., 2007). In the case of developing countries, Bennett and Estrin (2007) show how informal activities allow entrepreneurs to explore the profitability of their venture idea, acting as a 'stepping stone' towards more substantial businesses, allowing them to 'experiment cheaply in an uncertain environment'. Similar results are available for Russia and the Ukraine. Williams et al. (2007) show that 85 per cent of those small-scale entrepreneurs formally registered alluded to conducting part of their business informally, while another 90 per cent stated that they had started their venture on 'a cash-in-hand basis', thus progressing from illegal to legal business once their venture became more established. For Russia, Guariglia and Kim (2006) find that one quarter of newly self-employed entrepreneurs have been 'moonlighting' in the past. Aidis and van Praag (2007) confirm such positive benefits of illegal entrepreneurial experiences acquired under socialism to entrepreneurship and economic development in a transition period; Aidis (2003) demonstrates the entrepreneurship visible in traders at open-air markets.

Other authors emphasize the contributions of the informal sector to employment growth and economic development in its own right, regardless of whether or not informal enterprises necessarily transit to being legalized and/or registered. In analysing Latin American experiences, Maloney (2004, p. 1159) argues that the informal sector should be reinterpreted as 'the unregulated developing country analogue of the voluntary entrepreneurial small firm sector found in advanced countries'. However, in a transition country context, informality is often implicitly considered as a transient phenomenon that eventually will disappear once the business environment is functioning properly and the legal framework for entrepreneurial activities has been set. For example, despite their results confirming informality as a seedbed for more substantial entrepreneurial activities, Guariglia and Kim (2006) also confirm that 'moonlighting' is transitory, with people who want to shift jobs using this to test new employment possibilities.

The Heterogeneity of Informal Activity

In this context, it is important to recognize the heterogeneity of informal activity that exists, only some of which is likely to have real potential as a development route into more formal forms of entrepreneurship. Williams (2005b) for example, has distinguished four principal types of informal work: firstly, 'organized informal work', which involves people working on an informal basis for businesses that undertake some or all of their activity informally; secondly, 'informal work conducted by micro entrepreneurs', where informal activity is used by the business owner as a short-term risk minimization strategy, either to test out a fledgling business venture or to establish themselves; thirdly, 'informal work by more established businesses', as part of a 'getting by' strategy in a serial and ongoing manner; and fourthly, 'informal work by family, friends and acquaintances', where cash is given for favours and exchanges that perhaps in the past might have been unpaid. It is the second category of the Williams typology that would appear to be the most relevant to the proposition under investigation in this chapter.

The following sections examine the heterogeneity of informal activities and the question of whether or not they can be a seedbed for more substantial entrepreneurial ventures, based on empirical evidence from some former Soviet republics. The analysis seeks to identify antecedents and the factors influencing the transition to more substantial enterprises. Before that, we briefly present the methodology and data base.

METHODOLOGY AND DATA SOURCES

Empirically, the chapter uses in-depth case material, drawn mainly from a study of cross-border entrepreneurship and trading activity in the Ukraine, Belarus and Moldova. Within this project (Intas 04-79-6991), a total of 240 in-depth interviews (in each region 20 enterprises and 10 individuals/households) were conducted in a total of eight border regions (three border regions in the Ukraine and Belarus respectively and two in Moldova) between 2005 and 2007. Although these cases have been used as a basis for this exploratory paper, a larger set of case material from a number of research projects on entrepreneurship and small enterprise development in 'early stage' transition conditions, is in the process of being systematically analysed for a similar purpose. Interviews in all projects were semi-structured. The sensitive nature of some of the questions studied, together with the exploratory nature of the research, made a qualitative approach the most appropriate. Enterprises involved in cross-border activities were identified either through meetings with representatives of business associations, business support agencies and other local institutions, or through the snowball method. In the case of individuals involved in cross-border trading activities, the semi-legal nature of some of this activity was a practical problem facing the research team. In this case, respondents were identified by researchers at random, through observation of petty trading activities at markets and bus stations on both sides of the border and/or at railway stations at border crossing points. In some cases, researchers accompanied respondents in their cross-border journey, conducting an interview en route, representing a form of 'participant observation'.

Case studies have been analysed using NVivo software, in order to allow a systematic search for patterns of entrepreneurial activity in the semi-structured and unstructured data gathered from respondents, as described above. The aim is to investigate the entry into entrepreneurship, the motivation for that, and whether or not these motivations change over time; to analyse development paths over time; and to consider the implications for entrepreneurial behaviour, and for the contribution of entrepreneurship to social and economic transformation. Enterprise case studies have been analysed in order to identify and assess the origins of the business activity and any relationship with petty trading and informal activity; case studies with individual petty traders from the point of view of their development potential, in the context of the aspirations of business owners. Particular emphasis is paid to identifying the nature and extent of entrepreneurial activities, motives for engaging in such activities, the role of different members of the household, their entrepreneurial strategies and factors either inhibiting or favouring their entrepreneurial activities, as well as the development of such activities over time.

EXPLORING THE EMERGENCE OF ENTREPRENEURIAL POTENTIAL

So far, and adopting a cross-sectional view, our analysis suggests that those involved in petty trading activities may be divided into two broad categories: firstly, those driven by proprietorship-type motivation, where individuals lack the interest and ability for entrepreneurship and thus lack (currently at least) development potential (traders). The second, by contrast, is driven by more entrepreneurial individuals, whose motivation, drive and resourcefulness make them nascent entrepreneurs. The first category involves petty trading as an income strategy, where the main goal is driven by a need to gain, or to add to, a family's income. Such petty trading often is not a registered activity and is conducted informally. The second category contains different types of entrepreneurial activities, namely (i) shuttle trade on a larger scale, although since it operates mainly on an illegal basis, this limits the contribution of such activities to overall economic development; (ii) illegal or semi-legal petty trading as a starting point for more substantial entrepreneurial activities, often used later as an additional means to obtain working capital or as supplementary strategy to obtain input for legal entrepreneurial activities; and (iii) petty trading as a testing ground for entrepreneurial skills, also leading to more substantial entrepreneurial ventures in the long run. The latter patterns are similar to the second of Williams' four categories (2005b) of informal work, namely that conducted by micro and more established entrepreneurs.

Petty Trading Without Major Development Potential

In a transition context, an individual's decision to become involved in business activity is frequently linked to the needs of their household or family, rather than just their own individual needs. In this regard, the empirical results suggest that where households or families are involved in petty trading activity, the latter is usually the main source of household income in the case of pensioners and older respondents, but is an *additional* source of income in the case of younger participants. As a result of the transition process, during which unemployment or underemployment increased dramatically in countries such as Belarus, Moldova or the Ukraine, petty trading is a survival strategy for many respondents, contributing 50 per cent or more to a family's income (Box 15.1). 'Lack of money', 'too small pension', 'no job' are all commonly stated motives for entering the 'shuttle trade' business. Often, petty traders have to care for their parents and/or are single mothers, and/or their wages in formal employment are too low to cover household expenditures. In such situations, cross-border cooperation and petty trading become a 'life-saving activity', as one respondent in Belarus put it, stressing the hard nature of the daily work associated with this activity, as well as the fact that it is a constant headache. Others complained about constant harassment, health risks and the attitude of the state towards private trade. In no sense does this form of activity represent a soft option for those involved in it. Instead, those individuals engaged in it are demonstrating entrepreneurial attributes in terms of initiative and 'doing something for themselves', rather than simply waiting for others to help them. Regardless of their motives, such people are undoubtedly demonstrating aspects of entrepreneurial behaviour, even if their motives are those Scase classifies as those of 'proprietors'.

There are many motives for getting involved in petty trading and it is overly simplistic to classify all petty trading as a 'survival strategy' (Smith, 2002; Smallbone and Welter, 2006). Many traders emphasize how cross-border trading has allowed them to substantially increase their household income. For example, in one case, such activities not only helped to guarantee a steady income for the family members involved, but sufficient surplus was generated for the younger son to be able to build a house. Often, cross-border activities allow respondents to buy goods and services

BOX 15.1 PETTY TRADING AS A MAJOR SOURCE OF INCOME

1. This respondent had been divorced for five years (CS7HH/Vitebsk). In order to earn income, she started weaving tapestries, which she sold through art shops in Belarus, while at the same time going on regular trips to Poland, organized by her church. Initially, she took some of her tapestry with her as gifts, but she soon discovered that there was an opportunity to sell her goods through art galleries in Poland.

2. This respondent and her husband have made their hobby a profitable cross-border trading activity (CS6HH/Vitebsk). They both have been active in foot orienteering since school days, participating in championships during Soviet times and getting to know friends in Poland with the same interest. When transition started, they used this friendship to import electronic goods to Poland and to bring cosmetics and clothes to Poland. When the wife lost her job as an engineer in a television factory because of staff reduction, she saw a need to more seriously engage in cross-border trading in order to complement their household income. She now works for a low wage in a state regional association for out-of-school work, teaching orienteering to schoolboys. Additionally, she trades camping outfits that she receives from her Polish partners.

3. This woman, living in Cahul in Moldova (CS3HH/Cahul), has been involved in shuttle trading activities since the beginning of the 1990s, when she began with small lots that she could fit into one bag. Today, she brings merchandise for herself and for two small-scale traders from a neighbouring district. She specializes in stockings, socks and pants, importing from Turkey. Her main motive for entering petty trading has been to earn an income for herself and her son. Her activity is illegal, since it is not registered.

Source: Own interviews, Intas 04-79-6991.

they could not otherwise afford. In most cases, respondents also bring back goods and foodstuff for personal use. It can be argued that despite their low development potential, the individuals engaged in such activities are demonstrating attributes usually associated with entrepreneurial behaviour, even if the activities themselves may not be considered forms of entrepreneurship.

Petty Trading With Development Potential

Although the main objective of most petty traders is to generate income for current consumption, some use such activities to accumulate capital for more substantial entrepreneurial ventures, thus qualifying as 'entrepreneurs' in Scase's understanding. This is reflected in interviews which show that more substantial entrepreneurial activities can have their origin in former (or ongoing) shuttle trading experiences, which helped the participants to accumulate financial capital as well as the networks and contacts required to build up their ventures. Interestingly, such substantial entrepreneurial activities are not always operating within the law. However, our analysis also shows cases where substantial, albeit illegal large-scale shuttle trading activity evolved from 'simple' and small-scale petty trading activities (Box 15.2), thus adding another category of 'longstanding substantial informal entrepreneurial activity' to Williams's (2005b) classification.

This pattern is an interesting one insofar as it demonstrates entrepreneurial potential and also the (sometimes) substantial development potential of petty trading activities. At the same time, the cases also show the unwillingness of respondents to legalize their activities, which restricts the contribution of such activities to economic development. While some may choose to stress the ethical dilemma inherent in all informal activity, an alternative view is to emphasize the arbitrary nature of the regulatory regime in many 'early stage' transition countries, which means that informality is mainly a response to the absence of what in a mature market context would be seen as the basic framework conditions for entrepreneurship. Such illegal activities create employment not only for the shuttle trader him/herself, but for others also, particularly where shuttle traders are embedded in wider networks of cross-border activities, as some of the cases show. Intermediaries organize joint border crossings, negotiating with the customs officers and border police. Individuals sell their services as 'passengers' or goods transporters, thus giving additional meaning to Williams's (2005b) category of 'informal work'.

As a consequence, activities that start as simple trading activities on a small scale can subsequently evolve over a period of time into substantial enterprise activity with future development potential. All examples in this section

BOX 15.2   INFORMAL SHUTTLE BUSINESS ON A LARGE SCALE

1. This entrepreneur, 30 years old, had been unemployed (CS6HH/Cahul). After she got married in 1996, she was looking for ways to earn income for the family, and started trading foodstuff from Moldova to Romania. She used bus routes and transported the goods in large bags. In 2000, the family bought a minibus, which boosted their shuttle business. Today, both partners are involved in the shuttle business. The family started to buy agricultural products on a large scale from Moldovan cooperatives and/or small landholders without transport possibilities, who valued the higher price the respondent paid. Products are transported to the 'Market of Moldovans' in Galati in Romania. As the business activity is not registered, the spouses can only take 200 kg each in crossing the border, but they normally bring along other persons in their minibus, to increase their cross-border trading capacity. As a rule, people wait at the Moldovan customs for a possibility to help carry goods across the border for payment. However, customs officials also know that the respondent carries out her activity illegally and so the spouses have to bribe them to avoid long time delays at the customs. Asked whether she would legalize her activities, the respondent negated this, stating that she does not see any advantage as she can sell her goods without documentation in Romania and registration would only add to bureaucracy. Their trading activities have always been the main source of income, especially during summer and autumn. During the rest of the year, the husband sometimes goes to find work in Russia while the wife works at home.

2. A second entrepreneur, also a woman from Cahul, and 55 years old, tells a similar story (CS7HH/Cahul). Her shuttle business and cross-border activities started 16 years ago. Previously, she worked in a factory, which at the beginning of the 1990s only paid minimal wages. She quit and started trading various foodstuffs and other types of goods to Romania. She specialized in salted fish (of several species), biscuits, halva, tomato paste, natural juice, etc.

as well as illegally exported cigarettes. During the first five years of her business activities, she acted as a shuttle trader, transporting goods in bags on buses to the market in Galati (Romania). When she had acquired Romanian citizenship, she rented a market stall and started trading foodstuff and other goods brought by other Moldovans. The respondent rents a one-room flat in Galati as she usually spends three weeks per month in Romania and just a week in Moldova. She has arrangements with several persons in Moldova who supply her with goods. When she goes back to Moldova, she also buys foodstuff for reselling in Romania. The respondent is the main earner for the family, as the husband's wage is very low. They therefore have agreed that the husband keeps the house while the wife earns the income. Customs and border controls represent a serious barrier for her illegal activities, demanding bribes and sometimes confiscating illegal goods, which she tries to circumvent by only exporting small quantities of goods to minimize the risk of loss. When asked if she would legalize her business, her answer was that if she did, the business would cease to exist.

Source: Own interviews, Intas 04-79-6991.

demonstrate the potential for venture creation that exists from 'simple' petty trading activities, in a context where a more conventional approach (in the mainstream literature sense) to venture creation is difficult, because of the constraints imposed by a combination of institutional deficiencies and a lack of access to necessary resources. Trading activities in the cases described in Box 15.3 developed from simple sales activity to more sophisticated entrepreneurial activities, which are mainly legal. This involved an active search for customers and markets and was often based on some professional experiences in the field the respondents trade in. The age of the entrepreneurs appears sometimes to play a role, in that younger respondents appear to be more flexible in adapting to adverse environments and in locating and exploiting business opportunities, although this is not a consistent pattern.

The Context

While emphasizing the development potential that exists in some individuals engaged in petty trading activities, an adverse business environment

BOX 15.3 FROM PETTY TRADING TO MORE SUBSTANTIAL ENTREPRENEURIAL ACTIVITIES

1. This Ukrainian entrepreneur became involved in his father's shuttle business when still at school (CS18ENT/Lviv). The shuttle trade was launched in the early 1990s. The goods traded were exported to Poland initially and included a wide range, from deodorant sprays to TV sets, wheels and bicycles. In later years, the father concentrated on importing goods from Poland to the Ukraine. The business was semi-official, but trade was chaotic: wheels were handed over to friends at the market; two wheels were advertised for sale while there were many more that were added on a piece-by-piece basis. Traders did not keep accounting books or records. Today, the business is officially registered, it pays a fixed tax and since 1999, they have owned a small shop, although they still have to pay rent including a small fee to the market security guards for its location at the central market. Three years ago, the entrepreneur started focusing on trading goods made in Ukraine, as importing goods from Poland became more and more difficult.

2. This firm is located in Zakarpattya in Ukraine (CS18ENT/Zarkapattya). Since 2000, it has been an official representative of a Czech firm, selling second-hand clothes and footwear to a network of enterprises in Ukraine. By Ukrainian standards, it is a large supplier, ranking 13 in 2002. The company employs 11 persons, including four drivers in another small business providing cargo services. The entrepreneur is 37 years old. He attended the Kiev Institute of Light Industry, obtaining a degree from the Department for the Automation of Technological Processes. Since he was a teenager, he has occupied himself with trading different goods in order to earn money. Already in 1991, he registered as an individual entrepreneur. At that time, he mainly was involved in – illegal – shuttle trade, but he refrained from elaborating on this in more detail. After having earned some capital, he opened a company (with friends) selling input material and accessories for the light industry in Kiev. When moving to Uzhgorod in Western

Ukraine, he sold his share in that company and opened two enterprises, only one of which turned out to be successful. Nevertheless, for someone who started his life as a petty trader, this individual has acquired the attributes of a habitual entrepreneur.

3. This trader in Vitebsk, Belarus, is a 35-year-old trained engineer (radio engineering), formally employed by the public telecommunication company (CS1HH/Vitebsk). His first experiences with shuttle trading go back to when he was a student. This respondent began making regular trips to Russia when he decided to get married, in order to earn enough money for the wedding. His first activities were importing various goods such as clothes, telephone sets and electrical goods from Russia. However, later he switched to buying 'vouchers' for regular travels to Bialystok in Poland, where he shopped for housekeeping goods, tools and other goods. Some years ago, he decided to specialize in importing mobile phones, which is an area related to his regular employment. On demand, he buys in Poland and sells both in Belarus and Pskov in Russia, where, thanks to his wife's relatives, he has a ready-made distribution channel.

4. This entrepreneur, 36 years old, owns a private limited company in Edinet, Moldova, with currently seven employees (CS19ENT/Edinet). The company was established in 1996. The statutes stipulate several activities, at the moment the firm concentrates on the import and export of agricultural goods. From 1996 to 2001 the entrepreneur also developed TV activity in his region and provided cargo transport services abroad to domestic and foreign firms. Since 2001, he has exclusively concentrated on exporting and importing agricultural goods. This includes potatoes from Poland and Romania and exporting fruits mainly to Russia. In the early 1990s, the entrepreneur started with illegal shuttle trading, exporting and selling Russian and Moldovan-produced TV sets to Romania. Today, the cross-border activities are still partly illegal. Usually, when crossing the border he declares lower quantities in his documents and lower costs for his goods in order to avoid customs dues.

Source: Own interviews, Intas 04-79-6991.

that is common in transition environments can also restrict the development potential of petty trading activities. The cases in Box 15.4 demonstrate the difficulties of establishing a formal sector business by legalizing trading activities in an environment where rules and regulations are administered on an ad hoc basis and not implemented properly. While clearly such institutional deficiencies may contribute to the establishment of such forms of informal activity in the first place, they can also affect the potential for individuals engaged in them using the resources generated to support more substantial business activities. On the other hand, it must be stressed that we also have cases that have traded fully legally from the beginning, thus requiring a deeper analysis into the genuine reasons for informality.

This leads to traders operating semi-legally, in the sense that they use illegal cross-border trade in order to secure input for registered activities in their home country. This places them into Williams's (2005b) category of 'informal work by more established entrepreneurs' where the informality is used as a 'getting-by' strategy on an ongoing basis. A typical case is that of a woman trader who holds a licence allowing her to trade goods in the territory of Moldova, but not to import goods from Romania and Ukraine (CS1HH). Besides trading imported textiles from Romania and Ukraine, the respondent acts as an official distributor of medical products for a European company, whose products are also imported illegally. She named the high level of import taxes as the main reason for her illegal border trade. In the long run, however, such behaviour impedes business development as well as hindering these entrepreneurs from fully realizing the contribution they could make to economic and social development.

Identifying Opportunities

A particular feature emerging from the interviews is the inventiveness and entrepreneurial alertness of respondents currently engaged in petty trading activity to recognize opportunities, in which they demonstrate some of the key qualities associated with entrepreneurship. As suggested previously, this challenges a simple categorization of all petty trading activities as 'proprietorship', because some of the individuals involved are behaving entrepreneurially, even if their main motive in the short term is income generation. Often, opportunities are identified because respondents themselves miss a particular good or service or are looking for cheaper sources of supply (Box 15.5). Others react to demands made by friends or colleagues, which they then identify as a wider potential opportunity for shuttle trading. Moreover, the case interviews show respondents adapting to changing market conditions and demands in selecting the goods they trade.

BOX 15.4   EXTERNAL BARRIERS TO REALIZING
THE DEVELOPMENT POTENTIAL OF
PETTY TRADING ACTIVITIES

1. A typical case showing the difficulties involved in real-
    izing the development potential of petty trading involves
    two sisters, both in their 30s, who trade in window ledges
    (CS10HH/Grodno), helped by their mother. The business
    activity was started six years ago, mainly to boost family
    income. Today, they have two trading places at markets in
    Grodno, Belarus: one is a typical 'plastic cell' of 2 sq m.; the
    other is their own small shop. The respondents go to Poland
    to search for suitable products in markets there. The busi-
    ness is based on responding to requests from their custom-
    ers. They bring the products purchased to the border where
    they are distributed among the transporters, the capacity of
    which is one of the constraints on the development potential
    of this particular trading activity. A more substantial business
    in window ledges would require documents confirming the
    sales in Poland as a requirement for the respondents to reg-
    ister customs fees and to import goods beyond the individual
    customs-free limit. However, as most sales partners are
    operating semi-legally themselves, the sisters would have to
    change their business partners in order to operate entirely
    within the law.

2. The second case is an entrepreneur, 48 years old, who
    abandoned his job as an executive for 'Youth and Sports' in
    the commune Cucoara in Moldova, because of low wages
    (CS8HH/Cahul). For several years, he worked illegally as a
    construction worker in Russia and Germany. Having accu-
    mulated capital, he decided to start his own small business
    and obtained a licence for passenger transport in Moldova
    and Romania. When in early 2005, private minibuses were
    replaced by a government-owned firm he lost his licence
    several times and had to re-purchase it through bribes,
    until he decided to sell his minibus. Instead, he bought a
    small car and illegally began transporting passengers. He
    also started trading in illegal goods, namely cigarettes and
    petrol. Petrol is transported in his car's petrol tank and sold
    at a higher price in Romania. Cigarettes are permitted for

transportation in a quantity of 10 packets per person. The respondent buys cigarettes in Moldova and distributes them among his passengers before crossing the border. In 2003–04 he also traded vegetables, fruits and walnuts from his own land, but because of conflicts with customs (he choose not to elaborate on that) he stopped that activity. Income from all these activities does not contribute to sustaining his family, but according to the respondent is saved for opening up a more substantial business later on.

Source: Own interviews, Intas 04-79-6991.

BOX 15.5 ENTREPRENEURSHIP IN THE CONTEXT OF PETTY TRADING: INVENTIVENESS AND OPPORTUNITY IDENTIFICATION

This entrepreneur from Grodno in Belarus (CS2HH/Grodno) started importing baby carriages for twins from Poland, when his twins were born. At that time, he bought a baby carriage in Poland, which his wife did not like. As a result, he placed an advertisement in the newspapers to sell this carriage, which he did before going to Poland to buy another one for his family. Having earned around $50 from this sale, he started what became a flourishing trading activity and the Polish seller quickly agreed to establish a profitable partnership. Today, the entrepreneur, who works in a state company, visits Poland on average twice per month. Before specializing in baby carriages, he imported household electrical accessories, various accessories for car owners and gold, on an irregular basis.

Source: Own interviews, Intas 04-79-6991.

In this context, much of the entrepreneurship literature has emphasized that opportunities do not only 'exist out there' (Davidsson, 2003), but are also created. In this regard, respondents were often creating their own opportunities, or significantly developing what was initially an external stimulus, such as a request from a relative for a particular item. While the specific nature of some of the opportunities may be transient, the behaviour demonstrated by respondents overall shows a high level of sensitivity and responsiveness to the needs of customers, who are themselves heavily influenced by institutional conditions.

CONCLUSIONS AND IMPLICATIONS

With regard to entrepreneurship theory, Davidsson (2003) and Baker et al. (2005), for example, have emphasized the need for entrepreneurship research to acknowledge the heterogeneity of environmental conditions, outcomes and behaviours that exist. This chapter contributes to the ongoing discussion of the nature of entrepreneurship across different environments in a number of respects. Firstly, by focusing on the fuzzy nature of the boundary between formal and informal activity, the study contributes new evidence on one of the routes to entrepreneurship in resource and institutionally deficient environments. In this respect, the chapter makes an empirical contribution to the transition literature, which with some notable exceptions (e.g. Aidis, 2003; Aidis and van Praag, 2007) tends to concentrate mainly on entrepreneurial activity that is part of the formal economy.

In seeking to assess the entrepreneurial potential of those involved in petty trading activity, the case evidence is divided into four categories, describing different types of situation with varying development potential. While not all petty traders have such potential, some do, either as 'entrepreneurs' operating large-scale ventures within the informal economy, or by using accumulated resources to invest in the development of productive enterprises in the formal economy. It may be argued that individuals in both groups are demonstrating qualities of entrepreneurship, thereby emphasizing the rather static nature of the entrepreneur–proprietor type dichotomies, as proposed by Scase and others.

As well as exploring unique case data to investigate development potential over time, the chapter also contributes to the emerging literature emphasizing the embeddedness of entrepreneurship in specific social contexts, which in transition economies contain a number of specific features. In this regard, Williams (2005a) argues that coping practices in the informal sphere are not limited to poor and unemployed households/individuals but rather cut across socio-economic spheres and contexts. We take up this argument by extending his fourfold classification of informal entrepreneurial activities, suggesting that it may be more appropriate to think of a continuum of informality instead of attempting to develop exclusive categories. At the same time, the view that research should transcend the widely painted negative portrayal of informal activities as a hindrance to economic development because of its exploitative and low-paid nature and vice versa (Williams et al., 2007), is supported and extended by the evidence presented here.

In terms of policy implications, Maloney (2004) emphasizes the voluntary element of informality, which exists, he suggests, because of the laxity of enforcement and implementation, thus allowing entrepreneurs and small traders a choice regarding the 'optimal degree of participation in formal institutions' (Maloney, 2004, p. 1173). An alternative view is that in situations where the regulatory framework includes penal and/or continuously changing tax rates, the lack of an appropriate legal framework and other institutional deficiencies, activities that in some countries may be able to operate profitably and legally are only viable if they operate partly outside the law. To the extent that this can be demonstrated, the choice for business owners is to operate at least partly informally or not to operate at all. If petty traders and small entrepreneurs, as depicted in this chapter, remain informal (illegal) voluntarily, they manage to do so because the business framework is incomplete and/or is not enforced properly. This means that policies that focus on increasing the 'formality' of petty trading might clash or contradict with policies to foster entrepreneurship development: '[D]eterring informal employment will result in governments stamping out with one hand precisely the entrepreneurship and enterprise that with another hand they are so desperately seeking to nurture' (Williams et al., 2007, p. 409).

REFERENCES

Aidis, R. (2003), 'Officially despised yet tolerated: open-air markets and entrepreneurship in post-socialist countries', *Post-Communist Economies*, **15** (3), 461–73.

Aidis, R. and M. van Praag (2007), 'Illegal entrepreneurship experience: does it make a difference for business performance and motivation?', *Journal of Business Venturing*, **22**, 283–310.

Arzeni, S. (1996), 'Entrepreneurship in Eastern Europe: a critical view', in H. Brezinski and M. Fritsch (eds), *The Economic Impact of New Firms in Post Socialist Countries: Bottom-Up Transformation in Eastern Europe*, Cheltenham, UK and Brookfield, USA: Edward Elgar, pp. 52–8.

Baker, T., E. Gedajlovic and M. Lubatkin (2005), 'A framework for comparing entrepreneurship processes across nations', *Journal of International Business Studies*, **36** (5), 492–504.

Bennett, J. and S. Estrin (2007), '*Informality as a stepping stone: entrepreneurial entry in a developing economy*', IZA Discussion Paper 2950, IZA, Bonn.

Dallago, B. (1990), *The Irregular Economy: The 'Underground' Economy and the 'Black' Labour Market*, Aldershot: Dartmouth.

Davidsson, P. (2003), 'The domain of entrepreneurship research: some suggestions', in J. Katz and D. Shepherd (eds), *Advances in Entrepreneurship, Firm Emergence and Growth*, Vol. 6, Oxford: Elsevier/JAI Press, pp. 315–72.

Guariglia, A. and B.-Y. Kim (2006), 'The dynamics of moonlighting in Russia', *Economics of Transition*, **14** (1), 1–45.

Maloney, W.F. (2004), 'Informality revisited', *World Development*, **32** (7), 1159–78.

Pavlovskaya, M. (2004), 'Other transitions: multiple economies of Moscow households in the 1990s, *Annals of the Association of American Geographers*, **94** (2), 329–51.

Rehn, A. and S. Taalas (2004), '"Znakomstva I svyazi" (acquaintances and connections) – Blat, the Soviet Union and mundane entrepreneurship', *Entrepreneurship and Regional Development*, **16** (3), 235–50.

Scase, R. (1997), 'The role of small businesses in the economic transformation of Eastern Europe: real but relatively unimportant?', *International Small Business Journal*, **16** (1), 13–21.

Scase, R. (2003), 'Entrepreneurship and proprietorship in transition: policy implications for the SME sector', in R. McIntyre and B. Dallago (eds), *Small and Medium Enterprises in Transitional Economies*, Basingstoke, Palgrave Macmillan, pp. 64–77.

Smallbone, D. and F. Welter (2001), 'The distinctiveness of entrepreneurship in transition economies', *Small Business Economics*, **16**, 249–62.

Smallbone, D. and F. Welter (2006), 'Conceptualising entrepreneurship in a transition context', *International Journal of Entrepreneurship and Small Business*, **3** (2), 190–206.

Smith, A. (2002), 'Culture/economy and spaces of economic practice: positioning households in post-communism', *Transactions of the Institute of British Geographers*, **27**, 232–50.

Wallace, C. and R. Latcheva (2006), 'Economic transformation outside the law. Corruption, trust in public institutions and the informal economy in transition countries of Central and Eastern Europe', *Europe Asia Studies*, **58** (1), 81–102.

Wasilczuk, J. (2000), 'Advantageous competence of owner/managers to grow the firm in Poland: empirical evidence', *Journal of Small Business Management*, **38** (2), 88–94.

Welter, F. (1989), *Der informelle Sektor in Entwicklungsländern dargestellt an Beispielen in Afrika* [*The Informal Sector in Developing Countries, Illustrated with Examples from Africa*], Materialien und kleine Schriften des Instituts für Entwicklungsforschung und Entwicklungspolitik, 125, Bochum: Institut für Entwicklungsforschung und Entwicklungspolitik, Ruhr-Universität Bochum.

Williams, C. (2005a), 'Surviving post-socialism: coping practices in East-Central Europe', *International Journal of Sociology and Social Policy*, **25** (9), 65–77.

Williams, C. (2005b), 'The undeclared sector, self-employment and public policy', *International Journal of Entrepreneurial Behaviour and Research*, **11** (4), 244–57.

Williams, C., J. Round and P. Rodgers (2007), 'Beyond the formal/informal economy binary hierarchy', *International Journal of Social Economics*, **34** (6), 402–14.

Index